DESTINY'S PHONE CALL

David Stockman made Upton repeat the telephone number three times to make sure he'd written it down correctly. Upton made Stockman promise to call back with the news. Three minutes later his phone rang. It was Stockman. And he sounded very excited.

"What did he say?" Upton asked.

"Ronald Reagan said, 'You were the only one who bested me in the debates. I was two and one. I beat Anderson. I beat Carter. But I lost to you. So I'm going to offer you the toughest job in Washington— OMB.' "

"And what did you say?"

"I'll take it!"

STOCKMAN
THE MAN, THE MYTH, THE FUTURE

BY OWEN ULLMANN

ZEBRA BOOKS
KENSINGTON PUBLISHING CORP.

FOR LOIS AND CARA

CONTENTS

AUTHOR'S NOTE

When I first encountered David Stockman in late 1980 I was immediately impressed with the budget director-designate as a unique individual and an uncommon sort of public official. Journalists are always on the lookout for the unusual, and in Stockman we found a mother lode of talent, controversy and iconoclasm. While I have my personal disagreements with policies he has advocated, I find his background, his style and his approach to governance fascinating for the many reasons that I hope this book makes clear. So I set out with great excitement to write a biography about the remarkable career he achieved during his first thirty-nine years. I quickly discovered, however, that no one had written a comprehensive account of his life. Most of what had been published about him was the same information based on the same handful of sources and recycled from one magazine article to another.

I started, then, largely from scratch. Between late 1985 and early 1986 I interviewed nearly 200 people whose lives have crossed his: family members, friends from boyhood to the present, neighbors, teachers, professors, political assistants and colleagues, mentors, political enemies, journalists, members of Congress and their staffs, senior members of the White House staff, Cabinet members, other high ranking Reagan Administration officials, personal aides and officials at the Office of Management and Budget (OMB). Unless otherwise specified, all quotations used in this book are from those original interviews.

Most of these people spoke on the record, often quite bluntly and openly, allowing me to quote or paraphrase them by name. A number of individuals, however, granted interviews on condition that all or part of what they said be placed on "background"—journalistic parlance that means I could quote what they said but not by name. This cloak of anonymity can be abused by sources with an axe to grind. It allows them to make false allegations or claims that they would be afraid or embarrassed to make in their own name. Consequently I have tried wherever possible to check other sources in verifying the accuracy and assessing the credibility of claims and opinions offered on background. Many people who spoke on background were Stockman's political enemies and had obvious biases. Surprisingly, however, the majority of those who placed statements on background were friends or colleagues who expressed great fondness and admiration for Stockman but also had criticisms and insights about him which they preferred to discuss anonymously. To help readers draw their own conclusions, I have attempted to describe unnamed sources as specifically as possible in terms of their positions, their relationship with Stockman and their positive or negative feelings toward him.

Stockman was restrained under his own book contract from granting a formal interview for this project, which was completed prior to the release of his book. However, I have had numerous interviews with him throughout his tenure at OMB that I was able to use, including two two-hour interviews conducted in 1984. Although most of our conversations were on "background" at the time I had conducted the interviews, he has consented to my placing them on the record for the first time in this book. Many of his admissions and criticisms concerning the Reagan Administration and his role in it have the same candid and at times rather cynical tone of the statements he made in the Atlantic Monthly. This pattern underscores the fact that had the Atlantic not come along, he was bound to create a public furor at some later time in another news medium. Dave Stockman could never resist sharing his frank opinions with the world.

Much of the personal information about Stockman's life, inner thoughts and private statements come from those closest to him: his mother and father, his brothers, his wife, long-time friends and loyal assistants. They provided valuable insight and detail, and I am grateful for the time and cooperation they gave me. Although Stockman could not cooperate personally, he made no attempt to discourage

11

family members or friends from helping me, and for that, I thank him.

I also wish to thank the many senior officials in the government who made time in their hectic schedules to be interviewed, often at length. In several cases, to my surprise, they were refreshingly candid for the record. I salute them.

My regular employer, Knight-Ridder Newspapers, Inc, encouraged me to take on this project and to see it through, and for that I extend my appreciation. In particular, I want to thank my bureau chief, Robert S. Boyd, and my news editor, Clark Hoyt, for their steadfast support, patience and understanding; company President James K. Batten and Senior Vice-President Larry Jinks for their personal words of encouragement, and National Editor Walter T. Ridder for generously allowing me to use his office. Special thanks also to assistant librarian Ed Felker, who served as an invaluable research assistant, and to head librarian Jo Kirks, who repeatedly helped me locate information that I never would have found on my own.

To my family and all the friends who helped me cope with the stress of writing a book, I owe a debt of appreciation. None is owed more than my wife, Lois Kietur, who faithfully saw me through it all. I also want to single out Ellen Warren for her support and confidence when I needed it most.

Although I believe this book is the most complete account of David Stockman's life written to date, I hesitate to call it a comprehensive biography. Assuming he enjoys a normal life expectancy, Stockman has

12

barely passed the halfway point at this writing. If he lives the second half of his life the way he did the first, this book will have to be entitled, "Volume One."

—Owen Ullmann
Washington, D.C.
March, 1986

CHAPTER 1

INTRODUCTION

A fateful convergence of dramatic events is usually the stuff of fiction. But it struck David Alan Stockman in a very real way on November 10, 1981 — a date that proved to be both a chronological and political turning point in his life. The federal budget director had turned thirty-five that Tuesday, and was enjoying a rare respite from his normally frenetic work pace. During a morning meeting at the Treasury Department he was surprised with a birthday cake decorated with thirty-five little hatchets symbolizing the unprecedented package of budget cuts he had designed and steered through Congress earlier in the year. That afternoon, in his own second floor suite in the old Executive Office Building, his staff threw a surprise birthday party for him that included a clown who decorated him to look like a buffoon. It was one of those rare, light moments when the ever-serious, ever-calculating budget-meister allowed himself to look ridiculous in public. But the playfulness and gaiety masked a quiet dread that had begun building within Stockman an hour before, when his public affairs assistant, Edwin L. Dale, Jr., had stormed into his office and shouted, "The *Atlantic Monthly*'s out."

In a lengthy article published in the December 1981 issue of *Atlantic Monthly*, Stockman had committed the high political crime of candor. With breathtaking honesty and detail, he had granted a long series of interviews (that he subsequently claimed would, he thought, be released at a later date) in which he acknowledged all the shortcomings, failures, miscalculations and deceptions of Ronald Reagan's newly enacted "supply-side" economic program. The program's obvious defect — that it would produce record deficits instead of a promised balanced budget — had long been suspected by outsiders. But now, here was the President's chief economic wizard expressing the same misgivings in colorful language. There were no great new revelations in the article, nothing that most Reagan Administration insiders were not already whispering about privately and starting to hint at publicly. Nevertheless, honesty can be a liability in official Washington, giving as it does ammunition to political opponents. Not surprisingly, the immediate reaction was explosive. In spite of rumors of his summary execution from the Cabinet, Stockman kept his job after he publicly recanted his indiscreet remarks and pledged his lasting fealty to a forgiving Reagan. But the incident left him psychologically devastated. And it robbed him of the awesome power he had enjoyed for ten months as the President's trusted surrogate on economic policy. Forced into the background, he learned a lasting lesson about the

16

political system's resistance to change and its intolerance of honestly expressed opinions.

The *Atlantic Monthly* episode provides a dramatic glimpse into one of the most fascinating political figures of his generation. With the exception of Alexander Hamilton, never before in the nation's history had so young a man wielded so much power and influence. And never before had it been stripped away so quickly and unexpectedly. For part of 1981 it almost seemed David Stockman *was* President. And even after his great fall, he remained the most interesting and best-known member of the Administration, next to Ronald Reagan himself.

Stockman is fascinating because he is unique and complex. He is astonishingly competitive and ambitious, and living proof of the rewards that come from hard work and determination. And yet he does not see his own ambition because he has submerged it in the noble cause he believes he is leading. He is beneficiary of a string of lucky breaks, but also someone who has worked diligently and cleverly to create opportunities for advancement. He has a brilliant mind capable of solving the most complex technical problems, but an understanding of basic human motivations — including his own — escapes him. As the first member of the postwar baby-boom to make it into the Cabinet, he had a youthful, radical and anti-establishment outlook; but he also became an important part of the establishment and spoke on behalf of the traditional economic values embraced by an older, more conservative generation.

As the *Atlantic Monthly* incident underscored, he also is an uncommon blend of righteousness and deviousness. One part is the intellectual idealist driven to impose his consistent set of conservative principles onto, as he sees it, an unruly, irrational and unfair political system. The other part is the knowing cynic who understands that politics is a game of self-preservation based on keeping the most powerful interest groups happy with some federal handout. He can argue the morality and rightness of his ideas with the powerful self-assurance and, indeed, arrogance of the true believer willing to pay the price for his honesty. At the same time he can be brilliantly deceptive and manipulative to achieve his ends. His ongoing dilemma was finding a way to reconcile his rigid world of ideas with the compromising world of politics.

In fact, he never could reconcile those contradictory strands, and so he spent his political career sounding like the "angry young man"—filled with frustration, bitterness, contempt and a trace of the moral indignation that came easily to him. But he also had reason to be angry. In 1981 he had come into national prominence by boasting, like a sheriff vowing to clean up the town, that he would straighten out the chaotic federal budget once and for all. Four and a half years later he ended his stormy reign as White House budget director, admitting failure: The federal budget he had left behind was in its worst shape in history, unbalanced by a record $200 billion, all because the political establishment was too irrational and too irresponsible to take the strong medicine he had prescribed as a cure.

His contempt for the system when he left had carried him full circle back to 1975, when his climb to prominence as a budgetary genius had begun. As an unknown, twenty-eight-year-old congressional aide from rural Michigan, he had issued the same warnings and the same indictment of the political system in a scholarly article called "The Social Pork Barrel." In it he condemned conservatives as well as liberals in Congress for perpetuating fiscally irresponsible social programs of dubious public value. The article brought him to the attention of Washington opinion-leaders, who were impressed with his knowledge of the budget and facility with statistics, his clarity of thought and his yearning for a chance to reshape social policy to fit his view of what government should be. "The Social Pork Barrel" contributed to his rise to power as much as the *Atlantic Monthly* precipitated his fall.

The views about the role of government that he would express with such conviction and eloquence were shaped by his sheltered childhood and years of studying ideas that he found in books. Ideas were the most precious commodity in his world. They interested him far more than people, money or status, and they guided him on a strange political odyssey filled with abandoned and bitter mentors. As a teenager on his family's farm in southwestern Michigan, he was a Goldwater Republican. As an undergraduate at Michigan State University, he was a Vietnam War protestor who flirted with Marxism. As a graduate student at Harvard Divinity School, where he avoided the draft, he studied under leading neoconservatives. When Republican Congressman John Anderson of

19

Illinois brought him to Washington in 1970, he became a Republican again, but not a conventional one. He combined conservative views about the economy with liberal views about social issues, the war in Vietnam and Watergate. Later he would become a self-described "libertarian" who opposed government intervention in economic as well as social behavior.

Stockman played down his liberal views and played up his conservative ones to win election to Congress in 1976 from his Michigan district, one of the country's leading bastions of conservative Republicanism. His election was a textbook case in political strategy. Over the next four years he used his office as a public platform to spread his economic beliefs, demonstrating that what young House members from the minority party lacked in political power they could make up in influence and visibility. While many of his colleagues reveled in the prestige, publicity and perquisites of their office, Stockman's ambition was to change policy. He did not want the illusion of power, he wanted the real thing.

He was to get his chance by way of a succession of coincidences in 1980. His third choice for President, Ronald Reagan, won the Republican nomination and needed help in preparing for a debate against John Anderson, who was running as an independent candidate. Stockman was asked to impersonate his former boss in a practice debate with Reagan; three months later he was named to the new President's Cabinet. At age thirty-four he was the youngest member to sit at the Cabinet table in more than 160 years.

Until Stockman came along, federal budget directors toiled in virtual obscurity outside of the capital, with the notable exception of Bert Lance. But Lance's noteriety came from banking improprieties he was accused of committing before he assumed the post in 1977; what he did during his seven-month reign as OMB director got lost in the scandal that forced his resignation. Other previous directors, such as George Shultz and Caspar Weinberger, became well known only after they left OMB for more glamorous Cabinet positions. Stockman, however, understood the potential of the budget office, which functions like the brain of the sprawling federal bureaucracy. Virtually every executive-branch activity crosses the desk of the budget director at some point. The post can be even more potent when a President who likes to delegate power chooses a director who outstrips other Cabinet officers in energy, intelligence and creativity. Which is what happened on Dec. 11, 1980, when President-elect Ronald Reagan took a chance on a young, untested man half his age.

For a while Reagan and Stockman were a perfect fit—what one lacked the other possessed in spades. Reagan's political strengths lay in his personal charm, his smile and good looks, his folksy anecdotes and his ability to translate abstract issues into emotional appeals. No one ever credited him for his brain power and analytical talents; he followed his gut instincts and deeply held convictions, which were molded and set while Stockman was still in diapers. The budget director, by contrast, was all intellect and little charm. His mother, Carol, describes him as the least emotional of her five children. Colleagues from his days in Congress recall him shunning social events. Associates at OMB portray him as a youthful absent-minded professor with few social graces and no interest in small talk.

Reagan also personified the laid-back California lifestyle: work nine-to-five, watch the diet, exercise regularly and never show any tension. Stockman was all Protestant work ethic. Particularly in the first year, he worked like a demon, putting in sixteen-hour days six or seven days a week, chain-smoking cigarettes, gulping down pots of coffee, dining on vending machine junk food.

Politically they were both economic conservatives, but Reagan never shared the extreme view of limited government that Stockman advocated. On non-economic issues Reagan was a New Right conservative who championed school prayer and a ban on abortions. Stockman was a closet liberal who repudiated the New Right agenda as an encroachment on personal freedom. In their political perspectives both had their own distorted view of the world. Reagan's was based on a life of stories that became symbols of political truth about the way the world worked even though they had no basis in fact. And once he locked onto a belief, Reagan held it firmly and constantly. For Stockman, whose firsthand experiences in the world were limited, truth existed in the books he read and in the objective set of consistent and coherent facts he discerned through logic. And he would shed a belief as soon as he found a flaw in it that compromised his demand for certainty about the way the world works. Stockman also would distort the truth as he knew it for political purposes, but ultimately he would come clean in the name of intellectual honesty and righteousness. His compulsion for

22

candor showed itself in the *Atlantic Monthly* and in dozens of other statements he made during his tenure. He was obsessed with sharing his latest beliefs with the world. To his critics, it was pure hubris.

Until the *Atlantic* controversy drove them apart, Reagan and Stockman were an unbeatable combination. The Great Communicator, using his skills to reduce complex proposals into simple themes, sold his economic program to the public. Stockman, armed with his thick black books of numbers, skillfully argued the case before the skeptics: Congress, the news media, the lobbyists and private economists who make their living reading the fine print. There was much to be skeptical about. Reagan had claimed he could cut personal taxes, sharply boost defense spending and balance the federal budget—all at the same time. He also had said he could lower inflation without a recession and that he could reduce government spending on social programs simply by eliminating waste, fraud and abuse; worthwhile programs and benefits would not have to be touched. All this would come about as a result of his "supply-side" tax cut, which would stimulate an economic boom. It sounded too good to be true. During the 1980 presidential campaign George Bush had ridiculed the program as "voodoo economics" and John Anderson claimed Reagan could only achieve his objectives simultaneously by using mirrors.

Stockman was a belated—and, as it turned out, tentative—convert to the supply-side theory. His main focus was on cutting spending, not taxes, but he signed onto the idea and promised Reagan he could make it all work in 1981, even though conventional economic forecasts predicted Reagan's proposals would produce enormous deficits. To make everything add up to a balanced budget by 1984, as the Administration had publicly promised, Stockman played fast and furious with the numbers to produce the desired result. By mid-1981 he would be obliged to admit what conventional economists had been warning about all along — Ronald Reagan's economic program was sowing seeds for giant deficits.

After less than a year in office Stockman would change from a supremely confident leader of the Reagan Revolution into a frustrated political broker trying to repair the damage he had caused. He took them all on — both parties in Congress, the President, top presidential assistants, the Secretary of Defense, the Secretary of the Treasury, other Cabinet officers, and hundreds of lobbyists out to protect their clients' special tax breaks and government programs. He believed in an equitable assault on federal spending, so he tried to cut middle-class programs and business subsidies as well as low-income programs; in the end, the programs cut most were those that benefited the group with the weakest political voice in Washington — the poor. He also wanted to raise taxes to offset some of Reagan's 1981 tax cut, which grew bigger than planned when the White House bought votes in Congress with special tax breaks. But Reagan kept saying no, no, no. Stockman tried to pare back what he saw as an over-generous buildup in the military budget which he had, regretfully, left unchallenged in early 1981. But neither the President nor the Pentagon would go along. Stockman had some success at the margins, but Reagan's basic budget priorities remained in place. Repeatedly he would decry the hopelessness of the situation and wheel and deal with Congress to win a few budget cuts, but the determined idealist in him kept fighting for the conservative revolution to which his political brethren gave lip service but would not really embrace.

Stockman decided to give it one more try after Reagan's landslide election in 1984. When he failed — as he knew he would — he left to become an instant-millionaire author and investment banker on Wall Street. When he walked out the door of his OMB office of his own free will in the summer of 1985, he felt the vindication of a man who had been right, even if ignored. No one would say he was driven out by the *Atlantic Monthly*. No one would say he didn't try his best. And no one would soon forget that he had been there.

CHAPTER 2

WORKING AND
WINNING

As a member of the first class of post-World War II baby-boomers, David Stockman was born, appropriately, on an army base. It happened in the middle of Texas on November 10, 1946. But he was never meant to live the life of a Texan, and at five weeks of age his parents brought their infant son to his real home, the southwestern Michigan farm where family roots had been planted three generations before.

This was the setting that molded Stockman's personality and philosophy. It was classic Midwestern Americana—a slice of life that more than one native described as a model for Norman Rockwell paintings, complete with all the clichés: flat, rural landscapes broken by an occasional rolling hill, the country store at an intersection that served as the town center, the plain one-room school house, and even the little white-steepled church. Stockman's father, Allen, "is the kind of guy I imagine Rockwell would paint picking apples off a tree," said one long-time area resident. It was a stereotypical world of homogeneity, absolutes and certainty. Here thrived a community of industrious German-American farmers who embodied the old-fashioned values that became Stockman trademarks in Washington—the Protestant work ethic, stoicism, moral rectitude, self-reliance, a financial conservatism that equated both private and public borrowing with immoral behavior, and a political conservatism that viewed federal government as an unwanted and unneeded intrusion.

The community values provided the philosophical foundation, but the special traits that propelled Stockman toward an extraordinary career came from within himself and his family. Throughout his life he has revealed an intellectual obsession to understand how the world works, and he has been able to satisfy that obsession thanks to a gifted mind capable of absorbing, retaining and analyzing an enormous store of information accumulated from books and other reading materials. But it was not enough just to understand. He felt compelled to put that knowledge to practical use, as a result of a burning competitive drive to win and a long family tradition of political activism. That activism, rooted in a lofty Christian idealism about helping one's fellow man, seemed strangely at odds with the strong anti-government philosophy held by family members. More than anything else, the unbridled ambition, the intensity, the workaholic habits, the single-minded concentration and accumulation of political power that continually amazed his friends and intimidated his adversaries seemed to spring from his competitive drive. "You

27

know, that's the key to the whole thing," his younger brother, Steven, said. "He's very combative, very assertive, very aggressive. He likes a good fight, and it's kind of one of the things that really motivates him." Another younger brother, Dan, saw in that drive a striving for the ego rewards of winning. "He always wanted to be successful and a high achiever. You know, he was striving for power, recognition, all of that."

Stockman's competitive spirit and lust for winning, his shy and unemotional personality, his prematurely gray hair and pointed nose are inherited from his father's side of the family. But his cultural, political and philosophical makeup come from his mother's family, the Bartz clan. He grew up on Bartz soil and has the Bartz political blood in his veins. His great-grandfather, Albert Bartz, was one of five brothers who emigrated to the United States from Germany in the 1880s. One went to North Dakota, one settled in Montana, and the other three came to Michigan. Albert started a fruit farm on a tract of land in what is now Royalton Township, a tiny agricultural community eight miles southeast of St. Joseph, Michigan. He originally lived in a small wooden house, but around 1910 he built a larger two-story, red-brick farmhouse and planted a ring of silver birches around it. The homestead became known as the Birchlawn Farm. Albert's son, William, grew up in that house, as did his granddaughter, Carol, and his great-grandson, David. It was remarkably stable and tradition-bound family culture in which young Stockman was reared.

Although they made a modest living as farmers,

the Bartz family also was attracted to public office, with a particular penchant for managing the treasury. "The whole Bartz family was very interested in politics," Stockman's mother, Carol, said. "I guess it was a way of showing their very strong feelings of patriotism about the U.S. because they felt so fortunate to be free and to be able to do what they wanted to do." She recalled that one relative who settled in North Dakota went into the state legislature. Some of the Michigan relatives became township supervisors or treasurers. And her father, William, was a township supervisor and later served thirty years as Berrien County treasurer, beginning in 1938. "I figured when I was growing up that [this] was just the way everybody lived," she said. "I didn't realize everybody's not interested in politics."

William Bartz, who had two daughters, Carol and an older sister, Joyce, hired someone to run the farm while he served as county treasurer, a job that initially paid a few thousand dollars a year. Carol continued the family tradition in the early 1960s by serving as deputy treasurer under her father, who retired in 1968 at the age of seventy-five. Although women candidates were unheard of in the area at the time, she ran to succeed him that year and lost the election. But she never lost interest and ran again for the post in 1984, this time successfully. Fascination with politics was passed down to two of Carol's five children. David, the eldest, is the first family member to pursue national office. Brother Steven became a political analyst for the U.S. Department of Energy in Washington, D.C., and got elected as a supervisor in Loudoun County, Virginia, a distant suburb.

The Stockman side of the family also emigrated from Germany, but it had neither a political tradition nor deep roots in the Michigan soil. David's paternal grandfather, Matthew Stockmann (with two *n*s), settled in St. Joseph in 1914 and worked as a knitter in a local nylon factory that made stockings, parachutes and other nylon goods. The family name was inadvertently Americanized to Stockman in 1927, when David's father, Allen, was born and his birth certificate omitted the second *n*.

Allen Stockman and Carol Bartz were high school sweethearts. After his graduation in June 1945, "Al," then eighteen, was drafted into the army, where he was assigned to several bases in the South until winding up at Camp Hood, later renamed Fort Hood, near Waco, Texas. Carol, meanwhile, finished high school and attended the University of Michigan, where she studied political science. But she dropped out in March 1946 to get married and join her husband in Texas. She had just turned eighteen, and he nineteen. In December of that year, five weeks after David was born, Al was discharged from the army and Carol's parents drove down to see their first grandchild and take the family home to Michigan in time for Christmas.

Back home, Al carried on the Bartz tradition. He ran the eighty-acre farm. They had dairy cows and also grew an assortment of fruits and vegetables that included grapes, peaches, raspberries, strawberries and tomatoes. In the early 1960s, when David was a teenager, the Stockmans gave up the dairy operation because it was too small to remain profitable, the investment required to expand the dairy herd and increase storage facilities was steep, and the kids were too involved in sports and school activities to provide all the help needed. So, in place of the cows, the family added corn, soybeans and a few oats. Around 1970 the Stockmans rented, and later purchased, another seventy acres and concentrated on just three crops: grapes, corn and soybeans. Grapes became their most profitable crop after they joined a cooperative that supplied Welch, the grape juice company.

The Bartz fascination with local politics also rubbed off on Al Stockman. In 1957 he became a member of the Royalton Township board, and in 1961 he became township treasurer, a post he would still hold twenty-five years later.

David Stockman's childhood years were simple, sheltered and predictable, with all the activity revolving around the family and the work routine necessitated by farm life along Scottdale Road. The grandparents lived next door. The one-room school, which his mother and grandfather also had attended, was half a mile down the road in one direction, where it intersected with John Beers Road; the Evangelical United Brethren Church, later to merge with the Methodist Church, was mile and a half down Scottdale Road in the other direction. Family members worshiped and socialized at the little church, and they were buried in its graveyard. Except for an occasional trip into St. Joseph or its sister city, Benton Harbor, Scottdale Road provided the outer boundaries for Stockman's world in his first decade.

At first his family lived in the small house while his

grandparents, William and Madge, lived next door in the larger brick house. But they swapped houses when he was eight because his family had rapidly expanded to seven members and was feeling cramped. David was an only child for just eleven months. Linda was born in 1947, Steven was born in 1949, Daniel came along in 1950 and Gary followed in 1951. It was a spacious, comfortable house but a simple, utilitarian one with plain furnishings and little in the way of ornamentation. The farm provided an adequate living, but the family was never affluent.

David's love affair with books and learning surfaced almost immediately. In his baby album, on a page listing his favorite toys, the last two entries written by his mother state: "Seventeen months—David is beginning to enjoy being read to. Two years—Likes to look at books by himself." By third grade he had read every book in the schoolhouse at least once, an accomplishment made possible by the extensive independent study that is required when one teacher has to instruct eight grades. His favorite books, (according to his brother, Steve) were biographies about famous American presidents such as George Washington, Andrew Jackson and Abraham Lincoln. After fourth grade he left the one-room school to attend a two-room school, where he completed fifth and sixth grades in one year despite being sick that spring with hepatitis and the measles. As a young adult his voracious appetite for books, particularly history, amazed everyone who knew him. "He would read heavy nonfiction for amusement," said Frederick N. Khedouri, one of Stockman's closest aides during his years as a congressman and budget director. Other friends and co-workers recalled countless stories of him reading on dates, on vacations, early in the morning, during the day while closeted in his congressional or budget office and late at night before he went to sleep. Books became his principal companions. They provided vicarious knowledge about how the real world out there worked, a world about which he had intense curiosity but surprisingly little firsthand experience.

Stockman's wife, Jennifer, explains his thirst for reading as "just a real natural curiosity" and an efficient way to remember information. "It's easier to remember because he has such a broad knowledge on so many issues that everything he reads, it just plugs in the holes, the missing links," she said. "If you just read a subject for the first time that you know nothing about, chances are you're going to forget 99 percent of it. But when you build this foundation, everything just logically builds and it's easier to remember. That's his philosophy on acquiring information. The more he knows, the more he'll want to know and the more he'll remember."

His constant quest for knowledge, ranging from grand political philosophies to numbing detail about the federal budget, left little time for people. Indeed, his wife readily admits, he is much more fascinated by ideas than by his fellow human beings. Human behavior, motivations and emotions don't interest him except to the extent that they have a direct effect on political issues. Because of this inclination, a number of people who worked with or for him in Washington found him to be terribly arrogant, extremely self-centered, heartless, and thoughtless

33

about other people.

His family and his few close friends, however, would defend him as a shy farm boy who can be a warm, caring person in private but has never been able to show much emotion or feel comfortable making small talk or interacting in social situations. His self-centeredness would be defended as a benign neglect of people resulting from his intense concentration on his work. His lack of compassion would be explained as a reflection of the no-nonsense, stoical style of life on the farm, where emotions were suppressed. "I think Dave's always been basically shy. Takes after his dad," said his mother. "I think he would rather sit down and have a hard conversation about situations than just sit and talk about the weather." She said he also was the least emotional of the five kids. "Some people just don't show their emotions very readily." His wife said he developed a very thick skin that allowed him to fight hard for his political beliefs without taking the attacks personally. Susan Hause Runne, a former college girlfriend who would later work for him at the budget office, recalled Stockman explaining his shyness by telling about going to a bakery with his father, as a young boy, and being forced to buy something inside while his father waited outside in the truck. "He talked about how mortified he was," she said. He never seemed able to overcome his childhood emotions.

Whatever he may have lacked in emotional maturity, he more than offset through effort. If he was less emotional than his siblings, he also was more ambitious and achieved more. Linda eventually received a doctorate in education and set up her own consulting firm in Missouri. Steve earned a law degree and would dabble in real estate, construction and career counseling before going to work at the Energy Department as a specialist on energy relations between the United States and Canada. Dan, remembered by friends as the countercultural radical in the family during the late 1960s and early 1970s, moved to Springfield, Missouri, where he started a small landscape and gardening business. Gary stayed in Michigan, where he went to work for the state corrections department as a probation officer in the Lansing area.

Dave Stockman showed a liking for hard work, persistence and the rewards they bring at a remarkably young age, a trait he learned from both sides of the family. His two favorite bedtime stories were "The Tortoise and the Hare" and "The Little Engine That Could" (with its confidence-building refrain, "I think I can! I think I can!"). Steve: "My mother wore that book out reading it to Dave." Carol: "He was self-motivated. I think that was kind of a family tradition. My dad was pretty motivated. And Al is, too." She said all four sons worked diligently and rarely complained, but Dave always worked the hardest and seemed to require the least prompting. He got into the work routine at the age of five. "I was working out in the field and I'd have to take care of him," Al Stockman recalled. "And he'd have to follow me around. While he was there he was pitching in, doing whatever I was doing, or trying to." Al also had a rule that by age five, the kids were old enough to help milk the cows once in the morning, before school, and once in the evening, after school. They would put on their barn clothes and when they were done they would put on their school clothes. Added his mother, "He told us once that he was the only kid in kindergarten who had to come home and do work." In later years, Al said, "he was out there every morning at five or five-thirty before school to milk the cows. He'd help with the chores all the time. You'd just call him once, and there he was. You didn't have to go up there and drag him out of bed or anything like that."

That's not to say that David was a paragon. On occasion his father, a fairly strict disciplinarian, would use the strap in the barn, a boyhood memory that would surface in late 1981 in the famous "visit to the woodshed" metaphor he used in describing his meeting with President Reagan to discuss his *Atlantic Monthly* interview. But for the most part, family members recall, he was very well behaved and incredibly motivated. Partly, it was to win approval from his parents and grandparents, who set high expectations by teaching their children to give a task either 100 percent or nothing at all. "Steve one time made the observation that, 'You always expected the best of us, and so we tried to live up to it without ever saying anything.' And I think maybe that was the key," said Carol. "He said we never asked, 'Do you want to go to college?' He said, 'You just expected us to go.' " Partly, David's behavior came from a sense of responsibility or the pressure an eldest child often feels to set an example for his younger siblings.

More than anything else Stockman's brothers, other relatives, and boyhood friends remember him working harder and longer than anyone else, as if always in a competition. If there was still someone else working in the fields or orchards at the end of the day, he would stay until the other person left. "He always worked harder than everyone else," said Ron Both, a first cousin who grew up with Dave. "I remember working with him on my uncle's cherry farm, and he always picked more cherries, worked faster, was more intense. Maybe it had something to do with being first born, but no one came close to picking as many cherries as Dave. And he was like that with everything, playing football or baseball."

Brothers Steve and Gary attribute the work to an intense desire to win, a trait David inherited from his father. Steve said his father, who is a good athlete, revealed his own competitiveness during family games of basketball. As his sons grew bigger and became better at the game, Al would play harder to make sure his side won. "Dad would step on your feet or push you," Steve said. He added that he sometimes suspected his father of cheating on the score.

This competitive spirit first surfaced when Dave was about five and played checkers with his dad, who always played to win, and which made young Dave very mad. "At first Dave would lose and get angry, but he would work at getting better and eventually beat my father," Steve said, relating what Dave had told him about those early childhood contests. "The way Dave talked about it, I think the games of checkers were key. He really got upset about losing, and I thing he also felt it was *unfair* for his father to take such advantage of him."

Farm chores became contests as well. "No matter

what we did, whether it was picking strawberries, planting strawberries, hoeing strawberries or raspberries, Dave always made it a game." said Steve. "Who did the most rows, who picked the most quarts of berries, who picked the most bushels of tomatoes." The younger brothers, whom Dave referred to as "the three little guys," occasionally would pool resources — and still lose. "I could hoe faster than him for a while, like the hare," added Steve, "but he was like the tortoise, just kept going steady until he won." Gary said he has a vivid recollection when Dave was in grade school and got a new red J. C. Higgins bicycle from their father, who said he was rewarding his eldest son for working so hard. "I was really impressed by that," he said. Steve recalled a rare incident in a subsequent year when he managed to pick more containers of strawberries than his older brother one morning. "Is that so, Dave? Steve did best?" their father asked. "Yeah, but I'll crush him this afternoon," Dave said, and he did. Rather than pout and dwell on his failure, he would pick himself up, dust himself off and concentrate on getting even in the next battle. Steve saw work as the main ingredient behind his brother's success. "He's probably got an IQ around 135, 140, but I'd say it's 10 percent brilliance and 90 percent sweat."

He would display this nondefeatist attitude later on as a high school athlete, congressional staffer, candidate for Congress, member of Congress and director of the Office of Management and Budget. "I may not be the smartest guy in the world," he told Steve after coming to Washington. "I may not be the sharpest guy, the best talker, the best dressed. But one thing I know. I can outwork them." And he did. His work habits spawned dozens of stories of almost mythic proportions from awed friends and associates who would relate how he would persist at his tasks beyond what seemed humanly possible: how he showed up in high school once with severe sunburn because he had been working on the farm so long: his mind-boggling research and writing from his days in college on to his career in Congress: his legendary sixteen-to-twenty-hour days and 100-hour-plus weeks during fifteen years in Washington: the thick, detailed briefing papers he would personally write: his determination as budget director to spend as much time as necessary to be better prepared than any of his potential adversaries on budget issues. "I think Dave's been working eighteen hours a day consistently since he was twenty-three and came to Washington," said brother Dan. "I think he got most of his enjoyment out of work." And his own dedication to the work ethic became a major component in his arguments as budget director for curbing federal programs. During one discussion in his office about a proposal to put a $4,000 annual cap on college loans, one of his budget examiners asked how a student would be able to afford an expensive private school. Stockman, who was proud of the fact that he had earned money for college by working on the family farm during the summers, held up his hands: "He could use these."

But young Stockman did not throw himself into his work for its own sake or for the pure sport of it. He appreciated hard work as a means to an end, and he had ambitious ends in mind. Despite the harsh, closed-in life of rural Michigan, David had grand dreams in his early teens, as this story by Steve reveals:

"Ever since I can remember, when 'Bonanza' was real big on TV, he got us talking about the Ponderosa and we'd fashion ourselves as the Cartwrights. Dave would be the oldest one, Adam. He was the smart one and the diligent, hard worker. Me, being the next, was Hoss. And they had a cousin on there for awhile, the attractive good-looking one, that was Dan. And then Gary was always little, so he was Little Joe. And what we were going to do, we were going to make a dynasty on the farm. We were going to do different things — get hybrid tomatoes and have a greenhouse and have a big invention section. I was going to be the head of the invention section. We'd have helicopters and modern technology. Dave would be the mastermind or the president of the organization. We were going to buy out all our neighbors' farms and have a 2,000-acre farm and, you know, build nice houses for the help. Very progressive. We planned it for several years. We used to call my dad a stick-in-the-mud because he was kind of provincial. He went with the old farm, didn't try to expand."

Friends who would meet him and work for him in the 1970s said they got the impression that Stockman also appreciated work of the mental kind as a way to escape the dreary farm life. Fred Upton, a close aide for nearly ten years, said he recalled Stockman joking, "I know about cows and I realized early on that I'm not cut out to be a farmer, so I used my head to get out." Don Moran, another long-time, trusted aide, said he recollected Stockman explaining his capacity for total concentration and intense work as the result of his distraction-free youth and his yearning for something more exciting. "I recall a story he would tell about growing up in Michigan and how he felt utterly bored 95 percent of the time and vowed that he would never be bored again," said Moran.

One ambition he did not exhibit during his high school years was a desire to be an outstanding scholar. Although he seemed able to will himself to be the best at something when he concentrated on it, scholastic achievement was not a top goal and he did not especially apply himself to his studies. In college, in graduate school and in Washington, Stockman dazzled peers and mentors with his brilliance. But a dozen former teachers and fellow students from the Class of 1964 at Lakeshore High School in Stevensville, Michigan, remembered him twenty-two years later only as a good, mainly B-plus student who showed no talents that would have signaled an extraordinary future. "He was bright, but no genius," said Mike Ferris, a classmate who stayed in the area and operated a music store. Robin Campbell, who taught Stockman social studies and math and was his basketball coach, said, "To this day, I have not been able to recall anything that said, 'Aha! There's something that's going to make him big.' He did not stand out. He was not a loner but he was not the leader everyone followed."

John Adams, Stockman's German teacher for two years, recalled him as a good student who was on the quiet side. "But I must say, I was surprised that everyone in Washington regarded Dave as a genius. He was not a genius here. He was a good above-average student." Adams also remembered that young

41

Stockman "was always whispering behind his books. He could be a little sneaky. He had this smile that suggested he was up to something." His teachers and classmates, using the identical words, shared another common observation that would later become a cliché about him during his years as budget director: "He did his homework." Tom Porter, who taught math and geometry and was the only teacher interviewed who recalled giving Stockman A's, said, "He always did his homework, but I think he did it in the ten minutes preceding my class and then used the end of my class to do his homework for the next class. But he was smart enough to get away with it." And he did enough school work to graduate in the top twenty percent of his class and get accepted to a good college. Stockman's natural aptitude for math and numbers would serve him well after he became budget director.

Steve said his brother did not stand out scholastically because he was too busy with sports, extracurricular activites and farm work in the mornings and nights: "He was involved in a lot of other activities. He was on student council, he was playing sports every single night—basketball, football, track—and then when we would get home we'd have work to do every night and there just wasn't any time to do homework. Especially in the fall, we'd be picking tomatoes until eleven or eleven thirty at night. Soon as we'd get home from basketball practice we'd get a bite to eat, go and pick up the tomatoes out in the field, and then come in and crate 'em all night. We used to have a song about it: 'Pick all day and pack all night.' "

With all his high school activities, Stockman channeled most of his energies into sports. Although his father was a talented athlete, his eldest son did not exhibit any similar natural talent. But he made up for it through practice and determination, beginning in his pre-teen days, when he proved to be the best pitcher in Little League. "He was kind of wild but very fast and those poor kids would be up there shaking at the plate," said Steve. "They probably thought he was going to hit them or strike them out." In track, he set a high school record for the mile. In football, he was quarterback for a varsity team that had a 2-5-1 record in his senior year. In basketball that year, he was a starting guard on a quintet that finished its season with a 2-16 record. Glenn Arter, his football coach, said Stockman was on the slight side, about five-foot-ten and 150 to 160 pounds. "But he had grit and stuck in there. Those Stockman kids knew what hard work was." Campbell, who was both his assistant football coach and his basketball coach, said "Dave was not blessed with a lot of athletic talent, but he worked hard. He would come into the gym in the summer and work on his game. Whatever he took up, he concentrated his talents on. He gave it his all, and you can see that pattern throughout his life." Russell Bergemann, a close high school friend who was the center on the football team, said he always remembered Stockman "forcing himself to excel, whether it was pitching hay at his farm or playing football and basketball."

"I remember, even in ninth grade, he was very small but probably was the best tackle on the football team because he'd practice," said Steve. "I remember his

43

junior varsity coach coming up to me and saying, 'Your brother hits harder than anybody out there.' And a lot of times, when he would tackle somebody, you could hear it in the stands. Just cracking that hard. When he was a sophomore, he played offense and defense on junior varsity. Junior year, he started as quarterback and was pretty good. He taught himself to throw the ball very well. We didn't have a punter, and he couldn't punt particularly well, but he taught himself to punt and he punted for a pretty good average — he kicked 40-yard punts. And then he did the placekicking, too. Coach Arter wouldn't let his quarterbacks play both ways, but finally, when Dave was a senior, the coach just couldn't afford not to have him play defense. So instead of inside linebacker, which he played in junior varsity, Arter put him at outside linebacker, and no one could run around Dave."

He excelled in the 4-H. One year he won the prize for the grand champion cow at the county fair. Another time he won a state show on woodworking, for building a record cabinet. In 1964 he was named outstanding 4-H member in Berrien County and one of twelve outstanding 4-H members in Michigan. He also won a $500 scholarship that year to study agriculture at Michigan State University. Stockman was active in school extracurricular activities as well. He played alto saxophone in the school band, acted a minor role in the school play and was president of the student council in his senior year. Indeed, the family's attraction for politics was underscored by a joke among students that year that the council should be renamed the Stockman Student Council because, while Dave was president, Linda was secretary, and Steve and cousin Ron Both were members.

Dan explained his brother's penchant for athletics and extracurricular activites as a way to achieve prestige and popularity. "He was very status-conscious and prestige-conscious, part of wanting to be successful," he said. "Mention the word prestige and he'd get real interested. He always wanted to be somebody, to stand out above the ordinary, always striving to be larger than life, trying harder. He wanted to be a cool guy. He wanted to be popular, and he hung around with this group that thought they were all cool lover types." A yearning for prestige and status is why he did not want to live the life of a farmer, Dan added.

A few close friends said they also saw a striving for prestige in Stockman that he carefully hid from most people. One friend explained it was a basic insecurity about not having any as a kid and later being surrounded by people who came from very wealthy and powerful families. Although his family was not poor, it had to do without at times. Occasionally, Dan recalled, the kids didn't have school lunch money, and their clothes were not as nice as the ones some of their classmates wore. "Dave's just a poor boy trying to make good," said Richard Straus, one close friend.

But Stockman never neglected his cerebral development in pursuit of high school popularity contests. He continued to develop his mind and to learn through reading, even though he did not concentrate on getting top grades in school. On Sunday afternoons, Dan remembered, Dave would rather spend his time reading the works of Dostoevsky and other books than play basketball with his brothers.

Every account of those high school years forms a portrait of a happy, confident and successful youth living out the cliché of the All-American, cheerful farm boy. He was a good-looking and neatly dressed youth, with a trim build, short-cropped dark hair, flashing eyes and an appealing smile. He was popular with the teachers, his male pals and the local girls. He also would suffer an occasional, minor turbulence of adolescence. His pal Russell Bergemann remembered that one time in their senior year after a double date he had gotten a call at five or six in the morning from the mother of Stockman's girlfriend. She was worried that her daughter had not gotten home yet. It turned out the couple had had a fight and the young lady had gotten out of the car and walked home. On another occasion that year, he had gotten home after a midnight curfew set by his parents, so he removed the new pair of shoes he was wearing, left them in the shed in the rear of the house and crept in without being heard. The next morning, he was furious to discover that the dog had chewed up one of his shoes. But such incidents seemed to be the rare exception. Mostly the living was placid, the waters untroubled. Or at least so it seemed.

Although his boyhood friends and teachers spoke highly of him, they also remembered him as being on the quiet side, not overly sociable, and many said they would never have expected him to go into politics. "He was very straight, real nice, got along

46

with everybody, but he also was low-keyed," said Mike Ferris. "He was not Mr. Personality." Connie Cranci, who was in the 4-H with him, said, "he couldn't be any nicer. But he was very, very quiet. It was quite surprising when he got into politics."

Stockman went to Michigan State University in the fall of 1964 expecting to make a career of farming on the grand, Ponderosa-type scale about which he and his brothers had been fantasizing. At the time he was not thinking about a political career. Although Grandfather Bartz had instilled in his grandson a strong political consciousness, young Stockman was distracted by other activities. But in his senior year political thoughts began to enter his mind with increasing frequency, and he soon would set out on a ten-year philosophical odyssey that would take him across the political spectrum and ultimately back to the philosophical roots planted by his grandfather.

CHAPTER 3

CHILD OF LIGHT,
CHILD OF DARKNESS

In many households, politics and religion are "verboten" topics for dinnertime conversation. But in the Stockman household they were dominant themes. They were defined and enunciated repeatedly by the family patriarch, William Bartz. He was sociable and outgoing, personality traits that never rubbed off on his grandson, David. But his viewpoints had the earliest, and most lasting, influence on Stockman's ultimate philosophical makeup. "Dave always really looked up to my dad," said Carol, and Bartz imbued the youth with an old-fashioned bedrock Republicanism that worshipped the free-enterprise system, hard work and rugged individualism, and detested the growth of federal government and Communism. Bartz also instilled his grandson with a strong sense of fundamental Christian moralism that emphasized the importance of living a righteous life, distinguishing right from wrong and helping one's fellow man.

As budget director, Stockman reflected these political-religious strands. But he practiced his idealism on the highest, most abstract plane. He pursued policies that he believed were good for the country as a whole, but he was not one to dedicate himself to helping needy people on an intimate, one-to-one level. He did not focus on individual victims who might suffer under his policies because he felt convinced that from on high, he was advancing the greater good of society.

William Bartz, a 1914 graduate of Moody Bible Institute in Chicago, taught his grandchildren to practice Christianity more as a secular code of conduct that as a spiritual religion. Steve described his grandfather's influence as "a strong moral background. It was based on 'God knows right from wrong.'" Stockman became an agnostic as an adult, but he told friends that he never abandoned his Christian obligation to serve mankind. Religious and racial tolerance were an important part of his religious training, too, but in a community that was virtually all white and Protestant there were few opportunities to put that rule into practice. "We knew one black family, the Rileys, and we always liked them," Steve said. The Stockmans also were friendly with an old black man, a Mr. Bell, who worked on their farm and lived as a tenant on the second floor of the packing shed. Occasionally the kids would go up to Mr. Bell's room and listen wide-eyed as he told them stories and showed them copies of *Life* magazine, with its exotic pictures from around the world. "We were taught that you don't discriminate against anybody," said Steve. "Probably one of the first songs we learned from my grandmother is called 'Jesus

49

Loves the Little Children of the World,' and it goes: 'Jesus loves the little children/ All the children of the world/ Red and yellow, black and white/ All are precious in his sight.' And we'd always remember that one line and shout out, 'Red and yellow, black and white,' but couldn't remember the rest of the lines."

William Bartz also had very strong, unambiguous political views, and he was not bashful about expressing them and using politics to advance them. Although he stressed tolerance of people, he was intolerant of the federal government. "He was a dyed-in-the-wool Republican," said Al Stockman. Carol Stockman felt her father was a little too conservative, particularly because he was an enthusiastic supporter of Barry Goldwater's presidential campaign in 1964. "If I recall, I was not real thrilled with Goldwater," she said. Family members remembered frequent discussions generated by Bartz about the evils of deficit spending and the Democrats. "He was bedrock Republican. He'd talk about how [Franklin] Roosevelt and Social Security were ruining the country," said Steve. "My grandfather always spoke ill of the federal government and the bureaucracy. He thought Alf Landon should have won in '36 and maybe could have saved some things from going the way of the New Deal. He was a believer in Herbert Hoover efficiency." Bartz, who also preached anti-Communism, encouraged family members to stand up for their political principles and not be afraid to say what they believed.

Those beliefs left a major impression on Dave, who had a particularly close relationship with his grandfather. As budget director, his obsession with reducing the deficit, even at the price of higher taxes, stemmed from his grandfather's strict view that "you should pay for what you get" and that it was immoral to spend more than you have. His unusual penchant for public candor also was a Bartz trait.

In addition to all the talk, there was lots of political activity in the household, although young Stockman did not pay much attention until his teenage years. Every two years, his father or grandfather would be running for reelection, and while the campaigns did not amount to much, he would accompany one of them to a political speech or help put up campaign signs. There also was a steady stream of political conventions and dinners that William Bartz would attend with his eldest grandson in tow. One that stood out in family members' minds was a Lincoln Day dinner in the early 1960s that featured then Michigan Governor George Romney, a moderate Republican who had become a hero to Bartz for ending a twenty-two-year reign by Democratic governors. Bartz was also very active in the local Kiwanis Club and got his grandson involved in its junior auxiliary, the Key Club. With increasing regularity, Stockman would go next door to visit his grandfather and keep up on current events by reading *U.S. News and World Report*.

Bartz's fascination with political discussions, gatherings and elections were passed down to Carol, who passed it down to her children, particularly her eldest. "Ever since he was around twelve or thirteen, Dave was always interested in politics," said brother Dan. "We'd all go to political dinners or meet politicians who came to see our grandfather, but Dave always got off on it the most. Maybe because he's always been a leader type and always dreaming big." Dan also remembered that when they were working in the fields when the adults were around, "we'd talk about politics and what's going on in the news. My grandfather especially would talk about ideals, what's right and wrong. He'd talk about the debt being too much, or about FDR being the worst thing to happen to the country, how he really appreciated America, freedom, and individualism and he'd talk about it over and over again." When Bartz was not preaching these beliefs, Carol and Al were.

Few outsiders saw the Bartz idealism that family members spoke of with such reverence, but they were keenly aware of the political activism. Bartz had a reputation for being gregarious and well liked throughout the area, but his family also developed a reputation with some residents as a politically ambitious and opportunistic clan. "They always keep their eye on the main chance, particularly that Dave. He's extremely ambitious," said one family acquaintance.

Over time the religious training, the political indoctrination, and life as Stockman observed it in his bucolic niche of Michigan emerged to produce in him a world view that was based on simple truths and absolute certainty. There was no ambiguity; there were no exceptions. There were right ways for societies to function and there were wrong ways. Stockman's travels outside Berrien County were infrequent, but he did not have to go beyond his immediate environment to find vivid, empirical evidence to support his grandfather's political views. Stockman assumed that these basic truths about his narrow society applied to the rest of the world, too.

Geographically and culturally, Berrien County was particularly isolated. Lake Michigan stretched along its western border, Indiana was to the south, and the rest of the county was surrounded by small towns and farms. Chicago was only ninety miles southwest, but the family rarely went there except to attend a baseball game from time to time. Nevertheless, Stockman could find a world of graphic contrasts in nearby St. Joseph and Benton Harbor. Although known as the Twin Cities, they bear no resemblance to one another. They are adjacent communities, separated physically by the St. Joseph River where it meets Lake Michigan, but crossing the bridge that connects them gives one a jarring sense of having been transported in a time machine. St. Joseph is a neat, white and thriving county seat populated by hard-working Protestants. Benton Harbor is a black, devastated urban ghost town inhabited by welfare families.

When Stockman was born, Benton Harbor was the prosperous commercial and industrial hub of the area, and St. Joseph was a sleepy little bedroom community that had gotten into financial trouble during World War II. The Upton Machinery Company, later renamed the Whirlpool Corporation, was founded in Benton Harbor, and the city also had a number of steel foundries. During the war, a large number of blacks migrated from the South to work in Benton Harbor's factories, and they stayed after the war, settling in a ghetto area known as The Flats. As with so many other American industrial cities, Benton Harbor began to deteriorate during the 1960s. It began with the slow exodus of whites to suburban homes and shopping malls, and turned into white flight following racial riots in the city. Many of the white store owners and families settled in St. Joseph, and real estate agents allegedly discouraged blacks from following suit.

By the 1980s the two cities had become segregated societies living side by side. According to the 1980 U.S. Census, 98.2 percent of St. Joseph's 9,622 residents were white, while 86.3 percent of Benton Harbor's 14,707 residents were black, most of whom were receiving some form of government financial assistance. According to figures from the Michigan Employment Security Commission, St. Joseph had an 8 percent unemployment rate in the fall of 1985, compared with 34 percent in Benton Harbor. But the statistical contrasts do not begin to convey the jarring visual differences between the two downtowns. St. Joseph converted its commercial district into a quaint mall with attractive little shops and brick walks. It has a modern county courthouse and other attractive county buildings, new shopping strips, restaurants and a hotel. All of that ends at the foot of the bridge into Benton Harbor. For half a dozen blocks in all directions, the central district of Benton Harbor looks deserted, like a Hollywood movie set of a city that had been abandoned years before. All around are boarded-up office buildings, vacant store fronts, crumbling apartment buildings. A trickle of cars would pass by without stopping. Pedestrians would be rare sights. It is an eerie feeling.

Stockman had a chance to observe both cities as a boy. Every month or so, he and his family would visit his paternal grandfather, Matthew Stockmann, who lived in downtown St. Joseph. During the summers, Dave would accompany his father occasionally on trips through Benton Harbor to what is still the largest open-air farmers' market in the world. "To get there, you had to go right down through the black slums of Benton Harbor, all those falling-down houses," Steve recalled. "And, you know, we felt compassion for those folks." Once he was in Washington, David Stockman would relate to those memories in a dispassionate way. St. Joseph and Benton Harbor became his black-and-white analytical model of how the world worked. St. Joseph and its surrounding rural territory was an economically healthy area that survived nicely without federal assistance. That included the farmers who grew fruit for a profit without federal subsidies. Benton Harbor and its residents, on the other hand, had been the recipient of all kinds of government subsidies and grants — and was still deteriorating.

"Benton Harbor was my empirical example," he told a colleague in the Reagan Administration. Here is firsthand proof that the free market and personal initiative works and, therefore, is right, while the expanding social-welfare state is expensive, counterproductive and, therefore, is wrong. In Washington he would claim that Benton Harbor had received tens of millions of dollars in federal aid since the 1960s, and economic conditions in the city only worsened. Although racism and a nationwide demographic change from urban to suburban life contributed to the city's appalling decline, Stockman had but one simple explanation for Benton Harbor's despair — government welfare programs that destroyed personal incentive and perpetuated poverty. This was the view of government that his grandfather always expressed. Stockman rejected this view during a period of ideological questioning in the 1960s, but he embraced it again in the 1970s as a major tenet of his antigovernment belief system.

Jack Strayer, a Berrien County native who worked for Stockman during his first campaign for Congress in 1976 and then joined his congressional staff, said Stockman blamed the high number of welfare recipients in the county partly on the fact that people living in northern Indiana would move across the state border, because Michigan paid higher welfare benefits. Strayer, who came from an affluent family of surgeons in Niles, in the southern part of the county, said "my folks' cleaning lady originally moved up to Michigan from South Bend, Indiana, which was only a few miles away, just to get more welfare.

"Dave found that kind of repugnant," Strayer continued. "But he's not against the poor. He's against the kind of pampering and coddling, the cradle-to-the-grave system that we've created, a vicious cycle where in Michigan now we have the fourth generation of welfare people, where the great-grandparents never worked and there's no incentive to work. Dave felt the only way to stop the cycle is to get these people to work, no matter what kind of job it is, just so they have the responsibility of work. They have to go to work. And remember, the work ethic, the Protestant work ethic, is what motivates Dave."

Strayer recalled an incident in 1978, when Stockman, then a first-term congressman, was Grand Marshal for the annual Blossom Time Parade that winds through downtown St. Joseph and Benton Harbor:

"We walked across the bridge to Benton Harbor, and the crowd is all black on both sides of the street. And there's this cute little boy with his mother. She was probably twenty years old, and he was about four years old. Dave put out his hand to the boy, but the little boy was kind of shy, and his mother said something to the effect of 'Shake his hand, baby, it's the onliest thing you're ever going to get off of him.' And Dave looked her right in the eye and said, 'That's right, sweetheart, that's right,' and went on walking down the parade route.

"I think he must have felt that this was a welfare mother with lots of little welfare children, and she was ten or fifteen years younger than Dave. And it really frightened him that there were so many of these little children being born that were creating social problems later on — crime and drugs. He feels very strongly that most hardened criminals come from homes that are third and fourth generation welfare people, black or white. I think he felt that once we do something about the welfare system, we could curtail crime, drug abuse and some of the health care costs."

Stockman's attitude about welfare also reflected an elitist attitude that friends and family saw evolving out of his devotion to the work ethic. Dan Stockman said that during the early 1970s, when his brother worked for Congressman John Anderson, he would divide people in "high rent" and "low rent" categories. The former were highly motivated, successful people who achieved wealth, power and status through hard work. The latter were unmotivated nonachievers who wound up as nobodies. "He

57

doesn't like slothful, lazy people," said Dan, who described his brother as someone who could be both an idealistic do-gooder and "very elitist." Dan remembered discussions in which Dave would say he believed people were not created equal, that some people were better than others, and that there is an aristocracy composed of successful people who run the world and deserve to be at the top because they took risks, worked hard and took advantage of lucky breaks that came their way. "Those are his class of people," said Dan.

Stockman may have felt firm in his diagnosis of Benton Harbor's disease, but he had no cure beyond the magic of the free market, and even he knew that would not solve Benton Harbor's massive social problems. He readily admitted that he had no solution. He could say with certainty that A is wrong and B is right, "but the question is how do you get from A to B? I didn't have an answer," he confessed.

"His theories fall apart when it comes to Benton Harbor, because the only thing that's going to help Benton Harbor is government assistance," said Strayer. "No private investor's going to go in there, no venture capitalist is going to go in there. No church or United Way has the funds to bring that back. Dave thinks society should be more local, more philanthropic, rather than always counting on the government for solutions. But that's where his theory falls off, when you bring up Benton Harbor." So he ignores the problem.

Stockman's wife, Jennifer, acknowledged that he has no solution to the problems of Benton Harbor, "but it's not because he's unsympathetic or uncaring.

I think because he has such a big-picture view of the way the world should work, he does take a fairly hard line when it comes to solving immediate problems." Stockman believes the federal government cannot possibly solve every social problem, and the line has to be drawn somewhere, she said.

In December 1985, Michigan declared Benton Harbor its first "enterprise zone" under a state program that encourages economic revitalization of depressed cities by offering tax breaks to attract private business investment. As a member of Congress, Stockman had supported legislation that would do the same thing using the federal tax code. The concept appeals to economic conservatives because of its emphasis on private sector rather than government investment, yet it hardly conforms to the pure, free-enterprise philosophy that Stockman espoused. Tax breaks are a government subsidy and budgetary expense borne by taxpayers just as much as outright grants, and the government sets the guidelines as to the type of business activity that qualifies for the breaks. Thus the private investor becomes a surrogate for the government. A nongovernment solution to Benton Harbor's ills had yet to be found.

Stockman's certain and consistent view of the world came under challenge for the first time in the spring of 1964, when he was a seventeen-year-old high school senior. Through his local church, he had entered an essay contest sponsored nationally by the American Friends Service Committee, a very liberal, socially active arm of the Quakers involved in promoting civil rights and social welfare programs, helping the poor and minorities, and opposing the military-industrial complex. The theme of the essay was "what nonviolence means to me." Stockman, who would exhibit a special talent for writing throughout his career, wrote an impressive paper that he would describe twenty years later as "an ode to Martin Luther King, Jr., and Mahatma Gandhi." His essay was selected as one of the national winners, and his reward was a week-long political seminar in Washington conducted by the Service Committee. The trip included a side trip to the United Nations in New York. The event created a fair amount of cultural and political shock for a youth who had never strayed for any length of time from his rural Michigan home or his grandfather's bedrock Republicanism. For the first time in his life "I was immersed in liberalism," he recalled. "I was becoming idealistic. I had this idea of making a better world. I thought racism and poverty were bad."

The seminar called into conflict the religious and political views Stockman had absorbed from his grandfather. The Christian idealism about helping one's fellow man was consistent with what the teenager was picking up from the American Friends. But William Bartz's anti-New Deal Republicanism was not. The conflict was made even more pronounced by Bartz's early and enthusiastic support for Barry Goldwater's presidential campaign that year. But Stockman, always obsessed with finding a perfectly consistent philosophical viewpoint, refused to see a conflict at the time. "I didn't see Goldwater and Gandhi as being incompatible," he said. Goldwater's traditional values, anti-Communism and strong belief in free enterprise, did not have to be at odds with Gandhi's belief in nonviolent protest to help the oppressed. So, when the students were asked as part of the seminar to write letters to their senators urging their support of the 1964 Civil Rights Act pending in Congress, Stockman wrote to Goldwater, urging the conservative senator from Arizona to vote for the legislation because it was "the Christian thing to do." On June 19, 1964, the Senate passed the Civil Rights Act by a vote of 73-27. Of 33 Republican senators, only six voted against the act. Goldwater was one of the six. His vote put him in the company of southern Democrats who were avowed segregationists, and he would be attacked by members of his own party for abandoning its traditional support for equal opportunity. But as the GOP nominee, Goldwater would defend his vote by claiming the Civil Rights Act was just another attempt by government to encroach on individual freedom. Looking back at the episode, Stockman admitted he had been pretty naive in his political thinking. It was a trait that both friends and enemies said he exhibited during his years in Washington.

The ideas he was exposed to at the Friends' seminar started to pull him to the left before he left high school. He began questioning the Republican dogma with which he had grown up. "I remember in our senior year we had an economics class, and I was shocked because David was espousing liberal ideas about economic class and socialism," said William F. "Rick" Ast III, a high school friend who went on with Stockman to Michigan State University. Stockman's social studies teacher and student council adviser, Robert Fell, noticed the senior undergoing another change that clashed with his strict, authoritarian upbringing. "He was acting a little rebellious," said Fell. "He had that general attitude against authority that was common with those kids in the sixties."

Stockman, however, was not ready to make a clean break to a new political identity. With his grandfather's strong encouragement, he continued to support Goldwater. Steve recalled that his brother headed up the "Goldwater for President" organization in high school and, in what would be a harbinger of things to come, played the role of Goldwater in a mock debate in school. It was fateful training. Sixteen years later Stockman would play the role of another presidential candidate, John Anderson, in a mock debate with Ronald Reagan that would land him the job as the new President's budget director. "I was a country conservative from a Republican family. I thought Goldwater was the greatest thing since sliced bread," Stockman explained in an interview published by the New York *Times* magazine on March 15, 1981.

In the fall of 1964, David Stockman entered Michigan State University to learn how to become a farmer in the modern age. Instead, he became a Marxist.

Michigan State was a suitable choice for Stockman. Founded as Michigan Agricultural College, it has a more conservative political tradition than the University of Michigan and it places a lot of emphasis on agricultural programs. In the more cosmopolitan eastern end of state, it is known derisively as

"Moo U." William Bartz had taken a farming course there. In later years, as a member of the Michigan Farm Bureau, he would take Stockman to the campus in East Lansing, where the bureau was headquartered, and sometimes they would watch the Spartan football team take on a Big Ten opponent. Stockman became familiar with the quiet college town just outside the state capital of Lansing and decided this was the place for him.

Instead of finding reinforcement for his childhood values, however, Stockman was thrown immediately into an alien cultural and political climate. One of his dormitory roommates in his freshman year was unlike anyone he had known from home — a politically liberal Jew from New York who introduced him to his first bagel and kidded him for being a country rube. More significantly, Stockman took a course during his first semester on American thought and language that precipitated the disintegration of his entire Christian-conservative philosophy. The course was taught by a young instructor who was a Jewish leftist from Brooklyn, according to Stockman's description. During this course Stockman finally discovered the conflict in his views that was first raised by the Friends' seminar. "This professor just tore down all my old views, just tore them down," Stockman said. "First I lost religion, then I lost Republicanism, and then I lost capitalism."

Family members recall noticing his changing attitudes that fall, when he started questioning his support for Goldwater. By the spring of 1965, when he came home to visit, the changes had become more pronounced. He had let his hair grow longer, he had bought a guitar to pluck on, he introduced his brothers to Bob Dylan and Joan Baez records. He spoke with concern about the poor and oppressed. He sounded like a liberal. During the summer after his freshman year, he worked sweeping floors at a die casting business owned by an uncle. "You had some rednecks working there, and Dave would argue politics with them, and one time he said he almost got into a fight with one of the workers," Steve said. Stockman also started getting into frequent and bitter arguments with his father, first over his modestly long hair, then over his increasingly liberal politics, then over the war in Vietnam. It was a scene that was being repeated in hundreds of thousands of other homes across the country. The baby-boomers of the late 1940s were turning into the anti-authoritarian rebels of the late 1960s.

Stockman had decided to resolve his internal conflict. He embraced his left-wing, idealistic self who wanted to fight poverty and racism, and discarded his right-wing ideological self who believed in individual effort and the pursuit of economic self-interest. He became a believer in the Peace Corps, LBJ's Great Society, the War on Poverty and other elements of the Democratic social-welfare state. Although he had given up on Republicanism and capitalism, he did not abandon religion altogether. He told Steve about a Student Christian Athletes banquet he had attended in 1965. The guest speaker was Bob Timberlake, the All-American quarterback who had led the University of Michigan Football team to the Big Ten championship and the Rose Bowl during the prior season. "He was very impressed with Timberlake. In fact, he wrote a long letter home to my parents about it. He wasn't radical at the time. But he was changing," said Steve. "He was saying he wanted to give up agriculture and wanted to go into the ministry. I remember that my grandfather was delighted." In the summer of 1965, Stockman switched his major from agriculture to religion, a change of courses that would lead him to the forefront of the campus protest movement against the Vietnam War.

In his sophomore year Stockman had become "a hard-core liberal," recalled Robert Anderson, now chairman of the religious studies department at the university. Anderson was an associate professor at the time, and Stockman took five or six of his courses as a sophomore and junior. It was Anderson who recruited Stockman to help teach a Sunday school class for high school students in East Lansing at the Edgewood People's Church, an interdenominational congregation that later changed its name to Edgewood United Church of Christ. The church was the focal point for a group of liberal clergy and lay Christian activists opposing the Vietnam War. This was Stockman's connection to the campus antiwar movement.

"When I first met him, he had a crew cut," said Anderson, who took a liking to Stockman and occasionally invited him home for Sunday dinners. "He was a good-looking boy. He tended to be rather quiet in a large group situation. But in smaller seminars, he came on very passionately. He was very articulate." Anderson also remembered Stockman as mainly a B student who was fascinated with theology, read a lot of religious philosophy and considered teaching the subject as a profession. At the time, Anderson said, Stockman looked at theology more as someone who was looking for a philosophy of how the world works than as someone pursuing spiritual salvation or the ministry as a career. Anderson then added an observation that several of Stockman's high school teachers also had made: "I liked him very much, but he never impressed me as a wizard or genius. Of all the students I had, he was not one I would have figured to become a national figure."

"We were all just becoming bleeding hearts back then," said Stockman's cousin, Ron Both, who was one year behind him at Michigan State. "When we were growing up, we didn't know much about racism and ghettos. But when we went to college and found there were all these people without rights and unable to vote, we became liberal across the board. We became much more liberal than our parents or grandparents. We looked at them as being very narrowminded. I can remember a few times Dave was not on speaking terms with his father."

In his head, Stockman was turning more radical than either his religion professor or cousin realized. Intellectually, Stockman's search for the perfect-world theory briefly turned him into a Marxist, to use his own label. One major influence was Herbert Marcuse, whose 1965 Marxist tract, *One-Dimensional Man,* had become the rage on college campuses. Marxism, with its belief that men can use their capacity to reason and their innate goodness to create perfect societies, appealed to the idealistic side of Stockman. He also had become an agnostic, a change that would lead to occasional arguments with his grandfather. Life as an intellectual Marxist would prove to be relatively brief; Stockman would reject it by his senior year. But he remained an agnostic; he could not find certain proof that God exists.

Stockman's radicalization in thought coincided with the United States' growing involvement in Vietnam, a policy that he adamantly opposed. He began reading everything he could find about the history of Vietnam and analyses of the current war, and he read other books on history, economics, politics and philosophy. In the process he drifted further and further away from his family's belief that the United States was making a moral stand in Southeast Asia to halt the spread of Communism. He became convinced that the issue was not Communism but colonialism. The U.S. government was the aggressor, interfering in a civil war to protect the economic interests of major American corporations. To Stockman, Ho Chi Minh was the brave hero engaged in a nationalist struggle for independence.

Thousands of other draft-age men on college campuses had come to the same ideological point and were becoming more active in expressing their moral outrage about the war. And their outrage was sincere. Yet, beneath the veneer of intellectual opposition were raw feelings. The activism of those young men was precipitated and sustained in large measure by a gripping fear of being drafted, sent to Vietnam and winding up dead or wounded in the steaming jungles of Indochina. Together, self-righteousness and self-interest became powerful weapons against U.S. policy. And for someone with Stockman's strong moralistic upbringing, moral outrage against the war came easily. "I also became antiwar," said cousin Both. "And a lot of that was idealism. We believed we could make the world the way it should be. We were being very moral, and saw the war as very immoral."

But Stockman was not the typical antiwar protestor or intellectual. As with everything else he did as a child and adult, he threw himself into the protest movement with an intensity no one else could match. His intellectual obsession to understand how the world works and the Bartz political activism running through his blood propelled him into a leadership role.

Stockman's antiwar activism occurred mainly in 1967, when national protests against the war were expanding. Early that year he convinced his brothers that the war was wrong and gave them anti-war leaflets to distribute in high school. At the same time he became a leader of the Michigan State protest movement, but in a squeaky-clean kind of way. He worked through the auspices of the University Christian Movement and made a conscious point of seeking change through the system. He was no scruffy, bomb-throwing type of radical. He was the antithesis of the stereotypical countercultural militant thrusting his fist in the air, shouting "Off the imperialist pig!" and threatening to tear down the system, or at least rip it a little bit at the edges. Stockman may have traveled far from his roots philosophically, but in appearance and tactics he was still the conservative, mainstream, idealistic farm kid.

If there was a radical revolution going on in Stockman's head at the time, it didn't show on the outside. His black hair and sideburns may have gotten long by his father's standards, but photographs of him revealed a clean-cut and conventional kid by college standards at that time. His hair and dress were neat. He had a preference for blue jeans, button-down oxford shirts or work shirts, wool shirt-jackets, and tennis shoes or penny loafers. No one who remembered him from those days recalls him ever participating in or advocating any violent acts; rather, he advocated nonviolent protests in the tradition of Gandhi and King. And while many students deemphasized their academic studies to concentrate on campus politics, Stockman became a better student even as his activism increased. He started out as a B student during his first two years, but was getting A's consistently by his senior year, when he changed his major to humanities, with an emphasis on history. And he was able to graduate with academic honors.

He rebelled against authority figures — in particular his father, the Selective Service System, and U.S. foreign policy — but that was the extent of his revolution. If that made him a revolutionary, then he was a revolutionary as budget director when he rebelled against the authority represented by Ronald Reagan, the Cabinet, the Congress and the outside political forces that defended federal programs.

He was a radical to the extent that every student who actively opposed U.S. policy in Vietnam and avoided the draft was considered a radical in those days. But there was a big difference between being a radical at Berkeley, Columbia, or the University of Michigan and being a radical at Michigan State University. While violence erupted on some campuses, MSU was relatively peaceful and conservative.

Its chapter of SDS — Students for a Democratic Society — was not militantly left-wing as was its counterpart at the University of Michigan. Former SDS members looking back did not recall it being particularly radical at all. One big war-related event to hit the MSU campus came in 1966, when *Ramparts* magazine disclosed that the university had provided cover for a group of Central Intelligence Agency specialists who, posing as faculty members, helped train South Vietnamese secret police serving under the late President Ngo Dinh Diem's regime. But the project, which began in 1955, had ended by 1962, and so the matter already was moot by the time Stockman arrived. Students who went to school with him remembered only one major demonstration, a peaceful sit-in at the administration building over the firing of a professor. "That's about as radical as it got," said Susan Hause Runne, who became Stockman's girlfriend during his junior year. "I'd say he was more ultraliberal than radical," said his cousin, Both. "He wanted to change the system, not destroy it." By his own reckoning, Stockman was "a soft-core radical." That is how he described himself in a 1981 *Time* magazine interview, and it was an accurate description.

Stockman's most radical act came on April 12, 1967, when he signed an SDS advertisement that ran in the student newspaper. "WE WON'T GO," the ad declared in bold, black letters across the top. The text beneath stated:

We the undersigned, are young Americans of draft age opposed to United States intervention in Vietnam. We hereby form an anti-draft union

70

and declare our intention to:

1. refuse to fight against the people of Vietnam.
2. refuse to be inducted into the armed forces of the United States.
3. resist the draft.
4. aid and encourage others to do the same.

The names of thirty-three men appeared below in alphabetical order. The twenty-ninth name was David A. Stockman.

Stockman's support of so radical a statement, with its public vow to violate U.S. law, was out of character for him. His attitude throughout the period was better reflected the day after the ad appeared, when the *Michigan State News* ran a story about a campus peace group planning to send President Johnson a petition urging an immediate halt to American bombing of North Vietnam and recognition of the National Liberation Front in peace talks. The petition was being circulated by the Peace Coordinating Committee, a subsidiary of the University Christian Movement. The committee's chairman was David Stockman. In the article Stockman said the group evolved that past winter "as an expression of the change in the peace movement from a fringe of radical activists to a more moderate mainstream." He went on to say: "We don't expect any change in Administration policy from this action, but rather a change in the minds of Americans. The Vietnam War is not just a mistake or aberration, but is symptomatic of a failure in American policy to deal realistically with the developing Third World." He also said

71

the committee planned to set up "a draft counseling center" aimed at college and high school students. These were not the words of a radical.

The petition was circulated in conjunction with massive peace marches held in New York City and San Francisco on April 15 under the sponsorship of the Spring Mobilization Committee to End the War in Vietnam. Stockman was among those who turned out in New York. In an April 18 article on the march in the *Michigan State News,* Stockman said he was impressed with the large turnout of Negro civil rights workers and expressed hope that a coalition of civil rights and peace groups could make for a more effective alliance. The experience also heightened his involvement in the antiwar movement. "Before I went, I was quite pessimistic. I thought we couldn't do anything," he said. "This gave me a desire to get out and start working and organizing."

That's exactly what he did. In the summer of 1967 he became the only full-time, paid coordinator of "Vietnam Summer," a consciousness-raising project organized primarily by ministers associated with the Edgewood church. Its objective was to turn public opinion in East Lansing against the war through direct mail and door-to-door canvassing and weekly coffees at homes. In an interview published August 1 of that year in the East Lansing *Towne Courier,* Stockman noted that the project's volunteers included liberal Democrats seeking to change Democratic Party policy toward the war, those who were simply "morally outraged" by the war, and people who were thinking about starting a new political party because working for change through the Democratic and Republican parties was impossible. Stock-man spoke as one who identified with SDS members calling for major changes in the system, but he spent his time with older liberal Democrats, not SDS students.

It is easy to look at Vietnam Summer as an aberration in Stockman's life, a period of adolescent romanticism, a temporary search for ideals that he would shed as he matured and became wise in the ways of the real world. Yet looked at more closely, Vietnam Summer was very representative of his later life, character and ambitions. It set a very clear pattern that he would repeat again and again—at Harvard, as a congressional aide to Rep. John Anderson in Washington, as a member of Congress and as a member of Reagan's Cabinet. The sequence begins with a bright young man who is adopted as the star protégé of a group of older men with a strongly held political philosophy. He impresses them with his ability to advance their cause through his extraordinary talent for absorbing, synthesizing and articulating information, and the intensity with which he works. So, they give him responsibility. But he quickly grows disillusioned with their theory, abandons it in search of a new framework and, more often than not, leaves his mentors feeling betrayed, bitter and wondering whether he is an idealist driven to find the truth or a self-centered, ambitious striver seeking to get ahead. In fact, he was both.

As sincere as his opposition to the war was that summer, the project offered other major incentives that attracted Stockman. One was the fact that he received board and enough money so that he would not have to work on the family farm. The other attraction was that he had an opportunity to be where the political action was, at the cutting edge he found so fascinating. "David would always fill the void where there was a void in leadership," observed Stockman's former congressional aide Jack Strayer. "He saw in high school the way you got to be a leader and be popular was to be in sports. When he came to Michigan State he was a very good Republican right up until the moment he arrived, and then saw the whole leadership thing in college was based around the antiwar movement. That's how you work your way to the top, and he did. I wonder if his philosophy was as strongly antiwar as he said it was at the time. I don't think his actions reflect his beliefs as much as his desire to lead. He's always been driven to be the best." Stockman frequently has defended his antiwar activities as the result of a deep moral commitment, but he also has admitted that he was attracted to the leadership potential it offered as well.

Most of the other activists in Vietnam Summer were men who ranged from their late twenties to fifties and were members of Edgewood Church. Stockman was hired by David C. Hollister, an East Lansing high school teacher who later became a Democratic state representative. Stockman had responded to a newspaper ad for a full-time organizer. "He was very bright, very articulate, seemed to have a clear grasp of the issues on Vietnam," Hollister recalled. "He knew about the French and an indigenous group of folks who had been fighting for thousands of years and that the war was not part of an international Communist conspiracy."

Stockman's job was to run the office and direct volunteers who would first make door-to-door calls, then follow up the personal contacts with antiwar mailings, and then invite people to a weekly coffee that included films and speakers. It proved to be invaluable organizing experience that Stockman would use eight years later when he plotted his first run for Congress. Stockman also was chief spokesman for the group.

The campus pastor, H. Lynn Jondahl, who also would become a Democratic state representative in later years, remembered Stockman as being "very articulate and well informed." Jondahl described Stockman's personality and talents in precisely the same way associates in the Reagan Administration would speak of him fifteen years later. Jondahl remembers him mostly for his keen analysis of the war and his extensive reading that kept him abreast of all the current critiques of U.S. policy. "He would provide resource material and information to our discussions, and he was very serious about it. He also would write synopses of what was being written about the war in our newsletter," Jondahl said. "We spent a good deal of time together, but I don't think I knew him other than through our talks about interests and values. He seemed very intense." Jondahl remembered Stockman describing himself as a leftist who favored a shift in political-economic power in the country. "He clearly identified himself with a group who wanted more substantial change. He talked about the war being driven by major corporate interests who had a stake in Southeast Asia to control resources. But he never rejected the political system."

The Michigan State Policy, however, thought his activities sufficiently radical to keep tabs on Vietnam Summer through its political surveillance group, the "Red Squad." The file on the group's activities included a list of potential contributors, newspaper clippings and other published materials. Stockman's name was included in dossiers kept on Jondahl and Hollister, who saw their files in 1980, four years after a Michigan court ruled that the Red Squad's data-gathering activities were unconstitutional. The court also ordered the state to release the contents of the 38,000 files to the people on whom files were kept between 1950 and 1974. As a result of that order, Stockman's inclusion in the files came to light in late December 1980, a few weeks after Reagan had nominated him to the budget post and before the Senate confirmed the appointment. "This was basically a church group engaged in an entirely acceptable activity," Stockman said at the time. "It sort of strikes me as an archaic whiff of another era." He added that he did not believe the disclosure would hurt his chances for confirmation "unless expressing opposition to a government policy is something that is wrong."

When Vietnam Summer ended in September 1967, it evolved into a new group, the Greater Lansing Community Organization, which focused on social issues as well as the war. Stockman, who was beginning his senior year, became a member of the steering committee. From the outset, the GLCO had decided it would seek change through the legitimate political process, such as by fielding candidates for public office. That was how Hollister and Jondahl got elected to the Michigan legislature. The group also focused on projects aimed at helping welfare clients and public housing tenants organize to increase their political power. Other projects included draft counseling and a boycott of a local Sears store to protest discrimination against blacks in hiring. "David was big on helping people to achieve self-determination," said Betty Duley, one of the steering committee members. "He was a kind of strategist for us. He had keen insight into what made things work and how to use the media people. We'd sit around the kitchen table Saturday mornings and plot what to do."

In October 1967, Stockman was one of the main campus organizers for another antiwar march, this time in Washington. He thoroughly enjoyed his leadership role and helped drive the old bus that carried the MSU contingent to the nation's capital. This was the famous march to the Pentagon that would turn violent and be chronicled by Norman Mailer in his book *The Armies of the Night*. The Washington march was the culmination of a week-long, nationwide protest against the draft organized by the National Mobilization Committee to End the War in Vietnam. The crowd, estimated at 55,000 by police and 150,000 by march organizers, participated in a peaceful rally October 21 at the Lincoln Memorial, where one of the national organizers, David Dellinger, declared that the demonstration was "a beginning of a new stage in the American peace movement in which the cutting edge becomes active resistance." The movement was becoming more radical, just the opposite of the direction in which Stockman had wanted to go that spring.

After the speeches at the Lincoln Memorial, some

30,000 to 35,000 in the crowd, including Stockman, marched across the Potomac River to the Pentagon. A government march permit had restricted the demonstration to a parking lot and a grassy area a safe distance from the building, which had been ringed by 2,500 troops carrying clubs and tear gas grenades. Troops had been flown in from bases around the country including, coincidentally, Fort Hood, Stockman's birthplace. Within a few hours, violence erupted when several thousand demonstrators crossed the authorized lines and clashed with authorities. Tear-gas canisters were fired, bottles and eggs were thrown, clubs were swung and blood was splattered on the steps of the Pentagon. The majority of protesters, including Stockman, tried to stay clear of the melee. They left the scene and began heading home, but several hundred protestors who remained after the clashes had subsided staged a sit-down into the night near the main entrance to the Pentagon and were arrested. By October twenty-third, when the protest finally ended, authorities reported that 681 people had been arrested and that twenty-four demonstrators and twenty-three soldiers or U.S. marshals had been injured. President Johnson assailed the protest as "irresponsible acts of violence and lawlessness." Dellinger said the antiwar movement had decided to change its tactics from peaceful parades to "confrontations" with the government through sit-ins and other acts of civil disobedience. "We have been calling for a step-up to a new phase in the movement," Dellinger announced after an October 22 meeting of the mobilization committee. "We were gratified and enthused that so many people came in from all over the country ready for this."

Stockman, however, was not ready for this. In fact, he felt repulsed by the violence he had witnessed. "That's when the war really got radical," he later recalled. "You had those SDS-Pentagon demonstrations. I saw the violence, I saw it being provoked by our side. I reacted very strongly against it." Indeed, although he saw himself as a radical in thought, he was still the nonviolent Christian idealist in deed. As a result, the march became a turning point in his political development. His drift to the left had come to an abrupt halt, and he started to revert to his conservative roots. "Prior to the march, I was SDS-Marxist-oriented," he explained. "Then I shifted away from the anti-system radicals and identified with the traditional peace liberals, the social Democratic liberals." These were the activists at Edgewood Church. It was an easy transition since he worked and lived with them.

A key figure in this transition was the Reverend Truman Morrison, the Edgewood church pastor and the man whom Stockman described as "the guru who got me out of the radical left to a more mainstream position. Truman rescued me with [Rheinhold] Niebuhr. I became neo-orthodox and adopted a more metaphysical view."

Reinhold Niebuhr, who died in 1971, was one of the twentieth century's leading theologians. Always a strong anti-Communist, he saw himself as a Christian socialist who later came to see some good in capitalism provided it was restrained through government welfare programs, such as the New Deal. Unlike many nineteenth-century idealists who believed that

79

humans were innately driven to do good, Niebuhr saw a more ambiguous world in which people were constantly struggling between altruistic and selfish instincts. This was the main message in books such as *Moral Man and Immoral Society* and *The Children of Light and the Children of Darkness* (1944). In the latter he wrote one of his most famous statements: "Man's capacity for justice makes democracy possible; but man's inclination to injustice makes democracy necessary." The Children of Light were naive idealists who failed to appreciate how strong self-interest motivations are; the Children of Darkness were wiser because they saw the self-interest, but they also became more cynical as a result.

These writings had a profound intellectual impact on Stockman, who would mention them in letters to his family and in discussions with his brothers. Niebuhr provided a rational framework that accommodated the social idealism and economic self-interest that had been driven into him in childhood. Niebuhr provided the perfect fit, for Stockman personified the Child of Light and Darkness. He is driven, far more than most mortals, both by an extraordinary sense of idealism to do good as he believes it at the time, and by an intense self-interest to achieve and reap the rewards of success. These competing drives explain why he induces such strong feelings — positive, negative and both — in people who have known him: why some see him as a convincing, super-ambitious politician; and why still others see him as an ideological zealot; why others see him as an amazing mix of self-righteous true believer and self-centered master manipulator.

These conflicting strands would reveal themselves repeatedly during Stockman's adult years. They would show in a congressional voting record that reflected extreme ideological purity and occasional political expediency; they would show in the way he became a devotee of Reaganomics and then its most appalled critic on the inside; they would show in his contempt for the self-interests that shape the American political process and his willingness to exploit those self-interests to advance his policy objectives; they would show in the way he could speak with such honesty in public and play deceptive games with his political adversaries in private; they would show in the way he could be tolerant of religious and racial differences in people and also feel intolerant of those who did not work hard to take advantage of opportunities that came their way.

Unlike Stockman, however, Niebuhr believed that the ambiguity and creative tension resulting from the Utopian and selfish sides of people were positive forces that produced a balanced and realistic attitude needed to improve society. But Stockman never exhibited any tolerance for ambiguity. He always seemed to veer from one extreme to the other rather than settle on some middle course. He was both the fundamental Christian moralist and the unbending economic conservative of his childhood. He was both the idealistic protestor and anti-authoritarian cynic of the 1960s. He was both the dedicated public servant and ambitious striver of the 1980s.

"This is the irony of Stockman," said one close friend in the Reagan Administration. "He's very tolerant of different kinds of people and he is a deep believer in economic freedom. Yet he has kind of a totalitarian spirit when it comes to a free, pluralistic and democratic political process. He's highly disrespectful of it. He has near contempt for it because it keeps frustrating his policy objectives. And there's a danger to this kind of thinking. You can get a society and a world in trouble if you accumulate too much power and join with it too much certainty about the rightness of anything. History is filled with examples of people who have had excessive certainty linked with excessive moralism linked with excessive power."

In some ways Stockman's behavior and attitudes resemble the sharp facets found in adolescents before maturity and experience round off the edges. And in fact, like so many of his generation, he had an extended adolescence that lasted into his mid-thirties. He did not marry until age thirty-six and did not become a father until thirty-eight, and he spent the bulk of his first forty years essentially as a student-scholar—reading, learning, writing, analyzing. "David's still a child," one close friend said with affection, an observation that was echoed by many other friends and co-workers.

As a college senior Stockman did not have to settle any conflicts between idealism and self-interest. They merged at the right time to lead him on a path away from the draft and toward Harvard Divinity School.

During Vietnam Summer, Stockman lived off-campus at the home of John Brattin, an attorney who was part of the group of Edgewood Church liberals. Stockman wound up staying there for his senior year.

It was a big, limestone house with white columns, and although Brattin's wife, Alice Jean, had children of her own living there, she liked to take in young college men. "He was an exceptionally intelligent and exceptionally well-read young man," Brattin recalled. "He was an omnivorous reader. He read everything and was an independent thinker. He was so intense and always ambitious. He was very inquisitive and wanted to acquire as much knowledge as he could. He had firm views, was sure of his analysis and the breadth of his ability, but he was open to opposing viewpoints." Brattin also remembered Stockman as a rather smug young man. "He knew he was smarter than anyone else he came in contact with and he certainly was pleased with himself. He probably felt his intellectual ability entitled him to certain things that put him in conflict with my wife. I remember he used to like to leave his shoes in the living room even though Alice Jean kept telling him not to. So, finally, she just dropped them down the laundry chute. My children were a little unhappy with Dave because they saw him able to break the rules when they couldn't." Brattin said Stockman seemed to spend most of his final months of college at the university library, and when he wasn't there, he would engage in intellectual debates with the older men active in the church. "His emotions were always held closely under control. He took positions from an intellectual, rather than emotional, standpoint. And he didn't hang around women much."

At this point Stockman's interest in antiwar activism waned, but he still opposed the war and he was still a strong backer of the civil rights movement. In late 1967 he encouraged his brother, Steve, then a student at the University of Michigan, to enroll in an exchange program at all-black Tuskegee Institute in Alabama. Steve did, and brought one of the students home for Thanksgiving that year.

The only woman in Stockman's life at that time was Susan Hause, a sophomore when he was a senior. She met him on the antiwar march to Washington and became his girlfriend and reading companion. Their relationship continued at Harvard and in Washington, when he hired her to work with him on Anderson's staff. Their personal relationship ended then, but she worked for him again as a senior budget official when he became OMB director. She later got married, took her husband's last name, Runne, and in 1985 left OMB to become a vice president at Citicorp in New York City.

"The Brattins were part of the liberal-religious group," she remembered. "They subscribed to *The Progressive, New Republic, Commentary,* and magazines like that. Mrs. Brattin let Dave invite SDS speakers to the house, and I remember Dave would be sitting in front of a roaring fire until one or two in the morning debating the war. He adored debating, but not chitchat." Stockman did not have much money then, and they did not go on traditional dates, such as to the movies or to a restaurant. Instead they spent a lot of evenings going to antiwar meetings and potluck dinners, or just staying up late together reading at the Brattins. "He felt he had something to say about the burning issues of the day. Somehow he felt driven to have people listen to him." Runne also described Stockman as "very self-centered, but in a benign way," in that he did not seem to be consciously egotistical as much as he was absorbed in his ideas, and neglected other people without realizing it.

"He was a very nice guy, really. And he could be humorous," Runne continued. "But he also was pretty unemotional. I suspect that is part of the farm mentality. You repress your emotions." As for friends, "he had his debating partners and a girlfriend. I think his activism was a way to deal with people. He preferred to avoid personal contacts. Being personal would be to muse on some intellectual level."

During his final term in school, Stockman's friends and mentors remember him turning more conservative politically. And like most other graduating college seniors, he was growing increasingly concerned about the prospect of being drafted. "He started looking for a way to avoid the draft," Runne recalled. Added Truman Morrison, who had become his principal mentor: "I think he was genuinely concerned about war and peace, but he genuinely wanted to avoid the war. He didn't want to have anything to do with the whole damn war. He was repulsed by the immorality of it all, the fire strikes, the destruction of villages." His brother, Steve, said, "I remember he was very concerned when he was graduating from Michigan State. He got his 1-A classification [available for immediate induction] and he had to go to Detroit and get a physical. For a while, we thought he would be drafted, but then he got accepted at Harvard Divinity School and he got a deferment. I knew he was strongly against the war, but I don't know what he would have done if he had been inducted."

No one remembered who suggested it first, but Stockman and his mentors agreed that Harvard Divinity School provided the way out. At the time, the only graduate school work that qualified for an automatic draft deferment after college were medical school and study for the ministry. As Stockman himself would later admit, Harvard was a perfect choice for three equally compelling reasons: he could avoid the draft; he had a sincere interest in theology, although more as an academic pursuit than as a route to the ministry; and Harvard offered the prestige, intellectual excellence and opportunities for success that satisfied his personal ambitions. But most of all, said Runne, "it was the only option" to avoid the draft. Morrison wrote a letter of reference. So did Jondahl, who noted in his that Stockman had become reluctant to support the militant tactics of the antiwar movement. He got accepted on a one-year Rockefeller Foundation grant, designed to expose students to seminary work so they could decide if they truly were interested in the ministry. Edgewood Church also made Stockman a $500 interest-free loan to help him cover expenses in his first year. Thirteen years later, after he became OMB director and pressed for curbs on government student loans, it was disclosed that the church had sent him half a dozen reminder letters before he repaid it. Morrison said in Stockman's defense at the time that students were given an indefinite amount of time to repay the loan, and that the incident was being blown out of proportion.

"I don't know if he would have been a minister, but he was quite serious about theology," Jennifer Stockman said of her husband's decision to go to Harvard. "Of course he also, as he will freely admit, went to avoid the draft. So there was an ulterior motive to going to divinity school." Still, she added, he also saw getting into Harvard as a major personal achievement and an opportunity to mingle with "the people who were the country's brightest and who would accomplish the most." A life as a minister seemed less and less in the cards. "I think the more knowledge he had about theology, the more agnostic he became," she said. "He's way too pragmatic to really believe in a superior being or any spirit. I think he'd like to, because it gives you a real sense of security, but I don't think he can, intellectually, because he has no empirical evidence."

"As he was going to Harvard," Stockman's mother said, "I recall he said he didn't ever want to be an ordained minister. He said he would like to have been a writer." Added brother Steve: "I'd say one of the reasons he went to Harvard was because it was the academic elite. He went there for the challenge. He always had this thing of being the rural boy from a one-room school. In high school he didn't get the best grades in the world, but he got by and knew he could have been valedictorian of his class if he put enough time and energy into it. And at Michigan State he didn't get really good grades the first couple of years, but by the end he was straight A's. So, it was a challenge again. He was going to Harvard, where all the intellectuals were going, to see if he was a true intellectual."

Stockman's success at avoiding the draft seemed to have been more the rule than the exception for college men of that era, but his decision would dog him in his later years. In response to the "We Won't Go" ad that Stockman signed in 1967, Jerome Eckenrode, a graduate student and ex-Marine, wrote a letter to the editor of the *Michigan State News* a week later charging that the ad should have been called, "I'm Afraid to Go." Anyone who signed the ad, he said, "is a young draft dodger with a yellow streak down the middle of his back. One who is associated with this group knows that it's his turn to serve America and he doesn't have the spirit to face the situation." Similar charges came up briefly during his campaign for Congress in 1976, and they were whispered in the Pentagon throughout his OMB years once he started calling for reductions in Reagan's proposed military budget. Several top White House officials said they specifically recalled hearing Defense Secretary Caspar Weinberger refer to him when he was not present as "the little draft dodger" or "the blow-dried draft dodger." Weinberger, however, denied ever using either expression.

As a public official Stockman never fully repudiated his antiwar activism. He did come to reject the analysis of his student days that the war was a civil conflict, and decided instead that the global spread of Communism was the real issue, as his father had insisted all along. But he remained critical of the way the war was managed, believing that the Johnson Administration rushed into Vietnam at great cost without first developing a sound policy on how best to contain Communism in the region. Indeed, for the same reason he became critical of his own Administration's ill-fated decision to put military forces in

Lebanon.

Looking back at the way the Vietnam war ended, Stockman and other draft evaders could feel vindicated by history. But Stockman's father still has his doubts. "I do support my country in a war, one way or another," Al Stockman said as he recalled the arguments with his college-age son. "I'm not going to turn my tail on my country, right or wrong." Of course, he agreed, the way things turned out led him to reconsider his own earlier support for the war. Was he saying that his son was right in protesting the war? "Well," Al replied slowly, "I'm not saying anything now." Then he added, "I'm saying, if we did not have that opposition, would the war have turned out as we know now it did? How much effect did that opposition actually have?"

In the fall of 1968, with thoughts of the war far removed, David Stockman set off for a new life at Harvard. Alice Jean Brattin drove him to Cambridge, Massachusetts, and Sue Hause went along for the ride. The Brattins would never hear from him again. Mrs. Brattin, now deceased, felt disappointed that he didn't stay in touch. Lynn Jondahl and David Hollister felt disappointed that he turned to the right. Truman Morrison felt disappointed that his protégé's passion for economic conservatism excluded compassion for society's needy.

"I discovered him to be very inner-directed, not so much oblivious to other people as much as primarily self-oriented," Morrison said as he reflected on Stockman's reconversion from liberal to conservative. "I see David as representative of the person who operates out of a real sense of inner integrity. But what is lacking, even when he is part of a social movement, is a sense of belonging and of genuine solidarity with the whole human family, the kind of personal orientation which is expressed by the word 'compassion.' " Morrison added: "David is a real disciple of the truth as he sees it, but he has moved toward thinking in economic terms that everything can be quantified, and he does not take into account the moral factors that cannot be quantified."

Later mentors also would express disappointment in Stockman's philosophical shift away from their viewpoints after seeming to embrace them so fully. It is as if he has been on a perpetual, childlike search for the ideal theory for how the world works. At first sighting, he can be a passionate believer, but when he quickly sees an imperfection, he casts the theory aside and resumes his search.

Deputy Treasury Secretary Richard G. Darman, who became one of Stockman's closest friends and political allies when he served in the White House as deputy to the chief of staff, explained the pattern this way:

"David has been looking and looking and looking for an intellectually and morally defensible complete world view. He grew up in a simple world with simple truths and a high degree of certainty. I think anyone who grows up in a world like that has trouble adjusting to the realities of a much more complicated and uncertain world. When you grow out of his little community and get into the larger world, you find that the old framework is inadequate and you get

90

buffeted. The particular sequence as to whether you're going to get attracted in this direction or that direction is almost chance. I see these as intense explorations on his part of the potential that one of these world views would have for providing this complete framework of certainty, morality, justification.

"Yet they're all flawed. All these frameworks are flawed, so when you go to one you are ultimately bound to reject it, whatever the sequence, because if you've got the intellectual power that he does, you've got the power not only to understand, you've got the power to criticize, and that's what he's done. And each framework gets shed. He temporarily deludes himself into believing he's got the entire, complete package of truths at any time, but then he's also capable of being the best critic of the underpinnings of that supposed truth. He's his own antithesis. How much he'll develop and where he'll settle is an interesting question. How much can humans ever know? How certain can we ever be?"

Richard Straus, a journalist who became close friends with Stockman when both were congressional aides in the early 1970s, said he recalled hearing Stockman lament that "as soon as he figures out where the world is, then it moves on him."

Jennifer Stockman described her husband's relationship with ideas in terms that suggest an adolescent crush. "He gets infatuated with an issue or with a person, and he doesn't take it lightly. He really learns everything there is to learn." He also has a tendency, she said, to be "in awe of an idea or a person until he gets close enough" to see the flaws.

And that's been true of everything and everybody, whether it be Marxism or Ronald Reagan. "David was fascinated with Marxism as an alternative to our system, but I don't think he ever believed in it."

The conflicting strains of idealism and cynicism flowing through David Stockman are not, however, just the project of his placid childhood upbringing. He also is an elder statesman of the turbulent 60s, a time that produced many Children of Light and Darkness. College campuses were a breeding ground for utopian dreamers who crusaded against poverty and racism, denounced Third World oppression, and sought to build a new world community based on fellowship. But their activism also gave rise to strong feelings of cynicism when they came to accept that society ran on self-interest and was not about to change. Their cynicism was reinforced by a loss of respect for national political leaders and institutions. Social injustice, an unpopular war, and Watergate — all helped feed a growing contempt for the establishment. Within a decade many sixties activists would be clawing their way up the establishment ladder, but still toting the stark attitudinal contradictions of their generation.

Stockman was, though, unlike his generation in an introspective way. He never showed much interest in "finding himself" or "getting in touch" with his feelings, or other people's. He was so busy trying to figure out how the world works that he never bothered to figure out how individuals, including himself, work. He believed in ideas, not people. His closest friends have said he is disinterested in, even disdainful of, psychology. He seemed oblivious to his own inner motives and how his behavior affected the feelings and behavior of his colleagues in the government. He could become enraged with someone who fought him on a policy issue, and he could not avoid revealing his contempt for those he considered stupid—a category that included most of the people in the government. Yet his friends claimed he held no personal grudges and harbored no ill will toward people, and was never aware that people could feel that way about him. In other words, presumably he meant well but was terribly naive.

Stockman's numerous critics do not buy any of these explanations. They interpret his multiple political transformations as the mark of a pragmatic opportunist, not a seeker of truth. "I wonder," one of his chief adversaries in the Reagan Administration remarked scornfully, "whether David Stockman believes in anything but himself."

His supporters always saw the Child of Light. His enemies only saw the Child of Darkness.

CHAPTER 4

PURSUIT OF
POWER

When he arrived at Michigan State, David Stockman discovered a new political world. When he arrived at Harvard Divinity School, he discovered a new social world. In the fall of 1968, a still rather unsophisticated farm boy from the Midwest fell into the midst of an urbane, affluent and highbrow subset of the eastern elite, and he would never be the same for it. A rarefied scent of lofty intellectualism, power and prestige wafted through Cambridge, Massachusetts, and Stockman quickly picked it up. Whatever remaining interests he had in the farming life, theology or antiwar activism, he dropped them at Harvard. The secular world of ideas—the federal budget, politics and history—became his obsession.

Even before he left Michigan State, Stockman became more preoccupied with political thought than religion, and his politics were becoming noticeably more conservative. The Reverend Truman Morrison recalled a discussion shortly before Stockman headed off for Harvard in which the younger man expressed his fundamental disagreement with leftist analyses that saw economic power in the country concentrated within a small so-called elite. Stockman argued that he believed economic forces are widely dispersed in the United States. Nevertheless, he still saw himself as a Democrat when he moved to Cambridge, at least enough of one to vote for Hubert Humphrey in the 1968 presidential election.

During his first year at Harvard he lived in the divinity school dormitory, and although antiwar protests on campus were at their violent peak, he shunned them, spending his time instead as the model scholar. He studied continually, focusing on government and politics rather than seminary work. He was always reading, and writing copious notes in a tiny scrawl on index cards about everything he read; the index cards filled half a dozen file cabinets. His habit of taking incredibly detailed notes continued all through his years as budget director. The reason for them, he once claimed to Deputy OMB Director Joseph R. Wright, Jr., was that he memorized everything if he wrote it down.

"We spent a lot of time discussing our opposition to the radical response to the war," recalled R. Jeffrey Pollock, a Cleveland attorney who was Stockman's roommate for the 1968-69 divinity school year. "And we shared a mutual evolution in our thinking—away from a radical, or more liberal, position to a more reflective position on liberalism." Pollock also was bowled over, as was everyone else, by Stockman's mental prowess and prodigious work habits. "I consider David Stockman the smartest person I ever met.

And the hardest working. When he was named budget director, I wasn't surprised at all. He had this tremendous ability to absorb and assimilate information and ideas like a sponge. He'd bring back ten books and then work them through in a matter of days. He lived in a world of ideas, and everything else was kind of inconsequential." Stockman had little respect for psychology and sociology, according to Pollock, but was particularly interested in history, and wrote a huge paper on the Truman era that his professor described as being equal to a master's thesis. To satisfy his divinity curriculum requirements, he would take courses in areas such as church history. The only socializing Pollock could recall specifically was during the second school year, when they lived apart and he would invite Stockman to his home for dinner. "What else do poor graduate students do?"

Susan Hause Runne, who had transferred to Boston University to be with Stockman, said neither of them had money to do anything, so "he read a ton," cooked and ate his meals in a little kitchen in the dormitory basement and lived an ascetic lifestyle. But he soon discovered another, far more exciting, social lifestyle nearby that would set him on a course to Washington within two years.

The Divinity School was located on Francis Avenue, a fashionable street with large homes occupied by some of the academic community's most prominent scholars. Runne first discovered this social set when she transferred to Boston University to finish her undergraduate work and moved to Cambridge. In order to be close to Stockman, she found a family on

Francis Avenue that provided her with room and board in exchange for her taking care of their children. It happened to be the home of Justin Kaplan, the Pulitzer prize-winning biographer and writer for such publications as *Atlantic Monthly, Saturday Review,* the New York *Times* and the Washington *Post*. His wife, Anne Bernays Kaplan, was a novelist. It also happened that the Kaplans were good friends at the time with another family on Francis Avenue, Elizabeth and Daniel Patrick Moynihan. He was a professor of urban affairs at Harvard's John F. Kennedy School of Government and had recently become President Richard Nixon's assistant for urban affairs.

The Kaplans, the Moynihans and their circle of friends socialized frequently at each other's homes. Occasionally, when the Kaplans were entertaining, famous writers from New York would drop in. Respected by their elders as bright young students, Runne and Stockman were invited to mingle with the guests as they engaged in heady conversations. "He found the scene exciting," Runne said. "This was the New York-Cambridge liberal Jewish intelligentsia and it was highly charged."

As a new school year was about to begin in the fall of 1969, Stockman found out through the Kaplans that the Moynihans had lost their babysitter and were looking for a new student boarder to watch their children when they were away and to be the bartender for their parties. Stockman, impressed with Moynihan's intelligence and government position, jumped at the opportunity to be near him. It also was an opportunity to exchange his dreary dorm room for more comfortable quarters on Francis Avenue, and he lobbied the Kaplans to tell the Moynihans what a great candidate he would be. That connection was enough to guarantee him the job, Runne recalled. But Stockman never pursued an opportunity or challenge with anything less than full intensity. He thought Moynihan was looking for a research assistant — "my delusions of grandeur," he later explained — and prepared for what actually was a pro forma interview by reading everything Moynihan had ever written. As always, Stockman did his homework and was overprepared. Moynihan's political views and writings never came up in the interview; babysitting did, though, and he got the job.

Life with the Moynihans had a strong impact on Stockman both socially and politically. "Dave was out of his element at Harvard, and the Moynihans and Kaplans allowed us to be part of their scene," said Runne. "They had movie parties, cocktail parties, and Dave loved it." But there was still a lot of country hick in him. Runne recalled one party at which the Moynihans planned to serve clams on the half shell. Mrs. Moynihan had asked Stockman to help wash them. Having no prior contact with clams, Stockman ran hot water over them and the shells opened up, ruining them. "Liz [Moynihan] was mortified. I guess, so was Dave," said Runne. Stockman also became intrigued with life in Washington as a result of Moynihans's frequent trips to the capital. While there he would call his wife every night, "and we couldn't wait for Liz to relay all the goings-on about Washington. Dave thought that was real exciting," said Runne. By then, she added, Stockman had all but ignored divinity school and was taking courses in practical politics at the JFK School with professors who had government experience and were part of the Washington-Harvard network.

Politically, the milieu Stockman had fallen into was very much like the one he had left at Michigan State, except that instead of spending his time with a group of solidly liberal Christian mentors he had now become part of a group of Humphrey Democrats who were drifting to the right as they questioned the worth of liberal social-welfare programs. Instead of sitting up late at night before a roaring fire at the Brattin home criticizing the Vietnam war, he would be up late at night with Moynihan criticizing the Great Society. "Pat Moynihan would come home late at night and they'd sit by the fireplace, drinking brandy, discussing the great issues of the world," said Jennifer Stockman. "And it was just so high-minded that it was a fantasy for David to sit with this great man in his library, with a crackling fire, and talk about all these issues.

In addition to the Kaplans, the Moynihans spent time with people like Nathan Glazer, John Q. Wilson, Irving Kristol, Daniel Bell — all scholars associated with *The Public Interest*, a quarterly journal they founded in 1965 to subject traditional Democratic liberalism to academic scrutiny. Their initial goal was to make the Great Society work better. Some of them had been socialists before World War II who became more anti-Soviet and more hawkish in their foreign policy views and saw most regional conflicts as an East-West confrontation. They also grew more conservative on domestic issues as their studies of

99

social programs made them increasingly skeptical about the programs' value. At the heart of their skepticism about social liberalism, according to Glazer, "was a common theme of analysis—that the government was trying to do too many things or things it wasn't suited to do." The group believed in the minimum welfare state as generally defined by the New Deal, but questioned the need for new federal programs to cope with every social problem that came along, particularly if local government or community volunteers were better able to deal with the matter.

Most of *The Public Interest* crowd thought of themselves as liberals at the time. "One assumed everyone was liberal then. We all were," said Glazer. But they became known as "neoconservatives," a label coined by one of their sharpest critics on the left, socialist Michael Harrington. In later years the neoconservatives would scatter in different directions along the political spectrum. Kristol represented the extreme that moved to the far right on both foreign policy and domestic issues, while Moynihan represented the extreme that moved back to the left. After he was elected to the U.S. Senate from New York in 1976, Moynihan returned to traditional Democratic liberalism on most domestic and foreign policy issues.

Ironically Stockman, who adopted Moynihan as his mentor at Harvard, wound up closer to Kristol. In Washington, Stockman and Moynihan would remain personal friends. But they became political opponents, and Moynihan would bitterly disapprove of his protégé's views, just as one-time mentor Morrison had. As one of the speakers at a Washington Press

Club dinner in February 1982, Moynihan teased Stockman about his loose talk in his confessional-like interviews published the prior November in the *Atlantic Monthly*. Dressed in his academic robes, Moynihan suggested that Stockman had "lost his divinity" at Harvard. He then wryly added, "Stockman never did actually believe that confession is good for the soul. But he did discover that it was good for Stockman." In a more serious complaint in July 1985, the day after Stockman announced he would resign as budget director, Moynihan declared that Stockman had confided to him in 1981 that Reagan did not really believe his supply side tax cuts would raise revenue and balance the budget, as the president and budget director claimed publicly; rather, Reagan secretly believed the tax cut would lower revenues and drive up the deficit, thus pressuring Congress to cut domestic programs. "I can't remember any such conversation," Stockman replied in a terse statement through his office. "I can say only that I have a reputation for candor and Pat has a talent for embellishment." In fact, Stockman and other budget officials, in off-the-record meetings with reporters, frequently confided similar versions of Moynihan's account, except they added that Reagan naively believed sufficient domestic cuts would be made early enough to keep the deficit from climbing.

While Stockman was at Harvard, though, Moynihan was a key figure in his political development and the originator of many basic views Stockman would advocate as budget director. "He put me in a skeptical mode" about the liberalism embraced at Michigan State. "I just threw it all away," Stockman said, which is not surprising. After a schizophrenic ideological odyssey from Goldwater to the Quakers to LBJ to Marx to Niebuhr, he was ripe for another change to reconcile these conflicting views once and for all. Niebuhr, he felt, had put him on the right track, so he intensified his search at Harvard for the totally consistent framework that thus far had eluded him. "It was a time for him to turn inward," said Runne. During a visit to Cambridge, his brother Steve found him "very serious, very studious, disinclined to remove his concentration in any way, shape or form from academic pursuits at that time. He did go out to one party when I was there, but he didn't enjoy it. He left early. And he almost totally withdrew from any kind of sports activities."

Stockman, it seems, found what he was looking for in the book, *The Good Society*, written by Walter Lippmann in 1937. "Lippmann was really right-wing," he said. "This book was an attack on the New Deal as economic statism. It made a case for my grandfather's position. So I switched and became anti-New Deal." Just like that. He noted that Lippmann also was strongly anti-totalitarian, which was consistent with the anti-Communist views held by both Stockman's grandfather and by Niebuhr.

Actually the philosophical framework Stockman was looking for had been in his backyard all along. "Dave really reblossomed as a conservative at Harvard," said Dan Stockman. "Every time I saw him, he became more and more conservative." An economic conservative, that is. He was a free-marketeer again. But he also became a critic of the political process that gave rise to the Great Society and its successor

102

programs. Theodore Lowi's book, *The End of Liberalism*, convinced him that social policy was the random end result of a political free-for-all or open bazaar at which any group with political clout could get whatever it wanted; such a pluralistic system was doomed by its inability to set limits based on a rational set of guidelines. This belief became the focus of his thinking and the core of his frustration as budget director. *He* had devised the rational set of guidelines; he just couldn't get them implemented.

In later years he would read other conservative tracts that had a major impact on his thinking, such as Friedrich A. Hayek's *A Road to Serfdom*, a work he would reread every few years, and Milton and Rose Friedman's *Free to Choose*. These were books that equated economic freedom with political freedom, and he became a devout believer in economic freedom as a basic right. He decided virtually all government regulations and subsidies were bad economics because they either were inefficient or gave someone an unfair advantage. Over and over, his grandfather had told him and his siblings how fortunate they were to be living in America because of its sense of fairness, its respect for individual freedom and the abundant opportunities it offered those willing to work hard. Now he was reading towering conservative intellectuals who were saying pretty much the same thing, if in fancier language.

Yet one feels there remained a contradiction in his thinking that he did not recognize. His defense of absolute freedom to pursue economic self-interest collided with his rejection of a free, pluralistic political system that responded to that self-interest. He was libertarian toward the economic system and totalitar-

103

ian toward the political process. A close friend in the Reagan Administration had somberly made that point in warning that society puts itself in danger when it gives too much power to someone with too much certainty. Several other friends have joked that they occasionally see traits of a dictator in Stockman because he is so sure in his beliefs, though he would no doubt be a benevolent despot: "Once a long time ago, when I think we had too much to drink, I asked him what his highest political dream was, and he said it was to be Emperor of the Americas," former congressional aide Jack Strayer said, and then broke out laughing. "I thought, 'Okay, sorry I asked.' And he says, 'That's the only thing I want to be.' And he'd make a great one. I mean, he's the benevolent dictator we've all been looking for. If he was assured he'd be a dictator, he'd be benevolent."

As Stockman settled on a new philosophical framework, he tried to fill in the blanks by studying in exhaustive detail the programs of the Great Society, the War on Poverty and the political process that created them. A primary reference at Harvard was Moynihan's *Maximum Feasible Misunderstanding*, published in 1969, the same year Stockman moved in with him. Moynihan had written a highly critical account of how the Johnson Administration and Congress attempted to involve the poor in running anti-poverty programs through the creation of Community Action Programs (CAP). Instead of helping the poor, Moynihan argued, the programs were taken over by local government bureaucracies or militant

104

community activists who would siphon off federal funds for their own purposes before the money reached the people who actually were in poverty. After moving in with the Moynihans, Stockman pursued that theme in his graduate studies. He traveled to Washington to use the library of the Office of Economic Opportunity (OEO), which was administering the Community Action Programs, and gathered reams of material on the organizations that were receiving the funds. His conclusion confirmed Moynihan's: "The local social-welfare system was being co-opted by either local bureacracies or militants. The whole idea wasn't working," he judged. (As budget director, Stockman would make the identical argument in defending cuts in social-welfare programs targeted for the needy.) He wrote up his findings in a 130-page report for two related courses. Wilson, who taught Stockman in a political science seminar on organizational behavior, recalled his former student writing "a very long paper" on the Community Action Programs. "He was extremely bright and extremely hard-working," said Wilson. "He got an A, and I rarely give them." Glazer, who had Stockman for a seminar on social policy, said he remembered Stockman writing "a long, remarkable paper on poverty programs. It was an analysis of a group of poverty programs and dealt with statistics and budget numbers. He showed great ability."

Stockman also was heavily influenced by *Logic of Collective Action*, a book written in 1965 by economist Mancur Olson. Stockman had read it during Wilson's seminar, which examined how special interests such as business and labor affect political outcomes. Wilson said a major theme of the book was that as the number of members in an interest group expands, the members become more detached from issues and are less likely to become activists. Wilson said Stockman later told him that the book had a significant influence on him. "My guess is that it made him suspicious of how truly representative interest-group leaders are of their members. They claim to speak for thousands of people, but perhaps only a few are actually represented." Indeed, as budget director Stockman would argue that special-interest group spokesmen who argued against cuts in federal programs were not representing their members' concerns. Instead, he charged, they were expressing their own selfish concerns about losing the grants that funded their lobbying activities.

In a November 4, 1979, interview appearing in the Detroit *News*, Stockman, then a 32-year-old second-term congressman, confirmed that Wilson's seminar "totally changed my outlook" about the political system. "I decided that political parties, business enterprises and fraternal organizations—the building blocks of society—are motivated by the preservation instinct, by the need to survive and thrive. As you mature intellectually you begin to realize that some of the simplistic formulations and idealistic notions that are attractive when you're twenty don't seem very realistic when you're thirty. At twenty, it sounds great to say that self-interest is in the most destructive force in society and that capitalism needs to be abolished. Now I believe that self-interest is an inherent part of the human condition and what we need to do is harness it, not abolish it." Whether he was aware of it or not, Stockman was describing Reinhold Niebuhr's "Children of Darkness."

Looking back on this period, it is remarkable how consistently Stockman would apply his Harvard learning about federal programs and the budget process to his job as Reagan's chief budget-cutter a decade later. More remarkable is the fact that he had designs on the budget director's job *as far back as 1970*. At the time he wrote regularly to his brothers, telling them what he was learning and providing them with suggested reading lists. One book he singled out was *The Politics of the Budgetary Process*, written in 1964 by Aaron Wildavsky, a professor of political science and public policy at the University of California—Berkeley. "This book," Steve Stockman recalled, "said that all the decisions were made at the Bureau of the Budget," which was reorganized as the Office of Management and Budget in 1970. "That was a revelation to Dave. I remember him asking me to read it. I remember we talked about it quite a bit. It said the key to understanding the whole federal process was found in the budget. It talked about how the agencies pad their budget, then they go to the budget bureau and the bureau cuts them back, and they go to the congressional committees and the committees put the money back in. It was fairly enlightening. Both Dave and I agreed that if we ever got to Washington, if we ever worked in the government, the only worthwhile job in the federal government would be director of the Bureau of the Budget, because you could make real changes there."

Three years later, when the two Stockmans were in Washington and working for Anderson, they often made a point of walking past the house of then Budget Director Caspar Weinberger, who lived along one of the routes they could take on their way home from work. It is not unusual for impressionable young congressional aides to engage in hero-worship, but most would be expected to identify with someone in a glamorous job, at least a famous senator or, say, the Secretary of State or the Attorney General. But not David Stockman. "Weinberger may have been just this little green eyeshade to most people, but Dave really looked up to him," said Steve. "We both idolized him. Remember, he was 'Cap the Knife' then, the great budget cutter. We'd go by his house and see if he had gotten home from work yet and wonder if he was inside. And sometimes we'd see him and shout, 'Hey, there goes the budget director! There goes Weinberger!'" Yet Cap, too, would descend into the pattern of fallen hero-mentors. As Ronald Reagan's defense secretary, Weinberger would become "Cap the Shovel," a leading Stockman adversary, an object of ridicule and scorn to the same young man who had idolized him in 1973. As for Weinberger, he would come to view Stockman with both haughtiness and amusement. He never seemed to feel as personally bitter toward the budget director, as did Donald T. Regan, the Treasury Secretary turned White House Chief of Staff. Instead Weinberger regarded Stockman as a youthful numbers-cruncher who was still wet behind the ears and in need of some schoolboy lessons about teamwork and loyalty.

At the same time that he was becoming an expert on the budget and the political process, Stockman spent many of his Harvard days rereading his history, this time concentrating on books that discredited the leftist, pro-liberal, pro-Soviet views that had impressed him so much at Michigan State. His reading helped develop an intellectual framework that would justify his decision to turn away from the antiwar protests in which he had been so active just a few years before.

His strong negative reaction to the violent protests at the Pentagon was reinforced at Harvard, which was in the midst of its most militant antiwar period when he first arrived. "There were big campus strikes, and radicals tried to burn the ROTC building," he recalled in the 1979 Detroit *News* interview. "There was a sort of shrill absolutism of violence and of rhetoric that made me question the whole movement." But it was not merely the violence that made him lose interest in the movement. He was living with, studying with and mingling with people who obviously wielded influence by working within the political process, not by protesting from the outside. He developed a craving for legitimate authority. "When you hang around these impressive members of the intelligentsia it whets your appetite for power," observed Runne. "Dave found it very exciting to hear these people talk about national issues in personal terms: what happened at a meeting with the President or at a Cabinet meeting. Given the scene, it was all very lofty, and I think Dave was very much interested in Washington."

Besides, Runne added, Stockman was too preoccupied with his own poltitical development to get involved in anything else. "Liz [Moynihan] and Annie [Kaplan] would keep urging us to do something social together, go to a movie or out to dinner, but that didn't interest him. He wanted to read and study. He would get ecstatic about finding some new research study at the library."

Actually, the closest Stockman came to a demonstration at Harvard was as a disdainful spectator. Runne broke out laughing as she recalled the incident: "I remember we went as gawkers to watch a sit-in at Harvard Yard. We went with Justin Kaplan, and Justin put on this nice sports jacket and had a hankie hanging out of his breast pocket just so. And we would just watch like we were on a social outing. We were above it all."

The luck of the draw gave Stockman another compelling reason to lose interest in Vietnam. The draft system had been replaced by a lottery system that took effect in 1970. All draft-age men, which included Stockman, were assigned numbers randomly from 1 to 366, based on their birthday. Draft boards, starting with number 1, would call up names until the military needs were met. If the year ended before someone's number was chosen, he was free of the draft for good. In December 1969, when the first lottery was held, it was generally understood at the time that those in the first third almost certainly would be called and that those in the last third probably would not. Stockman and other men born on November 10 were in that last group; they received number 282. The Selective Service only got up to 195 in 1970.

Stockman's Harvard days had one additional lasting impact on him: a special identification with Jews. Most of the neoconservative crowd he hung around with were Jewish, and Runne recalled Stockman remarking at the time that "I think I have a little Jewish blood in me." In Washington, several of his most trusted assistants in Congress and at the budget office were Jewish, a number of close friends and confidants are Jewish. And his wife is Jewish. Until he went to Michigan State he had not had any close contact with Jews, but he soon became impressed with the scholarship and intellectual abilities he saw in the Jewish students and teachers he met. Jack Strayer, his congressional aide in the 1970s, said Stockman discussed religion frequently in those days. "He considered Jews intellectually superior. That was a given," said Strayer. Richard Straus, a close friend who is Jewish, winced in acknowledging that Stockman has made the same observation to him. "It is a naive view and it sounds anti-Semitic, but it's unfair to Dave because it's not what he really means," said Straus. "It's just that Dave admires people who are very bright, knowledgeable and curious, because he is. And it turns out that a lot of them happen to be Jews. It also turns out that Jewish culture is big on learning, and he likes that. He relates to it." Stockman's empathy with Jews and his interfaith marriage underscores the lesson about the religious tolerance he learned as a child. It also reflects the anti-traditional attitude he picked up from his generation.

"Dave has had an amazing string of coincidences and lucky breaks in his life," observed his brother Dan. "But he's also an opportunist. He takes advantage of opportunities when they come along. He's very good at cashing in on them." Stockman has said the same thing about himself in looking back at an amazing career in which he leapfrogged from babysitting graduate student to congressional aide to congressman to White House budget director in a mere ten years. His astounding success did not flow from passive fate, from just being in the right place at the right time. The supercompetitive achiever in him was always on the prowl for lucky breaks; he *tried* to put himself in the right place at the right time, and when the opportunity opened up he pounced on it. In 1970, he and destiny conspired to get him to Washington — the right place, the right time.

It so happened that David Broder, a political reporter and columnist for The Washington *Post*, spent the 1969-70 academic year at Harvard's Institute of Politics teaching a non-credit seminar for undergraduates. It also so happened that Broder received a telephone call at the start of the term from Pat Moynihan, who said he had a graduate student named David Stockman who was a live-in babysitter and who had signed up for the seminar but couldn't get in. Moynihan said Stockman was very bright and very interested in politics, and he asked Broder if he could find room for another student. Broder consented. "He started coming, but not regularly; he came when he wanted," Broder recalled. "He was not particularly active or assertive." Broder said he had written a column at the time that criticized the anti-establishment political tactics of the antiwar movement and suggested that more could be accomplished by working through the system — for example, seeking to remove from office politicians who supported the war. The column had provoked a strong negative reaction from the students, and the focus of the seminar shifted to the issue of opposition politics. As part of the course Broder would invite guest speakers from time to time, and it further so happened that one of his guests was John B. Anderson, a five-term Republican congressman from Illinois who had recently been elected chairman of the House Republican Conference—the forum used by House GOP members to caucus on issues and strategy. The chairmanship was the third-ranking leadership post in the party.

In the spring of 1970 Anderson wrote a letter to Broder, saying he had an opening for a young staff assistant on the House Republican Conference. Anderson remembered the bright students and stimulating discussions at the seminar, and wondered if Broder could recommend any candidates. Broder thought of Stockman. "He was clearly politically oriented and did not stand out as an antiwar firebrand," Broder said. "He was a bright guy and he was reading more than the undergraduates. I remember him talking about Senator [Arthur] Vandenberg [Republican from Michigan, 1928-1951], and I was struck by how much he knew about Vandenberg. I decided this was a guy who was ready for Washington."

And so he was. Stockman followed up Broder's tip, contacted Anderson and arranged to meet him in Washington for an interview. Naturally, and inevitably, he did his homework first. "He read everything he could find out about Anderson, his voting record, the current issues," said Runne. "I remember we went to the Cambridge local library, pulling out volumes of *Congressional Quarterly* to look up Anderson's record. And we'd talk about strategy, how he could get the job. Dave was very excited about it." Stockman got Moynihan to recommend him. He also got a recommendation from Broder. And he persuaded Anderson to hire him. In later years the names of Broder and Anderson would join the long list of former Stockman talent scouts who grew disenchanted with their prize find. Broder would later accuse him of being a "duplicitous" cynic who would play by the rules of the political game when he was winning and express self-righteous contempt for the political process when he was losing. Anderson felt an especially deep sense of betrayal in 1980, when Stockman impersonated him in preparing Reagan for their presidential debate.

In June of 1970, with the draft no longer a personal problem, Stockman, then twenty-three, dropped out of Harvard Divinity School without getting a degree and moved to Washington. Washington . . . a city filled with people who held power or hungered for it, their ranks now swelled by one the day David Stockman flew into town. As his taxicab passed the Washington Monument and he gazed up at its height, Stockman promised himself that someday he would conquer this town. Years later, after making that vow come true, he would retell that story to friends. And in relating it he would reveal a strong sense of pride and satisfaction in his personal success — which was rather out of character for him. Normally he took his greatest pride in his work — the budget changes he wrought, his analysis, his articles.

He usually talked of power as a tool for implementing, not as an ego-gratifying perquisite. He was not one to revel in his power, prestige or fame — at least not in front of others.

Like his prior moves to East Lansing and Cambridge, Stockman faced a culture shock during his first weeks in Washington, but this one was particularly traumatic. Stockman initially moved with another congressional aide into a townhouse in Lincoln Park, a neighborhood east of Capitol Hill that was a convenient twelve-block walk to work but also an area with a high crime rate. Late one night his roommate was driving home from a movie with his girlfriend and pulled his car up to the curb outside the townhouse. A group of teen-agers approached, and one of them grabbed the girlfriend's purse through the open car window. When the roommate got out to fight them off, he was shot to death at point-blank range. Stockman, who did not learn of the shooting until the next morning, promptly moved out of the neighborhood, finding a place with a group of congressional aides who lived in a two-story nineteenth-century row house, supposedly once occupied by Supreme Court Justice Oliver Wendell Holmes, Jr., that was a few blocks away from the Court and the Capitol. Seven years later, then first-term Congressman Stockman also became the victim of a street crime while seeing a girlfriend, Sue Gillespie, home late one night. The couple was approached by three teenagers who claimed to have a gun and demanded their valuables. Stockman surrendered his watch and his wallet, which contained among other things $100 in cash and the special voting card he needed for the electronic vote-recording system used by the House of Representatives. Luckily, the assailants then ran off. The next day, he was forced to walk up to the well of the House to record his vote manually for a $125 million bill proposed by the Carter Administration to reduce juvenile crime. His heart, and wallet, were clearly in that one.

Stockman started off as one of Anderson's legislative assistants with responsibility for answering constituent mail, a job often given to congressional newcomers. "Within the first two months Anderson pulled him off that," said Steve Stockman. "He was too valuable doing research and he wasn't doing that good a job on the mail anyway."

Donald R. Wolfensberger, then Anderson's chief legislative assistant, had the same first impression of Stockman that most people had: that of a serious, ambitious young man who read and worked interminably. "He had such a voracious intellectual appetite. He would work nights and weekends. He ordered up books and books and books from the Library of Congress. I remember we'd play softball sometimes, but he'd stay and work. He was a very quick study who had an amazing retentive power. He could pick up something quickly and integrate it. I was very impressed with his IQ; it's as close to genius as anyone I've met." Wolfensberger also said that Stockman had a good sense of humor and was easy to get along with.

Although he started out as Wolfensberger's deputy, Stockman's intense drive soon made him the chief issues man. Typical of his nature to seek out the toughest challenge, one of the first legislative issues he dove into was also one of the more difficult and surely least glamorous: cargo preference, related to legislation favored by the maritime industry and unions, requiring that a minimum percentage of shipping be handled by American-owned firms. Ever since his farm days Stockman seemed to thrive on challenges that most people would consider too complex or impossible or tedious. During a conversation in Washington with someone who also grew up on the farm, when asked what chore he liked to do the most, Stockman said, "pitching hay."

The exotica of cargo preference did not just speak to the competitive side of Stockman; it also got his intellectual blood boiling, since it was the kind of economic subsidy that he found so loathsome. "I remember he wrote a very long analytical piece on it," said Susan Runne, who had come down from Cambridge to visit him in Washington. "I remember his attitude was the same as with the Vietnam war. He was convinced that he knew all about it and had the correct solution and rationale."

Another issue Stockman got involved in was election campaign financing. Anderson and Congressman Morris Udall, an Arizona Democrat, teamed up in 1971 and again in 1974 to sponsor bills limiting spending for congressional and presidential campaigns. Stockman was one of the major authors of both bills, which essentially shaped the legislation that eventually would be enacted in both years. It was unusual for Republicans to push for limtis on campaign spending, but Anderson and Stockman worked hard on the issue. Nevertheless Stockman was always troubled that he couldn't find a totally equitable way to establish spending limits for each congressional district. Through his research he discovered that media markets differed dramatically among congressional districts. Some districts were located in the middle of several major television, radio and newspaper markets, while some districts (such as his own) were not in any and so had to rely mostly on direct mail.

As a congressman, Stockman supported campaign finance reform legislation because of his opposition to the clout special interests exerted through their campaign contributions. But he also appeared to switch sides on the issue from year to year, opposing public financing of campaigns and spending limits that he believed favored incumbents. He had staked out his own position on the matter, and it did not conform with those of either the Democratic or Republican leaders in the House.

Robert J. Walker, who worked part-time for John Anderson in 1971 and later served as chief domestic adviser for Anderson's presidential campaign, remembered Stockman as "the boy wonder" who worked all the time. "He was very bright, very cerebral and a workaholic. His work was his life." Interestingly, Walker also remembered that Stockman "had a Keynesian outlook. I had a number of economic talks with Dave, and I think Dave thought a lot along those lines—that the economy could be fine-tuned by the government, that tax cuts and deficits were stimulants."

Stockman's mother recalled similar discussions. "Well, I think when he first got to Washington, I'd say, 'You know, this deficit spending is terrible.' And he'd say, 'Well, now, they can justify it by blah, blah, blah.' We sometimes had long telephone conversations about it."

Could it be? David Stockman, mortal enemy of deficit spending, a Keynesian? Could he really have had anything kind to say about deficits? Well, yes. As a student, Stockman never studied economics in great detail and he did not have a firm economic philosophy at the time he joined Anderson. Even as budget director he was relatively unschooled in economics theory, and his more knowledgeable aides considered him somewhat naive on the subject. "Remember, everyone was a Keynesian around 1970, and the deficits weren't a problem," said Steve Stockman. "Dave was more concerned about how much the government spent and taxed than about whether the books balanced out exactly. When the deficits got bigger a few years later, then he really started to worry." Indeed, the government actually produced a $3 billion budget surplus in 1969. By 1972, however, the budget had back-to-back deficits of $23 billion. The budget was never balanced while Stockman was in Washington.

During his first year with Anderson, Stockman also wrote many floor speeches for the congressman. In doing so he displayed a habit of doing his best and most intensive work at the very last minute. One of the secretaries had put up a sign, "Flow Mount Vesuvius," near his typewriter because it always seemed that he would suffer writer's block for days, but then on the day before it was due, when the pressure was greatest, the words suddenly starting flowing out like molten lava from Mount Vesuvius and he would finish in an hour. This was how he worked as budget director as well. Stockman wrote his own speeches and briefing materials, which is unheard of for Cabinet-level officials, and he would work on them literally until the last minute, rewriting, perfecting, catching an error here, changing a number there. And he sometimes acted as if possessed by a demon. He would snarl at his assistants, dash in and out of his office looking for information. Sometimes he would be kneeling on the floor trying to assemble papers that had been scattered across the room. He got especially frenetic just before he was to brief the President. His briefing materials always were prodigious. He could assemble volumes of information with a clarity and organization that other officials found astonishing. And like clockwork, the thick black briefing books were plopped in front of the President a few minutes after they were due.

"Dave always worked on things up until the eleventh hour," said David Gerson, a close friend and adviser who served as Stockman's principal assistant for a dozen years, starting with Anderson and ending with Reagan. Typically, as OMB director Stockman would rush off to the White House for a meeting, and Gerson, who would have to insert the last-minute changes in the presentation, would come running and panting into the meeting a few minutes later to distribute the briefing books. "Dave just loves writing and he loves producing quality work under deadline," said Gerson.

Pressure may have been good for his mind, but it was bad for his nerves. Stockman did not handle the stress well emotionally, according to several trusted assistants who worked with him at the budget office. "Dave lacks grace, and he is basically insecure about social matters," said one senior lieutenant and personal friend. "It manifested itself in his very poor response to pressure. In a crunch situation, where a document had to be completed, or an analysis, or a paper for a Cabinet meeting or a [Capitol] Hill presentation was due, as the clock ticked to the eleventh hour, Dave would become extremely irascible, extremely short-tempered and unkind to his staff and his secretaries. And since his gentlemanliness was always low to begin with, you can imagine what it was like under pressure. In fact, this is what got him in trouble in Hill testimony. When he was grilled by somebody who knew what he was talking about, Dave would literally lose his temper on the stand, and that's where he would make statements that he would later regret. This hurt him a lot in his congressional relations because many people got tired of being insulted by Dave Stockman during a congressional hearing."

Stockman had been with Anderson for barely eighteen months when another one of those "lucky" breaks came along. The executive director of the House Republican Conference left in December 1971, and Anderson rewarded his hard-working legislative assistant by passing over more senior aides and naming him to the plum job. Having just turned twenty-five, Stockman became the youngest person ever to hold the post and the youngest person with floor privileges, excluding the pages.

Stockman would later claim he got the job because he and Anderson planned to collaborate on a book about moderate Republicanism. It would be their hostile reaction to the anti-civil-rights posture of the GOP under the Nixon-Agnew Administration. Stockman said Anderson had no idea what the Republican Conference did and thought his aide would have more time to work on the book as conference director. In fact, Stockman had even less time after he took over the conference because he began developing new services to satisfy House Republicans who, Stockman always worried, would kick Anderson out of his leadership spot for being so independent. Stockman figured if he kept the members happy they would keep Anderson in his job. Although he might have had Anderson's interests in mind, Stockman also found that the conference post advanced his own interests and ambitions.

Until Stockman took over, the House Republican Conference had been a rather dormant organization. To change that, Stockman started the *House Republican Legislative Digest,* a compendium of all pending legislation including the status of the bills and an analysis of the pros and cons involved in each issue. Stockman and his staff of eight spent most of their time on the *Digest*. It became an instant hit with Republicans, who previously had to rely on background material provided by the Democrats. It was done so well, in fact, that outsiders began subscribing to the *Digest* and used it as a basic resource material. Susan Runne, who move to Washington when Stockman hired her to be the editor of the *Digest,* said he started it as a way to express his opinions on various issues. It also was a way for him to learn about a variety of issues and to do what he liked best — read, write and analyze. It also showed his ambition: Stockman was never satisfied to work within the previously established parameters of a job; he always wanted to make it bigger, more important and more visible than it had been before. He did that at the conference. He did that as a freshman congressman from a minority party. He did that at the budget office.

Richard Straus saw the *Digest* as a way for Stockman to put his learning to immediate use:

"The thing about David you need to understand is that his reading was always focused on something that could be put into practice right away. He'd read all this stuff, it would get put in the *Digest.* Or he'd read a lot and then convince Anderson he's got a new bill to put in the hopper, or he's got to organize a new political something or other. David always had an outlet for these ideas. It was not enough just to think and learn. He would read voluminously, but then he'd have an outlet for it, a form of immediate gratification for his learning. I always thought that was the key to his ability to absorb. Who else in their twenties had such an outlet? A lot of legislative aides could read all this stuff, but they worked for boring congressmen who had been around for twenty years and didn't want to do anything, or they worked for someone who said, 'You can't do that,' because the people back home would hang him. But not David. He had a totally free route. Anderson was open to all sorts of ideas, his position gave him a national platform and he had freedom because he was a Republican in a Democratic-controlled House. It was the perfect place for someone with David's ability.

"I emphasize this point because I've always been struck by the way he has been able to mobilize everything that he learns for an immediate gratification. That is unique, and a key to understanding him. I've never seen anybody else able to do that. It started with Anderson, and it never stopped until he hit the stone wall in the second year of the Reagan Administration. And yet he kept going at it because he refused to believe that if he kept marshaling all of these things and reading more and finding out more than anybody else that he wouldn't surmount this obstacle as he had surmounted every other one intellectually. It always worked before, and now he had much greater power and access than he ever had before."

It has been generally assumed by political observers, and frequently written, that both Anderson and Stockman were moderate-to-liberal Republicans when they started working together in the early 1970s, but in subsequent years Anderson would move to the left while Stockman headed to the right. It is true that Anderson would desert his party on several issues, and that Stockman would become more of a hard-line conservative after his first year or two in Washington, but the popular version of their political relationship is not quite correct or so simple.

While they had fundamental differences on some issues, they were in fundamental agreement on others, and their political philosophies did not change that much over time. In most areas of macro-economics, both men shared similar views about reducing federal spending and eliminating government intervention in the economy, but Stockman was more fanatical on these from the very start of their relationship. On issues involving social-welfare programs, Stockman was a hard-line opponent from the day he arrived in Washington, while Anderson vacillated between supporting and opposing federal social-welfare spending throughout their association. Some of their disagreements involved political considerations more than ideological differences. On social-personal issues, such as abortion, the Equal Rights Amendment, school prayer and civil rights, both were liberals — or, perhaps more accurately, libertarians. Indeed, on fifteen key issues singled out in the 1980 edition of *The Almanac of American Politics,* Stockman and Anderson voted identically on all but three. The almanac also revealed, rather significantly, that in 1977 and 1978 the quasi-liberal Republican Ripon Society rated Anderson's voting record at 100 percent and Stockman's at 92 percent for the two years. Even as budget director, Stockman still identified himself as basically a Ripon Republican — a free-market conservative on economics and a liberal on certain social and personal freedom issues. Both congressmen were unique and complex political figures in Congress who did not lend themselves easily to specific political labels, particularly since the meaning of those labels have kept changing with the times. The two men also had a close personal and working relationship, something like a father and son. Anderson, twenty-four years older than his aide, stayed at the Stockman family home in Michigan on a few occasions and hired two of Stockman's brothers to work in his congressional office while the eldest brother worked at the Republican Conference. As a result of their closeness over five years, they exerted more influence on each other than either would later admit.

Anderson and Stockman came from similar districts made up of small towns and farms, overwhelmingly white and Republican, with heavy concentrations of northern European stock possessing a strong sense of the Protestant work ethic, self-reliance and moral rectitude. And in the same way that Stockman's district is politically different from most of Michigan because of its location along the southern and western border of the state, Anderson's district is politically distinct from the rest of Illinois because of its location in the northwest corner near Wisconsin and Iowa. Both men also showed a greater intellect and interest in ideas than most of their House colleagues, and both had a tendency to be political mavericks.

When it came to basic free-market principles, Anderson and Stockman saw eye to eye. "Basically we had a similar view of fiscal policy," Stockman later said. "He was against wage-price controls, he was big on free enterprise, he was against regulations and business subsidies. It was on social issues where we differed. He believed more in social-welfare programs."

John Anderson has stated their differences more bluntly. "He always was more conservative. David

Stockman is an old-fashioned conservative. He attaches mystical, if not magical, powers to the free market. I would disagree with him. There are limitations to the free market. I don't have a religious or ideological commitment to it." Anderson went on to say: "He tood a very hostile attitude toward the role of government in meeting people's needs, a lot of which came out of the civil-rights struggle. Significant elements of the population, mainly women and minorities, had been left behind by the economy, and the government had to do something to deal with the social injustice. I suppose he had a fundamentally different point of view all along, but he muted it while working for me."

The main point of tension in their relationship, as former colleagues recalled, was Anderson's tendency to desert the official GOP line and move to the left on all sorts of non-economic issues — from civil rights to campaign financing, to Vietnam, to Nixon and Watergate. When these controversial positions would put his leadership post in jeopardy, Stockman would work to keep him in the Republican mainstream and in his post. Which, of course, is what a loyal staff assistant is supposed to do. It also is what an ambitious young man who wants to keep his own job would decide to do. In early 1971, before Stockman became director of the Conference, Anderson had been challenged for his third-ranking leadership post by Ohio Republican Samuel L. Devine, who complained that Anderson's record on domestic issues was too liberal. Anderson survived by a close 89-81 vote, but the tight race left Stockman worried that his boss would be dumped in the future.

"John Anderson was a liberal across the board," claimed Richard Straus, who met Stockman in 1972 and established a close friendship that both have maintained since. Straus worked at the time as a legislative assistant to former Congressman Peter Frelinghuysen, a New Jersey Republican. He later turned to journalism, writing a newspaper column and publishing a newsletter on Middle Eastern affairs. "Anything Anderson wasn't liberal on was because of Stockman. I mean, Stockman pulled at him constantly and held onto the coattails to hold him back. John Anderson was a liberal. He may have been considered an economic conservative or moderate at the time, but he was a left-winger in his heart."

Stockman could keep Anderson conservative on economic issues involving fiscal prudence, incentives, business subsidies and regulation, where both had a basic agreement. In the summer of 1972, for example, Stockman prepared a thirty-page detailed analysis of Democratic presidential nominee George McGovern's budget proposals that Anderson used to attack the candidate. The study concluded that McGovern's program would drive spending up 37 percent, require a 53 percent increase in federal income taxes, "wipe out the middle class" and produce a $126 billion deficit. In 1973 Anderson showed his conservative colors when he tried unsuccessfully to amend a bill to increase the minimum wage with a provision to establish a sub-minimum wage for teenagers and farm workers. He also was consistent in opposing subsidies, helped defeat a price-support program for sugar growers in 1974, and became interested in deregulation of the trucking industry — a subject to which Stockman had devoted an entire issue of the *Digest*.

When it came to social-welfare programs on which Anderson would waver, Stockman sometimes prevailed. In 1973 Stockman persuaded Anderson to vote for an amendment to a farm bill that barred striking workers from receiving food stamps. The amendment passed by a narrow margin in the House but was eliminated from the version of the compromise bill that finally cleared both the House and Senate. Anderson went along in part because his stand would be popular in his district. On environmental issues Anderson was essentially pro and Stockman was con, because of his rigid anti-regulation view. "Dave was a very anti-clean air, anti-clean water when it came to federal regulation," said Runne. "It was all part of his anti-government philosophy." But Stockman also would do Anderson's bidding, as in 1973 when he worked with Udall's staff to develop an alternative to the Alaskan oil pipeline.

When it came to issues on which Stockman had no particular expertise and Anderson had strongly held views, Stockman wasn't able to keep his boss on the GOP reservation. In the fall of 1971 Anderson deserted the GOP leadership by supporting a stronger, Democratic-backed version of a bill to empower the Equal Employment Opportunity Commission to bring discrimination suits in federal court. Anderson generally supported the Nixon Administration on Vietnam, but he started to grow impatient with the continued fighting and voted in 1973 to override Richard Nixon's veto of a joint congressional resolution limiting his war powers. In that same year, as the

Watergate scandal grew, Anderson became one of the first Republicans in Congress to press for a full investigation and, later, for Nixon's resignation.

Such positions gave Anderson the reputation of being a rabid anti-Nixon liberal Republican, despite his economic record. It was assumed that Stockman and the other Anderson staff assistants at the House Republican Conference had the same views. Which, for the most part, was true. Stockman *looked* liberal. He was only in his mid-twenties and his assistants were even younger; his hair, which had not yet turned gray, covered his ears and reached down to the back of his shirt collar; he had joined the Ripon Society because the more senior Anderson aides had; he did not even vote for Nixon in 1972. Although he considered McGovern too far left, he disliked Nixon because of what the Anderson group called the "sleaze factor." They also didn't like the Nixon-Agnew attacks against the three social "A's — Acid, Abortion and Amnesty." So he left his presidential ballot blank. Like so many others his age, Stockman could boast that he had *never* voted for Richard Nixon, neither in the 1968 nor the 1972 election.

Much of the antipathy traditional Republicans felt toward Anderson and his youthful crew stemmed from the "Us versus Them" mentality that had developed. With the countercultural revolution in full swing and Watergate jeopardizing Nixon's future, the political scene was divided into two hostile camps: the liberal Democrats and their long-haired, pot-smoking radical friends (which included women, blacks and ethnics), and the straight, clean-cut, flag-waving white men who stood up for God, country,

130

Republicanism and Richard Nixon. Since Anderson was the only GOP leader who didn't conform to the second stereotype, and particularly since he was viewed as being so violently anti-Nixon, it was assumed he was a traitorous member of "Them."

This attitude bothered Stockman, particularly when he too was suspected of being one of "Them." After all, he had worked diligently to keep Anderson in step with the party, especially on Watergate. "That was the cutting issue for liberals and conservatives," said Richard Straus, "and David twisted himself into a pretzel trying to get Anderson to hold back. But Anderson wouldn't, because he was morally outraged by Richard Nixon. Now, David wasn't morally outraged. I suspect one of the reasons was because he had someone like Anderson, who had more than enough moral outrage for the two of them. See, I was in the opposite position. I worked for a guy who wasn't morally outraged, and it drove me up a wall, and eventually I quit because of it. I couldn't work for the Republicans anymore."

Straus added: "I remember one of the guys in my office said, 'The President's going on TV tonight. What are you going to do?' I said, 'I'm going to David's house to watch it,' He said, 'You going to throw tomatoes at the TV?' That kind of thing grated on David. But in fact, David did have a big picture of Nixon in his bathroom. It was a big formal picture like you'd see in a government office. And people would put whipped cream on it or they would draw horns on it or deface it in some other way. And David would always clean it up because he didn't like the image my Republican colleague had of him. Everyone would say, 'Anderson's got these young guys working for him and they're pushing him to the left.' Yet the truth of the matter was that David was pushing Anderson to the right, and he didn't want to seem like that wrong image people had of him, even if he personally did throw tomatoes at Nixon."

Straus, who was married at the time to a woman who worked for Stockman, laughingly recalled the day in 1974 when Nixon finally released all the transcripts from the Watergate tapes, which produced the "smoking gun" that would bring on his downfall:

"I can still remember the night Nixon released the expurgated 1,300 pages of transcripts. David read *all* 1,300 pages and then declared, to the enormous chagrin of a lot of people and the general mirth of my wife and myself, that, 'Yes, there is a case to be made here for Richard Nixon.' See, Nixon had doctored it in such a way that somebody could plausibly argue his case, I don't know who. Well, in this case, there was a who: it was David. He did argue it. And I remember my wife and I just thinking that this was the funniest thing we'd ever heard. And we just totally dismissed it and laughed. But he was dead serious because he had a purpose, which was to protect Anderson. He worried with good reason that Anderson was going out there and hanging himself by trying to lynch Nixon. The guy was head of the Republican Conference; he wasn't supposed to carry Ted Kennedy's water. Nobody suspected at the time that Nixon was going to fly off in a helicopter and leave the country to Gerald Ford. David had convinced himself there was a plausible case based on the transcripts. I'm not saying a tight case, but a plausible one."

Personally, Stockman hoped that the worst being written about Nixon in the Washington *Post* was true, and that he would be forced out of office. Professionally, however, he felt uncertain about the credibility of the allegations and whether, even if true, there was enough evidence of wrongdoing to warrant a President's impeachment. Only belatedly did he come around to the conclusion that the Nixon tapes contained the "smoking gun."

Despite much anguish about Watergate, Stockman did not have much impact on Anderson's thinking, according to the congressman's later recollections. "I don't recall that being a subject of many discussions," Anderson said. "On Watergate he was not a close confidant." Perhaps the same delusion of grandeur that led Stockman to think he was going to be Moynihan's research assistant gave him an exaggerated sense of importance of his Watergate counsel to Anderson.

Ironically, one of the reasons Stockman was so intent on protecting Anderson was because he worried that New York Congressman Jack Kemp would make a run at the Conference chairmanship. "Dave was always plotting and scheming to make sure Kemp couldn't do it," said Straus. Kemp never did challenge Anderson, but he did become Conference chairman in 1981 after Anderson had left the Congress. Kemp would become a mentor of Stockman's after he became a member of Congress, introducing him to supply-side economics and playing an important role as an intermediary to get his protégé into the OMB post. But Kemp also would become one of the many disillusioned mentors who felt betrayed by David Stockman.

Stockman, a creature of strict routines, had a personal life during his Anderson days that did not vary much from his last year at Michigan State and would remain the same at OMB: he read and wrote. His brother Steve, who lived with him during the early 1970s, gives this account of his schedule:

On weekdays he would get up at 6:30 A.M., leave for his office at 7:00 A.M., eat breakfast en route, eat a sandwich at his desk around noon, come home at 6:00 P.M., take a 30-minute nap, eat dinner, go back to the office around 7:30 P.M., work until 11:00-11:30 P.M., come home and either read or chat about his work, which consisted of reading, researching and writing. He would sleep four to six hours a night; he never needed more. Saturdays were pretty much the same, except he would knock off work a little earlier, and on rare occasions he would take the entire day off if he had an out-of-town visitor or a special activity planned. On Sundays he'd have breakfast at Sherrill's Bakery, go to his office, where he would read the New York *Times*, Washington *Post* and (now defunct) Washington *Star* until about noon and then resume his normal routine, except that he sometimes would take Sunday night off rather than return to the office after dinner. He had only one close friend outside of work — Richard Straus. He never watched television, never went to a sporting event, and only rarely saw a movie. "I remember we went to see 'A Clockwork Orange' one time," said Steve. "Dave thought it was a

134

bit weird, and it was. This was a time when we had some dates and we got there late. We were in the first row looking up at the screen. And there was a name we took from that movie. 'Droogs' [Friends]. And we picked that up and used to call each other the 'Droogs.' "

Stockman did not exercise or watch his diet. He ate fast food, drank coffee by the potful and chain-smoked Salem cigarettes, a habit he picked up from Steve who moved in with his older brother in 1971. His daily consumption of McDonald's cheeseburgers, barbecue potato chips, three pots of coffee and several packs of Salems became legendary during his OMB years.

After Steve Stockman graduated from the University of Michigan in 1971 he moved to Washington at the urging of his brother, who arranged a summer internship for him at the Conference. Steve said Dave also encouraged him to attend law school in Washington and helped get him a temporary job in Anderson's office while he studied law at Georgetown University. In 1973 Dan also got a job working in Anderson's office, and he moved in with his brothers at the row house on 408 A Street, Northeast. Dan left politics for the construction business in 1975 and moved to Springfield, Missouri, five years later. In the same year that Dan came to Washington, David Gerson came to work for the Republican Conference as a nineteen-year-old intern. A year later "Ger," as he was called to distinguish him from David Stockman, dropped out of Case Western Reserve University in Cleveland, moved in with the Stockman brothers and dedicated the next eleven years of his life to his namesake. Over time, Ger came to be regarded as Stockman's alter ego.

Like Steve, Dan remembered little about his eldest brother's activities other than work. The younger brothers, by contrast, were rather more socially inclined. "We'd have quite a few parties," said Dan, who also recalled that Dave *occasionally* could unwind after work like a normal twenty-eight-year-old. "Sometimes," he said, "Dave and Steve and I would sit around, drink some beer or smoke some pot and have these rambling discussions. We'd talk a lot about ideas."

Stockman's ideas usually had to do with the federal budget. Ever since his Harvard days with Moynihan, he seemed obsessed with it. Each year the President sent Congress a proposed budget that was at least 600 pages long, crammed with numbers on specific programs, budget trends, economic forecasts and the like. And Stockman read it every year, all of it. "He'd read the full federal budget, not just a summary," said Steve. "He'd read the thing page by page. Every single program. It would take him about a month after it came out, but in the evenings he'd go back and he'd look at it. He'd look at the expenditure levels and what they were for. And so he *knew* it."

The more Stockman read and mastered, the more critical and contemptuous he became of the ever expanding network of social-welfare programs that Congress would approve every year. But no one on the Hill seemed to share his passion, including his boss. "Dave got real interested in the budget," said Dan Stockman. "He wanted Anderson to do something, and even though Anderson was a fiscal conservative, he didn't do anything. No one would or could. It became hopeless. But Dave wanted to do something about the budget. He developed a real commitment. He has a heroic love for this country that we got from our grandfather, and he really wanted to do something for the country. He knew the problem required hard medicine, and no one else was willing to say so."

Stockman's inability to do anything about the budget made him increasingly frustrated with the political process, an attitude that would surface again and again during his years at the budget office. David Broder of the Washington *Post* would meet with Stockman periodically at the Republican Conference during the early 1970s to assess the latest party currents. Like so many others, Broder uses one word to describe Stockman — "intense." Broder was impressed with the young staffer's keen perception of the congressional political environment, something Anderson seemed unaware of. He also was surprised by the extent to which Stockman would reflect his own views rather than those of his boss, as most loyal and more cautious aides would. What Broder heard was the mounting disdain Stockman had for the whole political system. "He would make an intellectually rigorous critique of the Washington establishment, and I found it striking that this was coming from a Republican staff guy," said Broder. "He would say, 'Hey! Except for everyone's first vote, there's not much difference between the two parties on the Hill.' What struck me was that here was a guy with an awful lot of naiveté. He was against politics in general."

As Richard Straus had observed, Stockman needed an immediate outlet for his ideas about the budget. In the summer of 1974 he found one. He and Susan Runne collaborated on an article that mercilessly attacked the social-welfare state as a "social pork barrel" and assigned both political parties equal blame for maintaining it. Although Runne claimed she wrote half the article, Stockman claimed credit for the final draft, and it was published under just his name. And it turned into another one of those examples in which his abilities, ambitions and good fortune converged to create a break, this one helping to catapult him into national recognition and a seat in Congress.

Stockman got the idea for the article from a twenty-volume study on the entire social-welfare structure commissioned by the Joint Economic Committee of Congress, which had released a series of papers on the issue between 1972 and 1974. One of the most publicized and controversial portions of that study was a 1972 General Accounting Office survey that found substantial inequities in the cumulative effect of some one hundred different cash and indirect-aid programs that were costing the government $100 billion a year. The GAO reported that some jobless families were drawing multiple benefits totalling more than average wages in some areas, while other poor people were ignored. Congresswoman Martha Griffiths, a Michigan Democrat who had ordered the survey, said the findings demonstrated the inadequacy of the whole federal welfare structure, and the results impressed Stockman, who had become particularly critical of the inherent unfairness he saw in the system.

Using that as his inspiration, Stockman wrote "The Social Pork Barrel," which would be published in the spring of 1975 by Stockman's old neoconservative friends at *The Public Interest* magazine. The article was truly remarkable in terms of the consistency with which Stockman argued his case then, and again and again over the next ten years, first as a congressman and then as budget director. The general criticisms, the specific proposals for cutting programs, the colorful but inflammatory rhetoric, the warnings of doom and gloom—all distinguishing marks of his career at OMB—were reflected in "The Social Pork Barrel." He warned of a coming "budget crisis," resulting from a swollen deficit and the "uncontrollable" growth of programs that invariably start out modest and simple only to wind up huge and complex. "The federal budget process, potentially the basic forum for serious policy choices, has been reduced to a mere annual ritual of accounts juggling," he said. That line referred, perhaps unintentionally, to the kind of budgetary sleight-of-hand he would criticize, yet also practice, at OMB.

The article went on in great detail to explain how programs that had grown out of the good intentions of the Great Society had become economically counterproductive, much too expensive, ineffective and unfair. One of his most biting complaints was that social programs originally meant to help the poor had been turned into multi-billion-dollar subsidies for the middle class, the result of politicians guaranteeing their own job security by following the maxim: "the greatest goodies for the greatest number." Stockman's own thinking in 1974 went like this:

Black lung benefits should be paid by the coal industry, not the government. Disaster relief should be the responsibility of those who take on the risk of building on a flood plain or farming in drought-prone areas. The National Cancer Institute's budget should be curbed because despite regular annual increases, the Institute has produced "no noticeable improvement in cancer survival rates" during the prior fifteen years. The military retirement pay system should be reformed because it is too generous. Scores of outmoded military bases should be closed and the Pentagon should operate more efficiently. (Members of Congress would rather cut weapons programs than shut a useless base in their district). Social service grants for compensatory education, community mental health centers and vocational rehabilitation do not show any clear effectiveness, and benefits are distributed randomly to only a tiny fraction of those eligible. Hospital construction has produced an excess of beds and has led to the costly over-hospitalization of Americans in place of less expensive alternatives. The "notorious" Impact Aid program has grown from a tiny program of helping school districts located near military bases to a grant program assisting half of all public school children. The "regressive" Social Security system could eliminate poverty if benefits were directed toward the poor instead of across the income spectrum. College loans should be limited to low-income families rather than become a middle-class entitlement. Most veterans benefits go to "ex-servicemen who do not even have a hangnail to show for their harrowing experiences in uniform."

In 1981 Stockman would pull all of these programs on his budget chopping block.

His conclusion in the article was that "the care and maintenance of the social welfare spending pipeline that extends to each of the 435 congressional districts in the nation have now become a central preoccupation of members and their staffs." Instead of acting like legislators and statesmen, members "have more and more taken on the characteristics of constituency ombudsmen and grant-brokers. As a consequence the aims of social policy have been subordinated to the exigencies of the new fiscal politics, and what may have been the bright promise of the Great Society has been transformed into a flabby hodgepodge, funded without policy consistency or rigor, that increasingly looks like a great social pork barrel." He went on to complain that budget policy turns out to be the random result of "the tugging and hauling of parochial interests and constituency needs. It is hardly surprising that the results of this kind of raw democracy in action are hardly optimal by any kind of disinterested standards."

Stockman also expressed his "a-pox-on-both-your-houses" mentality, which as Broder had noticed seemed so odd for someone who also wanted to be part of the system he was condemning: "If the programs which comprise and the rhetoric which surrounds the social pork barrel are liberal in paternity, this distinction usually fades with the passage of time. Indeed, the political maintenance capabilities of the system are so strong that all except the most extreme and idiosyncratic conservatives are eventually brought into the consensus. There is, however, a process of evolution that often leads to the erroneous impression that there are serious ideological differences in Congress on social spending policy. In reality, there are not.

"George Wallace's old charge about there being 'not a dime's worth of difference' between the two major parties is not far from the truth in terms of social welfare policy," Stockman concluded, "Conservatives may profess to be vigilantly watching at the gates of the federal treasury, and liberals may profess to be striving to insure that America's least advantaged are given their due; but in reality neither side is doing very much of either task. In fact, conservative duplicity and liberal ideology both contribute to the dynamics and durability of the social pork barrel. Yet the resulting social policy stalemate cannot persist indefinitely."

Ten years later, despite an extraordinary battle over the budget, the stalemate would persist, and a soon-to-depart OMB director David Stockman would be giving forth with the exact same lament! "After four years I am convinced that a large share of the problem is us. By that, I mean Republicans," Stockman said in a July 1985 interview that was published the following February in, of all places, *Penthouse* magazine. "We talk about big government in the abstract, and runaway budgets, and reducing the growth rate in spending. . . . If you ask Republicans, 'Would you cut the government ten percent?' they'd say, 'Yes.' But for each piece that you have to start cutting, there is an enormously powerful cadre of people who protect it — on our side!"

What was missing from "The Social Pork Barrel" — and still missing in his later views, such as in the *Penthouse* interview — was a creative solution to the political stalemate he had viewed with such exasperation, or at least a slight acknowledgement that some pork may have redeeming social or economic value, or some recognition that a pluralistic political system responsive to so many diverse interests can't be *all* bad. But if anything, he had become only hardened in his antipathy toward the system. It was as if his political development had become stunted after years of abnormal growth. Whether he resumes his search for a new political framework will have to be answered by the future.

Stockman submitted his 1974 article to Nathan Glazer, one of the editors of *The Public Interest*. He then returned to Harvard, where he spent the fall studying at the Institute of Politics. While there he served as coordinator for an orientation seminar the Institute provides for new members of Congress. Jonathan Moore, the Institute's director, described Stockman at the time as "one of the most able and articulate aides on Capitol Hill," according to a December 18, 1974 story in the St. Joseph *Herald-Palladium*, Stockman's hometown newspaper. But Stockman had higher ambitions in mind than being just the best congressional aide. It did not take more than a year or two in Washington for him to decide he could do a better job than most members of Congress.

Initially Glazer and Irving Kristol, the magazine's

co-editors, were not overly impressed with the article, and they almost did not run it. "We rejected it at first," recalled Kristol. "We thought it was interesting but rather familiar, as if we had heard it before. So we looked at it again after ten days and changed our minds. Maybe it seemed more familiar to us than our readers. Maybe we had read something else that was similar but not so sharply done as this." Glazer remembered that he had mixed feelings about the article at first. "It showed good qualities — a command of detail, clear writing — but I thought it was too detailed. So we passed it up. Then we decided to publish it."

The article became the lead piece in the Spring 1975 edition of the magazine and swiftly made Stockman a name with the official gatekeepers of opinion on the east coast. It also set him on a fateful course to great power and a precipitous fall from grace. Meg Greenfield, then deputy editorial page editor of the Washington *Post*, read the article and was so impressed that she called to meet him for lunch. "I expected a fifty-five-year-old troll from the bowels of Congress," she exclaimed after laying eyes on the attractive young man who was only half the age she had imagined. The article also was praised by Irving Kristol in a column he wrote for the *Wall Street Journal*, which caught the eye of other opinion leaders in the country. Kristol's column left a favorable impression on business and political leaders in Stockman's congressional district just a few months after an editorial in the area's most influential newspaper had called for a change of congressmen and encouraged Stockman to run. The article was also read by Richard Darman, then an obscure Ford Administration official, who would assign it for a graduate course on government that he taught at Harvard during Jimmy Carter's presidency. Darman recalled being impressed by the fact that the article showed sophistication in both its economic and political analysis, a combination that Darman found rare. In another one of those strange coincidences that repeated throughout Stockman's life, the article immediately following his in that issue of *The Public Interest* bore the strange title "The Mundell-Laffer Hypothesis — A New View of the World Economy" and was written by someone with an equally strange name, Jude Wanniski. Wanniski wrote editorials for the *Wall Street Journal*, and it was his article that introduced the political world to supply-side economics.

It turned out that Wanniski would meet Stockman two years later, help convert him into a supply-sider and come up with an idea that brought Stockman to the attention of Ronald Reagan during his 1980 campaign for the presidency. It further turned out that Richard Darman would join the Reagan Administration after the 1980 election as deputy to the White House chief of staff, become Stockman's closest ally in the White House and teach his strong-willed colleague how to channel his idealism and skepticism toward a middle, pragmatic course. And it also turned out that Meg Greenfield would commission future Stockman articles for the Washington *Post*, which would spread Stockman's reputation and lead him to meet William Greider, who would chronicle Budget Director David Stockman's first year in office for a magazine called *The Atlantic Monthly.*

Meanwhile, John Anderson would feel both surprised and betrayed by the views expressed in "The
Social Pork Barrel." Anderson refused to discuss
Stockman's personality or motivations, but on matters of policy Anderson said coldly: "He didn't reflect
my views at all. The pork barrel piece did not
comport with my ideas of government."

Stockman later said he thought Anderson was
aware that he was writing the article, which he
showed to Anderson at the time. He remembered
Anderson's reaction was that he disagreed with some
of the points. Howard Moffett, a lawyer who worked
for Anderson as an aide from 1969 to 1972, said he
was surprised that Stockman and Anderson would
wind up at ideological odds. "There wasn't anything I
was aware of in Anderson's office or at the House
Republican Conference to suggest that David's views
were different from Anderson's," he said. "Anderson
would never favor gutting social programs as much as
David did without regard for the social consequences.
I think Anderson feels a little betrayed by the shift in
allegiance, and I think he is genuinely surprised and
hurt that Stockman, a one-time ally and supporter,
would be waving the banner for the other side."

Anderson's wife, Keke, did not share her husband's
reluctance to discuss Stockman's character. Although
the Andersons and Stockman were once good
friends, they had a falling out during the 1980
presidential campaign, when they went their separate
ways. Six years later Anderson sounded bitter but

restrained when he spoke of his protégé. Keke, however, sounded as though she was still in a rage, as if Stockman had inflicted fresh wounds on her husband while his back was turned. "Politically they had scholarship in common. They were both intellectuals, but David has a ruthlessnesss in his heart that occurs when one is interested only in himself," she said, the sharp-edged words flowing out rapidly. Calling him "the little dummy" in one reference, she said Stockman refused to talk to her during the 1980 primaries. She added: "David always wanted to be the winner. He is a driven young man, I know. He is trying to prove himself to his mother."

And so yet another mentor scorned. But Stockman still could not understand why people always took it to heart. He was neither good at nor interested in understanding others' feelings or motivations; they only got in the way of his search for ideas. In terms of their psychological makeup, "he basically sees people as a blank wall," said Susan Runne. Jennifer Stockman said in her husband's defense: "They [the Andersons] shouldn't take it personally, because David didn't mean it personally. Again, it's David's eagerness for new ideas and for what he thinks is right, whoever happens to be there. It had nothing to do with being anti-Anderson and not caring about him. It just didn't happen to be." Stockman's mother, Carol, added: "It seems to me like Anderson kind of changed his views more than Dave did his. I think John got more liberal, rather than less." As for Keke, Carol Stockman said, "She's very adamant about Dave. She very much wanted to be a President's wife. That was pretty evident many years ago."

If Keke had an eye on the White House, she was not the only one. Stockman did, too, while working for Anderson, according to Runne. "It definitely was on his mind that he could have an impact on the world and that it was too important to let personal relations get in the way," Runne said in recalling a conversation that would end their long intimate relationship shortly after he moved to Washington. "He said he wanted to be President."

Susan Runne paused, then added: "He still wants to be President."

CHAPTER 5

A KID GOES
TO CONGRESS

Submerged somewhere in the back of his mind, David Stockman probably set his sights on a seat in Congress after his first walk up Capitol Hill in 1970. By his own conscious reckoning it took about a year for him to settle on his next career move. After all, he was barely a Republican at the time and he wasn't even twenty-five, the constitutionally set minimum age for members of the House of Representatives. He also had a practical problem: there was no job vacancy in his district and none in prospect for the foreseeable future. In 1974, however, another one of those lucky breaks came along and, as always, Stockman was more than ready to seize the day.

The fourth congressional district of Michigan, where David Stockman grew up, was certainly suited to his archconservative, antigovernment, free-market philosophy. Geographically it is a very large L-shaped district in the southwest corner of the state, stretching 100 miles along the eastern shore of Lake Michigan and another 100 miles along the Indiana border. Politically, though, the district is very small. Considered to have one of the most heavily Republican constituencies in the country, the district has had only one Democratic congressman in the last 100 years and he only got in by holding onto Franklin Roosevelt's coattails in the 1932 landslide election. By the 1934 election the district had, as it were, come to its senses again and voted out George Foulkes. Stockman, tongue in cheek, wrote in The Washington *Post* in February 1979 that Foulkes had "tried to help end the Depression by selling postmasterships. During his second term they moved his office to Fort Leavenworth, Kansas." According to the Biographical Directory of the American Congress, Foulkes's political career ended in a somewhat less amusing fashion: after losing reelection he "resumed agricultural pursuits" in the midwest.

Whatever the truth about Foulkes's political demise, there is no dispute that the district likes its congressmen Republican and conservative. "In this area the Republican primary is the election," said Berrien County Circuit Judge Chester J. Byrns, another disillusioned Stockman mentor who had become the younger man's political confidant and adviser in the early 1970s. "If you're a Republican you can't lose the general election unless you commit treason or public sodomy." Foulkes was ousted in the 1934 election by Clare E. Hoffman, a rigid isolationist, fiscal penny-pincher and ardent anti-New Dealer who represented the district for twenty-eight years. On the issue of federal spending, Hoffman weighed in on the Neanderthal side of the political spectrum.

Fred Upton, a close Stockman assistant for ten years who would seek the congressional seat for himself in 1986, quipped that Hoffman was reluctant to vote for the declaration of war against Japan in 1941 "because he felt the war would be too expensive." Hoffman was very much a man after Stockman's own heart.

Besides fiscal conservatism, however, there also was a tradition in the district of support for moral rectitude and social tolerance, views rooted in the Republican Party platform of the nineteenth Century: clean and honest government, support for women's rights, and opposition to slavery. The abolitionist tradition in the district stemmed from the days of the underground railway, whose network included stations in Cassopolis and Dowagiac. Sizable communities of descendants of slaves who found their way to the district still live in those areas. But the district, like the national Republican party, turned more conservative on social and civil rights issues in recent years. Both the nineteenth-century traditional and latter-day Republican views of the district are embodied in Hillsdale College. Founded in 1844, Hillsdale was one of the first American schools to admit women; today it is a bastion of libertarian thought and boasts of its uniqueness in refusing to accept federal funds because of the strings attached, including requirements concerning how many minority students must be enrolled.

When Hoffman retired in 1962 he was succeeded by Edward Hutchinson, a colorless lawyer and former state senator who had been born into a wealthy industrial family in the area, spent his career in public service and became a conservative Republican across the board on entering the U.S. House of Representatives. Although he became a strong opponent of civil rights legislation — which went against his district's more racially tolerant roots — it caused no problems back home. "Hutch" was basically low-keyed; he did nothing particularly outstanding that anyone could recall during his first six terms, but then again, he did nothing terribly wrong either. Which satisfied his easy-to-please constituents, who did not ask much of their congressmen and allowed them considerable independence in Washington. Except for a few Democratic enclaves, mainly Benton Harbor, district residents made do quite well without assistance from the federal government, and they wanted to keep it that way. That was true as well of the farmers in the area, who generally have prospered. Varietal grapes, such as those on the Stockman family farm, were and are a major crop in the district, and there are no direct federal subsidies for them.

Edward Hutchinson was well-entrenched in late 1971 and early 1972 when Stockman first caught the attention of some of the district's political movers and shakers. Stockman had gotten around Berrien County Republican circles well before then, thanks to his grandfather, William Bartz, who had retired as county treasurer in 1968, and his mother. Both liked to show David off to their political friends. After he became executive director of the House Republican Conference, however, Stockman began receiving political notice in his own right. An article about his promotion in the Dec. 24, 1971, edition of the St. Joseph *Herald-Palladium* carried the headline, "Lakeshore Graduate Still a Quarterback, Joins Big

Washington Team," and quoted Stockman as noting the difference between calling signals for his high school football team and for House Republicans. The article was accompanied by a photograph of him with long hair reaching below a shirt collar that seemed too large for his neck. Stockman also mentioned a book he and John Anderson were writing on "a new approach to domestic and social policies in the 1970s." (He did not, though, say it would be about moderate Republicanism.) The newspaper article ended with him discussing his future plans: "I like Washington and may stay there for a while to look at the electoral scene. I may also return to Harvard and get my Ph.D. in government. I would like to stay involved in Washington in various advisory capacities."

Two months later, on Feb. 22, 1972, Stockman showed up again in the newspaper, this time with a larger photo of him addressing the Benton Harbor Kiwanis Club and a headline that proclaimed: "GOP Aide Sees Grave Threat to Free Enterprise." The article quoted him as saying, "Over a period of forty years we have allowed our private economy to become so shackled down and freighted with impediments and interferences that it is now no longer capable of functioning and responding like it should." The impediments he identified were excessive government interventions in the private marketplace, and he cited several pertinent economic statistics and examples of obtrusive legislation to make his case.

As he made the rounds, Stockman's intellect impressed people in the district more than his personality or appearance. "He was not a gladhander or one to command the attention of an audience," commented one local who remembered meeting him in the early 1970s. "My first impression of him was that he looked like a clerk at J. C. Penney."

It was about this time that Stockman hooked up with his first local political patron outside the family, Judge "Chet" Byrns. Byrns married into the county's most prominent family, the Uptons, heirs to the Whirlpool Corporation fortune. He also ran unsuccessfully in the 1962 GOP primary against Hutchinson, and so had no love for his former opponent. Byrns had become good friends with Stockman's grandfather William Bartz through the local Kiwanis Club, and young Stockman first dabbled in politics as a teenager by working as a volunteer on Byrns's 1962 campaign. So there was a natural cameraderie between them when Stockman sought Byrns out a decade later for political advice. "I took a great interest in David because he was young, very intelligent and oriented toward a government career," said Byrns. "I also recognized immediately that he had great political ambitions." Over the next couple of years Stockman would come to Byrns's house for breakfast when he was back home and they would talk politics for hours. "He was well informed," Byrns recalled. "He had this ability to analyze and judge. He was not just spouting the party line. He was an independent soul. I remember we talked about the war, and he was not pleased with it. It was great to talk with him about economic matters because there was no one else in the area I could talk to about it. And we talked about his work in Washington."

After Stockman became a congressman, Byrns,

who saw himself as a moderate Republican, would express surprise that his young friend had such conservative economic leanings. Like so many other mentors, Byrns would come to feel that Stockman was mostly a self-centered self-promoter who used people to get ahead and then discarded them, presumably, to give him the benefit of the doubt, realizing that they expected something in return from him — something like recognition, appreciation and friendship. But David Stockman never saw matters in terms of personal debts or obligations. It never seemed to occur to him that he might owe something to someone who helped him. And he did not see why his change of views and positions and his personal advancement should leave people from his past feeling embittered. After all, he let people use him the same way he used them. He saw nothing wrong or bad about that; it was all up front, no obligations on either side. No "markers" owed or owing.

Stockman's work in Washington absorbed most of his time during the early 1970s, but he kept one eye on the district, looking out for a political break to happen. The opportunity he needed began developing in 1972, although neither he nor anyone else would realize it for another two years. When Hutchinson first came to the House, he had to flip a coin with Republican Congressman Robert McClory of Illinois, elected the same time, to see who would have seniority over the other on the House Judiciary Committee, to which both were assigned. Hutchinson won. By 1972, after several senior members had retired, Hutchinson became the ranking Republican on the Committee, a proud accomplishment for a congressman after a relatively short ten years. But a coin toss that seemed like good fortune for Hutchinson in 1962 turned out to be a bad omen that would lead to his political downfall a dozen years later, thanks to Richard Nixon and television.

When the Watergate break-in scandal led to the televised Nixon impeachment hearings of the House Judiciary Committee in mid-1974, Hutchinson became nationally famous as the President's most indefatigable defender right up until the very end. That by itself would not have been so bad, but his defense seemed based on reflexive loyalty rather than on a sharp lawyerly case. He came across the television as inarticulate, uninformed and generally out of it. Residents of the fourth district, who had never seen their congressman in action before, were appalled by his lackluster performance. "I'd go back home and people would say, 'My God! Oh, Ed really embarrassed us. He was terrible,'" said Steve Stockman. Judge Byrns added: "Hutch came across as a nothing on TV. It wasn't the position he took, but how he did it. If he had really championed Nixon, that would have been fine. But he looked like a zero." Byrns had his own axe to grind from his 1962 primary loss to Hutchinson, but he nevertheless seems to have reflected the consensus view in the district.

Stockman, who was in Washington writing "The Social Pork Barrel" during the impeachment hearings, was quick to pick up an opportunity dropped by Hutchinson. Well before then, he recalled in a November 1979 interview with the Detroit *News*, "I

156

came to the conclusion that I ought to run as soon as I had the opportunity. Like a lot of other people I thought I was as capable as many of the members I saw ambling around the halls of Congress. So I started to plot how to get myself in position to do that . . . Well, along came Watergate, and with it, Ed's chance for stardom as ranking member of the Judiciary Committee. Simply put, he missed the brass ring." Stockman would not make that same mistake.

Ironically, one of Hutchinson's defenders was Stockman's own father, Al, who, not being a Bartz, never seemed quite as enthused about his son's political career as Carol Stockman, according to family friends. "That's the whole thing, that Hutchinson didn't come across the tube, you know," Al Stockman said. "And I don't think that's a criterion to judge a person, as to how well they come across. Some people are real articulate and they can make you think you're anything they want, and still not be doing their job. Another person might be a strong worker who can't speak properly but is still doing a good job." Enough district voters felt differently to vote for a little-known and underfinanced Democrat in the 1974 congressional election. Although Hutchinson won, it was by a surprisingly close 54-to-46 percent margin rather than the easy 2-to-1 landslides he had received in the past. In a prescient assessment after the election, the 1976 edition of the *Almanac of American Politics* noted that Hutchinson would not have to worry about losing to a Democrat in the foreseeable future, but should worry about a Republican primary challenge. Hutchinson easily survived his 1972 primary challenge, the almanac noted, "but the congressman's weak showing in 1974 must be construed as the district's comment on his impeachment hearings performance, and it is possible that future primary challenges could be more successful." Well before those words were written, David Stockman was busy making sure they would come true.

The impeachment hearings reinforced Stockman's notion of running for the seat. In August 1974 he came home to address a convention of the Berrien County Republican Party and check out the political sentiments about Hutchinson. According to his brother Steve, however, he was not then seriously interested in the congressional seat. Steve said he recalled the two of them talking during the summer of 1974 about a future challenge to Hutchinson. But it was Steve who wanted to make the race. "Dave will deny this, because we've talked about it since, but it's true. I said Hutchinson was vulnerable. *I'll* finish law school and go back to Michigan and run in '76. *He* wasn't interested in running at the time," said Steve. "I didn't think he'd ever want to go into elected politics. He kind of disdained it and just didn't want to do that public stuff and the hassles of an election. That would take him away from his primary interest—research, reading and writing. So he said, 'Yeah, that's good. Go ahead. But where are you going to get the money?' I said I didn't know. Then we didn't talk about it for a while."

Steve obviously had underestimated his brother's personal ambition, his desire for the power that would give him an outlet to implement the ideas he had developed. By late 1974, however, after the congressional election results were in, Steve got a different message from his brother, who already was organizing and plotting for a possible campaign and had come home for Christmas to consult with Berrien County Republican leaders. "When I brought up my running again, Dave said, 'No, I'm running.' When he said that I was very surprised because I didn't think he'd want to. He wasn't the type of person who was overly aggressive and social. I said, 'Well, it's *my* idea.' And he said, 'I don't care. I'm going to do it.' "

Before their conversation Steve had had no inkling that his older brother had been eyeing the seat for years. Yet even in 1974 it was becoming common knowledge in the district that Dave Stockman was likely to contest the seat two years down the road. Area residents pointed to the fact that Stockman's mother conveniently became chairman of the Berrien County Republican Party in 1974, a key political post that would aid her son's future primary run. "Everyone thought that," said Carol Stockman, but she insisted that her getting the post was just one of those lucky coincidences that kept happening to her son. "The chairman before me said he'd do it but only for one two-year term. In the meantime I started working in the office as the executive secretary and people started looking around for somebody who would take it next. Some asked if I would be interested. Well, goodness, there had never been a woman chairman in Berrien County before so I said I would take it. But I said, 'I want you to know up front there is a possibility that sometime Dave may run for Congress. If you think it's not a good idea for me to take it, I'll be happy not to.' But there's a lot of hard work in these political jobs and if you don't get somebody who's going to work hard, your organization falls apart. So I guess they thought it was worth the risk, that maybe I would work hard." Carol Stockman resigned from the post in early 1976, when her son formally declared for Congress.

Stockman spent late 1974 and early 1975 cultivating a small circle of wealthy party activists in the district who had been Hutchinson's principal financial benefactors. As it turned out, they were ripe for cultivation, not just because they felt Hutchinson had performed poorly on television but because he seemed to be forgetting to court the friends who had put him in Congress in the first place. Those who thought they were buying influence, or at least a congressman's ear, with their campaign contributions were discovering a Hutchinson who had grown too imperious and secure in his job. He stopped returning telephone calls, answering letters and doing those little favors that are so important to the egos of the deep-pockets back home. "Hutch began to think that he was entitled to the office," said one local political observer. "He was never very popular or well liked, and when he stopped listening to his main backers he was in trouble. Hutch goofed, he stopped doing his homework." That was something David Stockman would never stop doing.

Perhaps no one felt more annoyance than Willard J. Banyon, publisher and editor of the *Herald-Palladium*, Berrien County's largest newspaper. Banyon had been Hutchinson's roommate in law school and was among his most ardent supporters in earlier days. But by 1974, when Hutchinson stopped returning his phone calls too, Banyon started looking for someone new. He did not have to look very long or very far. That Christmas Banyon received a Christmas card from David Stockman, a young man who customarily would forget to send birthday cards to his mother. Banyon would become Stockman's most important convert.

Another disaffected Hutchinson backer was John Globensky, a prominent Berrien County attorney who was the county GOP vice-chairman while Carol Stockman was chairman. "In 1974 Carol knew I was disenchanted with Hutch . . . he acted like he had never met me before. So Carol said, 'Dave's thinking of coming back. I think he wants to run for Congress.' I said it was an excellent idea." Globensky would become Stockman's campaign chairman.

Stockman's first big break came on February 19, 1975, when Banyon published an editorial — "A Shadow Creeping Toward Hutchinson." It began: "Politics is forever, only practitioners are mortal." It went on to attack Hutchinson, arguing that it was time for a "new face." Referring to the previous summer's televised impeachment hearings, Banyon said Hutchinson showed "as much presence as a spear carrier in the fifth rank of the opera." Banyon also complained that "Hutch spent less time and had less zip in his reelection," and concluded: "It's not too early for those who would make hay in the 1976 election to think of sharpening the mower's blade . . . One is David A. Stockman." Banyon had given the signal to the district's movers and shakers that it was time to switch wagons, and Stockman made sure his was available.

On April 27, 1975, Stockman announced on the "Michiana Report," a Sunday television interview show broadcast out of South Bend, Indiana, that he was considering a run for Congress and would make a formal announcement within nine months. Although Hutchinson had given no hints of interest in early retirement, Stockman added in his interview that one factor in his political plans would be whether the seat opened up. Even then, Stockman would say later, he was uncertain about challenging Hutchinson in 1976 or waiting until 1978. And his brother Dan recalled a conversation around this time in which David expressed doubts about whether a run for Congress was too big a step. Within a month, however, there was no question that Stockman would, indeed, be off and running.

Stockman's TV interview was treated like big news the next day in the *Herald-Palladium*, which gave the story and an accompanying photograph prominent display with the headline: "Stockman Ready for GOP Race. Wants Hutchinson's job." The story did not note Stockman's qualification about whether the seat would open up.

Predictably, Hutchinson did not take too kindly to the prospect of a party challenge from this younger upstart, and according to Stockman tried to get John Anderson to fire him. Judge Byrns, in whom Stockman would confide regularly, said his young friend had expressed great alarm at the possibility. "Dave said he needed the job. He needed the political position and he needed the money." But Anderson stuck with his aide and Stockman plunged ahead.

Within days of the television interview Stockman

was back in the local news. On May 1 he gave a Law Day address at Andrews University in Berrien Springs and used the occasion to take a broad and disdainful swipe at Congress for being "inexcusably derelict in its duty to formulate law" over the past ten years. "Congress has done a poor job," he said, charging that the elected representatives gave important bills, such as the 1970 Clean Air Act, hasty and careless attention and left the details to the courts, experts and bureaucrats who didn't have to go before the voters. He complained that an environmental law that had just passed Congress "in almost total oblivion" would harm the economy with provisions stuck in by bureaucrats to delay construction of the Alaska pipeline and halt construction of 106 power plants. Similarly he charged that an inattentive Congress let "narrow interests" rush through an automobile safety bill that included an annoying seatbelt interlock system that prevented cars from starting until belts were buckled. Stockman said such laws undermined public confidence in the legal system. (The interlock provision was repealed soon afterward because so many people found a way to bypass the system, and those who didn't complained bitterly about it.) The contemptuous broadside against Congress echoed the criticisms contained in "The Social Pork Barrel," which had appeared in print that same spring.

Indeed, most of Stockman's campaign over the next eighteen months would be based on the themes of that article, and he would use the same inflammatory words and hyperbole that got him both noticed and in hot water in later years. In August 1975, he told the Benton Harbor Exchange Club that a new bill to increase employment by regulating industrial production was "the most dangerous piece of legislation to come along in some time." (The bill was a precursor of the Humphrey-Hawkins Full Employment Act of 1978, which he bitterly opposed as a congressman.) Later that month he told the Benton Harbor-St. Joseph Rotary Club that welfare encouraged family breakups and illegitimate births and destroyed the will to work. In April 1976 he called for federal spending cuts to keep the deficit from getting too big. That same month he also told a local association of insurance underwriters that national health insurance would be "a health care catastrophe from which the nation would never recover" because it would eliminate freedom of choice for doctors and patients. In July 1976 he assailed excessive congressional self-indulgence "on salary, fringes and allowances" in order to ensure reelection. And in September of that year he told a local association of clergy that basic moral values in the society were being jeopardized by the "free lunch syndrome." In a few words that captured the essence of his social-economic-political philosophy, he declared: "Self-restraint and self-reliance have long been essential attributes of the American people. But the easy availability of hand-outs and free federal money are influencing appetites and encouraging us to expect more than we can afford."

At the end of February 1975, Stockman left his $32,000-a-year post at the House Republican Conference but continued to work as an assistant to John Anderson until the fall, by which time he had moved back to his parents' home to campaign full time. His first tasks were to raise enough money to challenge an incumbent and to circulate among the party faithful. The district had no experience with big-time fundraising or modern campaign techniques, but Stockman would introduce it to both. One major angel was Willard Banyon who, after a chat with Stockman, wrote out a check for $1,000 on the spot. Instead of depositing the check immediately, Stockman held on to it for a while to show other potential contributors, who were duly impressed.

John Globensky, Stockman's campaign manager by then, was another key fundraiser. "I took him by the hand to all my friends and I would ask each one for $500," he recalled. "I don't think we struck out more than one in ten tries. Everyone who supported Hutch came on board. They were looking for something new, fresh and vigorous, and Dave exuded those qualities. All you needed to do was to get Dave to talk on any subject to get money. It was as if he was God. By the time Hutch was ready to run, we had all his old supporters lined up." Globensky also recalled that Stockman had told Globensky's daughter, Janet, that summer that "he wanted to be President some day."

Judge Byrns helped raise money by inviting a group of potential donors, including much of the wealthy Upton clan, to his home in the fall of 1975. "Dave impressed everybody," said Byrns. "He had this bad habit of covering his mouth and he had this Prince Valiant haircut, and these business people noticed things like that, but one-on-one Dave convinced everybody that he was an individual of great potential who could be successful."

One of the people who attended that meeting and

was instantly impressed was twenty-two-year-old Fred Upton, one of the Whirlpool heirs and a recent college graduate who was intrigued by the prospect of working in a political campaign. "I remember Dave talking about welfare reform, and I went up afterward and said, 'Dave, I'm real enthused. You need some help.' So we got together later at a bar in Benton Harbor and he shared his 'secret plan' with me—the way he could pull it off. He talked about getting lists of the 20 percent who vote in primaries, and the costs, and using Wang machines to send out personalized junk mail. No one had seen anything like this before in the district. In the past all you did was get into a car, drive to the city hall in the next town, shake a few hands and then go on to the next town."

The "secret plan" was in fact a wonder to behold, not just to a political neophyte like Fred but even to professional campaign operatives in Washington like Steven F. Stockmeyer, then executive director of the National Republican Congressional Committee. Stockmeyer, who later opened his own lobbying firm, remembered the plan vividly:

"He approached me around the fall of 1975 and said he wanted to run and would like to bounce his plans off me. I told him I couldn't do anything because we supported incumbents. The last thing we could do was help one of their opponents. But he persisted and finally said, 'What if we happen to bump into each other on the outside?' So I said okay, and a week later I run into him at a party. I sat down and read his campaign planning document. It was this big thick binder and it was the most elaborate, ambitious, detailed complete plan I ever saw, before or since, and I've been involved in politics a long time. It was a beautiful document. It had a schedule of what would take place where and with whom; it was almost a day-to-day scenario. It called for extensive use of computers. That was cutting-edge stuff at the time. He had this plan to meet someone and then follow up twenty-four hours later with a letter tailored to the discussion. He would do it by getting young volunteers to punch names into a computer based on particular issues, such as Social Security. I told him it was terrific, and if he ran I fully expected to see him in Congress. And he actually implemented it, which was really something for a laid-back and rural district that had never seen a modern campaign."

Everything was falling into place by now. Stockman was picking up important backers, he had his campaign plan, he was starting to raise money, he was making the rounds with local party officials and impressing them. There remained just one small question about his politics: other than economics issues, was he conservative enough for his district? But he had thought of that, too. "There was no secret that Dave was seen along with Anderson as being in the moderate-liberal Republican philosophy," noted a long-time political friend. "He was a member of the Ripon Society, he hung around with the liberal-moderate Republicans. So I asked him how he would be able to modify his views to run in his district and I remember his answer very distinctly. He said, 'Don't worry about that. I'll be the most conservative guy you've ever seen in your life.' And we both laughed after he said that. So I got the distinct impression that he made a calculated shift in the way he presented himself in Washington at the time versus the way he campaigned in his district. It was a very calculated, opportunistic decision at the time. And I thought, here's a very calculating guy who knows he has to make a point of being conservative for his district."

Once in Congress, Stockman generally voted his conscience on important issues. He became a champion of the conservative economic views he had adopted from his Harvard days, but he also would vote his libertarian views on personal issues, such as abortion. Despite considerable pressure from Right-to-Life groups, for example, he voted against a bill that would ban federally funded abortions.

Stockman's "secret plan" was possible only because he had a "secret weapon" to help draft it and implement it — David Gerson. At the time "Ger" was a twenty-one-year-old whiz kid who had dropped out of college the previous year and moved in with the Stockman brothers to work full time with Stockman at the House Republican Conference. Although Stockman later got a reputation as a numbers wizard and computer genius it was Gerson who really deserved the reputation. Stockman was the conceptual man; Gerson was the technical and organizational genius who made it all work. Gerson was the one who ran the nuts-and-bolts election campaign. Later, Gerson ran the congressional office. At the age of twenty-seven, he was the chief administrative official at the Office of Management and Budget. Stockman may have known a lot about the budget part of OMB, but he knew nothing about, and cared nothing about, the management part. He had another little-known blind spot. Although gifted with an amazing recall of numbers that he could recite back in machinegunlike bursts to defend his arguments and mow down his opposition, he was not particularly good at mathematics. He could do simple addition and subtraction—the latter being his favorite, budget aides would joke—but if anything more complicated were involved he would get on the phone to Gerson with an S O S: "Can you do these compound growth rates?"

Stockman understood the importance of organization, but it was up to Gerson to provide it. Stockman also was keenly aware early on of the potential of computers and made great use of the information they could provide, but here he had a third blind spot: he did not know how to operate them by himself. In his personal aptitudes and techniques he was low-tech. He wrote everything in longhand on legal-size yellow notepads, including his lengthy memoirs on his years in the Reagan Administration. He was one of the first members of Congress to automate his office, but he did not touch the computers himself. As budget director he used a handheld calculator, but it was the simplest model available. And although he had a computer terminal installed in his office, it just sat there gathering dust. One night during Stockman's last year as budget director, an assistant who was working late ran into Stockman and his wife, both dressed in formal evening wear and huddled over his terminal. They were on their way to an official function and Jennifer was trying to teach her husband how to use it. Ironically, they had met in the 1970s when she was an IBM technical representative who would visit his congressional office to teach the staff how to use the computer. Her future husband turned out to be one of her worst students. "It's funny, he believes in all these toys," she said, "but personally he's not someone who likes a lot of change. I suppose I should have made him use a word processor or something, but he refused because he was afraid that the learning curve could slow him down."

Gerson displayed his talents in early 1974 when John Anderson was considering whether to run for the U.S. Senate against first-term Democrat Adlai E. Stevenson III. Stockman and Gerson teamed up to prepare an election analysis that concluded Anderson should not run. Anderson, who commented that the analysis was better than professional polls he had used in the past, followed its advice.

Stockman's own campaign plan was based on the fact that there were no television stations that broadcast from his district, so he and Gerson knew that television advertising was out. Direct mail and personal contacts would be the best way to reach people likely to vote in the district's Republican primary. But Michigan's open primary system does not require party registration. So they methodically went through precinct voting records to put together a list of the 20 percent of registered voters who had voted in the last few congressional primaries on the assumption that regular primary voters in the district almost certainly were Republicans. The lists were fed into a computerized system, designed by Gerson, that used several Wang word processors programmed to send out personally addressed letters. An initial mass-mailing would introduce Stockman and provide a list of some twenty issues. Voters would be asked to check off the issues they wanted more information about. The word processors then would be able to respond immediately to requests for information with personalized-sounding letters on the issues that had been checked. Later, during the formal campaign, they would feed personal information about people Stockman met into the system so they could generate folksy-sounding letters that would mention names of voters and tailor responses depending on their occupation, such as farming or medicine. Later personalized letters from computers, as any recipient of junk mail well knows, would be counterproductive; but at the time, it was new-frontier politicking for Michigan's old-fashioned fourth district. Stockman's youthful volunteers also would stay up late at night writing personal letters to people the candidate had met during the day, so that a voter would get a letter within twenty-four hours that would begin: "Dear John, It was great talking to you at the drugstore in Sturgis yesterday . . ." And so forth. People were impressed.

Among the few seasoned professionals Stockman turned to during the campaign was Robert Teeter, a political pollster based in Detroit. Teeter originally did some polling for the campaign, but Stockman and Gerson later did the polling themselves after figuring out how Teeter did it. Teeter remembered the campaign as "very modern, very up-to-date. It was state-of-the-art."

While Stockman and Gerson worked like busy little bees, Hutchinson started getting agitated and finally picked up the telephone to assemble his long-neglected angels to help him stop this upstart challenger. He was in for a shock — his old backers had been coopted by the new challenger.

On Monday, Feb. 2, 1976, chosen because it was Groundhog Day, twenty-nine-year-old David Stockman officially announced for Congress. He planned to make the announcement seven times that day, once in each of the district's seven county seats, with the help of a helicopter. But it was a cold and snowy morning and he got off to a bad start. The helicopter he originally hired would not start. Forced to find one somewhere else, he had to settle for five stops that day. Which was about as much adversity as Stockman would meet up with during the whole subsequent nine months.

His announcement of candidacy was vintage Stockman, containing as it did the same personal philosophy, the same political hyperbole, the same arguments, the same colorful imagery and cogent writing style, the same contempt for government that would become his rhetorical trademark for the next ten years. It even included some of the very phrases that showed up five years later in his controversial *Atlantic Monthly* interviews, with one noticeable difference: The defeatist attitude about changing the status quo, that he would express after leaving OMB in 1985, was absent. Here, he was the young congressional hopeful of 1976, filled with optimism and gung-ho spirits about the battle to come:

We enter our third century as a nation under a dark cloud of uncertainty and danger. We teeter on the brink of fiscal catastrophe after having added nearly one-quarter trillion dollars to the national debt during the last decade alone. [Ironically, during Stockman's five years as budget director, the debt increased by nearly one trillion dollars.] The most productive economic machine in the world, our free enterprise economy, has been nearly ground to a halt by a flood of bureaucratic edicts, government paperwork and regulatory interference . . . The stout independence and resourceful individualism that has traditionally characterized the American people is being deeply eroded by the corrosive promise of cradle-to-grave financial security and by a brooding Big Mother in Washington who attempts to protect us even from the unavoidable daily scrapes and minor mishaps that we have always cared for ourselves.

Fortunately, the American people are now recognizing that we have strayed far from the beaten path, and that we are rushing headlong toward a rendezvous with national calamity. But they feel helpless to rechart the course because we have a Congress in Washington which literally fiddles while the priceless heritage of two centuries burns. Yesterday's conservatives have lost so many battles that they no longer expect, let along aggressively struggle, to win the war. And Congress as a whole has become little more than a cozy club of careerists concerned primarily with maintaining their license to feed at the public trough tomorrow instead of fighting for the interests of the public today. . . .

Yesterday's politicians cannot spare us from the impending disaster. This includes yesterday's conservatives, too — no matter how strong their persistence [sic] of innocence. For they have had their chance and failed . . . I do not buy the argument that we are outnumbered, outgunned and doomed to perpetual defeat. I think we need only commit ourselves to working harder, devising better answers and communicating our message more persuasively. The national agenda is clear. We need to do nothing less than anesthetize the sprawling federal octopus, lay it on the operating table and undertake a decade of sustained, unrelenting surgery.

We must start by overhauling from top to bottom a runaway welfare system that is destroying families, eroding the work ethic and crushing the taxpayers. We need to abolish or drastically curtail those encrusted regulatory agencies like the ICC which have become a haven for special-interest favoritism and privileges rather than a watchdog for the public interest. We need to launch a relentless campaign against waste and stupidity in the federal bureaucracy and drastically reform a civil service system which rewards incompetence and sloth at the expense of the taxpayers. We need to get the federal government out of the business of concocting ways to improve tricycle safety and the like, and drive Big Motherism from Washington before it smothers us in our own nest.

174

And most of all, we need to stop the reckless hemorrhaging of the federal budget before we place the entire nation in the same financial trauma now confronting New York City.

I would not suggest that there are easy answers or ready panaceas in any of these areas. I do not imply that the job can be done in one year or even one term, and certainly not by one man. But I do believe that the American public is ready to respond to new leadership and to new ideas aimed at rescuing us from the thicket in which we are now ensnared. I do believe that the entrenched special-interest groups and self-perpetuating bureaucracies which dominate Washington can be defeated if we elect aggressive, resourceful fighters to public office. . . .

I have had the good fortune of being raised on a farm, of attending a one-room country school, of growing up in modest economic circumstances, of paying for my own education, of having had to scrap for everything that I have been able to achieve. Out of that has come a perspective which I think . . . could help lead the nation toward a more promising and confident future. But the hour is late and we have hidden our light under a barrel long enough. If the voters of the fourth district are willing, I can promise they will at last have a voice that Congress and the nation will hear loud and clear."

Stockman never mentioned Edward Hutchinson by name, but the reference to "yesterday's politicians" was obvious. And if people failed to get the picture from his words, he had more graphic material ready. Jack Strayer, who had joined the Stockman campaign as a top assistant, said Stockman had obtained photographs of the House Judiciary Committee's impeachment hearings that showed Hutchinson asleep while key White House officials were giving testimony. "We had these pictures, like the back of [former White House Counsel] John Dean's head, and you could see Ed Hutchinson with his head way back in his chair and his mouth open, and he's sound asleep. And we thought these would be great to use."

But Stockman never had to use them. On Wednesday, Feb. 4, 1976, two days after Stockman's formal announcement, Hutchinson announced in Washington that he was retiring because the fun had gone out of being in Congress. "Hutch was born with a gold spoon in his mouth," said Judge Byrns. "He never worked hard in his life and he had no stomach for rough-and tumble politics. He saw all his old supporters had become disillusioned or bored with him. This was his chance to get out with honor rather than get beat." Other local party activists said Hutchinson had come to believe that he owned the congressional seat and felt very bitter that he was being forced out rather than allowed to run for one more term and then retire. Hutchinson, who lived out his remaining years in obscurity, died July 22, 1985, in Naples, Florida. Associates said he carried his bitterness to the grave. Actually, according to several friends, Stockman realized from the start that it would not be easy to beat an incumbent, and was prepared to run again in 1978 had he lost the first race.

Stockman was campaigning at the county courthouse in Coldwater when he was called out of the middle of a meeting by an urgent telephone call from campaign headquarters in St. Joseph; it was David Gerson with word of Hutchinson's retirement. At first Stockman did not believe it. Then he became very excited. He and Fred Upton, who was with him, sensed immediately that they had just won the election. Still stunned by the news, Stockman and Upton went into a private office. "Fred, I can't believe it," Stockman said, shaking his head. "One thing about politics, you have to be in the right place at the right time, and I've had an amazing string of good luck behind me."

Stockman did not appreciate the extent to which he had helped Lady Luck along. He once referred to his election in 1976 as a "pure fluke." Ed Hutchinson had self-destructed and he just happened to be there, Stockman told friends. He was too modest . . . he had mined the political fields back home for years in advance so that he would benefit from an unexpected opportunity. "Lots of people go prospecting, but I kept striking pay dirt," he once said. He also wielded his pick harder and longer than most prospectors.

After 1976 seeming good luck would continue to fall Stockman's way, and he would help it out by making sure he was in the right place, at the right time.

While Stockman was raising his visibility back home, he was also starting to attract increased notice in Washington. In 1973 he had been singled out by the monthly magazine, *Washingtonian*, as one of the dozen most promising young aides on Capitol Hill, and his selection in 1974 as a co-director of Harvard's one-week orientation session for new members of Congress gave him additional recognition. "The Social Pork Barrel" brought him fame in the world of public policy. In addition to the Washington *Post* and *Wall Street Journal*, the article was cited in several national publications. It also caught the approving eye of national opinion leaders such as political columnist George Will, who would become both a personal friend and public fan of Stockman. Alice Rivlin, who had just become the first director of the newly established Congressional Budget Office, was so impressed with the piece that she arranged to have lunch with "this kid who works for John Anderson," just as had Meg Greenfield, the *Post*'s deputy editorial page editor. Greenfield also commissioned Stockman to write a piece for the newspaper's opinion page in the fall of 1975. Entitled "The Redistribution of Wealth," the article was a condensed version of "The Social Pork Barrel," contending that a set of programs that had started out as well-meaning welfare for the poor had been transformed unconsciously into "the beginnings of a major national income redistribution effort" that dispensed benefits in ways that defied both economic needs and equity. In Michigan, he wrote, a welfare mother with "savvy" could achieve the equivalent of a middle-class income by taking advantage of all available social programs. At the same time, he said, increasing numbers of middle-income families who were not in great need could not meet eligibility requirements for food stamps, school lunches and other forms of government assistance. Stockman proposed that a system he viewed as an irrational and growing hodgepodge of narrowly focused programs be replaced with an explicit national income-distribution policy based on a single cash-transfer program administered through the federal income-tax code.

By winter 1976, with Hutchinson out of the race and no other Republican opposition, everything was going Stockman's way. At first it seemed Stockman would win the election without even a primary fight. His only announced opponent by early spring was the same Democrat who had lost to Hutchinson in 1974—Richard "Mike" Daugherty, a fifty-four-year-old United Auto Workers union official from Sister Lake. On March 25 the two men held a debate in St. Joseph, during which they discussed their stands on several issues and discovered that they were in agreement on most: No anti-abortion amendment to the U.S. Constitution; no busing to desegregate schools; no gun-control legislation.

On April 21, 1976, Stockman was formally challenged for the Republican nomination by Lee Boothby, a forty-three-year-old Berrien Springs attorney with only modest local government experience. Boothby had run against Hutchinson in the 1962 GOP primary. This time he ran at the urging of a vengeful Hutchinson and GOP ultraconservatives who found Stockman's conservative credentials suspect. Stockman would overcome the political challenge rather easily, but he also faced a personal challenge more difficult to surmount. He had to force himself to overcome his instinctive shyness and develop more of the social graces expected of public figures.

Stockman, it seems clear, loved politics for the power—the opportunity to turn his views into social policy. But he hated politics for the personal demands it made on him. Most politicians get high marks for the social aspects of the job. The slick smiles, the cocktail party chitchat, the charm and grace all seem to come easily. David Stockman had few social graces and dreaded the mingling with strangers required of him during the campaign. He forced himself to be more sociable because he knew he had to, but he never overcame his natural shyness. Even as budget director he avoided virtually every social invitation. A quiet dinner with a small group of friends was as gregarious as he got. He never saw himself as a politician in the usual sense. Rather, he was a practitioner of politics preoccupied with pushing his ideas. He simply tuned people out.

He was at his best with a group, large or small, once he was talking about his issues. Invariably he would wow his audience with his articulate responses to their questions, his command of facts, his intense speaking style. "Dave knew three times as much as the entire district combined when it came to the issues, and people would come away shaking their heads in wonder," said one close friend. Breaking the ice, however, was always the problem. The solution was to cultivate a network of social butterflies around the district who would volunteer to stand at his side and introduce him at the endless series of coffees and teas he would attend several times a day. These intimate meetings of four to twenty people, held at the homes of volunteers, became his principal forum for meeting voters.

"David was always in another world. He just was not conscious of social amenities or graces," said one of his social aides, Georgianna Holcomb, a former beauty-pageant contestant from Coldwater who took Stockman around her native Branch County. Holcomb was a Republican Party activist in her mid-thirties when she met Stockman in the spring of 1975. "He was testing the waters then and we were so impressed with him. He was so full of facts, and prepared, and he would answer every question in a very articulate way. But he also seemed like such a loner. He was very shy and found it difficult to meet people. He had all this ability but he was afraid they'd eat him alive. So I offered to take him around the county, and he had someone like me everywhere.

"He was a terrific young man and we spent days traveling to these coffees," Holcomb continued. "Yet he always resisted the social graces. I'd always have to make a joke of reminding him to let the ladies go in the door first. He'd never say, 'May I help you with this.' He just went along and did his thing. It's not that he was impolite, he was just oblivious. He is one of those people whose work is his play. I was always afraid he'd never get married or get out of the office." She recalled that Stockman had one social talent: "He had this incredible, incredible faculty for remembering people's names." A priceless commodity for a politician.

Stockman's graying hair, which had now become shorter, his eyeglasses and his serious demeanor helped make him seem older than his twenty-nine years, but he had another image problem as a candidate for Congress. He tended to favor ill-fitting clothes, with the same tie, day after day. Holcomb said she was amused to see later pictures of him in Washington wearing the same red paisley tie she had bought for him during that first campaign. She also said she got a laugh out of a 1986 magazine article that mentioned him as an example of a fashion plate. "I think all the kudos have to go to Jennifer," she said.

Georgianna Holcomb also made two observations about Stockman shared by other friends and acquaintances in the district who have stayed in touch with him. One; Success did not change him. "He's still David. He's the same person we knew ten years ago. Very nice and down to earth. He's not pretentious." The other: He is one of the most impressive political figures they ever met and is destined to be President some day. "I still think so," Holcomb said.

Jack Strayer, son of a prominent Berrien County surgeon, had the same first reaction as Georgianna Holcomb to Stockman's personality and dress. Strayer was twenty-four and working temporarily as a salesman at a men's clothing store in Niles when a county Republican official brought Stockman by the store to meet him one afternoon in November of 1975. "He was very shy. He wasn't dressed particularly sharp or anything like that. I wasn't very impressed with this guy." But Strayer agreed to have dinner with Stockman that evening, and after he had a chance to hear what Stockman had to say he became very impressed, particularly after discovering that both were fans of theologian Reinhold Niebuhr.

Strayer picked up the $40 dinner tab and, having decided previously to drop out of graduate school, volunteered on the spot to work for Stockman. He soon became a regular campaign hand and, after the election, worked in Stockman's congressional office until 1979.

Strayer, who came from a more prosperous background and was a stylish fellow, decided Stockman needed a better wardrobe and became the candidate's fashion consultant. "Dave wore a lot of double-knit pants and jackets with funny ties and collars that were too big for his neck. He didn't have a lot of presence. Now, I'm not saying I'm a great guy or anything, but I think he liked what he saw in me . . . the way I handled myself, my manners, my hair style, my clothes. Remember, he was a farm boy who didn't really have to dress up when he worked for John Anderson. At Harvard he never had to dress up." So Strayer took him shopping.

"One time during the campaign"—Strayer broke up with laughter—"he said, 'I want a leisure suit.' I said, 'Why in the world do you want a leisure suit?' He said, 'Well, I went to the Coldwater Jaycees and I was the only one there who didn't have a leisure suit.' I told him he would be wasting his money, but he insisted. So, he bought this white leisure suit. It was linen and it was lightweight and it had wooden carved buttons and all. He wanted to wear it to another function in Coldwater, only this one was at the country club. And the only other person who had on a leisure suit was the bartender. In fact he had on the *same* leisure suit that Dave was wearing. Dave also was wearing black or navy blue underwear, and you could see it through these white pants. Everybody was laughing at him because they could see right through his pants. Afterward he said, 'Why didn't you tell me, goddamn it.' I said, 'I hadn't had time to check you out.' So, Dave never wore a leisure suit again."

By all accounts Stockman hated to campaign. He hated to shake hands at shopping centers or country fairs. He found the coffees and teas impossible after four-a-days for months on end, and the nonstop driving across his huge district wore him out. Here was someone who thrived on hard work throughout his life, but it never got to him the way politicking did. "This is the hardest work I've ever done," he told his brother Steve during the 1976 campaign. "I am so tired I can't believe it."

Strayer said Stockman did coffee meetings for six months and hated every one of them. "He just didn't want to go to them. After almost every coffee he'd get into the car and he would be so relieved that it was over . . . And he did such a good job, I could never imagine why he was so anxiety-ridden. It's not that he was nervous. He just thought it was a waste of his time, an inefficient use of his time. But then I'd see him wasting all kinds of time—what I'd call wasting time—just sitting in a chair with his hands folded, looking at the ceiling. To him, that was nirvana. Really. That was when he was happiest." Strayer, who grew up in a much fancier social circle, always figured that Stockman's shyness in social situations came from a basic insecurity about his modest background. "When Dave is sure of himself about something on an intellectual plane, he forgets his shyness and his aloofness because he's very confident of what he is saying. In a social situation he doesn't have the same confidence."

While Stockman was on the hustings his "secret weapon," David Gerson, was masterminding the operation in the basement of a St. Joseph insurance office that served as campaign headquarters. Gerson shared Stockman's discomfort about the social requirements of the campaign, but for a different reason. He was a young Jew from a Washington suburb in Maryland, and that made him an outsider on two counts in Stockman's parochial and Protestant district. Gerson detected some anti-Semitism and was sensitive about how his association with Stockman might hurt the campaign, according to Strayer. As a result Gerson rarely attended any functions, thinking it best to let the local campaign officials be the visible ones. "I don't think that the area is anti-Semitic," said Strayer. "It's just still white-bread country. Ger became friends with members of Benton Harbor's relatively small Jewish community, and although most were Democrats, he persuaded many of them to contribute to Stockman's campaign and to vote for him."

If Stockman never really loosened up to the social requirements of politics, he did what he had to do and showed, on occasion, that he had, in fact, a quite normal range of emotions. Strayer, for example, recalled a June campaign appearance at a Berrien County air show in Galien at which a stunt pilot's plane crashed. An ambulance rushed the pilot to the hospital in Niles, and Stockman, who had been sitting next to the pilot's wife in the stands, was asked to take her in his car to the hospital. Strayer, who did the driving, recalled speeding behind the ambulance in a car with a big Stockman sign on top and streamers fluttering madly in the wind. "Anybody who saw us would think some angry farmer finally shot Dave Stockman," he said. But Strayer also remembered Stockman trying his best to console the woman all the way to the hospital, where the pilot was declared dead. After a stiff drink, Stockman and Strayer drove on to another tea. As Strayer remembered it: "Dave said on the way over, 'Now, when we get to this house, don't mention anything about the plane crash. I don't want it to detract from my presentation. Maybe later we can tell them.' And I said, okay. When we got there, the minute the door opened, Dave right away said, 'God! You won't believe what just happened to us!' And he went into all the gory detail. He never did talk about government or anything, he was so keyed up."

And Strayer cited another time, when he urged Stockman to help hand out medals at a local Special Olympics for handicapped children. At first Stockman refused. "No, I'm not going to do that. It makes me nervous, it upsets me," he told Strayer, whose mentally retarded nephew was participating in the meet. "Well, my nephew's going to be in it and I'd really like you to do it for me," Strayer told him.

186

"Don't play on my heartstrings, I don't want to do it," Stockman insisted. But he finally relented. "We'll go for just a few minutes." They spent four hours there. "I'll never do that again," he told Strayer afterward. The next day the South Bend *Tribune* carried a picture of him holding a little girl with Down's syndrome over his head. Good press, Strayer thought, and Stockman apparently got into the event despite his initial reluctance.

"I'll tell you a thing that was amazing about him," said friend Richard Straus. "Sometimes after his first political campaign, David developed this ability to be affable, to be outgoing, to be charming in the political arena. It's almost as if he *willed* himself out of that shell of his because he knew that more was required of him in a social sense. I don't mean that he partied with the other Cabinet husbands and wives. He was never that kind of person. He was never interested in it. But he became a much more sophisticated political animal, and that required a certain social sophistication which I can only assume came as the result of an act of will. It wasn't picked up because he started hanging around fancy people. I think it's because he realized he had to do it and went out and did it."

Stockman knew he was going to win the GOP primary. His and Gerson's polls showed he had no serious opposition. In later years Stockman would make fun of his lightweight opposition and his lack of accomplishment in making it to Congress. Even so, his first primary fight got dirty and put him on the spot by forcing him to defend his conservative credentials. At Stockman's first face-to-face debate with Lee Boothby in May 1976, the two men were asked to name their presidential choices. Boothby, who had a case of laryngitis and no microphone, refused to endorse a candidate for the GOP presidential nomination, although it was widely known he favored Ronald Reagan over Michigan's favorite son, President Gerald Ford. Stockman strongly endorsed Ford, but added, "I could live with Reagan."

Privately, the Stockman family did not like Reagan. "I thought Reagan was too conservative at the time," said Carol Stockman. "Now, probably, I've changed. I don't think he's too conservative now. Maybe he had different people surrounding him then, but the way he was first portrayed seemed like he was kind of a rightwinger." She also disliked the tone of the Reagan campaign against Ford. "I always thought Jerry Ford was such a nice guy, and it didn't seem like they were very nice to him." Stockman shared his mother's feelings. Although he agreed with Reagan's economic policies, he detested Reagan's conservatism on social issues and thought of him as being too much of a "cowboy." In the political circles where Stockman traveled, Reagan was "Ronnie Ray Gun," and sometimes Stockman would use that mocking name himself. While watching the 1976 GOP convention on television with Strayer at a constituent's house, Stockman groaned every time a state delegation unexpectedly went for Reagan. Stockman resented the way Reagan curried favor with what he called "the irrational Right Wing and screaming Moral Majoritarians," whose views on issues such as abortion and school prayer struck him as improper government encroachment on personal freedoms. "I had a chip on my shoulder about them," he later said. And he still does.

Stockman's unhappiness with Reagan also stemmed from the fact that he was a big fan of Ford in 1976 because of the way he carried the country into a post-Watergate era. "I remember him coming home right after Nixon resigned and making a speech about how you could feel the difference in Washington by just walking through the streets," said Carol Stockman. "It seemed like there was again a vitalization in the capital that almost had felt like a death watch before."

It was as the August primary approached that the campaign turned mean, as Boothby tried to paint his opponent as a closet liberal, raising the issue of Stockman's antiwar protests and his avoidance of the draft, his connection to John Anderson and his association with the Ripon Society. Fred Upton remembered Stockman volunteers yanking Boothby flyers off of cars soon after they were put on the windshields. Upton also recalled, "They had this damaging radio ad: 'Ever hear of the Ripon Society? Left-wing, liberal groups accept money from them. Did you know that David Stockman accepted a loan from them?' Dave had, in fact, accepted a loan from the Ripon Society [$1,000], but he quickly paid it back and we scared the stations into yanking the ads." The Ripon Society, founded in 1962, may have been too liberal for the district on certain foreign policy and social issues, such as abortion, but its generally libertarian stance on economic issues would be pretty much consistent with voter attitudes in the area.

But Stockman took no chances. A week before the primary Stockman issued a press release, in response to a Boothby mass mailing that suggested Stockman favored socialized medicine and a welfare plan based on a guaranteed annual income. In rather overheated prose Stockman's release said, "I abhor the concept of giveaways to able-bodied people. I am committed to completely scrapping the current work-killing, family-destroying, bureaucracy-ridden welfare system and replacing it with a stringent workfare plan that will not give a dime to an employable person until he sweats out 40 hours per week in any available job." He went on to declare that "I absolutely oppose" compulsory national health insurance, and he said Boothby's "innuendo that I have been running for Congress on the congressional payroll . . . is absolutely false."

In any case, District voters did not seem to buy Boothby's charge that Stockman was a liberal on economic issues, but the Vietnam War issue did cost him some support, even from a close relative. His uncle, Edwin Bartz (now deceased), who was the circuit court bailiff at the time, told friends he would not help his nephew's campaign because he was so upset with his antiwar protests and because Dave had urged people to go to Canada to avoid the draft. Stockman's high school German teacher, John Adams, recalled there being "a lot of criticism of that fact that he went to school in theology during Vietnam until it was safe to drop out."

Neither the ghost of Vietnam nor Boothby's eleventh-hour attacks were enough to slow Stockman.

When the results of the August 3 primary came in, Stockman had drubbed his opponent by better than two to one: 28,871 to 13,564. Two late entries into the race, Helen Take, twenty-eight, a substitute teacher, and David S. Frazer, thirty-five, who was unemployed and campaigned in a green station wagon with a green canoe on top, managed another 5,000 votes between them. As a fund-raiser Stockman proved to be an even bigger powerhouse. A report filed with the Federal Election Commission showed Stockman had spent $74,798 from Jan. 1 through July 15, compared with $6,422 by Lee Boothby. Including the last two weeks of the primary campaign, Stockman's camp estimated it spent a total of $90,000. It also was revealed that Stockman, who had been saving much of his congressional salary for a rainy day, lent his campaign $15,500. . . .

On primary night Stockman and Jack Strayer had dinner with a wealthy supporter in Sturgis and then listened to the returns on the radio as they drove back to the Holiday Inn at St. Joseph, where campaign workers had assembled. When they arrived, Strayer remembered, stoical David Stockman did something much out of character:

"It was ten at night and I bet there were a thousand people waiting for him inside the hotel. I remember walking in first and, of course, the lights came up and the cameras started to roll. He came in, and there was this sustained cheering. And he went around and hugged, just grabbed everybody he could get his hands on. And no one had ever seen him be physical or emotional before. To see this kid, tears in his eyes, hugging everybody, picking little kids up over his head, it was really kind of heartwarming."

During the general election campaign Stockman was again confronted with the controversy over his stand on the Vietnam War and his antiwar protest days. People had whispered about the issue throughout the campaign, but it became more open and direct in the last month before the election. Stockman found himself forced to deny accusations that he had burned an American flag and his draft card during his student days. He also came under attack from the right-wing American Independent Party candidate, whose camp distributed literature calling attention to Stockman's earlier protest activities. During an October 10, 1976 candidates debate taped by a South Bend television station, according to an account published the following day in the *Herald-Palladium*, American Independent candidate Karl Friske defended distribution of the material. "If Mr. Stockman participated in un-American activities, people should know it." Stockman replied: "I did dissent from our policy in Vietnam. I was a student in college a decade ago. I signed a petition to stop the bombing." He added that his war opposition was not un-American, and that his foreign policy views had since become "more conservative," though he still opposed the war. On this issue the normally candid Stockman was very circumspect—he did not mention his leadership role in the antiwar movement, nor did he note that he was one of the signers of the SDS ad that vowed to resist the draft, refuse induction into the armed forces and encourage others to do the same. His opponents hadn't raised those other actions, and he was not about to volunteer them.

(Interestingly, when the debate turned to economic issues Stockman said that a $30 billion tax cut, together with "fiscal responsibility," was the best way to prod the economy into creating more jobs. Ronald Reagan would propose a similar economic plan four years later and tap Stockman to make it work.)

A week after his cautious statements about Vietnam, Stockman returned to his usual candid self. During a televised debate on October 18 Mike Daugherty asked why Stockman had received significant contributions from professional groups, including physicians, for his primary contest against Boothby. Stockman lost his cool. Strayer, who watched the debate from the back of the hall, heard his usually self-controlled man blurting out: "The reason I got so much money from doctors was because the biggest ambulance-chasing malpractice lawyer in Berrien County was my opponent."

"Dave just looked right into the camera and said it," Strayer recalled. "And, of course, it was on the news that night. Dave really got in trouble with the Berrien County Bar Association, among others. It was true, but it also created a considerable brouhaha. Stockman resented Lee Boothby so much because his campaign detracted from what Dave saw as the real issues—inflation and government spending."

Apparently realizing he had put his foot a ways in his mouth, Stockman publicly apologized to Boothby in an equally candid letter he circulated to the news media on October 20. He did not beat around the bush:

"This is to offer my sincere apology for the inappropriate, inaccurate and ungentlemanly remark that I made at the Dowagiac High School on Monday concerning the reason certain doctors contributed to my primary campaign. Throughout the course of my ten-month campaign for fourth district congressman I have set high standards for myself and have refrained from any comments whatsoever of a personal nature about my opponents. My comment characterizing you as an 'ambulance chasing malpractice lawyer' was therefore a total and egregious departure from that standard. I regret this very much and fully retract the statement because it is untrue and without factual foundation.

"I can assure you that it was not made with malice aforethought. It occurred in a heated debate with my Democratic opponent in response to defamatory insinuations by him as to why certain businessmen, bankers, doctors and other professional and occupation groups have contributed to my campaign. There is nothing to apologize for in regard to these modest contributions, but in my eagerness to score debating points in my own behalf, I spoke with unthinking disregard for their impact on your professional reputation and personal integrity.

"In order to demonstrate my good faith in this matter, I am sending copies of this letter to all local news media which carried the original story. I am man enough to admit my mistakes—especially under circumstances as serious as these—and hope that you will receive this statement in the same spirit."

Stockman's bluntness and willingness to accept the consequences of his behavior "like a man" was in character, but his apology was not. Stockman almost never apologized; he rarely was willing to admit he made a mistake. His only other public apology came in the wake of the controversy over his *Atlantic Monthly* interviews five years after the Boothby incident. In that one Stockman apologized to Ronald Reagan for his careless use of inflammatory phrases and the political trouble he had brought on the administration. But he never apologized for the basic thrust of his arguments. To the contrary, he believed he was right. He still does.

Neither the Vietnam War nor Stockman's candid outburst proved to have much impact on his campaign in its closing days. And he continued to pick up glowing notices outside the District. The generally liberal Detroit *Free Press* endorsed him as an "exceptional Republican candidate . . . who has the potential to be one of Michigan's outstanding congressman." The newspaper praised his extensive congressional experience and added: "His sensible view of what government should be, and how elected representatives should serve their constituents, is a welcome contrast to the demagoguery so often apparent in an election year."

On election night Stockman moved to an easy victory with 61 percent of the vote. The final tally over Daugherty was 107,881 to 69,655. In the fund-raising department, Stockman spent a district record $163,733 on his primary and general election campaigns, four times as much as Hutchinson ever spent. Daugherty spent $23,769 in his losing effort against

Stockman.

Stockman's victory was a moment of great pride for his family, particularly William Bartz, who stood at his grandson's side, flashing a big smile and a V for Victory sign for photographers.

Even though Stockman and his supporters had anticipated the victory for months, their celebration did not lack enthusiasm. A local contributor who owned a winery had donated $1,000 worth of Michigan champagne, and none of it went to waste.

But Stockman was not one to savor victory. He had work to do. The 1978 edition of the *Almanac of American Politics*, in another prescient observation, wrote after his election: "Stockman may be a good example of the kind of Republican—neither liberal nor conservative in terms his party has been arguing about in the last twenty years—of whom we may see considerably more in the next few years."

Within days of his election, Stockman was back in Washington trying to make those words come true.

CHAPTER 6

FROM THE BACK
BENCH TO THE
FRONT RANKS

It's bad enough being a freshman congressman in a system where power derives from seniority. It's even worse to be a backbencher when your party has just lost the White House and is outnumbered nearly two to one in the House. But David Stockman always relished a tough challenge and prepared for this one with the same zeal he directed at everything else.

Even before his election Stockman was so confident of victory that David Gerson went to Chicago to check out IBM computer systems for their congressional office. Stockman, meanwhile, concentrated on getting the best possible committee assignment. Legislative power, as he well knew, is in the committee structure, and assignment to an important committee can bring great influence and visibility to an enterprising lawmaker. The two most powerful House committees for someone as fascinated with federal finance as Stockman are Ways and Means, which raises the money, and Appropriations, which spends it. But those are much sought-after assignments that usually go to more senior members. So Stockman tried to find the next best thing. In his letter to the Republican Committee on Committees, which handles assignments, he said he would prefer to get a seat on Ways and Means or Appropriations, but since that was unlikely he would be happy to get on the Interstate and Foreign Commerce Committee (renamed Energy and Commerce Committee in 1981). The committee had far-reaching jurisdiction in numerous areas of economic policy that interested Stockman, including regulation, energy, health care and consumer affairs. Energy and health were also blossoming into major national issues, and Stockman saw an opportunity in becoming an expert on both. Using his connections with House Republican leaders, including John Anderson and Guy Vander Jagt of Michigan, chairman of the National Republican Congressional Committee, he landed a seat on the Commerce Committee.

"David knew how the system worked," said Richard Straus. "He knew what a long shot it would be to get on Ways and Means or Appropriations. So rather than go that foolish freshman route, he went right for a committee that maybe freshmen didn't have an easy time getting on, but if you request it and pull a couple of strings you get it. He saw the scope that the committee offered." Stockman was not as fortunate with his second committee assignment. He had asked for the Science and Technology Committee, but because of his prior Hill experience and knowledge of campaign finance laws he was sent to the House Administration Committee.

Stockman also began assembling his congressional staff, which would gain a reputation for being one of the youngest and brightest in Congress. Stockman, who had just turned thirty a week after the election, surrounded himself with aides who were mostly in their mid-twenties. Gerson, then twenty-three, became the administrative assistant and put together a computer system that, among other things, would handle constituent mail and thereby free up Stockman's staff to help him with research and writings on legislative issues instead of spending time writing endless form letters to the folks back home. After learning from a relatively crude system he had assembled during the campaign, Gerson put together a sophisticated IBM letter-writing system among the most advanced in the House. The system was based on a thick notebook containing numerous paragraphs stating Stockman's positions on more than one hundred issues that were fed into the computer's memory. When a constituent wrote a letter on a particular subject the computer could be instructed to spew out a response containing the appropriate paragraphs in coherent order, and presto, out came a perfectly typed letter ready to be mailed. Gerson would spend the next eight years running Stockman's office and a good deal of Stockman's personal life, first in Congress and then at OMB. Gerson also would play matchmaker to Stockman and his future wife, Jennifer Blei.

Other campaign assistants to join the congressional office in Washington were Fred Upton and Jack Strayer. Upton handled a variety of jobs and later became Stockman's liaison with constituents. Strayer handled correspondence and became Stockman's personal assistant until leaving in 1979. Stockman went outside his campaign staff to hire bright legislative assistants who would help him on the issues—two in particular becoming very close advisers and key members of the Stockman brain trust.

One was Frederick N. Khedouri, a descendant of a long line of prominent and prosperous Jews from Iraq. Born in 1950 in New York City, Khedouri could trace back his family tree several thousands of years. One of his more contemporary ancestors, his great-great-great-grandfather, was chief rabbi of Baghdad, a position of great authority at the time. In the summer of 1972, following his graduation from the University of Chicago, Khedouri followed his girlfriend, Sarah, to Washington, where both worked for Ralph Nader's Congress Project, which produced profiles and voting studies on members of Congress. Ironically Khedouri's supervisor at the time was Joan Claybrook, a Nader lieutenant who would do battle with Khedouri over auto regulation five years later, when she was pushing air bag requirements as head of the National Highway Traffic Safety Administration and Khedouri was opposing them as a legislative assistant to Stockman. Khedouri spent eight months with Congress Project and said he did it for the money, not because he shared Nader's liberal politics. Writers were paid $50 for each congressional study they wrote, he said, "and I quickly earned the distinction of being the highest paid person in the Nader organization because I've always been a very fast worker. I turned out three of these things in one week, which meant I got $150, which was more than Joan herself was paid at the time." Because of his association with Nader, Khedouri was assumed by his congressional colleagues to have been a liberal who was converted to conservatism by Stockman. He scoffed at that. He said he has been a lifelong Republican who got punched out in fifth grade for bad-mouthing John F. Kennedy, played in tennis proper white attire at college while radical students were demonstrating against the Vietnam War, and voted for Nixon in 1972—which was more than Stockman did. He did not serve in the military during the war, he said, because for some mysterious reason his draft board never called him up even though he had a low lottery number. But just in case, he said he was prepared to flunk the physical: "I've always been thin and I found out what the minimum height-weight relationship was for passing the physical," he said. "I realized I was within five or six pounds of it anyway, just my natural weight. So it would be no big deal for me to lose the small amount necessary to get under."

After leaving Nader in 1973 Khedouri went to the University of Texas, where he got a law degree, but by the fall of 1976 he had a hankering to return to Washington. It turned out that his girlfriend Sarah, whom he later married, was the daughter of Nathan Glazer, the Harvard professor and editor of *The*

Public Interest magazine. Glazer mentioned to Khedouri that a very bright young former student of his had just been elected to Congress and was looking for legislative aides. Khedouri, then all of twenty-six, interviewed for and got the job. As Stockman's legislative director in Congress and later as an associate director of OMB, Khedouri became an expert on energy, environmental and farm issues, and would write policy papers that many of his political allies — and adversaries as well — described as brilliant. But Khedouri found his boss even more impressive intellectually. "He is absolutely one of the smartest people I've ever met. He is one of the only people I would admit being a good deal smarter than I am," said Khedouri, an impeccably well dressed fellow whose thinning hair had turned prematurely gray, like his boss', and who speaks in a whispery, almost conspiratorial voice. In the spring of 1985 Khedouri left Stockman to become deputy chief of staff for Vice-President George Bush.

Stockman's other close legislative assistant was Donald W. Moran, one of the few natives of the south side of Chicago to grow up in a middle-class, half-Irish (on his father's side) family that also was rock-ribbed Republican. Born in 1951, Moran went to the University of Illinois, where he majored in abstract mathematics, minored in cultural anthropology and graduated with honors in 1973. Initially he joined the Young Republicans but became bored and dropped out after his freshman year. Cards and music replaced politics as his major passions. In fact, he played bridge and hearts well enough to earn significant spending money, and later would become an avid tournament bridge player. He also grew long hair and played guitar with folk and rock groups. Later, at OMB parties, he would pull out the guitar and strum Bob Dylan tunes. As with the other members of Stockman's inner circle, Moran did not get snared by the draft. In his case a high lottery number kept him out. After college Moran moved to southwestern Michigan, where his parents had retired, and went through several short-term jobs, including work as a crop insurance salesman and a car salesman. In the fall of 1974 he became administrative assistant to the Cass County Board of Commissioners, a political appointment under which he administered grant programs. From 1975 to 1977 he started managing federal job-training programs in Michigan financed under CETA—the Comprehensive Employment and Training Act. At OMB he would help the Reagan Administration eliminate $4 billion a year in CETA public service jobs—the largest single federal program to be wiped out in the 1981 round of budget cuts. Some might call this biting the hand that fed one—a charge not unfamiliar to Stockman as well.

While with CETA, Moran started dabbling in local GOP politics, which led to a meeting with Stockman at a Lincoln Day dinner. "I was ambivalent about the prospect of losing Hutchinson," recalled Moran, a tall thin man with blond hair, a basso voice and an intellect that several OMB colleagues described as more powerful than even his boss'. "But Dave struck me as a smart guy," Moran went on. His job prohibited him from working in the campaign, but in

February 1977, after the election, Stockman asked him to serve on one of several district advisory committees that he had set up to stay in touch with his political base. Moran agreed to be on the human resources panel; in May of that year they met again, and soon after, Gerson called and asked if Moran would like to come to Washington as a legislative assistant specializing in health issues and social-welfare programs. Moran could sound like a professor with his use of arcane and abstract metaphors, but at other times he sounded like a street-smart Chicago pol with his knowing references to "the boys" at the White House. Moran toiled at Stockman's side until 1985, when he left to become a health-care specialist with an economic consulting firm in Washington.

The last member of Stockman's inner circle, David Gerson, (unlike Stockman, Khedouri and Moran) started out as a Democrat, or at least he was born into a Democratic household in Kensington, Maryland; his mother was a psychiatrist and his father did market research and political lobbying. "But I was always pretty conservative. A libertarian," he said. Gerson attended Tulane University and Case Western Reserve University, but the lure of Washington drew him away from college before he earned a degree. Unlike his older colleagues he did not have to worry about being called into the military. He had not even reached the minimum draft age of twenty when the draft was stopped in mid-1973. Gerson's average build, short brown hair, glasses and conservative dress perfectly fitted the Washington stereotype of the earnest young man whisking through the corridors of government. Supervisor of "the body" (Stockman) as well as the office, Gerson developed a reputation among his staff as a perfectionist and demanding taskmaster, particularly with women. He would counter Stockman's own politically daring talk and actions by extreme caution, either in the way he would edit a speech or in his rare, circumspect conversations with reporters. Gerson left OMB in 1985 to become an executive with General Motors in Detroit.

During the eight years this foursome worked together they operated as a remarkably integrated unit. It was as if Gerson, Khedouri and Moran were extensions of Stockman. Fiercely loyal and utterly devoted to him, they worked endless hours in his shadow and contributed a fair portion of the brainpower that won Stockman instant recognition in Congress and in the national news media as one of the brightest minds in government. They all operated on the same political, social and generational wave length, and considered themselves libertarians — true-blue disciples of individual freedom in both economic and personal affairs, and ideologically against government intervention in either area. None was a social butterfly. They preferred to party among themselves or to attend small dinner parties rather than to travel the Washington cocktail circuit. All were young and innocent of any military experience, and all participated to some extent in the counterculture of their generation, whether through music, drugs, the social informality or the rebellious attitude toward authority figures. All shared a conceit about their abilities and beliefs. All shared an idealism bordering on missionary zeal that *their* views of government should prevail, and all shared a belief that incompetence, self-interest and lack of principle ruled the halls of Congress and the suites of the White House. It was David Stockman, however, who won all the attention while the "team" worked quietly, and in relative anonymity, in the background.

"I think Moran, Gerson and Khedouri are three of the brightest staff people anybody's ever had," observed one high-ranking Reagan Administration official — a good judge of intellectual talent and a friend of Stockman's. "Yet they never had as much credit as they deserved, and that's a curious thing about Dave. It's my impression that in a non-selfish way he's like a child in his egocentricity. Not that he's trying to serve himself, but his world-view has himself as the center and the key moving force. I wonder if Stockman fully appreciates, consciously at least, the extent of their contributions. I think to some extent they have been assimilated in his mind as an extention of himself. It's all part of himself. It's true that they probably wouldn't be what they are and were had it not been for him, and they all act as if they owe fealty to him. But why is there no record of his debt to them as well? I think the answer is that he has an excessive notion of his own importance."

Except for a few notable exceptions, in which he proved he could be as politically and selfishly motivated as anyone in Congress, Stockman did try diligently to be faithful to his rigid nineteenth-century laissez-faire, free-market, government-is-incompetent philosophy—in the bills he introduced and supported, in his floor speeches and in the extensive research and analysis he kept producing from his congressional office. He tried to be the force for truth, justice and goodness that his grandfather had raised; he was Reinhold Niebuhr's "Moral Man" up against the "Immoral Society," which in this case and in his view meant Congress. From his first weeks in the House of Representatives he made it clear he was more interested in taking on the club than joining it. On February 1, 1977, just short of his first month in office, Stockman assailed a proposal to raise the salaries of members of Congress by twenty-nine percent, from $44,600 to $57,500. "For the Congress to grant itself a pay increase that is greater than the median income of this country can only set a bad example. It makes us hypocrites as we call on others for restraint," he said in remarks inserted into the *Congressional Record*. The raise, of course, went through anyway.

On February 9, in another unusual anti-establishment move for newcomers, Stockman and a freshman Democrat, thirty-two-year old Dan Glickman of Kansas, cosponsored a bill that would change House terms from two to four years and limit service in either House to twelve years. Speaking in defense of the bill on the House floor, Stockman said if there were a limit to a legislator's term, "a senator or representative [would be] less likely to forget the people to whom he [would] return." With a longer House term, he said, lawmakers could devote more time to their legislative work rather than spending half their time campaigning; also less influence would be exerted by special interest groups, "leaving the legislator better able to react to his own best judgment . . . By reducing the power of incumbency, we would open the possibilities for far more citizens to run for office. That occurrence might not sit well with many of us here, but we have talked a great deal lately about ethics and integrity. The question is: Do we have the integrity to do what is right for the country, regardless of personal aggrandizement? Twelve years in each House is adequate time in which to press for those pieces of legislation near and dear to the congressman and his constituents, but not usually enough time to become a professional politician whose main goal is reelection and maintaining a residence in Washington, D.C." It was not the kind of speech to endear a new member to his congressional elders. And, predictably, the legislation went nowhere.

Stockman had little respect for the institution of Congress or for its members, and he enjoyed ridiculing them in public. In an interview published in June 1977 by *U.S. News & World Report,* he declared, "This institution is even more profoundly undemocratic than I thought." He condemned the committee structure as a system that concentrated power in the hands of a few senior members and interest groups. And members of Congress were so busy meeting their constituents, he said, that they were ill-informed on the issues. "If you could go to the floor and suddenly freeze everything and give a little third-grade test on the issues, you'd be appalled by how much people don't know about what they're voting on." But he also admitted that as a freshman "I tend to take a negative perspective," and that despite the defects "the decisions that come out are somehow, miraculously, not as bad as they could be." Two years later, though, he sounded even more critical: "I'm more interested in ideas than votes because we can't make rational policy in a country this complex unless we're guided by ideas," he said in a Detroit *News* interview published November 4, 1979. "Time and time again we get into trouble because we're guided by pure expediency and political pragmatism. Congress simply drives me crazy that way. It's very frustrating and disillusioning when the greatest country in the world can't seem to produce a level of intelligence in its highest legislative body greater than what is frequently displayed here."

After serving as a key cabinet officer in the Reagan Administration, he would make the same observation in private about the President, most of his Cabinet, and the large number of "assholes" on the White House staff.

Stockman disdained the wheeling and dealing of the political process. He was not a coalition builder. For him political office offered power to shape society according to his distinct vision, not to build a lifetime career. Except for a Wednesday night discussion group on issues, called the Clearinghouse for the Future, he was, according to then Congressional Budget Office Director Alice Rivlin, "a loner and a maverick at a time when being a junior Republican didn't give you power over anything. But he was a lot of fun to spar with. He seemed much more interested in getting to the intellectual root of problems than in having a political discussion." Columnist-commentator George Will, who became a good friend, remembers that his first reaction on meeting Stockman was that he was "one of those rarities — a proper intellectual in politics, someone who was interested in ideas and believed they mattered . . . [Stockman] is more compelled by intellectual curiosity than by moral passion. He wants to figure it out and then see how far he can carry it." But Stockman also like to experiment on a grand scale . . . "His lab is a continent," Will added.

Dan Glickman, who socialized with Stockman occasionally and discovered him easygoing outside of work, said the kind of anti-institutional harangues that got Stockman attention were common at the time among many younger members. "A lot of us, Democrats and Republicans, railed wholesale against the system," he said. "It was a big issue then. But now you don't find new members doing that." Nor, for that matter, are Glickman and the other rebellious young Turks of the late 1970s still trashing the establishment; they're climbing their way up the pole. But Stockman has become even more anti-establishment, or at least anti The Reagan Administration establishment; note the title of his book, *The Tri-*

umph of Politics: Why the Reagan Revolution Failed.
"He was not afraid of bucking the institutional system. He obviously wasn't planning to work his way up," said Glickman, who attributed Stockman's behavior at the time to the reality of being a member of a powerless minority party and to his rigid ideological conviction. "Whether it was farm price supports or water projects, he took a libertarian view of government on almost everything," said Glickman.

Stockman thrived on risks, controversy and breaking the rules. It took a lot of self-righteousness, self-confidence and nerve, and his track record of success seemed to confirm him in the "right," as he saw it. "He's never worried for his job," said Steve Stockman. "I mean, a lot of people are quiet because they don't want to ruffle the feathers of the people back in Michigan. But if he lost an election in Congress, that wouldn't be the end of the world. He'd do something else. If he got fired from the Cabinet, it wouldn't be that big a tragedy. He knew he could do something else. He's always been in demand."

He was in demand in Congress even though he went against the flow because his abilities stuck out. Colleagues in both parties quickly recognized and respected him as a man of unusual intelligence, drive and ambition who had an extraordinary understanding of the issues and legislative process from his prior experience, and who could articulate the case for conservative economics better than anyone else. House Republicans named him chairman of a GOP task force on economic policy a month after he took his seat.

"Dave distinguished himself immediately in Congress," said Robert J. Walker, the former Anderson aide who worked on the staff of the House Republican Conference during Stockman's first term. "You had all of these old guard Republicans who had a gut reaction against government intrusion and high taxes . . . but Dave added an intellectual justification. He gained the respect of members for doing his homework." In 1979, during a House Republican caucus to discuss President Carter's standby gasoline-rationing plan, Walker recalled, members spoke in opposition to the plan but it was Stockman who stood up and said, "Here's why it's not going to work." And the others responded with, "Gee, Dave, You're right." Added Walker: "He showed a degree of intelligence rarely seen in the House. The members liked Dave for that . . . they needed an intellectual backbone for their positions. They were floundering and Dave was a real breath of fresh air. He was always more convincing than Jack Kemp."

Kemp, the former Buffalo Bills quarterback turned congressman from New York, was one of the few "new-idea" men among conservative House Republicans at the time, his big idea being tax cuts to stimulate economic growth. Kemp became one of Stockman's few friends in Congress and later became one of his many disillusioned mentors when they split over Stockman's repeated efforts to raise taxes to reduce the deficit. "We were immediate friends by virtue of our interest in economics," Kemp recalls of their earliest encounters. "He was bright, articulate, well-versed in free-enterprise economics. And he understood that the political future of conservatism had been weakened by simply opposing much of the agenda that the liberals had established. He knew that he had to be on the offense to be a good politician. So he was basically interested in action, ideas, reforms." Kemp also says he was not one to be offended by Stockman's disdainful attacks on Congress as an institution: "There's nothing wrong with being anti-establishment when the establishment is wrong. He did it within the framework of the whole democratic process. He wasn't sneaky about it. He did it openly, proudly, disdainfully of those mistakes, and I think there was a lot of room for skepticism in the seventies. When you look at the performance of the economy, it was a mess. Dave questioned in an iconoclastic way some of those programs and policies. It's good to have someone like that, because out of that comes good public policy . . . I give Dave credit for challenging some of these cherished notions."

Another one of Stockman's few congressional friends was Phil (Gramm-Rudman-Hollings) Gramm of Texas. First elected to the House as a Democrat in 1978, he switched parties in 1983 after openly working with the Republicans on a budget policy and won election to the Senate the following year. "Clearly Stockman was the smartest member of Congress," says Gramm, who is regarded by colleagues as the closest thing to another Stockman in Congress — bright, doctrinaire on free-market economics, hardworking, very ambitious and less than a winner in the charm department. "One of the appealing things about Stockman," Gramm adds, "was that he started sooner, worked harder, and knew more than anyone else. He did his homework and in so doing stood out from the crowd."

Members on the other side of the aisle agreed. Congressman Jack Dingell, a Michigan Democrat, was chairman of the Commerce Committee's energy and power subcommittee when Stockman joined it in 1977. "We developed a friendship," says Dingell, who became chairman of the full committee in 1981 when Stockman became OMB director. "He was very bright, very conservative—basically a free-market purist. I found his word to be generally good, although he could blind-side you," says Dingell, a House member since 1955. Because they were both from Michigan, the two men often found themselves on the same side, such as in fighting efforts to regulate automobile safety and exhaust pollution.

But at the same time Stockman was earning his colleague's respect for his intellectual abilities he also was inviting their resentment with his attitude. Although the few members who got to know him socially say they found him pleasant and likable, most saw him as a smug young know-it-all who was intense, serious and overly ambitious, and who wore his consistency on economic principles as too shiny a badge of honor. Inflexible, he infuriated older members of both parties who were accustomed to playing the game according to the rules as they saw them.

In 1978, for example, Stockman refused pleadings

from then House Minority Leader John Rhodes of Arizona to help pass a water projects bill that Stockman considered right out of the old pork barrel. "John Rhodes physically grabbed Dave and said, 'I need your support on the water project vote,' " recalls Stockman legislative aide Fred Upton. "And Dave said, 'No.' Well, in 1979 when Dave wanted to get off the Administration Committee and onto Appropriations, Rhodes screwed him." Eldon Rudd of Arizona who had the same seniority as Stockman but had voted with Rhodes on the water projects, got the committee seat instead. "I suspect Dave had no way of knowing the importance of water in Arizona. You can't have economic growth without it," says John Globensky, Stockman's election campaign chairman. "Here's this Michigan farm boy who didn't realize what he was doing. To him, it was just pork barreling."

"David was not unimpressed with his knowledge," says Dingell, "but he combined two unique disadvantages: he had the convictions of the divine and of the economist. That makes one inflexible and less pragmatic, but he still could be very capable in working on legislation."

Many other members did not appreciate his cunning legislative tactics, particularly his use of the surprise element. They preferred to do political combat in the open, and felt Stockman did not always level with them. One of his favorite tactics as a member of a hopelessly outnumbered House minority was to defeat Democratic legislation through "Trojan Horse" amendments that were not what they seemed: after attracting bipartisan support, the amendments would prove to undermine the intent of the original legislation. Some Republican members who did not want their names used complained that Stockman was often abrasive and would step on a lot of toes. While some members were trying to build coalitions, "Dave was interested in making headlines and a name for himself," complained one junior member.

On the Democratic side Stockman really put some noses out of joint. "He was always a member of the flamboyant and not particularly effective minority of the minority," says Michael W. Kitzmiller, a member of the Commerce Committee staff who later became staff director under Dingell. "You could always count of him being a wise-ass. He'd take a contrary position from the leadership just to be contrary." Kitzmiller remembers a dispute in 1979 when the committee passed a bill to save helium, discovered with natural gas, from escaping into the atmosphere. He said Stockman scoffed at committee projections that helium supplies could be depleted within fifty years, and charged that enormous amounts of energy would have to expended to recapture the helium. Said Kitzmiller:

"He argued we should just let the helium go and that the market would find a way to recapture it. And he offered an amendment to rename the legislation the 'flat earth' bill because the theory that helium resources are finite is the same as the theory that the earth is flat. He loved those kinds of sorties. He never made any constructive proposals. He always was on a raid to torpedo something or embarrass members. He could be very sarcastic and malicious, and he had this nervous little giggle that made him obnoxious. I've worked in Congress for twenty years and I can't think of any member I feel less respect for except those convicted of crimes. I've known this kind of person. He's a man of absolutely no principle, a total opportunist. He'll always be a graduate student who is very interested in religion when there's a war on."

A perhaps more balanced estimate would be that Stockman the congressman was a man of principle *and* one who saw the main chance and seized it. In his district the two were compatible, and he could say with pride how true his voting record was to his personal convictions. When his principles collided with his district's politics he could opt for politics, or vote his principles. It depended . . .

Candidate for the most unprincipled vote of his congressional career is the one cast during his third month as a member of the House. President Carter's first executive order, issued January 21, 1977, granted a pardon to Vietnam draft-evaders. The action drew considerable opposition in Congress, and the House went on record with its objection March 16 by adopting an amendment to an appropriations bill that prohibited funds from being spent in connection with the amnesty program. Congressman John T. Myers, an Indiana Republican who sponsored the amendment, said the vote was "possibly the only opportunity you will have to express your views on this issue of the pardon." Stockman, who ten years earlier had signed a petition vowing to "resist the draft" and to "aid and encourage others to do the same," voted in favor of the Myers amendment, which passed by a narrow margin. Stockman later would admit that, yes, indeed, his vote had been based on district politics and that he had been "hypocritical." Such reflective honesty was one of Stockman's more endearing traits, made him likable to a lot of people — but not everyone. Keke Anderson cites that vote as "my greatest disappointment in David Stockman. I asked him once how he had ended up in divinity school, and his response was very quick: 'I didn't want to go to Vietnam.' It gave me the chills."

Stockman's legislative aides cite one particular vote by which he betrayed his free-market principles for district politics. The issue involved a 1977 ban on the sale of children's sleepwear treated with Tris, a flame-retardant chemical found to have cancer-causing properties. Companies adversely affected by the ban persuaded Congress to pass legislation ordering the federal government to reimburse them for losses incurred as a result of the ban. One of those companies was in Stockman's district, and he agreed to co-sponsor the legislation. His staff was later nonplused to discover that he had voted for it. The bill passed Congress in 1978 but it was pocket-vetoed by Carter, who said it would represent "an unprecedented and unwise use of taxpayers' funds." Privately, David Stockman agreed.

Fred Upton recalls other instances when Stockman would vote against some program reauthorization, such as Urban Development Action Grants, and the relevant federal agency would call urging him to reverse his vote, and Upton would persuade him to "take a walk" when the issue came up again. And in March 1977, Stockman and three other Michigan congressmen sponsored a bill to provide financial assistance to Michigan farmers who had lost livestock poisoned by a flame retardant, polybrominated biphenyls (PBB), which accidentally had been mixed in with feed distributed throughout the state.

But such flights from Stockman's standard ideology were unusual. Gerson, Moran and Khedouri would play a guessing game about how Stockman should have voted on an economic issue based on the principle involved. When they checked his actual vote, they found they almost always guessed right.

Even so, Stockman's vote against federal pork did not deter him from grabbing all the chops he could for his own district. In fact, his office had programmed its computer system to be on the lookout for grants and loans that would help his constituents. "If the money is going to be allocated, then we're going to do our part to see that our constituents get a fair share," Gerson told a group of district businesses at an April 1980 conference on how to become a government supplier. Stockman sounded more cynical when he was quoted in the *Atlantic Monthly* the following year: "I went around and cut all the ribbons and they never knew I voted against the damn programs." Stockman saw no conflict in voting against federal water projects, then helping Decatur, Michigan, obtain a $575,000 loan from the Farmers Home Administration in 1977 to improve and expand its water system. Budget Director Stockman had no problem in 1981 about trying to eliminate the Economic Development Administration, the same agency that Congressman Stockman had written to in 1978 in hopes of obtaining a $266,000 grant for an industrial park in Adrian, Michigan.

Mostly, Stockman's voting record on issues related to the budget and economy was predictable during his four years in Congress—the evidence is in the high ratings he earned from conservative and business groups opposed to government spending and the low ratings he got from liberal and labor groups favoring social programs. His record on other issues was considerably more varied. He did not follow a conservative GOP line reflexively but voted a more independent line that largely reflected his personal views: as noted previously, in 1977 and 1978 the Ripon Society, the political club created by young Republicans who considered themselves progressive, liberal or libertarian, gave him a 92 percent rating.

On most military-spending issues he was a strong supporter who voted for increases in the Defense Department budget and construction of the B-1 bomber. Nevertheless, colleagues also recall him expressing some private misgivings about pork in the military budget. When he became budget director he made his doubts very public after first helping to push a rapid escalation in defense spending through Congress. He saw foreign aid as overseas pork, and generally voted with his conservative colleagues to reduce foreign assistance spending. But he also departed from the GOP line on several foreign policy issues. In March 1977, for example, he was one of a small group of Republicans to support a Carter-backed bill to ban imports of chrome for Rhodesia's white-ruled government. In a more surprising departure from his GOP colleagues he voted in June 1979 for final passage of a Carter-backed bill that implemented the Panama Canal treaties. Only 35 of 157 House Republicans voted that way. Opposition to the treaties was a big issue with conservatives at the time, and although Stockman voted with the conservatives in attempts to attach crippling amendments to the legislation, he deserted them at the end. "We had sent out all these red-meat, anti-canal letters to the district," recalls Fred Upton, "and then Dave said, 'I just couldn't do it. I had to vote my conscience.' And I said, 'Oh, no. How could you?' " The year before, when Stockman had surveyed his district on the issue, two-thirds of the respondents said they opposed Senate ratification of the treaties. In general, though, Stockman did not spend too much time thinking on foreign policy issues, except for their budgetary impact.

On social issues he usually voted his libertarian instincts — on the side of perceived individual freedom of choice over government intervention. So depending on the issue, he sometimes was aligned with liberal Democrats and sometimes voted with conservative Republicans. He generally favored the pro-choice position on abortion, supported the Equal Rights Amendment, voted against school busing to desegregate schools, opposed affirmative action guidelines to correct racial imbalance, opposed gun control and mandated school prayer.

In 1977 he was one of only twenty-one Republicans to oppose an amendment to prohibit the use of federal funds to finance or encourage abortions. Although he found out from his 1978 survey that a slight majority of his district was pro-choice on abortion, he still had to fend off pressure from a strong anti-abortion organization back home. In his second term "he would take a walk for the anti-abortionists," when a key vote was up, according to Upton. David Gerson remembers having to urge Stockman not to buckle under to the anti-abortion forces.

In 1978 he supported a resolution to extend the deadline for ratification of the Equal Rights Amendment by thirty-nine months, a position opposed by most members of his party; but he also voted for a GOP amendment that would have allowed states that had ratified the ERA to rescind their ratification during the extention.

In 1979 Stockman joined conservatives in voting for a constitutional amendment that would prohibit forced busing to achieve racial balance in schools. He also voted consistently against gun control, knowing his district was strongly opposed to any federal regulation of firearms. He personally objected to school prayer legislation but occasionally would support a measure calling for voluntary school prayer because it was a very popular issue back home.

For the most part, though, Stockman tuned out social policy issues the way he tended to ignore foreign policy matters. He was just too involved with his work on the budget and economic matters to pay much attention to the so-called social agenda, which he regarded as a "silly" diversion. He became interested in social issues only to the extent that district politics forced him to be. "In rural Michigan you have to be against gun control, for example," says friend Richard Straus. "So he develops this very finely argued position against gun control, and it reminded me of his defense of Nixon, which was ridiculous. So I laughed at him and started to argue with him. It showed he was willing to do what had to be done. He doesn't care about school prayer or gun control, but he has to do certain things. If he thought about it, he'd probably say there shouldn't be 400 million guns in the country. But it's not a central issue. He'll drop the subject the minute he can because it doesn't interest him and he's not comfortable with it. If he had run for the Senate or had a job where he really had to stake out those positions, I honestly believe he would have a hard time. For all the opportunism he's accused of, I think that on the social issues he'd have a hard time playing the game over a prolonged period because they're anathema to him. They don't stand up against good, solid, historical, analytical research, which he applies to everything."

One of the few non-budget issues that interested him more than superficially was campaign finance reform. He had developed expertise on the issue as a legislative aide to Anderson. He also saw it as a way to reduce the influence of special interest groups, which he held responsible for perpetuating the social pork barrel. Yet he took such a complex position on campaign finance that he could seem both a big supporter and a leading opponent. He was an original sponsor of a 1977 bill to provide limited public financing of House general election campaigns, but disagreed with some specific provisions and helped bottle it up in the House Administration Committee that year. In 1978 he voted with the losing side that tried to keep campaign financing reform alive in the House that year, but when the issue came up again a year later he helped defeat it in committee. Later he would explain that he always opposed the idea of public financing of campaigns, but he was willing to go along as a way to neutralize the impact of special-interest political-action committees, which have become major backers of campaigns. "That's how we allowed the squeaking wheels to get too much influence," he said. So he favored matching federal payments to candidates who could raise money from smaller, non-PAC contributors, but he also complained that the spending limits set by the Democratic-backed bill favored incumbents, and in the end he would not support the legislation.

When campaign financing was not on the front burner, Stockman devoted his four years in Congress to leading the opposition to government spending and regulation. He opposed public subsidies for Amtrak and the creation of new national parks and forests in Alaska. He opposed establishment of an Energy Department and a consumer protection agency. He opposed emergency aid for farmers and federal regulation to curb hospital costs. And he fought federal regulation of energy supplies across the board, from oil- and gas-price controls to standby gasoline rationing. And he made the case for fiscal conservatism better than anyone had before. As a member of a badly outnumbered minority he could not hope to implement policies of his own, but he showed he could help defeat policies being pushed by the Carter Administration — such as its hospital cost-containment package and its proposed standby gasoline-rationing plan. This was a novelty for more senior Republicans, who had been accustomed to mouthing their opposition but not being able to *do* anything about it.

One of Stockman's most effective forays came in mid-1978 when he played a key role in defeating Carter's hospital cost-control package. During Commerce Committee consideration of the legislation, Stockman offered a highly complicated amendment that undermined the basic but unstated assumption of the administration's bill: that costs would be lowered by curbing hospital admissions. Stockman's amendment kicked out the underpinnings by removing the provisions that would have discouraged patient admissions and replacing them with incentives to increase admissions. The amendment, which passed the committee by one vote, was so complicated that administration supporters didn't understand at the time of the vote how damaging the measure was. Only days later did administration officials seem to realize that the Stockman amendment had essentially gutted the intent of the original bill. A month later the legislation was scrapped by the committee, dealing a stunning loss to Carter. Don

Moran, who helped Stockman draft the crippling amendment, proudly calls it "the ultimate Trojan Horse."

Which was typical of how Stockman operated. He didn't build coalitions or count heads to defeat the administration. He was the ideologue and mastermind who provided the intellectual arguments and the technical gimmicks. "He was devastatingly accurate in his critiques of the Carter Administration," says Washington *Post* political columnist David Broder. "He was very, very good at recognizing programmatic flabbiness and political ineptitude."

Stockman managed this by turning his congressional office into a think tank that cranked out a torrent of long, sophisticated position papers. He would send out lengthy "Dear Colleague" letters to other House members every week or two to state his case on the issues. With help principally from Khedouri and Moran, he would write 50-page analyses filled with statistics on why, say, hospital cost-control legislation or emergency farm aid or gasoline rationing was wrong. And he would put them into the *Congressional Record,* which was filled with long studies of this sort, except rarely were they authored by the members of Congress.

Stockman was a different animal.

Congressman Stockman was really an academic in mind and a kid at heart. Over three elections he never overcame his intense dislike of the social requirements of the job. He got a little better at campaigning in

226

1978 and 1980, and didn't need the social crutches who stood at his side in 1976, but his attitude was still: the less politicking he had to do, the better. During his first year in office he went back to his district forty-four weekends, by David Gerson's count, but with each successive year he cut down on his trips: by 1980 he went home only about half a dozen times, according to Fred Upton's count. He made sure, though, that the district was being taken care of in his absence. Two regional offices and a mobile van tended to local business, and Upton and Gerson would stand in for him at numerous district events. After a while his staff would joke that most of Stockman's constituents thought Upton or Gerson was their congressman. Actually, Stockman had the luxury of being able to stay in Washington because he had a "safe district" and did not have to worry about being reelected. In 1978 he had no primary opposition and swept to reelection with 71 percent of the vote. In 1980 he won another term with 75 percent of the vote.

"It's not that I mind the time spent talking with people or making speeches," he told the Flint *Journal* in a September 2, 1979, interview. "It's the travel time. Spending two hours in a car getting from one end of my district to the other, I'm not doing anything constructive. I can't read or mend political fences." Similarly, he told the Detroit *News* in a November 4, 1979, interview: "I don't dislike campaigning, but if I had my choice between reading a 500-page report on auto-industry regulations and a day of campaigning, I'd take the former." The Detroit

News article went on to say that Stockman appeared bored at some district visits and tried to avoid the crowds at others: "At a David Stockman Night at the Berrien County Fair, the congressman stayed safely inside the Republican Party tent, venturing out into the crowd only once—for a cup of coffee." He never changed. In December 1980 when he called a friend to break the news that he had been named budget director, he said: "The best part is I'll never have to spend another weekend in Michigan."

Stockman never really fitted the congressional stereotype. Despite his gray hair he had boyish features, did not dress as well as his colleagues and had to be reminded by his staff to get his hair cut or to buy some new shoes. He could pass for one of his aides, which occasionally proved helpful when he was trying to avoid meeting some constituents. Where other members would take advantage of the perquisites of office, he found them loathsome and avoided congressional "fact-finding" junkets that were always scheduled during the recesses. As a point of pride, Gerson would try to operate the office below budget so he could return leftover funds. Since Stockman hated to squander time, he would eat most of his meals in cafeterias or at his desk rather than take the time to dine leisurely at a plush restaurant. Always the creature of habit, he and Gerson, Moran and Khedouri would go to the cafeteria in the Longworth House Office Building at 8:07 each morning ("that's when the line dwindled down," says Gerson) and Odessa Ferguson, working behind the counter, would automatically serve up the same breakfast for Stockman—two eggs over medium, a double order of bacon and toast. Lunch usually was a tuna fish sandwich in the office. He was also constantly smoking Salems and gulping down coffee.

The cigarette smoking drove Gerson up the wall. He was always hounding Stockman about it, and although Stockman never quit he did become embarrassed about his weakness and was forever trying to hide it from Gerson, from constituents and almost every else. A few times he started little fires in his desk drawer or the wastebasket trying to hide a burning cigarette in his ashtray. Each time he managed to douse the flames with coffee. Sometimes he would go down to the basement of the office building to smoke so Gerson wouldn't see him. If he was making a speech in his district, Fred Upton recalls, he sometimes would run into the bathroom to smoke, leaving his constituents wondering where he'd disappeared to. He continued to hide his smoking as budget director by not lighting up in public. At one social function, Federal Reserve Board Chairman Paul Volcker's wife had stepped out onto a balcony for a discreet smoke herself, only to run into Stockman puffing away.

Friends who socialized with him often remarked that one of Stockman's charms was that he never acted status-conscious or seemed impressed with his position. To them he was just plain Dave, a hardworking bachelor in his early thirties who happened to be a member of Congress. On the rare occasions when he was not working, he could actually be quite informal and funny. At small parties with close friends he would be very much a product of his generation—wearing jeans, listening to old folk or rock music, even smoking marijuana. (Once he became budget director, however, he made a point of keeping his distance from illegal drugs and rumors of cocaine use at OMB. Nicotine and caffeine were his drugs of choice.)

At work, Stockman used his congressional office like a professor's study. "The closest way you could describe him would be as a professor," says Steve Stockman. "When he got to be a congressman he had a staff with research assistants, like professors used to have, and he could, with a budget of about one million dollars a year, have his own computer. It was like his dream come true. He could research anything he wanted to. He could have complete access to the Library of Congress. And then there were the political things he would have to do as part of the deal to be this kind of professor. I think OMB is kind of a continuation of the professor role, only with a much bigger research staff at his disposal."

"He'd have the curtains drawn in the middle of the day, and he would be smoking and reading crunched over his desk," says Diana Moore, his personal secretary and office manager from 1979 until he left OMB in 1985. "His In box was always filled with a two-foot stack of books. He always asked for a huge stack of books, even when he went on vacation." Sometimes, she recalls, he was so focused on his work that he acted like an absent-minded professor—wearing two shoes that didn't match, showing up in a suit jacket with the wrong trousers, misplacing his wallet or keys. "And he just hated to waste time, which is why he avoided social things — almost too much. He'd say, 'I don't want to do another M and M [mix and mingle] or G and G [grip and grin.]' Dave was basically a loner until Jennifer came along."

Jennifer Blei came along in 1978. Born in the Philadelphia suburb of Willow Grove, Pennsylvania, Blei joined IBM right after college and by 1977 at the age of twenty-two had become the company's technical representative for customers at the White House and on Capitol Hill. In her job teaching customers how to operate their systems, one of her regular stops was at Stockman's office. Like Stockman she was very bright, ambitious and resourceful. She switched to sales in 1978, and within a few years had become one of IBM's star performers. She also was, and is, attractive, with light brown hair, blue eyes and a trim figure, and she dressed smartly. Her visits were exciting events to the young, sometimes very young, men in Stockman's office, who would make suggestive comments or pant behind her back or both. "Frankly, Dave surrounded himself with a bunch of immature sexists," said one woman who worked for him and preferred that her identity not be disclosed. "But he wasn't one himself, maybe because his mother was a good role model for feminists. And Jennifer, too. In fact, he always had women in responsible jobs — in Congress and at OMB."

At first neither Stockman nor Blei paid much attention to the other since each was dating someone else. Stockman was seeing Sue Gillespie, a hometown girl who had gotten a job in Washington, but then they stopped seeing each other after about a year. Jack Strayer says Gillespie had gotten tired of spending all her time reading books with Stockman, and finally announced that she did not want to spend her life with a professor or monk. "For three or four months after they broke up he wasn't doing any more dating, and I could see that he was going to become a kind of little old hunchback man with nobody in his life," says Strayer. "He was kind of moping around." Meanwhile, Blei also had ended her relationship. The time, it seemed, was ripe.

In the spring of 1978 Gerson decided to throw a garden party at his new house, and Strayer wrote it down on Stockman's schedule. But Stockman said he wasn't going: "I don't have a date," he told Strayer, who told Gerson, who was not happy to hear that. Just then, Blei walked into the office. "Ger and I looked at each other and he said, 'Aha. Why not?,'" recalls Strayer. "So Ger got up and talked to Jennifer for a few minutes about computers, then went into Dave's office, came out and said, 'Jennifer, Dave wants to talk to you.' So Jennifer goes into his office. Half an hour later they walk out and disappear down the hall. Dave came back a little while later and said, 'Well, I'm taking Jennifer to Gerson's party.' They were only at the party for about half an hour, and that was that." Soon afterward they began living together.

"Ger was very intent in having the two of us meet," says Jennifer, who married Dave in 1983. "I still don't know why. I'm sure Ger has his reasons, but I don't know. I'm just thrilled that he did and will forever be thankful."

At the same time that he began taking up with Jennifer Blei, Stockman started attracting national attention for his views on energy, which was now the hot topic of the day. He had, naturally, become an expert on energy and the most articulate voice in Congress for a 180-degree reversal in policy from government control to total reliance on the free market. In February 1978 Stockman inserted into the *Congressional Record* an article by Irving Trust Company economist Arnold E. Safer that predicted the rise in oil prices would produce world oil surpluses in "the years ahead." Using that as a springboard Stockman, with Khedouri's assistance, laid out a similar view in a lengthy article that appeared in *The Public Interest* in the fall of 1978. The article refuted government predictions of an oil shortage in the mid-1980s by arguing that the high price of oil from OPEC (Organization of Petroleum Exporting Countries) would push down world demand and drive up production by non-OPEC sources so long as the U.S. government did not interfere with the marketplace by keeping price controls, which he said were unnecessary because prices would fall on their own as supplies increased. "We need do little more than decontrol domestic energy prices, dismantle the energy bureaucracy and allow the U.S. economy to equilibrate at the world level," he wrote. "Energy supply and demand will take care of itself, no less efficiently than commodity soybeans or Saran

Wrap."

His analysis proved out, and he went on to warn that the real danger was not an energy shortage, but that "we will squander massive amounts of economic resources on a continued futile and foolish quest for energy autarchy. The economic pie will inevitably shrink as a result. And in the process we will saddle our economy and the American people with enormous amounts of political interference and bureaucratic management of their lives, so that the sphere of personal freedom will shrink as well."

Stockman believed very strongly that government proposals dictating how people should conserve energy not only were bad economics but amounted to totalitarianism—"statism," as he liked to call it. Stockman had written a shorter article on the same theme in the spring of 1978 for the Washington *Post*. Both articles won him more national attention, just as "The Social Pork Barrel" had. One of his new admirers was William Greider, a Washington *Post* reporter who recalled being "stunned that a guy who could write so well and do his own thinking was a congressman." Like Meg Greenfield, Greider rang up Stockman for lunch and the two started a relationship that would rock the capital and both of their careers three years later with the publication of Greider's *Atlantic Monthly* article—"The Education of David Stockman." When they first met, Greider considered himself a political liberal who opposed Stockman's laissez-faire economic philosophy and his attempts to dismantle the social-welfare state, but admired the congressman's intelligence. So when

Greider became editor of the *Post*'s Sunday opinion section he invited Stockman to write several more pieces. Most were on energy and made the same free-market case in arguing against gasoline rationing, regulation of natural gas prices and a $60 billion-plus program to develop synthetic fuel.

Stockman had found a unique political formula. With his blend of scholarly research, colorful rhetoric and devotion to the free market on virtually every economic issue, he was making a name for himself and his cause while other junior members of the junior party in the House were toiling in obscurity. Standing up for his beliefs, taking risks, being controversial, going against the grain was surely paying off.

And it made him increasingly bolder. During the 1978 protests by grain farmers seeking higher price supports for their crops, Stockman stood firm in his opposition to a farm bill that would increase price supports. Although most of his constituents supported him, his stand brought some local farmers who were hurting into his office. Jack Strayer, who scheduled constituent appointments, says Stockman had no sympathy for the farmers in trouble. He believed most of them didn't really want to farm. "These guys had inherited a job they didn't want," says Strayer. "Their fathers had made the money and now lived in Florida. In fact, about a quarter of the addresses of the farm mailing list we had were in Florida. They had winter homes there. The parents had done all right, but the new generation didn't want to farm because they couldn't make the money their parents made."

Strayer recalls Stockman delivering essentially that same blunt speech during face-to-face meetings with local farmers who spent several weeks in Washington participating in the American Agricultural Movement demonstrations:

"He basically told these people, 'Look, there isn't anybody in this room over forty. All your parents are in Florida. You guys are lazy, you mismanage money.' After about six weeks he got tired of these people coming in every day, so finally he put his foot down and said, 'Jack, I will not see another farmer from the fourth district.' I got very angry with him and said, 'These people are spending a lot of money and a lot of time; they're your constituents. You owe it to them.' And he threw me out of his office.

"But pretty soon this couple came in and they'd been living in a tent. They were very old, they looked messy and they smelled like kerosene. They said, 'We're with the American Agricultural Movement. We want to see the Congressman.' Well, it turns out they were from a town in Michigan that wasn't even in the district, but I was still so angry at Dave that I said, 'The Congressman will see you right away.' I just opened the door and said, 'Dave, these are the Joneses,' or whatever, 'from Greenville.' This couple walked in, and Dave had this blank look on his face. He spent about ten minutes with them.

"When they came out of his office, he said, 'Thank you very much for coming,' and then turned to me, saying, 'Jack, can I see you in the office for a second.' He sat me down in this big leather chair for visitors—

I never sat in it before—and said, 'Sit down, let me get you a cup of coffee.' I figured he was going to fire me. Instead, he set the coffee down, got on his knees right in front of me, put his hands together like he was praying and said, 'I'll do anything you want. I'll see any farmer you want. Just don't bring people like that into my office ever again.' "

Bluntness and political hyperbole were means of calling attention to his ideas. Convinced that his beliefs were the truth, he thought that if he could publicize them, people would ultimately see the light. In a March 1979 interview published in the Automobile Club of Michigan's magazine, Stockman claimed that the Environmental Protection Agency's regulation of auto exhaust emissions was not intended primarily to protect the public health and quality of the air. "Their real, underlying motivation, and I'll use a strong term, 'their hidden agenda,' is to use these regulatory powers to undermine the entire auto industry." He went on to charge that the "so-called clean-air coalition," which included at least one top EPA official, weren't candid about their objective: "It's not clean air or air quality that's adequate for breathing that is their goal. It's really an effort to get rid of the automobile."

In June 1979 he assailed a proposed six-month moratorium on new nuclear power reactors as "an effort to legitimize and give congressional sanction to all the half-baked and unsubstantiated conclusions being shamelessly propagated by the windmill and woodstove people." The following month, on a similar note, he argued against spending $1.2 billion to build the Clinch River, Tennessee, nuclear breeder reactor. In the past the project had been opposed largely on environmental grounds, but Stockman argued against it on the economic grounds that it was too costly for the energy it would produce. In making that point, he argued, "I'm not a namby-pamby, bird-watching environmentalist, but I'm still opposed . . ." His ever-cautious aide, Gerson, thought that was a little strong, even for his boss. So, using congressional prerogative, Gerson edited out the line before Stockman's speech was printed for history in the *Congressional Record*. But a reporter for an environmental newsletter happened to hear the remark on the House floor and published it. When Stockman became budget director he would find himself defending the Clinch River project for a simple political reason: Senate Majority Leader Howard Baker, a Republican from Tennessee, wanted it spared from the 1981 round of budget cuts.

For audacity, cynicism, irreverence and self-deprecating humor, little could compare with a personal piece Stockman wrote for William Greider on Feb. 11, 1979, to inaugurate a "Company Town" series, in which Washingtonians would write diarylike accounts of a week in their life. This was not the scholarly, serious and idealistic David Stockman. This was the adolescent, earthy David Stockman, the clever sixties kid who could thumb his nose at an establishment he had voluntarily joined, poke fun at himself and figure he could get away with it — which, of course he did:

Monday. My second swearing-in ceremony. The chamber was slightly reminiscent of a busy day at the zoo: women and children everywhere, and not a few peacocks strutting around in full dress. Taking the oath definitely swells the sense of self-importance. It also dulls the recollection of how you got here. To hear it in the cloak-room, it was all brains, savvy and superior ability. The truth is, it's often purely a matter of default. Thus far, my competition has consisted of a cocktail waitress on leave, a roofing sales-man who couldn't seem to move enough shin-gles, a lawyer who was trying to advertise HIS, and a man who drove around the district with seven kids inside the car, a canoe on top and an unemployment check in his pocket to finance it all. So much for personal prowess.

Tuesday . . . Now that [House Democratic Leader] Jim Wright says the people are entitled to send crooks to Congress, at least a guy can enjoy being sociable again. Last year, I didn't accept many invitations from lobbyists. With the House legislating itself into an ethical chas-tity belt last session, one couldn't be too careful. Now we are gaining some perspective. So I decided to venture out last night. Jennifer and I were treated to the works: dinner at the George-town Club; a chauffered ride to the National Theater; excellent seats for 'A Chorus Line'; more drinks afterward. This was all courtesy of a husband-and-wife lobbyist team. He repre-sents a drug company. She lobbies for the insurance industry. I'm supposed to feel slightly compromised—because I'm on the public health subcommittee—but frankly that's silly. The chauffered ride can be justified under any circumstances. Now that the honorable Secretary [of Transportation] Brock Adams is promoting Model A's, Detroit needs the business. Besides that, the limousine was actually a bus.

The great Victorian Secret must be told. Lobbyists are positively timid about bringing up business on social occasions. By the time we got through the subjects of tennis clubs, the Super Bowl and favorite scenes from 'Animal House,' the third round of drinks had already arrived. This prompted a brief discussion of the 'generic' drug issue. I am still not certain, however, whether they are good, bad, illegal or only available at the White House pharmacy. As long as there is a convicted felon sitting in the House of Representatives [Michigan Democrat Charles C. Diggs, Jr.], I'm not going to get too worried about who paid for the Duckling a L'Orange. . . .

Thursday . . . No speeches, committee meetings, floor session, visiting constituents or evening engagements . . . A rare opportunity to delve into some heavyweight material. During office hours this turns out to be a bulky EPA document entitled, 'Air Quality Criteria for Ozone and other Photochemical Oxidants.' It purports to demonstrate the public health necessity to sharply curtail future industrial growth in

Brothers romp in bed at home, 1958. From left, David, 12; Dan, 8; Gary, 7; and Steven, 9.

The Stockman homestead, built around 1910 by Stockman's great-grandfather, Albert Bartz. Large birches around house provided the name for the family farm, Birchlawn.

One-room schoolhouse in Royalton Township, Michigan, which Stockman attended from kindergarten through the third grade.

Photo of Birchlawn barn, 1961, from family album.

Twelve-year-old Dave helps
with the milking chores on
the farm.

Official high school year-
book portrait, 1964.

Always the leader: as student council president in
high school.

As quarterback of high school football team in senior year; not big or talented, but competitive.

As guard on high school basketball team; they rarely won but kept trying.

Candid shot of Stockman as recent graduate from Michigan State bound for Harvard, June 1968.

As college junior, left, Stockman gets into campus newspaper for his role in organizing Michigan State contingent for April 1967 antiwar protest in New York City. Credit: The State News.

Thirty-three male students at Michigan State sign April 12, 1967, SDS ad in Michigan State News vowing to resist draft.

Giving speech to Berrien County, Michigan, Kiwanis Club in 1973. At the time Stockman was serving as 26-year-old executive director of House Republican Conference. Credit: Benton Harbor—St. Joseph, Michigan, Herald-Palladium.

Proud grandparents William and Madge Bartz on night of Stockman's first election to Congress, November 2, 1976. Credit: Benton Harbor—St. Joseph, Michigan, Herald-Palladium.

Allen and Carol Stockman flank son on night of his victory in Republican primary for Congress, August 3, 1976. Credit: Benton Harbor—St. Joseph, Michigan, Herald-Palladium.

Stockman and House Speaker Tip O'Neill recreate new congressman's swearing-in on January 19, 1977—two weeks after the real thing—for a hometown publicity picture. Credit: Benton Harbor—St. Joseph, Michigan, Herald-Palladium.

Mr. Stockman goes to Congress, 1977. Benton Harbor—St. Joseph, Michigan, Herald-Palladium.

Relaxing with wife, Jennifer, Labor Day 1985.

Back home in Michigan in August 1984 at 20th reunion of Lakeshore High School Class of 1964, with, from left, former German teacher John Adams, friend William Cesaroni and wife, Jennifer.

At high school reunion with former classmates, from left, Donna Cayo, cousin David Bartz, Lee Hendrix, William Cesaroni and Yvonne Vidt.

Starting out as one happy economic team, February 1981, from left, chief White House economist Murray Weidenbaum, President Reagan, Treasury Secretary Donald T. Regan, Stockman. Credit: Jack Kightlinger/The White House.

Praying for strength? Stockman awaits his turn to tell House Budget Committee at October 2, 1981 hearing that more cuts are needed to balance budget. Credit: AP/Wide World.

Attention to detail: one of numerous precisely drawn charts Stockman sketched on yellow legal pads for aides to reproduce and put in briefing packets.

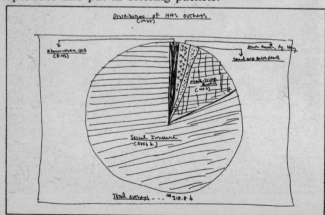

Typical harpooning by cartoonists in early 1981 turns Stockman into fearsome budget slasher. Credit: Reprinted by permission of Tribune Media Services.

Forcing a smile for surprise 35th birthday party, November 10, 1981, moments before Atlantic Monthly controversy breaks.

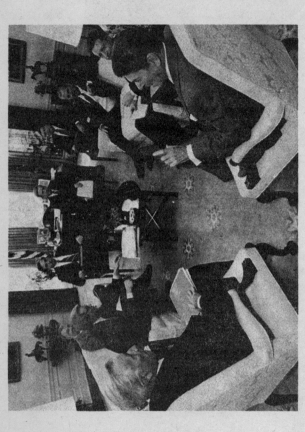

President Reagan, lower right, discusses policy issues in Oval Office with senior advisers, clockwise from left, Regan, Stockman, Edwin Meese, Richard Darman, Robert McFarlane, M.B. Oglesby, James Baker, Caspar Weinberger, March 1984. Credit: Bill Fitz-Patrick/The White House.

Briefing the President, October 1981. Credit: Michael Evans/The White House.

President Reagan's farewell gift to Stockman, July 31, 1985, framed and personally autographed. Credit: Garner, Washington Times.

Talking about taxes with Donald Regan, left, and Assistant Treasury Secretary John "Buck" Chapoton, January 1984. Credit: Jack Kightlinger/The White House.

At July 26, 1985 farewell party OMB staff present "640-dollar" toilet seat containing portrait of Stockman's favorite Cabinet Secretary, "Cap" Weinberger. Credit: Barbara Ann Clay.

order to reduce ozone—smog—to naturally occurring levels. Failure to do so may result in episodic outbreaks of cough, headache and ticklish throat among 1/100th of the U.S. population. The evening is devoted to further progress on Barbara Tuchman's *A Distant Mirror*, wherein the vulnerability of pre-industrial society to pestilence and famine is meticulously chronicled: one-third of the known population was wiped out by the Black Plague and earlier famines during the fourteenth century. Apparently risks are inescapable, but at least our pandemics are getting more benign.

Friday. Breakfast in Williamsburg with the new class of freshman members . . . Rep. Al Gore, the Tennessee Democrat, and Dave Stockman performing. It wasn't really an even match. At age thirty, Al is already a major league politician in the essential meaning of the term: witty, personable, ultrafluent, possessed of a brilliant instinct for the rhetorical jugular. With ambition, poise and charisma to match. The Great Mentioners haven't discovered him yet, but they will. I'd give him higher odds for the brass ring than his father, the former senator, ever had. Unfortunately, he inhales populist nostrums as naturally as he breathes. If there is one great service I can perform for the Republic, it may be to teach Al Gore some basic economics before it is too late. (Privately, according to Strayer, Stockman once observed, "You know, Al Gore is almost as smart as I am. He's brilliant.")

When Stockman's brain trust saw a draft of the article, they couldn't quite believe it. Fred Khedouri saw it as another case of Stockman trying to be too cute. "He always wrote things like that and we would tone them down. So he would hide his drafts from us." Don Moran stumbled across a copy of the draft and thought, "Is this some kind of a joke? Is Dave just letting off some steam?" Stockman just liked the exposure. "He figured this was a neat opportunity . . . 'They're giving me a chance to be cute and clever,'" a close friend said. Stockman's detractors would point to articles such as this—and later the one in *Atlantic Monthly*—as evidence of his hubris and being a smartass.

Still, who could argue with success? The system he kept railing against kept rewarding him.

By coincidence on the same Sunday that Stockman's "Company Town" piece appeared in Washington, the Detroit *News* carried a piece about the Michigan political outlook for 1982. Stockman, it said, "is the odds-on choice for bigger and better things. Though deemed a moderate, his stand on taxes—he was part of the GOP's national tax-cutting roadshow last fall—has earned him admirers on the right. He has a knack for getting into the news. As a former aide to John Anderson, he has congressional contacts he can call on in a U.S. Senate race. Winning in his fourth congressional district on the shores of Lake Michigan is hardly a challenge." Others in Washington were saying the same thing, and Stockman and his staff also were talking about a possible run for the Senate in 1982, when Michigan Democrat Donald Riegle's term was up. "We knew he was destined for higher grandeur," says Fred Upton.

And the rave reviews kept rolling in. The August 1979 *Time* magazine ran a cover story on achievers under fifty, and included the thirty-two-year-old congressman in its list of "50 Faces for America's Future." The article noted that Stockman "has in three years earned a reputation on Capitol Hill for effectively delivering his moderate to conservative views."

Soon after that article appeared Stockman, once again as iconoclast, found a dramatic way to drive home his free-market convictions. He decided to oppose Chrysler Corporation's request for federal loan guarantees in 1979 to hold off bankruptcy. And he didn't just oppose the loan; he led the charge against the company, even though it was based in his home state. He had railed for years against spineless members of Congress who would put parochial self-interest above even their lip service to principle. Here was a grand opportunity for him to set a high-minded example.

Indeed, for Stockman, Chrysler was tailor-made. He could argue that in a truly free market, failure is a necessary fact of life; in fact, the very threat of failure is a main incentive for business management to strive for efficiency, low cost and the kind of products consumers want. If a company flunked the test of the marketplace, it *deserved* to fail. Since Stockman was from Michigan he could also show how he could rise above parochial interests, although actually his district did not have a heavy concentration of workers or companies dependent on Chrysler, which was headquartered on the other side of the state in Detroit.

Chrysler Chairman Lee Iacocca had based his case for government help on the claim that the company's trouble had been at least partly the result of overzealous government regulation. Stockman conceded the point but argued it was not sufficient cause for a huge government bailout. In September 1979, as an alternative to the Carter Administration-backed loan guarantees, Stockman proposed legislation that would help the struggling automaker by scaling back federal fuel economy, car safety and exhaust emission regulations. That same month he wrote an article for the *Wall Street Journal* criticizing the loan as a reward for failure. This type of thinking, he warned, would lead the United States toward "the arthritic condition that has crippled Britain's economy."

On December 9, 1979, with a House vote on the $1.5 billion loan guarantees just one week away and with lobbying by Chrysler and the United Auto Workers union at its frenetic peak, Stockman wrote a lengthy article in the Washington *Post* entitled, "Let Chrysler Go Bankrupt." It began: "It is not Chrysler Corp. that needs saving. It is the nation that needs to be spared the heavy economic and political burdens the bailout portends." The article went on to describe the loan guarantees as "an appalling escalation of narrow, self-pleading politics." He then laid out a case, backed by statistical analysis, to prove that Chrysler's failure would not have devastating consequences. He argued that in time many of its dealers, suppliers and employees would be absorbed by other auto companies or related businesses. And the workers permanently "orphaned" had special unemployment benefits that kept them at nearly full pay until they could be retrained for new work.

It was a nimble exposition of how the marketplace might adjust efficiently to economic change. But it said nothing about how humans adjust emotionally to sudden changes. There was not a single recognition in the article of the fears, uncertainties and trauma that the potential collapse of the giant automaker would have on the hundreds of thousands of people who worked for Chrysler or did business with it. Undoubtedly some people would lose their businesses or homes, marriages would break up, families would be forced to move, neighborhoods near the big auto plants would collapse. There would be an enormous amount of pain and suffering as people "adjusted." Presumably Stockman considered all that the implicit price society pays for the potential rewards the system offers.

Of course, it is easy to agree in the abstract until one becomes a loser in reality. David Stockman always saw the bargain in the abstract. He never has believed that the squeaking wheels of what he perceives as economic selfishness or self-interest might sometimes also be the screams of genuine desperation. It was like Benton Harbor: He saw the macroeconomic problem but not the microhuman suffering — and not because he did not care but because the emotional factors did not fit into his quantitative formulas. He would argue that he does

245

care, but someone has to look at the bigger picture and do what's right for the larger society. He would not convince his critics. To them, he was and is all brain and no heart.

On December 18, 1979, the House approved the loan guarantee by a two-to-one margin. Of Michigan's nineteen-member delegation, all voted for the legislation except one: David Stockman. The vote infuriated other members of the delegation in both parties as well as the moderate Republicans who dominated the state, such as Governor William Milliken. Some political observers predicted that the vote killed any hopes Stockman might have had of winning a Senate seat. "There was a lot of ill will toward him because of that vote," says John Dingell. "Michigan wouldn't have him." Dingell and other Democrats in the state's congressional delegation felt Stockman had such a myopic view of the world that he failed to see any virtue in government's role as a helping hand in time of need. "Ebenezer Scrooge would look like a generous man compared to him," Dingell says.

The Detroit *Free Press* endorsed him for reelection in the fall of 1980 even though it objected to his vote on Chrysler. The newspaper praised him for attaining a national standing on conservative issues consistent with his district. But on his Chrysler stand it did hit hard at his blind spot: "David Stockman is a cerebral GOP conservative who would probably feel quite at home discoursing in a parlor full of eighteenth-century libertarians. His intelligence and ability to articulate theory have made him the favorite conservative of publications such as the *Wall Street Journal*; on occasion, though, that devotion to theory leads him astray. We thought his opposition to helping Chrysler was a clear case of elevating abstraction over reality and, indeed, of misperceiving or refusing to perceive the social and economic costs of a Chrysler failure."

Stockman, however, was very proud of the vote. He had been taught to stand up for his beliefs, and he had. Indeed, when his friend Richard Straus later asked him how Jack Kemp, another outspoken free-market conservative, had voted on a $2.3 billion federal loan package for New York City in 1975, Stockman smiled and said Kemp had voted for it. "That's the essence of David as a political-intellectual," said Straus. "There's a relish in doing it. He enjoyed going against the grain." In retrospect, supporters of the loan guarantees became convinced they were right and Stockman was wrong. After all, not only did Chrysler survive, but it became profitable and repaid its loans, with interest, in the fall of 1983 — seven years ahead of schedule.

But Stockman still thought he was right six years after his vote. "I think he's pretty convinced if there's another recession, Chrysler just might not make it," says Jack Strayer. "He still thinks he's going to be vindicated." Richard Straus adds that Stockman took particular pride that, despite his vote, Lee Iacocca would call him toward the end of his OMB tenure "and congratulate him on being the only man in the administration making any sense on economic policy."

Stockman's vote against Chrysler may not have gone over well in most of Michigan at the time, but it was generally applauded in *his* district, although he had to do some missionary work among some of local business people with ties to Chrysler. A number of Chrysler-dependent businesses had reacted very strongly against his position initially, so he toured the district to calm them down and shame them. "I thought you were for free enterprise?" he would ask, and they usually agreed. One dealer admitted that he wasn't making any money selling Chrysler cars, anyway, and pointed across the street to a profitable Toyota dealership that he owned.

Stockman also got some more notice nationally. A week after the vote the U.S. Jaycees named him one of the nation's Ten Outstanding Young Men. And despite his controversial vote he was not ruling out a possible Senate bid. Publicly he expressed ambivalence about seeking higher office because the full-time politicking required would limit the time he could devote to the issues, but it was clear from private conversations he had with friends back home at the time that he was more enamored with politics than he would admit in public. "I remember we were sitting around bullshitting about his political ambitions," says Russell Bergemann, Stockman's high school friend and football teammate. "We talked about Congress and the Senate, and the Presidency did pop up. He said the right pieces would have to fall in place for that to happen." Stockman's cousin, Ron Both, recalls a conversation during the Christmas holidays in 1979: "Dave and Steve and Linda [Stockman's sister] and I talked about a Senate race, and we thought it wasn't a good time. And we talked about him running for President in '88 or '92. We were only half-serious, but he was very agreeable to the idea. I think it's still an aspiration for him."

In 1980 Stockman turned his attention to the federal budget. In March he and Congressman Phil Gramm, the Texas Democrat (later turned Republican), teamed up to propose their own alternative to the Democratic leaderships' alleged balanced-budget plan for the upcoming fiscal year. Arguing that the leadership plan actually would produce a $26.4 billion deficit, Stockman said his budget proposal really would balance the budget for the first time since 1969 by cutting $26.4 billion out of domestic programs. His plan proved to be an early blueprint for the budget cuts he would be assembling nine months later as Ronald Reagan's budget director. CETA public service jobs and federal revenue sharing would be eliminated. Spending on food stamps and unemployment benefits would be cut. Higher income families would be made ineligible for school-lunch subsidies. A ceiling would be placed on Medicaid payments to the states. Urban mass transit subsidies, education programs and social services would be cut. A freeze on government hiring would be imposed along with cuts in agency administrative budgets for travel, equipment and publicity. Defense spending, however, would not be cut. The Democratic-controlled Congress rejected the Stockman-Gramm budget and stuck with its own "balanced" budget.

Wendell M. Belew Jr., chief counsel to the Democratic-controlled House Budget Committee from 1977 to 1986, recalls the Stockman-Gramm proposal as a comprehensive across-the-board approach to budget cutting that was rejected by the committee staff for being too simplistic. "Looking back, the only remarkable thing about it was that it was not technically astute or innovative,"says Belew. "It gave no hint of his later facility with the budget."

In spring of 1980 Stockman prepared an analysis of the Democratic budget, inserted into the *Congressional Record*, in which he labeled the so-called balanced budget "A Trojan Horse by any other name." Stockman lambasted the budget as "a fabulous political fiction—a legislative hoax worthy of Orson Welles's 1930's radio broadcast on the landing of the Martians . . . the proverbial house of cards." His analysis predicted the deficit actually would soar, possibly above $40 billion.

Events would take an ironic turn. Little more than a year later, Stockman would see his own stinging charge leveled against his own balanced budget plan, except that his deficits would soar far above $40 billion. And his penchant for the "Trojan Horse" metaphor—one of the favorites in his vocabulary— would land him in Ronald Reagan's woodshed.

Indeed, in the spring of 1980 who would have guessed that David Stockman, even with his knack of being in the right place at the right time, would ascend to the White House and the front ranks of power?

CHAPTER 7

FATE AND
A DEBATE

"Ronald Reagan may be a great politician, but David Stockman is a great actor."

Such was the reaction of Martin Anderson, Ronald Reagan's chief advisor on domestic issues, after watching Stockman impersonate his former boss, Congressman John Anderson, in a mock debate with Reagan during the fall of 1980. Stockman had been called in to help prepare Reagan, the GOP nominee, for a presidential debate with the independent challenger. Martin Anderson's review was not unique. Everyone who witnessed the mock debate came away in amazement. The young congressman from Michigan had been sensational in his Andersonian role. With a flurry of rhetorical jabs and accusatory uppercuts, he had the Gipper on the ropes. Reagan's debate with the real John Anderson that September was child's play by comparison.

David Stockman an actor? His only prior experience was a bit part in high school when he played a G-man in "You Can't Take It With You." For that matter, he had never even been in a formal debate

251

before coming up against Reagan. But once again Stockman seized the day. He prepared himself for the performance of his life, and then he gave it. It paid off less than three months later when he got a telephone call from Reagan offering an even better role: director of Office of Management and Budget.

That Stockman wound up at OMB to implement the Reagan Revolution is an astonishing tale of second choices, lucky coincidences, good connections and seized opportunities. Reagan was not Stockman's original choice for president, and Stockman was not Reagan's first choice for budget director. But destiny seemed determined to bring this strange duo together.

Stockman's path to Ronald Reagan's side started at the feet of Jack Kemp in late 1977. Kemp, his mentor at the time, introduced him to supply-side economics. Supply-side was a new name for an old school of classical free-market economics dating back to Adam Smith's writings in the late eighteenth century. Let men pursue their economic self-interest without hindrance, Smith said, and both prosperity and social harmony will follow as if society were guided by "an invisible hand." Of course, things never worked out that neatly, but mainstream economic thought in the industrialized societies in the nineteeth and early twentieth centuries was still based on the premise that free enterprise with minimum government interference was the most efficient route to progress; personal industriousness would increase the supply of goods and services, and the supply would create its own demand, although an occasional brief recession might be necessary to correct any imbalances between supply and demand. The Great Depression of the 1930s destroyed that notion. It was replaced by British economist John Maynard Keynes's remedy: increase government spending to raise demand until demand was in balance with supply again. In the post-World War II period this became known as Keynesian economics, and the stimulus took the form of tax cuts as well as federal spending. The formula seemed to work well for a few postwar decades. But by the 1970s it was clear this approach had its problems too. Inflation and economic stagnation had set in, despite ever higher levels of federal spending and taxation. Free-market critics of these policies complained that the government, under both Democrats and Republicans, had put too much emphasis on increasing demand and in the process suppressed supply through oppressive tax rates that discouraged the investment, saving and risk-taking required to expand production. Out of this came what would be called the supply-side school in the mid-1970s. Its proponents argued that government should return to the old days of encouraging saving, investment, entrepreneurship—the basic ingredients for economic growth. The chief way government could turn things around, the supply-siders argued, was through broad-based cuts in individual, corporate and capital gains tax rates to stimulate investment.

This wasn't just theory; there was some empirical evidence to back it up. Tax cuts designed by Treasury Secretary Andrew W. Mellon in the 1920s, when laissez-faire economics flourished, and the Kennedy-Johnson tax cuts of the early 1960s both stimulated economic growth without inflation. Congress also enacted a small income tax cut in 1978 to offset higher tax burdens caused by inflation and increased Social Security taxes. But it included a reduction in the capital gains tax, which had been pushed by the supply-siders. So far, this all seemed like mainstream economics. What transformed supply-side from a conventional tool for economic growth into a fringe cult was an exaggerated claim by some of its proponents that seemed too good to be true—that a deep across-the-board tax cut would pay for itself by triggering an economic boom; the surge in economic growth would then send revenues pouring into the Treasury and balance the budget. The proof was provided by the "Laffer Curve," named after Arthur B. Laffer, an economics professor at the University of Southern California. Laffer and his curve—which, legend holds, was first drawn on a cocktail napkin— were popularized in the mid-1970s by Jude Wanniski, the *Wall Street Journal* editorial writer who became chief publicist for the supply-side movement. Wanniski's articles appeared in the *Journal* and in magazines, including the same 1975 issue of *The Public Interest* that had carried Stockman's attack on the social pork barrel. Neither man knew it at the time, but many of the policies advanced by each of them in their back-to-back articles would be thrown together in 1980 to form the foundation for the so-called Reagan Revolution.

The Laffer Curve was supposed to answer Democratic critics' charges that a massive tax cut would produce a record deficit and soaring inflation. But the Democrats shrugged off Laffer's geometric hyperbola as economic hyperbole. Even some Republican supporters of supply-side tax cuts complained that the basic supply-side argument—that tax cuts stimulate economic growth—was discredited by those who oversold the advantages. "Academicians have to sell parts out of context and exaggerate them as a way of calling attention to their theories," says Senator Phil Gramm, the conservative Texas Republican, himself a former academician. "Any conservative knows there's nothing new under the sun."

Jack Kemp became the leading supply-side disciple in Congress and together with Senator William V. Roth, Jr., a Republican from Delaware, introduced a series of tax cuts, including one in 1978 to slash personal tax rates by one-third over three years. Kemp, perhaps the most dynamic Republican in the House, believed that the GOP had been the minority party for decades because of its preoccupation with balanced budgets and gloomy talk about "austerity, pain and sacrifice." It was time for a positive message. "We had to talk growth and jobs and getting America moving again," he says. "I bought the whole Kennedy notion of coming out of the recession of the sixties with tax cuts. He didn't talk about spending cuts, he talked about growth." Kemp was never big on domestic spending cuts the way Stockman was "because I just didn't think you could ever get there without getting the economy healthy enough so people could accept a cut in spending. It's very difficult, if you're black and unemployed in Cincinnati, Ohio, to think about an administration cutting the budget. The first emphasis should come on expanding the size of the pie to remove the fear that

Cousin Willie was going to lose his job in a slow-down." Unlike Stockman, who came from a rural area, Kemp represented Buffalo, N.Y., a district that had grown accustomed to social benefits from government. Political reality made him look for an alternative to budget cuts.

Kemp's interest in a new, or at least repackaged, idea appealed to Stockman, and Stockman's brains appealed to Kemp. The New York Republican, looking for recruits to the cause, took his young friend under his wing and introduced him to his supply-side circle of friends as "the smartest guy in Congress." A few times a year during 1977 and 1978, Wanniski and Laffer would rent adjoining suites at a downtown residential hotel and throw football parties, complete with beer and hot dogs, for "the cabal"—some twenty-five people who worked for Kemp and Roth. Wanniski met Stockman in December 1977 when Kemp brought his protégé to one of these parties. Wanniski had just finished writing a book in praise of supply-side tax cuts, *The Way the World Works*, which was published in 1978. Wanniski gave the manuscript to Stockman to read, and the congressman, according to the author, was impressed. "We all sat on the floor and talked about how to take over the world," recalled Wanniski, who left the *Wall Street Journal* in 1978 to start up an economic consulting firm. "Stockman bought the tax cuts. He joined the movement and participated with us thereafter."

Tax cuts, which the average person could understand, were only part of the supply-side gospel. The other part, which was obscured by the publicity about tax cuts, was a more arcane anti-inflation "monetary

256

policy." This entailed new rules for stabilizing the value of money in the economy, which was a responsibility of the nation's central bank, the Federal Reserve Board. The supply-siders wanted a return to a gold standard that would fix the worth of a dollar again and keep it from losing value to inflation. Most people blamed inflation on large budget deficits, but the supply-siders blamed it on the Nixon administration's decision in 1971 to end the fixed rate of gold at $35 an ounce and let it float. They disagreed with the "monetarist" school of thought, which blamed inflation on Federal Reserve policies that let the supply of money in the economy grow too fast relative to the increase in the supply of goods and services. This was pretty abstruse stuff, even for a smart guy like Stockman, who told Wanniski during one discussion, "One of these days, I'll have to get a briefing on monetary policy." He might have waited too long. More than any other factor, it was monetary policy that brought the Reagan Administration's balanced budget plans crashing down on Stockman's head in 1981.

In 1978, however, Stockman was fully on board the supply-side team, Laffer Curve and all. He later admitted as much, and friends recall him trying to explain to them how the Laffer Curve worked. Stockman had fallen in with another group of intellectual mentors bound by a view of how the world worked. Just as he had picked up the banner for his antiwar friends in East Lansing and his neoconservative friends in Cambridge, he now waved the flag for his supply-side friends in Washington. He fought in 1978 for passage of the cut in the capital gains tax rate, gave speeches on the House floor praising the Kemp-

Roth tax bill, calling it "the only new fiscal policy idea that has been proposed in decades," and was a member of the Republican team that traveled the country that year to promote tax cuts. Two years later he amazed Republican staff members of the Senate Finance Committee by drafting a statement to accompany a new Republican tax cut proposal. "This is what the *staff* is supposed to do. It was incredible to see a member of Congress write it and do such a good job," recalls one committee aide.

The 1978 tax cut bill went nowhere in the Democratic-controlled Congress, but it would be embraced by a Republican candidate for President named Ronald Reagan. Reagan bought Kemp's call for a new Republican economic pitch based on sunshine and optimism instead of gloom and doom. Kemp's tax cut and Laffer's Curve provided the painless way to economic growth and prosperity. Reagan wanted to campaign for lower inflation and lower taxes, but conventional economic theory argued that the former would require a recession and the latter would mean a higher budget deficit. That was unacceptable to Reagan, who believed that Carter's pessimistic attitude and calls for self-sacrifice were his political downfall. So the supply-siders were very appealing. Reagan may not have bought the theory, but he loved the sunny message, which was underscored in a campaign memorandum on economic policy drafted in August 1979 by domestic adviser Martin Anderson. The nine-page memorandum, which proved to be the skeleton of Reagan's 1981 economic program, argued for a plan that would promise simultaneously to stimulate economic growth, increase employment, reduce inflation, cut taxes and balance the budget—all within a year and without pain. "It is thus possible to reduce inflation and stimulate economic growth without having an economic bellyache, recession or depression," Anderson wrote. It would prove to be pure fantasy.

In the fall of 1979, Kemp and the other supply-siders decided to throw in with Reagan. Except for Stockman. He decided to go with John Connally, the former Texas governor and Treasury Secretary in the Nixon Administration. That struck the supply-siders as particularly strange, since Connally represented all the economic policies that Stockman opposed. As Treasury Secretary, Connally had presided over wage-and-price controls and a loan guarantee for Lockheed Aircraft Corporation. Now he was running for President as the candidate of big business—one of the loudest squeaking wheels of self-interest that Stockman was always assailing. Kemp would argue with Stockman about his support for Connally. Kemp says his recollection of Stockman's position at the time was that "he didn't think Reagan would get elected. When he thought about his vision of who should be President, in terms of personal charisma and leadership, he probably saw Connally—the appearance, the silver tongue, the forceful manner—and didn't think in terms of policy. He thought Reagan would never get elected." Kemp also recalls that when he and Stockman had breakfast with Connally and raised the candidate's earlier economic views, Connally was still defending them.

Wanniski remembers Stockman giving a different reason for supporting Connally: "He said Ronald Reagan wouldn't have the guts to do the bad things needed to cut the budget. He thought Connally was going to win and the country needed someone like John Connally to do the tough things, like cutting back environmental regulations. Dave saw him as the man on horseback." When Wanniski pressed Stockman about Connally's economic views, the young congressman said the supply-siders would be able to turn him around once he was in office. "Don't worry, don't worry," he would tell Wanniski, who replied, "Okay, Dave, the supply-siders will spread their bets around."

One former high-ranking White House official who became a Stockman antagonist speculated that Connally appealed to Stockman because "he was the candidate that had a clear answer for every problem. When you're an absolutist guy who's big on certainty like David Stockman is, Connally is your man."

Stockman, however, later said that he really backed Connally because he thought Connally could defeat Carter, and Reagan could not. He also said that he was repulsed by Reagan's stand on social issues, such as abortion and school prayer. He still had the same antipathy toward Reagan's embrace of the New Right that he had in 1976. "Reagan's thrust on the social issues was that of a rightwinger," he has said. Steve Stockman says his brother told him he agreed with Reagan on economic issues, but had added, "He's too ideological. He can't win an election. You're talking about Goldwater all over again." Stockman's mother, Carol, says her eldest son "just thought John Connally was, I guess, more moderate." Stockman's assistant, David Gerson, tried unsuccessfully to talk him out of an early endorsement, but Stockman told Gerson he thought Connally was more likely to win. Robert Walker, Stockman's former colleague from their days working for Anderson, says he was surprised to see Stockman support Connally. "On ideology, they were poles apart," says Walker, who became chief domestic adviser during Anderson's 1980 run for the presidency. "But Connally was a very hot property at the time Stockman went for him. The momentum was with Connally." A close friend adds: "I think at this point David's probably a little embarrassed about supporting Connally. But at the time, he couldn't imagine that Reagan would be a decent leader. He just was not terribly enthusiastic about Reagan then. He's still not."

Like so many other people before and since, Stockman had underestimated Ronald Reagan's political prowess. As he would do many times later, Stockman also overestimated his own political prowess. On March 9, 1980, John Connally pulled out of the presidential race. After spending $12 million and months of travel on his campaign, he had but one delegate to show for all his money and time.

Wanniski says he recalled Stockman bailing out of the Connally campaign before it formally ended and jumping to George Bush's campaign. "After Bush won the Iowa caucuses, Stockman became a Bush supporter and met with the Bush people," he says. "It was only after Reagan seemed to have it locked up that Stockman went for him." Actually, Stockman never went for Reagan completely. Although he formally endorsed Reagan in mid-April of 1980, he privately voted for Bush the following month in the Michigan primary because he felt closer to Bush ideologically. Bush, who had scored Reagan's economic program as "voodoo economics," upset Reagan in the state, but pulled out of the race within a week when it was clear that Reagan had the nomination locked up.

At this point Stockman was only at the edge of the Reagan campaign. But through his ties to Kemp and the supply-siders, he stayed in the thick of Republican Party action, which had now focused on the platform Reagan would run on in the fall. Party policy had split into two factions. There were the old-fashioned, balance-the-budget fiscal conservatives who talked about spending cuts and anti-inflation austerity; and there were the new-generation supply-siders who talked about tax cuts and economic prosperity. Both factions had engaged in an intense fight to determine where economic policy should head under a Reagan administration. Reagan decided to keep one foot in each camp. It was a straddle he would maintain throughout his presidency, producing a lasting and bitter conflict within his administration. Part of Reagan was the traditional crusader against wasteful government spending and budget deficits, a view reinforced by his old-guard advisers from California—men like George Shultz, the former budget director, Labor Secretary and Treasury Secretary, and Caspar Weinberger, also a former budget director and former Secretary of Health, Education and Welfare. But Reagan also was personally attracted to the arguments of the supply-siders, who put spending cuts and balanced budgets far behind tax cuts on their list of economic priorities. Reagan refused to choose between the two schools. He wanted both, and let his advisers struggle with a way to reconcile them, a task that ultimately proved impossible.

During the summer of 1980 the supply-siders blitzed the Republican national convention in Detroit to make their case, and Stockman was one of them. NBC television correspondent Chris Wallace, who met Stockman in 1978 while covering Congress and later became a good friend, recalls spending two hours in a revolving cocktail lounge at Detroit's Renaissance Center while Kemp and Stockman tried to sell him and his producer on supply-side economics. "I had the sense he was very much on board at the time," Wallace says of Stockman. At the convention Stockman got involved in writing the Republican Party platform, but ironically, not the part about economics; he was the chief author of the energy plank.

As part of their strategy for influencing party policy in a Reagan administration, the supply-side group had put together a list of candidates for key Cabinet jobs. The choices were based on a survey of the group that Wanniski had made before the convention. For Treasury Secretary, the consensus choice was supply-side advocate Lewis E. Lehrman, the millionaire founder of the Rite Aid drugstore chain who would later run unsuccessfully for governor of New York. For budget director, the consensus candidate was William M. Agee, chairman of Bendix

Corporation in Detroit. Wanniski wrote an article publicizing the choices, but Agee was not interested. "I had a party at my house for Jack Kemp during the convention," Agee said in an interview published March 15, 1981, in the New York *Times* magazine. "Just as Dave was about to leave he said, 'If the governor is elected, there's an appointment for you,' referring to OMB. I said, 'No, I'm a private enterprise man. But that's the job for you.' "

The job might have been right for Stockman, but he would not have landed it had it not been for two fortuitous coincidences. One was that Bush had been selected as Reagan's running mate, and Bush's political operators were now major players in Reagan's campaign. The other was that Reagan had agreed to a nationally televised debate on Sept. 21 with Stockman's former boss and mentor, John Anderson, who had abandoned his losing quest for the GOP nomination and launched an independent candidacy for president. The Bush people came up with the idea of preparing Reagan by holding mock debates.

The supply-siders were growing worried as the debate approached. Reagan had already agreed to push the Kemp-Roth individual tax cut and a business tax cut during the campaign, but the "cabal" feared their fresh message would get drowned out by Republican orthodoxy. "The Californians were running Reagan as the great budget-cutter," says Wanniski. "We were getting nervous about the debate with Anderson because we feared they wouldn't brief him the right way. We wanted to prop him up on the issue of growth through tax cuts instead of the old austerity stuff. So, I suggested that Kemp call the Bush people and remind them that Stockman once worked for John Anderson. The idea was to get a supply-sider into the room to help brief Reagan. We didn't know there was going to be a mock debate."

Coincidentally, as Kemp was recommending Stockman to the Reaganites, David Gergen, a Bush campaign aide who was now helping prepare Reagan for the Anderson debate, was looking for someone to be Anderson's stand-in for a practice session. Gergen had worked on President Gerald Ford's election campaign in 1976, and mock debates were used to prepare Ford for his encounter with Jimmy Carter. For the Anderson debate, Gergen thought of Stockman. Gergen knew Stockman's reputation as a bright young mover in the House and had been impressed with the congressman's articles on energy policy that he had read in the Washington *Post*. Figuring Stockman would make a worthy opponent, Gergen recommended him to James A. Baker III, who had managed Bush's campaign and was now a senior Reagan political adviser. Baker agreed that Stockman would be an ideal Anderson stand-in for practice debates. Baker figured a dress rehearsal would surely help an old actor like Reagan. It also would help the Bush people ingratiate themselves with the Reaganites, who had lingering suspicions about the loyalty of a crew that had been political adversaries only four month earlier. So Baker called Stockman, who readily agreed to help. "I remember the Bush people boasted that they had the guy who had worked for John Anderson and that he agreed to come and debate Reagan," recalls Reagan domestic issues adviser Martin Anderson.

Stockman now set out for the Wexford, Virginia, estate where Reagan was living temporarily during the general election campaign. As a joke his personal assistant, Diane Moore, and his legislative assistant, Don Moran, bought a bottle of Chablis and a wheel of Brie, put it in a brown paper bag and planted it in Stockman's car. Stockman did not have to be reminded that Anderson was the darling of the cheese-and-wine set; he didn't overlook anything in preparing for his first face-to-face encounter with the man he was now sure would soon be President of the United States.

A garage on the estate had been set up to look exactly like the studio that would be used for the actual debate in Baltimore. The plan was to have a series of debates. Each candidate would stand behind a podium and campaign advisors would play reporters asking the questions. For the first debate Reagan was dressed informally in a bright red sweater. He would see a lot more red by the end of the day.

Stockman was brilliant that first afternoon. Too brilliant. "Stockman was terrific. He laid Reagan out," recalls one of the participants. "I had my head in my hands. I said, 'Oh my God. There goes the campaign.' Stockman was incredible. He had all the Anderson mannerisms down. He knew the arguments cold. He had a lot of critical things to say about Reagan. He quoted Reagan back at himself, which raised all sorts of problems. It was scary."

Anderson had tried to undermine the credibility of Reagan's economic program by charging that the only way he could cut taxes, raise defense spending and balance the budget at the same time was with "mirrors." It was a variant of George Bush's earlier "voodoo economics" crack, and it struck at the Achilles' heel of the Reagan program. During the practice debate Stockman came at Reagan on the "mirror" argument like a Mack truck. "These arguments drawn on a napkin are preposterous," one of the eyewitnesses recalls him telling a stunned Reagan. "How could anyone possibly believe in something so crazy and unorthodox? It doesn't add up. The math is wrong. The revenue feedback won't be there. If you raise the defense budget and slash taxes, you're going to have deficits that'll curl your hair."

"It was a hell of a performance," says another participant. For Stockman, however, it was not all an act. Within the past few weeks he had examined the Laffer Curve more closely and decided it was flawed. Tax cuts would *not* pay for themselves in the short term, particularly if inflation were lowered. If Reagan was intent on going ahead with his tax cuts and defense budget increases, the only way to keep the deficit from soaring would be to go the old austerity route — deep domestic-program cuts. Stockman did not share those concerns with his supply-side friends or the Reaganites at the time, but the arguments that Stockman-as-Anderson had made in the garage at Wexford turned out to be prophetic. He would repeat them in the privacy of the White House during the spring and summer of 1981, and he would share them with the world in late 1981, through the *Atlantic Monthly*.

Stockman came on so strong in the first debate that Reagan got visibly upset and angry. "Why are you

267

doing this," he blurted out at one point, according to a participant. In fact, it was so bad that Reagan and his wife considered scrapping the remaining rehearsals. Nancy Reagan felt her husband would do better with a more relaxed form of preparation. But Baker argued to Michael Deaver, Reagan's closest personal aide, that it was important for Reagan to go ahead with the debates, to try to improve his performance. Deaver and the Reagans finally agreed.

"So we had another round the next day, and Reagan caught him this time. He was as good as Stockman," says one of the observers. "And the third day, the last practice round, Reagan took him." Other eyewitnesses say Reagan had become relaxed by the second debate and enjoyed the last two rounds. When it came to the actual debate with Anderson, Reagan was more than ready and held his own. "The real John Anderson proved to be a pale David Stockman," says Martin Anderson. "Everyone was very pleased with Stockman." Adds Gergen: "Reagan never faced anything as difficult or as challenging as that first debate. And it was from that that the relationship between Reagan and Stockman really blossomed. Stockman certainly had earned his keep before he got to the White House."

Reagan came away from the practice debate greatly impressed with this brilliant young congressman who was less than half his age. Stockman came away with a strong impression of Reagan, too, but it was not a favorable one. "After that first debate, when he got to know him, David was appalled at how poorly Reagan did. Just appalled," declares one close friend. "But he still wanted to believe in him."

John Anderson, for his part, felt he had been betrayed by a former aide who had exploited their personal relationship for political gain, and what had once been a close friendship ended in animosity. "In 1980 David refused to talk to me," said Keke Anderson.

In the supply-side camp, meanwhile, the "cabal" immediately sensed Stockman's reservations about their proposals, even though he had said nothing. "I thought he was going to push our views for the Anderson debate; instead he pushed the social pork barrel," Wanniski says. "I felt queasy."

Wanniski would feel even queasier a month later when the Reagan camp asked Stockman to help prepare the candidate for an October 28 debate with Carter. "This time I didn't think it would be such a great idea for Stockman to be there," Wanniski says, but the Reagan people assumed Stockman would be the perfect Carter surrogate. Having never worked for Carter, Stockman found the assignment more challenging, but he gave it his best shot. His aides remember that on the morning of one practice round he was up by 6:00 A.M., scrambling to organize all the little index cards he had written for each issue. The consensus opinion of his performance this time was that he was good, but not as good as he had been impersonating his former mentor. "Frankly, he was not as effective playing Carter as he was playing Anderson," says David Gergen. But the Reagan camp did not see the debate preparation as being so crucial this time. "We had been through all the paces before, so in terms of the intellectual push, this was not as arduous a routine," Gergen adds. Stockman, meanwhile, had become more favorably impressed with Reagan this time. He confided to friends that he thought Reagan had performed much better during the Carter practice rounds. "David was really kind of pulling for him," says Jennifer Stockman.

By now Stockman had good reason to pull for Reagan. He had decided he wanted to be budget director in a Reagan Administration, a post he had described as potentially the most powerful job next to the presidency itself. "Surrogate president," is how he had described it to friends. Once again good fortune and Stockman's ability to seize an opportunity would team up to drop him in the right place at the right time.

After Reagan's landslide victory, early speculation about his Cabinet choices figured Stockman as a possible Secretary of Energy because of his expertise on energy policy. But that was not the job for him; in fact, he thought the department should be abolished. Stockman had just won his own reelection by a landslide and would rather have stayed in Congress than take the Energy post. He wanted the budget job. If Reagan were a true conservative, Stockman felt he would have a once-in-a-lifetime opportunity to kick over the social pork barrel.

The supply-siders cooled on Bendix Chairman William Agee in October, when he got embroiled in a mini-scandal that put him out of the running. Rumor had it that he was having a romantic relationship with a twenty-nine-year-old assistant, Mary Cunningham, whom he had promoted rapidly to the post of vice-president. She resigned that fall, and later married Agee. With Agee out, Wanniski suggested that the supply-siders push Richard Fox, a top Reagan campaign official in Pennsylvania, for OMB. When Wanniski told Stockman that Fox was interested, Stockman replied, "I'd be interested myself." Wanniski was surprised, "You would?" he said, never suspecting before that Stockman was interested in giving up his seat in Congress. Wanniski and the other members of his group agreed to back him, in spite of their reservations about his devotion to the supply-side doctrine. "I figured they'd be happy to get Stockman," says Wanniski. "He was a bachelor, he'd work hard and he knew the issues, and we would have one of our own in the administration." Or at least Wanniski thought he was essentially one of their own. Kemp and company then began spreading out to push Stockman for OMB and Lewis Lehrman for Treasury with their various Republican contacts.

To call attention to themselves and their policies, Stockman wrote—with some input from Lehrman and Kemp—a twenty-three-page memorandum outlining the supply-side proposals for a new Reagan Administration. Stockman had always won attention in the past with his writing, and felt it might work again. The memo, which was circulated among Reagan's top advisers, had Stockman's trademark: a flair for the dramatic. Entitled "Avoiding a GOP Economic Dunkirk," it outlined a package of tax cuts and budget cuts and argued that the program could succeed only if Reagan declared a "national economic emergency" right after his inauguration; this would create the crisis atmosphere needed to rush the program through Congress, turn economic conditions around and avoid a lasting defeat for the Republican

Party. Reagan rejected the idea of declaring a national emergency, but he embraced many of the memo's specific proposals, and he tapped the chief author to implement them.

As it turned out, Stockman had no serious challenger for the job. "This isn't to take anything away from Dave, but I think there were several people who probably were ahead in the race or in the running for it who didn't really want it," Jack Kemp says. "Of the three or four people who were prominently mentioned, I don't think any wanted it. Dave did, and I think he deserved it."

His only apparent rivals were two old hands: Weinberger, who had the job under Nixon; and Alan Greenspan, chairman of the Council of Economic Advisers under President Ford and a top economic adviser to the Reagan campaign. Either could have had the job for the asking, many Reagan hands said, and David Stockman would have gone down a more obscure road. But neither of them wanted the job. "Cap" had his eye on the State Department or Defense Department post—as the world knows, he got the latter—and Greenspan was looking at the Treasury Department, which he didn't get.

Ironically Weinberger, the former Stockman idol who would later become Stockman's chief nemesis, played the decisive role in bringing the young congressman in as Reagan's budget director. During the transition period between the November 4 election and the January 20 inauguration, the president-elect had asked Weinberger, because of his prior budgetary expertise, to oversee a preliminary task force for putting together lists of potential budget cuts that could be pushed by the new administration. It was not a task Weinberger relished. "The President also indicated that he was interested in having David's expertise in the government," Weinberger recalls. "And I had talked with Dave in connection with some of these lists and thought he would do very well at OMB. To be perfectly frank about it, there were a lot of rumors that I might do that job again, which I did not want to do, having done it once. So I was very interested in finding acceptable substitutes, and so I recommended him [Stockman] in strong terms." When Weinberger had compiled his list of budget cuts, he presented them to Reagan. "I said, 'Here are the ways that you can make these cuts you asked me about, Mr. President, and I'm going to give them to whomever you designate and Dave Stockman seems the logical one.' And he said, 'That's fine.'"

Everyone in Reagan's inner circle was high on Stockman. Within weeks of the election he had become the consensus choice for budget director, indeed the only choice. "He had the optimal set of credentials," says Martin Anderson. "He knew the process and as far as we knew at the time he was in line with Ronald Reagan on the whole range of economic issues." Senator Paul Laxalt of Nevada, Reagan's campaign chairman and political confidant, recalls that Stockman had a clear shot at the OMB job. "I don't believe it was competitive."

Stockman had first come to Laxalt's attention when the senator read his article in the Washington *Post* against the Chrysler loan guarantees. "It was a gutsy position," Laxalt said. "It showed he was a courageous, principled and very intellectual man."

Stockman's help in the debate preparations had reinforced Laxalt's belief that this was a man Ronald Reagan could use. Two other close Reagan aides who would hold top jobs in the White House, Michael Deaver and Edwin Meese III, had also found Stockman very impressive during the debate rehearsals and supported him for the budget job. James A. Baker, who would join Deaver and Meese as part of the ruling triumvirate in the White House, recalled that Reagan had not wanted to fill his Cabinet with sitting Congressmen because he would need all the Republican help he could get to push his programs through Congress. But he made an exception in Stockman's case.

By Thanksgiving of 1980 Stockman knew well enough where he was headed to discuss it with his family. Steve Stockman remembers their father saying that if he took a Cabinet job he would lose political visibility in Michigan. "Dave agreed that it would probably hurt his chances of ever getting in the Senate," says Steve. "But at the same time he'd worked a long time trying to promote efficient government policies and felt that at OMB he'd probably have his best crack at it. And I reminded him about our former discussions about Aaron Wildavsky's book on the budget. And he said, yes, he could see OMB as a central point of bringing all of the elements of the federal government together, of rationalizing them and having one control point. And if there's any place to go, it's OMB."

On the night of Dec. 4, 1980, exactly one month after Reagan's election and ten years after Stockman and his brother had first fantasized about Dave being budget director, the telephone rang in his congressional office. It was 9:30 P.M. and Fred Upton picked up the phone.

"Dave Stockman's office."

"Is Dave there?"

The voice sounded familiar to Upton, but he couldn't quite place it. "No, sir, he's not."

"Well, gosh, I'd really like to talk to him."

"Well, I think he'd like to talk to you, sir." By now Upton realized who was on the phone.

"This is Ronnie Reagan calling from California."

"I know, I recognized your voice, Governor."

Upton, still a little stunned, congratulated Reagan on his election, and after another minute of chitchat said, "Dave's at dinner, but I can track him down for you."

"Well, I didn't want to disturb him."

"Oh, no. No problem at all."

"Well, I'm going out to dinner. So if you get him in the next ten minutes, great. If not, we can talk tomorrow."

"I'll track him down."

Reagan left his telephone number, and Upton ransacked the trash can looking for Stockman's daily schedule. He quickly found it and read that Stockman was having dinner at the home of Richard and Ann Fairbanks, whom Stockman had met through Kemp. Richard Fairbanks was working on the Reagan transition team and would later become an ambassador-at-large at the State Department. First Upton called to tell Fred Khedouri; both had promised to call the other as soon as any word came about an administration job. Then Upton called the Fairbanks and got Stockman on the phone.

"What are you disturbing me for?" Stockman asked rather testily.

"You just had a very important call from California."

"Who?"

"Who do you think?"

"Come on, I'm at dinner. Don't play games."

"Reagan. And he wants you to call him."

"Oh. OH. Hold on, just a minute, let me get a piece of paper."

Stockman made Upton repeat the telephone number three times to make sure he had written it down correctly. And Upton had made Stockman promise to call right back with the news. Three minutes later, the phone rang in the congressional office. It was Stockman. And he sounded very excited.

"Well, what did he say?" Upton asked.

"Ronald Reagan said, 'You were the only one who bested me in those debates. I was two and one. I beat Anderson. I beat Carter but I lost to you. So I'm going to offer you the toughest job in Washington—OMB.' "

"And what did you say?"

"I'll take it!"

CHAPTER 8

THE GIPPER AND
BOY WONDER

They were the oddest couple. The oldest President in American history and the youngest Cabinet-level appointee in 166 years. Yet they made an incredible team. Ronald Reagan provided the heart, David Stockman provided the brain, and between the two of them they launched the Reagan Revolution, brief as it turned out to be. More than any other person in the Administration, Stockman was responsible for turning Reagan's economic program into reality. And when he saw what he had wrought, Stockman worked harder than any other person in the Administration to try to redo it over the next four years. Ultimately he failed, and he left in abject frustration. That he stayed so long attests to his belief that hard work, reason, and "the truth" as he saw it would prevail over irrationality, inertia, incompetence and the self-interest institutionalized by the political system. But his perseverance also underscored a fundamental misunderstanding of Reagan and what he stood for. Not surprising, since in personality, cultural background, world outlook, and habits Ronald Reagan and David Stockman were as dissimilar as two men could be. As political figures, one personified the fading generation of leaders shaped in the turbulence of global depression and world war; the other embodied the emerging generation of high-expectation baby-boom leaders spawned in an era of peace and growing prosperity. Still, for wholly different reasons, Reagan and Stockman shared a passionate belief that the federal government had grown too big for its britches. It was on that common ground that they forged a dynamic partnership to cut the government back down to size. In the process they discovered they had far different visions of government and the exercise of power than either had imagined. The explosive conflicts that followed were inevitable.

Like Stockman, Reagan grew up in the Midwest, but in the small town of Dixon, Illinois, not on a farm. And while Stockman was reared in a Republican household with no use for the federal government, Reagan was raised in a Democratic home that was aided by the government. Reagan's father, Jack, was an alcoholic who held a variety of jobs as a salesman. On Christmas Eve in 1931, while Reagan was home from college, his father was fired from his latest job, a traumatic event that destroyed Jack's hopes of being part owner of a shoe store. Out of work, Jack became active in local Democratic Party politics and worked on the Dixon campaign for Franklin D. Roosevelt. After Roosevelt was elected in

1932, Jack got a job running the Dixon welfare office, which helped all the other victims of the Depression. His father's experience left a lasting impression on Ronald Reagan. Washington *Post* White House correspondent Lou Cannon, in his 1982 biography, *Reagan*, wrote, "When I asked Reagan during the 1980 campaign to name the single most important influence on his life, he replied without hesitation, 'the Depression.' "

The Depression years, however, were good to the future President. He went to Eureka College, where he excelled at athletics, drama, dating and having a good time. He was a leader briefly in a student strike over plans to drop some classes, but that was his only fling with campus activism. He was neither the hard-working scholar nor the dedicated protestor that Stockman was during his collegiate years. After Reagan graduated in 1932, although the Depression was at its depth, he managed to get himself a job as an announcer at a radio station in Iowa. From there it was up, up, up to fame, fortune and political power. Remarkably, he did it all with seeming ease, luck and a fair amount of fun along the way. Hard labor, brainpower and stoicism—the ingredients of Stockman's success—were not part of the Reagan formula; his natural gifts, including a handsome face, pleasing smile, golden voice and uncanny political instincts, carried him to the top. He had his share of disappointments and setbacks, including a failing movie career after World War II, a divorce, a fading television career and a losing quest for the presidency. But just when he was about to lose it all, good fortune came along to propel him on to greater triumphs. No wonder Ronald Reagan was such an optimist.

During World War II Reagan's poor eyesight kept him out of combat; instead he made military training films in Hollywood and would later speak proudly about his part in the war effort. After the war, when the Stockman generation was starting a baby boom, Reagan was undergoing his political transformation from New Deal Democrat to conservative Republican, thanks to several personal experiences that dramatically changed his political outlook. His movie career was finally making him rich, but the federal government was taking much of his money away with income tax rates that exceeded 90 percent. Then his movie career started to falter as movie companies were forced to sell off the theater chains they owned, a move prompted by government anti-trust actions. Reagan became president of the Screen Actors Guild at a time when the union became embroiled in a controversy over infiltration by Communists.

It was not surprising, then, that Reagan became a fervent opponent of high tax rates, government intrusion in the economy, and communism—cast-iron views he would hold onto for the next four decades. Unlike Stockman, who changed political ideologies with the time and place, Reagan made one mid-life change from liberal to right-wing. Period.

In the fall of 1967, while Stockman the radical was organizing campus protests against the war in Vietnam, Ronald Reagan, governor of California, was condemning those campus radicals as traitors. "I don't see how the American people can continue to buy their sons being asked to fight and die when the same government is defending the right of the dissenter to take his dissent actually in aiding the enemy that is trying to kill their sons," Reagan fulminated at a Des Moines, Iowa, news conference on Oct. 25, 1967. By 1974, when Stockman the neoconservative was assailing the explosive growth of government spending, Reagan was completing eight years as governor, during which time he had presided over the largest tax increase to date in California's history and a doubling of state spending to $10 billion. During the 1980 campaign, while Stockman was targeting specific federal programs for elimination on the ideological grounds that they were improper government functions, Reagan was condemning only in fuzzy terms all the "waste, extravagance, abuse and outright fraud in federal agencies and programs." Politically, they were never in step.

When Reagan tapped Stockman for budget director, he knew he was getting a very bright workaholic who would do a lot of the administration's dirty work. One of Reagan's political successes has been his ability to divorce himself from his unpopular actions by letting his assistants take the heat while he keeps his distance. It was always Stockman's budget cuts or Cap Weinberger's extravagant spending for defense or Interior Secretary James Watt's controversial environmental proposals. But it is doubtful that Reagan suspected that in Stockman he would also get his own antithesis as a human being, political leader and policy maker.

By every account Reagan is an amiable, sociable, laid-back and very secure Californian who made a lot of money outside of government without slaving for it, relishes the sweet fun and material rewards of life

281

over the hard work and modest lifestyle, plays the role of the macho cowboy and espouses traditional family and religious values—although he was divorced and does not attend church. He is anti-intellectual, a populist in his praise for the wisdom of the common man, a flag-waving, teary-eyed patriot in his love of country and its political institutions. (It's just the Washington "bureaucrats" and professional second-guessers he doesn't like.) As a leader he is committed to an order based on team play and loyalty, concentrates on broad themes and leaves the details to his staff, defends his positions with colorful anecdotes rather than cold analysis, talks a tough, confrontational and consistent line but takes a softer, compromising and pragmatically weaving course. He is a grandmaster of politics who offers hope, optimism and a free lunch.

Stockman, by contrast, is a serious, asocial, intense and insecure young Midwesterner who slaved in government without making a lot of money, relishes hard work and the ascetic life, rejects material ostentation, embraces anti-traditional personal values common to his generation—from extended adolescence and agnosticism to premarital cohabitation and an anti-institutional bias. He is intellectually rigorous in forming a belief system that must be totally consistent, is not a flag-waver who wears his patriotism on his sleeve, and is an elitist in his contempt for the competence of government institutions and the political process. As a government official he operated as a loner whose commitment to principle transcended team play or loyalty, was obsessed with detail, used confrontation, devious tactics and a mountain of analysis to make his case, and fought tirelessly for radical changes that had to meet the test of ideology and reason. He was the anti-politician demanding sacrifice, equity and full payment for services rendered.

Each man had a vision that did not quite square with the ambiguities of real life. Reagan's stemmed from distant memories of a way of life that no longer existed, and from the make-believe world of Hollywood. As president he could say things that were not factually correct, yet he was convinced they were true. He would tell "true" stories that never occurred, recite statistics and facts that were wrong, or deny taking positions even though the record showed otherwise, whether it had to do with Social Security or South Africa.

Stockman's world derived from the Christian idealism drilled into him by his grandfather, his childhood yearning for certainty and a lifetime of book-reading rather than firsthand experience. He would argue the general rule based on an intellectual principle, but in his sheltered life he had little knowledge of the real-life exceptions and contradictions.

His contemporaries in the White House recalled learning in 1984, with shock and amusement, that Stockman, by then a thirty-seven-year-old Cabinet hotshot and former Congressman, had to get a passport for a trip to the Middle East because he had never before been out of the country except for brief vacations in the Caribbean. "He had never even been to Canada or Mexico," claims his former aide Fred Upton. "When Jennifer found out, she said, 'You mean, you've never been to Paris?' And Dave got embarrassed and said, 'Ssh! Ssh!' " The Stockmans went to Israel that year for the wedding of Jennifer's sister, and they also visited Egypt to see the pyramids. The trip produced one of those classic Stockman-esque tales, in which he corrects their professor-guide for making a mistake about Egyptian history, a subject about which he had, of course, read extensively. Joseph R. Wright, Jr., Stockman's deputy director at OMB, and his fiancee joined the Stockmans on that sojourn, and he laughs about how his fiancee and Jennifer were "on Dave's case like you wouldn't believe because of the shoes he wears, the funny little hat he wears, the little gallon jug of water he carries in the Valley of the Kings all the time. And Dave is the only person I know that corrects a historian with a Ph.D. in Egyptology. It's amazing."

In many ways the fundamental differences that emerged between Reagan and Stockman were not unlike those often found between a father and son — the older man turned more pragmatic and cautious by the years, feeling wiser and more secure in his tempered judgments; the youth still impetuous, rebellious and convinced he has all the answers. And when they differed, each could be equally stubborn about changing his mind. Reagan and Stockman never bridged the generational gap that separated them, a failure that was a persistent source of conflict.

One of Stockman's major discoveries about Reagan was that the President did not share his enthusiasm for eliminating government programs on the grounds that they should be performed by the private sector. "We're the only true libertarians in the government," Stockman used to tell his inner circle at OMB during his many moments of frustration. "The President *likes* all these programs." Stockman came to see Reagan as a big-spending New Dealer who only wanted to get rid of that nefarious "WFA"—waste, fraud and abuse. Privately Stockman ridiculed the concept because he knew that WFA accounted for only a pittance of the federal budget. The big money was in programs that accomplished things, but things that Stockman thought government ought not do—provide cash benefits to middle-class people, subsidize local mass transit, build regional water systems, subsidize farm crops, pay for low-cost electricity in the South and Northwest, subsidize a variety of economic projects in cities across the country. Stockman made this point repeatedly in a lengthy interview he granted the author on Feb. 24, 1984, with the understanding that his remarks could not be made public until after he had left OMB:

His [Reagan's] view is that there probably is a legitimate need for most of the things we're doing and we should be able to do it more cheaply. . . . On most things as they come along, he'll say, 'Okay, can't we just reduce the overhead?' One good case I remember was grants for local sewer systems. I tried to get rid of them. Anne Burford [head of the Environmental Protection Agency] said she wanted to keep them. So, he decided in favor of keeping them. From a conservative perspective, you shouldn't have a federal government building

285

local sewer plants. It's a local responsibility. Local taxpayers ought to pay for it. It only benefits the immediate region.

Find a good speech where he has named something we shouldn't do? I leave you that challenge. I would come in saying that education is a state and local responsibility. They pay 92 percent of it; the eight percent isn't going to make much difference anyway, and if you're going to have strong decentralized local education you have to keep the federal dollars out. I'd say, 'You shouldn't have maritime subsidies, you shouldn't have farm subsidies, you shouldn't have programs that tax one region of the country to provide subways in another, or you shouldn't tax New York to provide sewers for Oklahoma.' I think in the abstract he would agree with that, but he has never pressed the point. He's never asked, 'Why aren't we getting rid of all these regional subsidies?'

The White House rhetoric, the speeches, have always been on overspending, not, 'Isn't it really, really wrong to subsidize riders in New York to be taxed out of the pockets of the hard-working people in Oklahoma? Does it make sense to tax the people in New York in order to have cheap sewers in Texas?' You haven't heard anything like that."

Stockman, then, saw the Reagan Revolution as superficial symbolism. The government was not being reshaped, it was just being put on a diet to get rid of some of the flab — except for defense spending.

Stockman's obvious frustration grew out of a sweeping belief that, without exception, anything the federal government did was either inherently unfair or could be done better and more efficiently by local government or private enterprise. He did not see the United States as one community of common interests and needs. He did not see the country as an integrated network in which Texans, because they were blessed with the good fortune of sitting on top of a sea of oil and gas, should use their revenues to help pay staggering social welfare costs in New York City, which had the burden of aiding the immigrants, artists and social outcasts because it happened to be a place that attracts large numbers of people in financial need. Stockman only saw the federal government as an incompetently run system that could not solve the problems of racism and poverty, that badly botched a distant war and that squandered national wealth on the wrong people for the wrong reasons and without regard for equity. Reagan did not rationalize his views of government the way Stockman did, but intuitively he believed the federal government had made things better when millions were suffering during the Depression, and he knew the government had won a noble war that saved the world from tyranny. His only complaint was that the government got sidetracked by the liberals during the 1960s.

"Ronald Reagan, in the end, is a gradualist and Dave Stockman is a revolutionary," says Lawrence A. Kudlow, a private economics consultant who served as chief economist at OMB from 1981 to 1983 and became a close Stockman friend and adviser. "When it came to implementing the limited government philosophy they both shared, as it turns out, Reagan was much more inclined to preserve some of the New Deal than Stockman was. So the real tension between these two guys on policy, in my opinion, was the go-slow, go-fast tension. And that policy tension significantly translated into a personal resentment that would fill Stockman to brimming over, occasionally, after losing. And at those moments, Dave would make a lot of comments about Reagan that he shouldn't have made."

Kudlow says Stockman's indiscreet comments generally were in the category of knocks at Reagan's intelligence. But Kudlow also claims Stockman said them only in the heat of anger. "I don't think Dave was as negative toward Reagan as either he himself or other people might have thought, based on these occasional statements. Dave was sort of befuddled at the extent of Ronald Reagan's political success, given, in Stockman's view, the President's limited intellectual capacity. The thing that Stockman could never quite figure out is, if he's not so smart, how come he's so damn successful politically? And I think it bothered him because here's Stockman, who is obviously smart, and his political future was going down the drain. In his last year, though, I detected a softening toward Reagan. I think Dave started to realize that this Reagan presidency in many ways was becoming bigger than life and that Reagan was going to be a towering historical figure whether Stockman liked it or not. And he was part of it. And I think in his mellower moods, Stockman realized that Reagan saved him from the *Atlantic* controversy and allowed him to remain in the Cabinet and to exit gracefully with his pride and dignity."

If Stockman had mellowed toward the President, other colleagues failed to notice it. Several friends and associates have said Stockman liked Reagan on a superficial level. But he also developed a deepseated contempt for the President and many of his trusted advisers because he thought they were intellectually dull, lazy and incompetent. That view was reinforced within Stockman's small circle of young bright libertarians. There was something of the "Us versus Them" attitude—the so rational and efficient men at OMB against the slothful and dense, as they saw it, Californians in the White House.

Sometimes Stockman made fun of Reagan's age. One friend says he joked that the President might be getting a little senile. Murray Weidenbaum, chairman of the White House Council of Economic Advisers during the first eighteen months of the administration, recalls one meeting at which Reagan joked that Stockman was young enough to be his son, and Stockman replied, "grandson." Adds Weidenbaum, "I thought to myself, 'Davey, boy, you're pushing your luck.' "

In interviews with reporters Stockman would disparage Reagan's intelligence and complain about his stubbornness. In another private interview with the author, to be made public only after he left OMB, Stockman said Reagan had a mind "like a trench—narrow but deep." Stockman also would marvel at Reagan's apparent memory of obscure details that bolstered his limited view of the world, at the same time resisting facts that might contradict that view. "If you made the argument, it wouldn't sink in," he said.

A Republican member of the Senate told a similar story about Reagan midway through his first term. A group of Senate Republicans had come to meet with the President to express their concern about the large deficits the White House was projecting for years to come. To dramatize their case for reducing the deficit through major budget surgery, they brought with them a graph that showed the explosion of the national debt under Reagan. It consisted of a vertical bar showing all the debt that had accumulated under the administrations of every prior President, and then showed the debt doubling under Reagan's steward-ship. As the senator remembered the meeting, a visibly angered Reagan looked at the graph, then turned to Treasury Secretary Donald Regan. "Is this right, Don?" Don Regan hemmed and hawed a little, said the graph was based on the latest forecasts for future economic conditions, and then turned to Stockman. "Isn't that right, Dave?" Stockman replied firmly, "Yes, sir." Reagan threw the graph down and then, as if he had forgotten the entire discussion, talked about how the government needed only to abandon wasteful projects such as an expansion of the Redwood National Forest in California.

One close Stockman friend who held a top job in the administration says Stockman sometimes acted like an elitist who believed in a meritocracy. Other times he seemed like a revolutionary. Whatever his role, he always saw "himself at the top. . . . The Reagan Administration would not have had a Reagan Revolution without David Stockman. There would not have been a particularly interesting administration without David A. Stockman—except in its blunders, perhaps. But notwithstanding all that, David Stockman tends to have a somewhat exaggerated sense of his own role in history. He thinks of himself more as a revolutionary, and revolutionaries tend often to have an inflated notion of the powers of a particular individual as opposed to other historical forces.

". . . In a sense, he saw his mission as larger than these people who happened to be here, like the President and some of his assistants who were of little or no significance. They were, in a way, the obstacles to progress that the political system had produced, and Dave was the force for truth, right, justice, goodness and all of that. And why should he be stopped in his missionary pursuit by these mere flawed mortals who happened along the way to do something exceedingly dumb or to create a big flap out of the *Atlantic Monthly* when they didn't have to?

"He had utter contempt at times for Don Regan, for Ed Meese, for Cap Weinberger, for the President, for a lot of people. To some degree even Jim Baker, because he thought Baker was too purely political. Why? Because if you ask, How knowledgeable? Not very knowledgeable. How industrious? Not very industrious. And those things are important to Dave. It's not just a question of being political. You've got people like Mike Deaver; he'd be gone at 5:30 or 6:00 o'clock every evening, never work on Saturdays, never work on Sundays. The President, of course, worked less than that. Meese would go to three cocktail parties a night. And you take the combined substantive knowledge of Meese, Deaver, to some degree Baker, and Reagan, and you really have to wonder if these people are the grand powers governing the society. And you're sitting over in your office saying, 'My God! These people don't know anything.' So, why should he allow his life to be steered by those people for whom he had a fair amount of contempt? But he stayed, because staying is governing and leaving isn't. And he kept thinking that intelligence ultimately would win out."

One of those top presidential assistants that Stockman's friend has referred to said the budget director suffered from the smugness of youth. "I think Dave was so smart that he sometimes believed nobody else had a view that mattered," the aide says. "In that sense Dave was not a good politician. He was either really naive or obstinate as hell. He continually believed, for instance, that the solution to the budget problem would be that the President one day wakes up and recognizes he had to raise taxes. Dave never, NEVER understood the depth of the President's commitment."

A close aide at OMB concedes that Stockman had a healthy sense of self-righteousness and arrogance about his points of view. "He'd always complain that he was surrounded by *no comprendo* guys, including the President and Meese. The problem was Dave was basically an Old Testament guy. He believed in work and self sacrifice. The President was an Evangelical Christian—push a button and the sun shines. And Meese embodied the decency and inconsistency of a Community Chest chairman in a good-sized city. He didn't have a cutting mind. And Ronald Reagan used to drive Dave crazy for the same kind of reason."

A top official at the White House who worked closely with Stockman says the young budget director could never dissuade Reagan or Meese from believing that the deficit could be eliminated through economic growth and an attack on government waste. "Dave tried so many ways with multicolored graphs and charts to show how we won't be able to grow out of these deficits, and the President would say, 'Don't suggest a tax increase. I won't accept it.' "

Michael Deaver, who left his post as White House deputy chief of staff in 1985 to become a Washington lobbyist, says Stockman suffered from a basic misperception of the world. "Dave always had to take the negative or pessimistic view. And that is contrary to the President's nature." A top White House official close to Meese, and highly critical of Stockman throughout his OMB tenure, complains: "Stockman thought of the President as a grandfather figure to be condescended to and indulged. He never understood the man and the politician that Ronald Reagan is — the most important political fact of our decade."

Kudlow says one of Stockman's problems was that he tried to convince Reagan on his own terms: "We weren't very persuasive with the President on many subjects because Ronald Reagan is not the kind of person who is going to be bowled over by the numbers. And that's putting it mildly. Ronald Reagan is a guy who is a storyteller. And I felt that in controversial areas where there was policy contention among the members of the senior Cabinet, we ought to be telling him a story back. Instead, we were doing it numerically. Okay, we think the deficit is too big. But why is it? We never really explained to Ronald Reagan, to his satisfaction, why the deficit was so bad. Ultimately, Stockman and Jim Baker were able to get antideficit decisions only because the deficit became a political problem."

Stockman's frustration about the budget was particularly keen when it came to national defense. Colleagues said Stockman could never win Reagan over in a battle with Weinberger about military spending because his was the antiwar draft-dodger generation and Reagan and Weinberger were from the "fought in World War II" generation. "On this, Weinberger had the President's complete trust," says one White House official. "Of course, anybody in that [older] generation who was more or less alive and able took that war to be their obligation just like breathing and off they went. Similarly, in Stockman's generation almost everybody who was educated didn't go. So Stockman happened to be of the second generation in the President's eyes and, though he didn't say so, it's quite safe to assume that the President would have felt that Cap was more surely patriotic. So when it came to worrying about protecting the United States, if Cap disagreed with the budget director, the President couldn't disagree with Cap."

Weinberger complained that Stockman's main fault was an unwillingness to support the President's priorities rather than his own. "I think the thing that bothered me most was the attacks he made on the President's budget after he had helped formulate it," Weinberger says. "And after it had gone to the Hill he would try to get a lot of it changed by members of

Congress with whom he maintained contact. That was undermining what we were trying to do . . . I didn't think there was all that much commitment to the President's programs and philosophy that I assumed all of the people in the government felt."

Martin Anderson, who served as chief White House domestic adviser in 1981, says Stockman's value to the older Cabinet members was his expertise on the budget, not his opinions, a point the youthful Stockman may never have realized. "As someone gets older, his judgment counts a lot. But when you're young you need a lot of facts," Anderson says. "At Cabinet meetings Stockman's judgment was not valued. No one ever said, 'What does Dave think?' or 'What's his opinion?' Rather, it always was, 'What are the facts?' "

Several of Stockman's close friends speak in high praise of his good intentions, sincerity, brilliance and remarkable dedication to doing what he honestly thought was best for the country. They claim motivations based on personal ego were subjugated to the cause of public service. Yet at the same time they describe his enormous sense of self-righteousness, his fanaticism and his extreme frustration as signs of adolescent behavior, and of a deep-seated insecurity he probably was never in touch with.

Says Jack Strayer, his former congressional aide: "Sometimes, I think he acts a little immature because his life experiences have been so limited. Sometimes you would see an immature little outbreak at a public hearing when he'd get real excited and lose his temper."

And from another good friend:

"One of the outstanding features of his personality is a deep-rooted insecurity. He feels he must have the last word in a debate or conversation and must take credit for ideas. He takes ideas from his staff and adopts them as his own without giving credit. And he wants desperately to make people believe that he knows every conceivable detail. . . .

"Dave never learned the art of quietly making a point or quietly pulling a punch. I mean, he was the direct opposite of the old-shoe type, the Eastern Ivy Leaguer. Things he said which made good sense were often said in such an antagonistic way that it created a backlash which undermined his analytical truth. And Dave Stockman almost never admitted he was wrong, and that's part of the insecurity.

"And I think the root of the insecurity is the lack of money. I think he's going to be a better, more confident and mellow human being once he starts banking these big dollars from his book and Wall Street career.

"Now, having said all that, let me balance it by emphasizing that he has some extremely positive traits. One is his tremendous ability to learn. He's a sponge at absorbing information, analyzing it and synthesizing it. He's brilliant at that. He's not a creative genius, but he's a genius at adapting. He's a dictator, but he can be very kind."

This is a portrait of a man operating on an entirely different psychological wave length from the man in the Oval Office. Unless he hides it even better than David Stockman, Ronald Reagan is not insecure about his abilities, his social graces, or money. Reagan, the Great Delegator, has a sign on his desk:

"There is no limit to what a man can do or where he can go if he doesn't mind who gets the credit." Unlike Stockman, socializing has been easy and basic to Reagan's career. As for money, Reagan is a millionaire surrounded by multimillionaire friends; he seems to take his and their wealth for granted after years of living the rich life.

Stockman has never been diffident about his thirst for power and influence, but he has played down any yearning for money. Indeed, he always gave the impression that he could not care less about it. In a Cabinet populated by millionaire businessmen, Stockman was a relative pauper who actually lived on his $71,000 salary and had no assets other than a part ownership in the family farm. And although he could keep close track of billions of dollars in federal spending, he never has seemed able to keep tabs on his own money. His aide Fred Upton says that in 1981, when Stockman received the prestigious Thomas Jefferson Award for Public Service, the $5,000 that came with it arrived not a moment too soon. "He would have been in the red that year without that award," says Upton, who also recalls American Express calling up around that time about an unpaid bill.

Stockman may have seemed a rare Republican in high office who didn't come from wealth and wasn't concerned with acquiring it, but according to numerous friends his lack of it was much on his mind for years. "Dave is a fairly money-motivated person," claims Jack Strayer, his former congressional aide. "He never had the money that he wanted as a child. He never had the money he wanted in college. Even in

Congress he'd say, 'You know, I'm not going to make any money being a Congressman.' One time he said if he could just have one year, he could make a million dollars through investments. But he knew he would make sacrifices until he was in his thirties, and then he'd make his money." Strayer adds that when Stockman left Washington at the end of 1979 he owned just one share of stock. "It was from that Kapok Tree restaurant chain down in Florida. You can buy them while paying your bill and his grandmother bought it for him. I think it was worth seventeen cents."

Strayer notes that both he and Fred Upton come from wealthy families, and that Stockman has spent a good deal of time at both their homes and apparently was very impressed with their elegant lifestyles. "He would say, 'Don't ever forget how lucky you are to be raised the way that you were,' or 'You're a spoiled brat and you have it made.' And I think Dave really liked our lifestyle, and Fred and I opened a lot of doors to other people who had a lot of money. But I also think there was a kind of resentment too. I think Dave still feels uncomfortable around people who have lots of money. He wasn't exactly poor, so I don't think it was that. I think part of it was the work ethic."

As a Congressman, Stockman used to ask Strayer rhetorically to look up the salaries of government bureaucrats with whom he had just met to see if they were worth their pay. And Upton recalls Stockman as budget director making jokes about Treasury Secretary Donald Regan's estimated $30 million-plus fortune from his career on Wall Street. "He would make a crack about Regan paying off the national debt out of his personal wealth, or say that the mortgage on Regan's house is equal to the national debt."

But in those first months of the new administration in 1981, David Stockman had no time for cynical jokes. Destiny, as it were, and his own hard work had conspired once again to give him a truly golden opportunity to make history. Which to David Stockman meant he had a lot of work to do.

CHAPTER 9

AN IMPOSSIBLE
BALANCING ACT

"David Stockman is the most brilliant man I've ever met in my life. David Stockman is also the most naive man I've ever met in my life. I will never meet another one like him."

The words flow out of Jonna Lynne "J. L." Cullen's mouth like thick honey from her native Mississippi. J. L. had met a lot of extraordinary men in a dozen years as a congressional aide in the House of Representatives. But none of them could compare with the driven young man she would team up with in late 1980 when she became head of OMB legislative affairs. That was the polite title for the White House lobbyist who would oversee all the sweet-talking, arm-twisting and deal-making that would be required of Stockman to get members of Congress to support his budget cuts.

Indeed, the task that Stockman willingly took on at the end of 1980 required nothing short of breathtaking brilliance and incredible naiveté. In barely two months he would have to take a rough sketch and turn it into a detailed blueprint for erecting the sweeping set of budget and economic changes that came to be known as the Reagan Revolution. Yet it was a project that seemed certain to collapse from the outset. In fact, several of his closest aides and colleagues now claim they realized within the first month of the Administration that Reagan's plan to cut taxes, boost defense spending and balance the budget in three years or less would never work. Of course the benefit of hindsight might have produced revisionist memories that were not so clear at the time. But David Stockman believed with the conviction of a Holy Crusader that it would all work out—even as the facts to the contrary kept mounting. Only by mid-1981, when the truth was unavoidable, did Stockman finally accept that he had laid the groundwork for the largest budget deficits in American history.

Many of Stockman's critics insist he was too smart with numbers, too knowledgeable about the budget really to believe he could pull off Reagan's program. To them he was the ultimate cynic, the Child of Darkness, who made a Faustian deal with the Devil to win a powerful and prestigious post that, for a while, approached the authority of the President himself. And when the plan started to come apart he would use all the arguments and sleight-of-hand tricks he could find to prop it up until it collapsed. But his friends knew him as the idealistic Child of Light who was capable of great self-delusion, at least for a while, because he was convinced beyond any doubt that what he was doing was right and that it would work out because he wanted it to work out. It represented his need for certainty about the way the world worked.

For Stockman, being named budget director in December of 1980 was like an athlete being selected for the Olympics after a decade of dedicated training. He had spent years as a powerless congressman seeking to cut the federal budget. Now he would have the power to make those cuts. It was a moment he had dreamed about, it was an enormous personal and political opportunity. He had so much work to do and so little time to do it. There was no time to question the soundness of the basic program. It became an article of faith.

On Dec.11, 1980, one week after his phone call from Ronald Reagan, David Stockman was formally designated as director of the Office of Management and Budget. Just one month past his thirty-fourth birthday Stockman would become the youngest person to sit in the Cabinet since 1814 when Richard Rush became James Madison's attorney general at the age of thirty-three and a half. Along with Stockman's appointment, Reagan also had announced seven other top Cabinet posts. Most were men in their fifties and sixties. Among the appointees were Donald T. Regan, then sixty-one, as Secretary of the Treasury, and Caspar Weinberger, then sixty-three, as Secretary of Defense. Within a year Stockman, Reagan and Weinberger would clash bitterly over both policy and personality. But for now they were all one, happy team.

It was on that December day, as the Cabinet appointees were paraded before the national news media on a hotel ballroom stage, that Stockman displayed for the first time the oversized pair of aviator glasses that became his trademark and helped typecast him as the Administration's bionic brain. The day before, his old pair had shattered when he bent over to pick up a paper. Knowing he needed a new pair for the Cabinet announcement, he rushed over to an optician, where he had arranged to meet his personal assistant Diana Moore. She remembers him picking out a large pair of glasses that struck her as too large for his face, but he liked them so she did not object. Later she would admit with a giggle that she had always felt a little guilty that she didn't talk him into choosing smaller, less conspicuous glasses.

Within the first days of his appointment Stockman went up to New York to visit several major investment houses on Wall Street, a tour arranged by supply-sider Jude Wanniski and by Richard Whalen, a Reagan campaign adviser. Wanniski, Whalen and Jack Kemp joined Stockman as he visited Merrill Lynch, Morgan Stanley, Bear Stearns and the firm that would become his future employer, Salomon Brothers. There, he met renowned economist and supply-side critic Henry Kaufman. The visit gave Wanniski the same queasy feeling he had after Stockman impersonated John Anderson in the mock debate three months earlier. "All through the day, all he talked about was the budget, not tax cuts," Wanniski says. "I got nervous and said, 'You're talking about all that old stuff,' And he said, 'You knew where my heart is.' "

The group then went to the University Club on Fifth Avenue, where Stockman met Alan Greenspan, the Ford Administration's chief economist, who now had a private consulting firm in New York. Greenspan was a traditional, fiscal conservative Republican who served as an economic adviser to the Reagan campaign. Later he would become a close personal friend and adviser to Stockman. While Wanniski watched, Greenspan and Stockman huddled in a corner talking about different programs that could be cut. An exasperated Wanniski picked up a handful of cocktail peanuts and dropped them one at a time on the table in front of them. "A hundred million here. Two hundred million there. It's peanuts. Peanuts," Wanniski said. "We're talking about billions [in tax cuts]." It was becoming obvious to Wanniski that Stockman was shedding his sunny supply-side belief in growth and prosperity through tax cuts, and going for Greenspan's gloomy Republican dogma of pain and austerity through budget cuts. Kemp came away from the trip suspecting that Stockman had become infatuated with elitist economic analysts like Greenspan and Kaufman who concentrated on technical economic details and lost sight, as he saw it, of the big picture — how to expand the economy so everyone could get a bigger share of the nation's wealth.

Stockman did not believe he was obliged to choose between tax cuts and budget cuts. He was convinced both were needed to keep from driving up the budget deficit. Without accompanying budget cuts, he feared, a higher deficit would block the economic expansion the tax cuts were supposed to trigger. Actually his view should have been no surprise to the supply-siders, since he expressed it in the "Dunkirk" memorandum he had written after the election. The memo, which Kemp had taken to Reagan's top economic policy advisers, said the tax cuts required to spur the "supply-side of the economy" could push the 1981 budget deficit into an unprecedented range of $60 billion to $80 billion. So "unless the tax cut program is accompanied by a credible and severe program" to curtail federal spending, he wrote, the rising budget deficit would raise fears in the financial markets about inflation and fiscal mismanagement. By now Stockman was fully on board the conventional argument that tax cuts would stimulate economic growth and increased federal revenues over the long term, but would not pay for themselves in the short term as predicted by the Laffer Curve. If the deficit were to be eliminated, there would have to be some pain too.

No question, reducing federal spending had been Stockman's preoccupation throughout his government career. "Dave would do just about anything to rip a dollar out of the spending stream," says David Gerson. As budget director that feeling was only reinforced. Although he appreciated and supported the incentive effects of supply-side tax cuts, he favored them for more traditional reasons. He figured that if the government didn't have the revenue it couldn't spend the money on the social pork barrel (although the record deficits of the past few years proved otherwise). He also felt that on pure free-enterprise grounds the less money controlled by government and the more kept in private hands, the better the economy would be.

As it turned out, Reagan would share this view to a considerable extent during his presidency. Reagan believed from his own personal experience the half of the Laffer Curve that showed the government losing revenue when tax rates get too high. Reagan knew from his Hollywood days that oppressive tax rates discouraged wealthy people from working and investing because they knew they could keep only 10 percent of their additional profits. Why make another movie? But Reagan never publicly embraced the part of the Laffer Curve that predicted lower tax rates would increase revenues sufficiently to eliminate the deficit without spending reductions. In fact, in his first economic address to the nation, on Feb. 5, 1981, he made the "starve the beast" case: ". . . There were always those who told us that taxes couldn't be cut until spending was reduced. Well, you know, we can lecture our children about extravagance until we run out of voice and breath. Or we can cure their extravagance by simply reducing their allowance."

Where Stockman and Reagan parted company was over what to do when the children kept up their spending by using a credit card. Stockman, like all good budget directors, wanted above all to balance the books. So he tried to impose a credit limit; and when he became convinced that wouldn't work, he wanted to pay the bills with tax revenue. Reagan, however, had an entirely different set of priorities. He wanted to take the credit card away from everyone but the kids at the Pentagon; and he figured the bills would eventually get paid by someone else. When forced to choose between tax increases and continued deficits of unprecedented magnitude, Stockman opted for the former, based on his strict "pay-for-what-you-get" midwestern conditioning. Reagan opted for the latter, based on his magical "there'll-be-a-happy-ending" Hollywood days. This was the side of Reagan that bought the supply-side argument that the economy could grow its way out of the deficits.

"I don't think Dave ever was anything more than a part of the supply-side movement," Jack Kemp says in retrospect. "Clearly, Stockman wanted to shrink the government by shrinking revenues. That's where I departed. Not that I don't want certain aspects of government to come down, but my whole goal was noninflationary economic growth so that you could shrink the size of government by making some of the government less needed. In other words, if the economy were growing as fast as I thought it could grow and unemployment were dropping as far as I thought it could go, you would, by nature, drop some of the social-welfare aspects of government. The way to reduce government spending is to reduce the need for government spending. Dave, apparently, had the view that if you cut the tax rates we lose revenue, and that takes away the oxygen. Thus, the spending shrinks. And Reagan kind of had one foot in each camp."

In those heady days right after he was named to OMB, Stockman's only thoughts about taxes and deficits were ways to cut them, and he was brimming with enthusiasm and confidence as he prepared for the challenge. . . . One evening at Tiberio's, an expensive Italian restaurant where he, Jennifer Blei, Chris Wallace and his wife celebrated the Cabinet appointment, Stockman talked excitedly about "how the world works." Wallace recalls that "he spoke with a certainty that he really knew what to do and that he was going in with a plan." It would be one of the last fancy dinners Stockman would allow himself over the next eight months. Time was too precious to squander over veal Tiberio and spinach-filled agnolotti. It also would be one of the last evenings he would be spending with Jennifer Blei for several months.

Stockman and Blei had been living together during his second term in Congress, but he moved into a separate apartment after his appointment. It would have been a little unseemly for a Cabinet member in this conservative Administration to be living out of wedlock, so why encourage the wagging tongues? Reagan might have fooled around in his younger days in Hollywood, but this was dowdy Washington in 1980, and for sure the likes of Jerry Falwell and his flock would not approve. Besides, Stockman would be so busy on his mission he wouldn't have time for a serious relationship.

"Frankly, it was no big secret that we lived together. I think everybody in our generation lived together," says Jennifer. "Soon after David knew he was going to become OMB director we said it's going to be a matter of days, if not hours, before people realize that we're living together. So we either should get married or not live together. We just didn't want to be pressured into getting married when we weren't ready. And we weren't ready.

"But we didn't feel like being gossiped about. We

308

would have become an item. The Moral Majority influence in this Administration would have taken a negative view of it. It just wasn't worth the exposure. I mean, it was a shame and we were kind of sorry that that had to be, but we were also quite pragmatic about it."

It turned into an actual separation that strained the relationship for a while. Stockman was spending every waking hour working on the budget, which left four hours a day or less to sleep, and no room in his life for Blei—although he did date other women until they got back together, with separate legal residences, later in 1981. "David had his thing to do. I mean, the last thing he wanted to worry about was his personal life. He didn't even want to eat and sleep," Jennifer tells it. "He just knew he had to survive. All he wanted to do was to get this so-called revolution off the ground. He looked at this as a once-in-a-lifetime opportunity, which it was. So he didn't want anything to distract him and I was plainly a distraction. But that shows how dedicated he was to the cause."

It also shows how dedicated he could be to his work, as Susan Hause Runne and Sue Gillespie had discovered earlier. Stockman did not easily separate work time from play time. Once when he and Blei had gone away on a vacation together Stockman had given Jack Strayer a list of twelve books on a variety of esoteric topics that he had wanted to take with him. Strayer dropped the couple off at the airport but intentionally left the books in his trunk as a favor to Blei. "No offense to Jennifer, but he would have read them otherwise," Strayer says.

Meanwhile Stockman was picking up some political flak back in his district because his campaign chairman, John Globensky, was running with his backing in a special election for the congressional seat Stockman had to resign. Amid complaints that Stockman was trying to "anoint" a successor, district Republicans turned Globensky away and nominated Mark Siljander, a young state representative with strong backing from fundamentalist Christian groups. Siljander went on to win the election and represented the district throughout Stockman's OMB tenure. In 1986 Stockman associate, Fred Upton, returned home to challenge Siljander in the GOP primary.

With his personal life on hold, Stockman concentrated on putting together his OMB team. For the most part it consisted of the young turks from his congressional office. David Gerson became his executive assistant and an associate director in charge of running the 650-person budget office. Don Moran and Fred Khedouri became associate directors. Diana Moore came as his personal assistant, Fred Upton worked on the legislative affairs staff under J. L. Cullen, and Susan Hause Runne came back to work as a senior budget analyst. Most of the other top jobs were filled by Republicans with various administration connections, but a few of Stockman's key appointments were far afield.

One key job, that of OMB chief economist, went to Lawrence Kudlow, who worked at Bear Stearns and who happened to meet Stockman the day of his Wall Street tour in December. Wanniski had read some of Kudlow's analyses, which were supportive of the supply-siders, and thought Stockman should meet him. Within six months Wanniski would view Stockman and Kudlow as traitors to the cause. Kudlow, a year younger than Stockman, grew up in a wealthy Englewood, N.J., family but went through a political conversion similar to Stockman's. He canvassed for Goldwater in high school. Then, as a student at the University of Rochester, he became an active Vietnam war protester and signed SDS petitions against the draft. Allergies spared him from military service. Kudlow also was a registered Democrat who had voted for Humphrey in 1968 and McGovern in 1972. He had worked for eighteen months at Common Cause, the liberal government watchdog agency — which some longtime Reaganites at the White House thought should have barred him from administration work. Kudlow then started turning conservative and Republican in the mid-seventies and became a speechwriter for former Treasury Secretary William E. Simon after Simon had left the Ford Administration. Kudlow, who would become a close Stockman adviser, saw himself as a 1960s-generation libertarian and as anti-establishment, like the other members of the OMB inner circle.

"There's a very strong anti-authority, antigovernment strain that comes through all of us," he says. "We would argue that government is bad whether it dictates economic resource allocation or whether it dictates social behavior. . . . You could say we were a bunch of younger baby-boom alumni who wanted to rid society of the albatross of government in all of its forms. The deficit was simply a political expression, and a rather useful political expression at that. But the root cause of our behavior as policy advisers was

311

the issue of government and the heartfelt opinion that we had to cut it back and get it out of our lives." Kudlow, who left OMB in 1983 to start his own economic consulting business, saw a link between that philosophy and the antiwar attitudes of the group. "The New Left was essentially anti-authoritarian in nature, so for me the leap from New Left to neoconservative is not as large a jump as you would think. In many ways we were in the Reagan Administration providing an antigovernment economic policy which is quite reminiscent of an antigovernment feeling concerning foreign policy." Like Stockman, Kudlow now considers himself a staunch anti-Communist: "Fifteen years ago I didn't really deal in those terms. I dealt in terms of the draft, which struck me as especially oppressive."

As his general counsel Stockman chose a "bleeding-heart" Democrat turned Reagan Republican, Michael Horowitz, one of the few non-baby-boomers to become a close adviser. He also was one of the few with a military record. Born in 1938, Horowitz served in the Marine Corps Reserves. In a 1980 article explaining his conversion to the right, Horowitz wrote, "I am Jewish, was student body president at City College of New York, taught civil rights law in Mississippi during the sixties . . . The best man at my wedding was a Democratic congressman with a 100 percent ADA [Americans for Democratic Action] rating . . . I was formatively influenced by a trade-unionist immigrant grandfather who regularly admonished me to see America as the blessed land." But by 1976 Horowitz said his disillusionment with liberalism had made him into a conservative. Like many recent converts, Horowitz became a darling of the Reaganites, and he played the informal role of defending Stockman from critics on the right who thought the budget director was not sufficiently conservative.

As his chief public spokesman Stockman selected Edwin L. Dale, Jr., a highly regarded newspaperman who had spent the previous four years working for the Democratic-controlled economic stabilization subcommittee of the House Committee on Banking, Finance and Urban Affairs. Dale, who was fifty-seven when he joined Stockman, was the elder statesman of the OMB inner circle, but like his youthful boss he had an amazingly broad knowledge of the federal budget and brought a candor and bluntness to his job that was unheard of in government public affairs circles. A native of Philadelphia, Dale served on a Navy destroyer during World War II and graduated from Yale. After a brief stint reporting and writing editorials for the Worcester *Evening Gazette* in Massachusetts, Dale came to Washington in 1951, where he spend four years covering economics for the old New York *Herald Tribune*. Dale moved to the New York *Times* in 1955, where he specialized in economics coverage for the next twenty-one years. As a staff member of the House economic stabilization subcommittee, Dale had handled legislation on the New York City rescue plan, the Chrysler loan guarantees, Carter's Council on Wage and Price Stability and the government synthetic fuel subsidy program — issues to which Stockman had been fundamentally opposed (although he later came to believe the New York City bailout was the right thing to do). Dale, however, was a registered Republican and was known on the committee as the "staff conservative," he says.

As a former journalist, Dale took his job as a public information specialist literally; he dispensed information accurately and efficiently, a rarity in Washington. Most of his counterparts in the Administration, particularly at the White House, functioned as public relations specialists and publicity agents who were hostile to the press. They knew very little about the substance of issues and thought mainly in terms of projecting their boss in the best possible light. That often meant playing dumb or being naturally so, ducking embarrassing questions, stretching the truth or lying outright. They felt justified because they assumed most reporters were closet liberals and anti-establishment cynics out to get Reagan the way they got Carter and Ford and Nixon and Johnson. Dale did not have that bunker mentality and tried to avoid playing deceitful games. He honestly admired Stockman, shared most of his views and did not feel it necessary to shape the budget director's public image. When he disagreed with Stockman on an issue, he was not too bashful to say so. That was fine with Stockman, who had a long relationship with journalists and felt confident he could handle selective contacts with opinion leaders in the press on his own. One of his earliest contacts was with Washington *Post* editor William Greider, who would start meeting with Stockman over breakfast on Saturday mornings. Stockman, who would be remarkable candid if reporters agreed to quote him anonymously as "a senior administration official," found this back-channel approach very useful in influencing administration policy, which is very sensitive to public opinion. Ultimately, the tactic would bring about his undoing.

Dale specialized in faithfully returning telephone calls and quickly providing information about the federal budget or explaining Stockman's views for reporters working under deadline pressure. He hated to talk about administration infighting, saying it was nothing but "silly gossip" that only detracted from the important substance involved. If a reporter pressed him for information that he knew but was not yet supposed to make public, he would not lie that he did not know, which is what most public affairs specialists do. He would just snarl, "I'm not going to tell you. What's your next question." When a reporter asked a stupid question or drew an improper inference — which happened often, given the arcane nature of the budget — Dale would become impatient and shout, "No! No! NO! Gee, I'm surprised at you. I thought you knew this stuff." Then he would insist he had to get off the phone because his "sea of yellow," as he called his pile of telephone messages, was threatening to engulf him. One time early in the Administration, Dale made front-page news by contradicting one of Reagan's frequent misstatements about budget programs. Dale later said he thought he had been responding to a hypothetical question from a reporter and did not know that Reagan had said anything in public.

Stockman's selection of Dale as his director of public affairs was proof of the budget director's strong confidence in his views about the role of the federal government. He did not need a salesman, he needed a credible spokesman who could provide the facts and let them speak for themselves. Stockman wanted to educate reporters, tutor them in the truth as he saw it.

While selecting a staff, Stockman also started working feverishly on assembling a detailed package of budget cuts. He saw a chance to attack the social pork barrel as never before, but it would have to be done quickly while Reagan's landslide victory was fresh and the Democrats were still disorganized over losing the Senate to the Republicans. But Stockman had to work within a policy strait jacket. For all practical purposes, Reagan's economic program was drafted in Chicago on Sept. 9, 1980, when he laid out his economic agenda. It called for a 30 percent cut in personal tax rates over three years, a big tax cut for business, a steady increase in defense spending, a dampening of inflation and a balanced budget by 1983. The plan was long on objectives but short on specifics, particularly for the spending cuts that would achieve this balanced budget. Thrown together somewhat haphazardly by Alan Greenspan and a few other senior economic advisers, the plan said Reagan would cut federal spending by at least 2 percent in 1981 and the number would grow to at least 7 percent by 1985. That sounded like a modest enough goal considering the government was spending more than $650 billion a year. Surely $15 billion or $25 billion a year in waste could be extracted easily enough. But Stockman knew that was an unrealistic and simplistic view. "The whole approach to domestic spending was just some little rule of thumb and there was never any hint of where it dealt with Medicare or jobs programs or whatever," Stockman said in a February 1984 interview. "And I don't think he [Reagan] focused on it that much. They just told him this was a pretty good target." Stockman knew that the detailed cuts would have to go beyond just trimming fat.

Right after the election Caspar Weinberger had been put in charge of developing a list of budget cuts to meet the balanced budget goal, but when Stockman took over in December and looked at what Richard Nixon's one-time budget director had put together, he threw it away. "My first recollection is of him saying that the work done by Weinberger was useless crap and they had to start over," says one high-ranking White House official who had joined the new administration a month before the inauguration. Weinberger's problem was that he had not been budget director for nearly eight years and had lost track of the budget trends and numbers. Steve Bell, staff director for the Senate Budget Committee throughout Stockman's tenure, recalls a meeting with Weinberger shortly after the election at which the cost of an appropriations bill for the Treasury Department and Postal Service had come up. "What is that, about a $4 billion bill?" Weinberger asked. And Bell was a little stunned because the bill was $8 billion. It had been $3 billion when Weinberger was budget director, and he had not realized how rapidly federal spending had increased and how complex budget issues had become. "Dave Stockman was simply the only person in the administration who knew anything about the federal budget," says Bell. "I think they were lucky they got Dave Stockman."

So Stockman had to start from scratch, collecting everything he could find: budget-cutting proposals he had pushed in Congress, proposals that had been floating around for years in the Congressional Budget Office, proposals that the career professionals at OMB had drafted but had gone nowhere in prior administrations. This was Stockman's meat. He was not especially creative; he was not the person who would discover a new theory of physics or write a sonata for piano or establish a new school of political thought. He was the ultimate problem-solver—the man who could put a 10,000-piece jigsaw puzzle together before anyone else so long as he was given all the pieces. He could absorb, adapt, analyze, synthesize and reconstruct enormous amounts of material, and he could keep it up at a frenetic pace when most others would have suffered third-degree brain burn. Yet even Stockman had not anticipated initially just how big a problem he would have to solve.

As soon as the Cabinet appointments were announced Stockman and his brain trust moved into the Reagan transition headquarters and began compiling as many proposals as possible for cutting the budget. "We wanted the biggest damn list we could get our hands on," says Don Moran. Reagan might have been thinking in terms of getting rid of waste, fraud and abuse, but Stockman was thinking in terms of a wholesale redefinition of government services. That meant cutting off or reducing food stamps, welfare, Medicaid, subsidized housing and other benefits to people who were not in abject poverty; barring upper-income families from school lunch subsidies and student loans; eliminating or trimming economic subsidies for farm programs, economic development, energy development, local government employment, mass transportation and the Postal Service; and curbing federal spending on a smorgasbord of programs that included education, energy and science, health care, housing, land conservation, the arts, space exploration, foreign aid and consumer safety. Stockman, as he saw it, was going after all the "squeaking wheels" that Congress oiled with taxpayer's money — the low-income people who abused welfare programs, middle-income people who were not deserving of aid intended for the poor, professional lobbyists for the poor who were siphoning off poverty money into their own pockets, upper-income people who were getting free lunches and free rides, businesses large and small that were depending on the government instead of the free market, and local and state governments that were looking to Uncle Sam to solve their problems.

First Stockman and company start with the "A" list, the things Stockman had wanted to do for years. Then there was the "B" list, savings proposed by other people that could be used, and there were "C" and "D" lists of relatively minor programs that could be trimmed or cut. Everything was included in Stockman's black book of budget cuts unless the staff thought it outrageous. "If something came up that struck us as being too loony, we dropped it," says Moran, "because what we wanted to do was start out with a list of everything we thought was defensible in the way of a program reduction. And we were going to try and ram that through the system. Anything we thought had some policy reason for reducing we would try to take a whack at." Susan Runne recalls the staff working frantically to finish its Herculean task within sixty days. There was no time to second-guess what they were doing. "We accepted on faith that all these changes we were making were the right thing to do. We didn't consider all the consequences they would have as one integrated package working its way through the [economic] system."

One area they did not pay much attention to was the rapid buildup in the Defense Department budget, which was being put together at the Pentagon. It was an oversight Stockman would later regret. But Stockman was so busy working on the domestic portion of the budget that he did not have the time to focus on Pentagon programs. So in late January, he and Defense Secretary Caspar Weinberger, using a hand calculator, determined a set of budget numbers for the Defense Department over the next five years so that Stockman could plug them into his overall budget. What they came up with was a five-year, $1.3 trillion spending plan that would allow the Pentagon's annual budget to jump from $159 billion in 1981 to $336 billion in 1986. Although Weinberger insists his budget was based on previously calculated military needs, Stockman has maintained emphatically over the years that the numbers "came right out of thin air." And once they were printed as the President's budget, they became locked in as Reagan's defense "policy." For the next four years, Weinberger would defend the numbers and Stockman would try with only marginal success to get Reagan to cut them back. It was indeed ironic that Stockman would exhaust himself trying to carve $40 billion in domestic savings out of the budget; and then would put nearly as much back in for the military with a flick of a calculator switch.

The huge defense buildup proved to be considerably larger than Reagan's advisers had estimated in Chicago when they put out his economic plan. But that was only the latest of numerous problems that would frustrate Stockman as he tried to fulfill Reagan's pledge to cut taxes, lower inflation, increase military spending and balance the budget by 1983. In the few months since Reagan had outlined that program, the economy had gotten weaker and the budget appeared headed into even deeper debt. Stockman knew that would make his job of balancing the budget that much harder. Most private forecasters considered the job impossible. Using conventional economic assumptions, they estimated that Reagan's tax cuts and military buildup would produce the largest deficits in history. But Stockman was not planning to use conventional economic assumptions. He had a different view of how the world should work, and he was convinced it would help him achieve his objectives. His critics would accuse him of using phony economic assumptions, but in Washington, it was a time-honored tradition to assume the best about the future at budget time. Stockman knew that well. With righteous indignation he had been accusing the Democrats of budgetary duplicity for years. In 1981, he and the Democrats would switch roles.

To understand how easy it is to manipulate budget numbers, it is perhaps useful to understand how they are estimated. Writing a federal budget is like predicting the weather. The meteorologists start out with some basic assumptions about how seasonal changes and major weather systems work. Then they refine their outlooks based on local conditions. The meteorologists may predict it will rain in three days based on the current movement of a low pressure system, but the system could break up or change direction, and the local area has sunny skies. The budget is subject to hundreds of variables, and the more distant the forecast, the more chance of major error. Estimating how much the government will actually spend one, two or three years down the road requires predictions about several things: how much will the population grow; how many people will retire, lose their jobs or get sick; how much inflation will increase various benefit programs; how a rise or fall in interest rates will affect government payments on the national debt. Estimating how much the government actually will take in requires similar predictions about how much inflation increases taxable earnings, how much payrolls and profits increase or decrease, how interest rates will affect loans owed the government, how many people will take advantage of the dozens of tax loopholes, and on and on. Like the weather, precise predictions about the budget are impossible until it is upon us. But unlike the weatherman, who tries to give an accurate forecast, the government always tries to predict sunny skies.

Back in May of 1980 Stockman angrily accused the Democrats of passing a phony balanced budget for 1981. He predicted the deficit would run $40 billion or higher. Seven months later, as budget director-designate, that prediction would haunt him. The projected deficit for 1981 was running close to $60 billion, a near record at the time, and it meant his task of balancing the budget by 1983, as Reagan had promised during the campaign, was out of the question. Even before Reagan's inauguration the incoming Administration was backing away from some of its campaign pledges. Stockman would now try to balance the budget by 1984, which meant other adjustments as well. The three-year, 30 percent cut in individual tax rates, which was supposed to go into effect retroactive to Jan. 1, 1981, would be postponed to July 1. Stockman later said the tax cut was delayed so that the government would not have to mail rebates to taxpayers, but the move also saved revenue.

In place of conventional economic forecasts that had shown huge budget deficits, Stockman relied on a novel economic model developed by Claremont Economic Institute, an economic consulting firm of which Lawrence Kudlow was a part owner. Kudlow helped Stockman use the new model and wound up staying at OMB. Most conventional forecasts were predicting high inflation and interest rates and stagnant economic growth over the next year, the set of conditions that produced the huge Reagan deficits in the computer run. But this new model was based on a "rational expectations" theory. It predicted that investor expectations about the economy could be turned around almost overnight, that Wall Street would react to Reagan's economic proposals immediately, and concluded that strong, noninflationary growth was coming. With expectations of future stagflation reversed, interest rates would plummet, the stock market would soar, the economy would be off to the races and—with the budget cuts Stockman and his staff were preparing—it would be possible to balance the budget by 1984. In retrospect, Kudlow says the scenario would have required "a miraculous" turnaround in investor attitudes.

Even with the new computer model of economic behavior, Stockman still had to iron out some fundamental differences with other incoming officials about the kind of economy Reagan's program would produce. The supply-siders never cared that much about the bottom line of the budget: they wanted to show strong economic growth, with or without deficits. At the same time, the monetarists' primary concern was to reduce inflation by limiting the rate at which money and credit was pumped into the economy. That normally entailed higher interest rates and lower growth, but the supply-siders and Stockman needed to show strong growth and low interest rates. So they came up with a hodge-podge economic forecast that met everybody's objectives—strong economic growth *and* falling inflation. In late January, after Murray L. Weidenbaum was named chairman of Reagan's Council of Economic Advisers, he became so upset over the obvious inconsistencies in the forecast that he demanded modifications. So did Senator Pete Domenici of New Mexico, who was taking over as the Republican chairman of the Senate Budget Committee. "If you go with a crazy forecast, I will not sign onto this budget and I will oppose it," Domenici declared at a meeting of senior economic advisers in the OMB conference room. The group finally agreed to some slight readjustments, but the final forecast that was published to support the balanced budget plan was so hopelessly optimistic, it became derisively known as the "Rosy Scenario." Domenici still didn't like it, but reluctantly went along. As things turned out, inflation came down even faster than had been predicted, but the forecast left out one rather important ingredient — the pain of a deep recession and high unemployment that would be required to wring inflation out of the economy.

Alan Greenspan, who had functioned as ad hoc chairman of the Council of Economic Advisers prior to Weidenbaum's appointment in late January, sat in on those economic debates and remembers Stockman calling the final shots. "Dave ultimately made the decision to do what was required from a standpoint of both politics and economic credibility," Greenspan says. "We needed a forecast that would not be screamed down by the economic community. The issue was how to reconcile it with the political objectives. What was not being discussed was what would be the best forecast objectively. The focus was to make it work politically by taking what seemed like a diametrically opposite [economic] belief." Noting Reagan's campaign plan to balance the budget in 1983, which Greenspan helped write, he added, "We knew in Chicago that we would need an awfully large shoehorn. Dave's job was to do what he could." Stockman thought it was possible to achieve it at the time, Greenspan says, because "Dave always starts at the top. He has to start with a perfect world."

More than any other single factor, the recession was the main undoing of Stockman's balanced-budget plan, but he had failed — or refused — to recognize that an economic price would have to be paid for reducing inflation. It always had been paid before, despite Reagan's vow to do things differently. Stockman had become so obsessed with the details of the budget, he forgot to pay attention to the broad dynamics of economic policy. He should have gotten that briefing on monetary policy when he first raised it with Jude Wanniski in 1978. "Dave could be naive about macroeconomic and monetary policy," says Ed Dale, who specialized in those issues as a reporter. A high-ranking administration official has said the inconsistent economic forecast became an early indication "of the fatal flaw in the design of the program." Because of his naiveté and his determination to achieve the impossible, Stockman was not prepared to accept what was coming.

During all this frenetic activity, Stockman still had to be confirmed in his post by the Senate. On Jan. 8, 1981, he appeared before the Senate Governmental Affairs Committee, which held a hearing on his appointment. As in so many earlier situations, he came across as a young man with a sharp mind and loose mouth. When questioned about his use of the phrase "coast-to-coast soup line" in his "Dunkirk Memorandum," which Wanniski had leaked to the New York *Times* in December, Stockman replied, "Sometimes my metaphors may be not quite as exact as they should be." As the *Atlantic Monthly* would demonstrate within the year, he never overcame that weakness. Stockman also was grilled about his colorful but strident attacks on farm subsidies in a 1978 letter to then Agriculture Secretary Bob Berglund. The letter began: "This is to express my unabated rage at the Department of Agriculture's recently announced intention to prop up the price of Idaho potatoes. After you spread the taxpayers' and consumers' gravy on the Russets, where will you strike next? Broccoli? Turnips? Peppermint?" The letter ended, "Your Department's supine capitulation in this potato caper makes the best argument yet for congressional enactment of a 'cold turkey' policy for American agriculture." The letter prompted Berglund to write, "Dear Congressman Stockman: This is in further reply to your juvenile letter of December 28 . . ."

Even so, the senators seemed to delight in Stockman's quick-witted responses and his willingness to take a strong stand on issues. On Jan. 27 the full Senate unanimously confirmed his nomination. As always, he could play the smart but sassy kid and get away with it. Their admiration was summed up at his confirmation hearing by Thomas Eagleton, a Missouri Democrat: "I am very impressed with Mr. Stockman as an exceedingly bright individual and a tremendously hard-working individual. Obviously I don't agree with every philosophical viewpoint that he has expressed. I am delighted that he has a viewpoint. I am delighted we don't have the kind of vacuous nominee that frequently comes before us, from both Republican and Democratic administrations. A nominee comes through, [and] he has no views on anything. He has no idea what he will do. This man at least has given a heck of a lot of thought to a lot of issues. In fact, I want to vote to confirm him for head of OMB and also Secretary of Energy at the same time. I would rather have him doing both jobs than having that other fellow, the one who said that the only drilling he knows about is drilling a tooth. Boy, if that isn't wonderful." That other fellow was James B. Edwards, an oral surgeon and former governor of South Carolina, who would become one of Stockman's many bitter enemies in the Cabinet. Edward's animosity was well founded: Stockman wanted to get rid of the Energy Department and thought Edwards was ignorant.

Deep cuts in energy programs were just part of some $40 billion in savings on the spending side that Stockman eventually would propose for 1982 to put the budget on the path toward balance. That was a huge sum, given the limited portion of the budget Stockman could even touch. Although federal spending in 1981 totaled $678 billion, one-fourth of that went to the military, and Reagan wanted to boost that part of the budget, not cut it. Another 10 percent went for interest on the national debt, which the government was obliged to pay. And another 37 percent went for Social Security retirement benefits, veterans benefits and a few other cash-benefit programs that Reagan had declared off-limits, mostly for political reasons. The net left for Stockman was only about $200 billion, or less than one-third of the budget, with which to achieve the bulk of his $40 billion in savings. The simple arithmetic made it obvious that some very major cuts would have to be made and that the resistance from the affected federal agencies, their protectors in Congress and their lobbyists on the outside would be fierce.

To Stockman's delight, Reagan went along with almost everything with the exception of a few but very large political sacred cows. These included the main Social Security pension program and its Medicare health payment plan for senior citizens, the two largest domestic programs in the budget. Veterans' programs, regular unemployment compensation and general welfare for the lowest-income groups also were thrown into this category. Most of the Social Security, Medicare and veterans' benefits went to middle-income and upper-income people, but the administration needed some rationalization to explain why these programs were not being touched. So the concept of a "Social Safety Net" was concocted by Stockman. Its purpose was to create a public impression that despite major surgery in the budget that went beyond anything ever attempted before, Reagan was not going to let the government turn a cold shoulder to those in genuine need. In that sense, the Social Safety Net was supposed to be Reagan's modern translation of the New Deal. It could rather more accurately have been called Reagan's Political Safety Net; as former presidential economist Murray Weidenbaum points out, "it protected the popular middle-class programs like Social Security . . ."

Moreover, the Safety Net had been stitched together so haphazardly in the first month of Reagan's presidency that some of the wrong programs got tossed in by mistake. Don Moran says the White House had been getting nervous over rumors that every single program in the budget was being cut and reporters were demanding to know what programs would be exempt. "My recollection is that somebody at the White House felt compelled to give out a list of those things that were not being cut. So we hurriedly put together a list of basic things that we're not cutting and gave it to [White House deputy press secretary] Larry Speakes to put out. And that somehow got interpreted as being the Social Safety Net." The unintended items included Head Start, summer youth employment and school lunches — all programs for low-income children — and a subsidized meal program for the elderly. Stockman did not plan to cut them in 1981, but he did not intend to put them in the safety net either, because he might need to axe them in later years. Reagan and his speechwriters were just as confused, and the President wound up including those four programs in the Safety Net when he unveiled his economic proposals before a joint session of Congress on Feb. 18, 1981. Within three months, Stockman would be trying to rip huge holes in the net to obtain his elusive balanced-budget goal.

At first Stockman was surprised that Reagan would go along with so many budget cuts that went beyond elimination of mere waste, fraud and abuse. Other than the major Safety Net items, Reagan bought just about everything except cuts in Merchant Marine operating subsidies; Reagan was a big fan of the Merchant Marine. So, no doubt feeling his oats even more, Stockman tried to sell Reagan on a list of tax "loophole" closings. Stockman saw these loopholes as just another type of federal subsidy that was granted on the tax side rather than on the spending side. His list included elimination of the oil depletion allowance and a ceiling on home mortgage interest deductions. From an ideological standpoint, Stockman considered these items to be government subsidies for the rich, and he opposed them as much as social-welfare spending for the middle class. From a political standpoint, he felt it was important to have a balanced program that cut everyone's pet subsidy on an equitable basis, pro-business Republicans on the upper end of the income scale as well as pro-welfare Democrats on the lower end of the scale. To Stockman they all amounted to pigs feeding at the public trough. But Reagan saw most of the loophole closings as tax increases and wouldn't buy them. He did, however, go along with one of Stockman's revenue proposals—to reduce government subsidies for airports, boat harbors and such facilities by increasing "user" fees on private aircraft, boats and barges. When word of Stockman's proposal to eliminate the oil depletion allowance leaked into the newspapers, some of the core supply-siders concluded they had lost him for good. "I went to see him," says Jude Wanniski, "and he was defensive and said, 'I'm busy. I have an appointment.' And he just left me sitting there."

The supply-siders concluded that Stockman had been co-opted by his job. He had become the nation's top green eyeshade and was determined to balance the books at any expense. "I think he got into OMB and looked at the figures and looked at what was happening and came away overwhelmed by the urgency of the problem," says Jack Kemp. "Whereas I thought we could be celebrating an end to inflation, a reigniting of the engine of growth and a restoration of the entrepreneurial dream and opportunity—what America was meant to be—Dave only saw the deficit as the sole criterion by which to judge economic policy. We used to argue about that time after time after time. It really drove us apart politically." A Kemp ally, Republican Congressman Newt Gingrich of Georgia, has charged: "Stockman played the role assigned to him at each level. At OMB he became an accountant. He became committed to the traditional GOP attitudes — cheap and negative. It goes back to the ways of the stupid party." Gingrich added that Stockman's relationship with the supply-siders "wasn't a marriage; it was a date."

Stockman got most of his spending cuts approved by Reagan because he had moved at exceptional speed. He already had his list of cuts developed by the time of the inauguration, and so was able to build a consensus for them within the Administration before any opposition could mobilize. And Reagan usually went along when his staff was in agreement. Normally, the first line of resistance to budget cuts comes from the departments, but the new Cabinet secretaries were just finding their way around their offices and most of them knew nothing about their budgets. Their assistant secretaries, who normally would have the budget expertise, were in most cases not even appointed yet. So Stockman had a virtual free hand the first month of the new administration. He became, to a degree, a surrogate President. One White House official recalls a preinaugural Cabinet meeting at which Reagan pointed at Stockman and said, "He's going to work with you." The unspoken message was, "This guy is doing what I want. So cooperate."

To reinforce that message, Stockman put together a budget review process that was designed to intimidate the Cabinet officer and guarantee favorable action on his cuts. Stockman, Presidential Counselor Ed Meese, White House Chief of Staff Jim Baker, Council of Economic Advisers Chairman Murray Weidenbaum and Domestic Policy Adviser Marty Anderson formed the budget review committee. "They would sit on one side of a table, like the Spanish Inquisition, and we would bring the Cabinet secretary or secretary-designate with one or two new staffers and sit them down on the other side," says Don Moran. "And then we would open up our black books and slap them down in front of the Cabinet secretary. Let's say there were fourteen items within his jurisdiction. We would go through them one by one and explain our reasons and then ask him to show cause why they shouldn't be on the list. And most of the time they said, 'Hmmmmm, I don't know anything about this.' "

While the Cabinet members were revealing their ignorance, Stockman was dazzling them with his budgetary wizardry. A White House official adds: "In my opinion, Stockman was making almost all the decisions, and he was railroading them by most everybody else, including the President. We had a couple of sessions with the President in which Stockman, with lightning speed, would go page after page after page in these big black books in which Reagan would just be informed of what the decision was. And if he wanted to object, he could object, but he didn't. The Cabinet was in a similar position. Most of them didn't know crap about their departments." Round One was no contest. But the Cabinet would catch on to Stockman's game pretty quickly, and over the next four years of his tenure he would never again pull off what he accomplished in the first fifteen days of Reagan's first term.

Despite an occasional setback within the administration on one of his proposed cuts, things were going well for Stockman. He was on the verge of completing the largest assault on the federal government ever attempted; history was about to be made. But then, in early February, things started to fall apart. Stockman had been working so furiously to meet a February 18 deadline, when Reagan was to unveil details of his program, that he forgot to make sure everything was adding up properly. Working around the clock, Stockman and his staff had done an incredible job assembling budget cuts — they had come up with $41 billion of savings for 1982 and $74 billion for 1984. But when he finally got around to checking the totals, Stockman discovered an enormous gap. Two weeks before Reagan was to announce his proposals to the nation, Stockman finally ran everything through the computer and found that he was still $76 billion short of a balanced budget by 1984. He was stupefied. "He was semi-hysterical. He couldn't believe it," said Runne. Despite all his efforts at budget-cutting, he was only half-way to his 1984 goal. Then, one of those lucky breaks came along to help him out at the right time; possibly, it even saved the Reagan Revolution from failing before it could be launched.

Stockman had discovered his problem around the time that Murray Weidenbaum had come on board as chief White House economist and was raising a fuss about the economic forecast. Stockman's initial computer run had been based on the compromise he had brokered between the supply-siders and the monetarists. Weidenbaum, an economic eclectic, complained that the forecast was ridiculous in that it had inflation virtually disappearing within five years. So he demanded that the forecast for inflation be raised. Although the change would produce some glaring inconsistencies with other parts of the forecast, namely money growth, Weidenbaum and Stockman worked out new inflation assumptions and insisted that the other economic advisers go along. Stockman was desperate for final numbers because he was barely a week away from his deadline for producing a finished budget. But Weidenbaum's insistence on taking some of the pink out of Rosy Scenario's cheeks had a serendipitous result for Stockman—it put him closer to a balanced budget. Higher inflation means more tax revenues and the computer now said he was only some $40 billion short of his 1984 goal. Only.

It was too late to scrounge around for budget cuts big enough to fill gaps of that magnitude in a few days, and the President couldn't back down so soon on his balanced budget pledge. But Stockman figured he could hide the shortfall temporarily. He did that by showing a balanced budget for 1984, but with the help of several "plugs." One was a line that said "budget savings to be presented subsequently:" $21 billion in 1983 and $31 billion in 1984. (Senate Republicans later dubbed this "the magic asterisk.") Another plug was hidden under a line that said "smaller reductions that have been identified." Stockman later would laugh that they were "identified in our minds." Similar but smaller plugs were scattered throughout the budget plan, his aides later admitted. Stockman justified these tricks as a way to buy some time. He would come back later and really identify those savings so he really could balance the budget. He also knew that without the promise of a balanced budget, Congress would not go along with so many drastic spending reductions. So, Stockman figured a little duplicity in the short run would serve a noble purpose in the long run. He did not see all the telltale signs that his plan was unraveling. He was too busy keeping it together.

He had another last-minute problem to resolve well before the budget plan was unveiled by Reagan. Stockman had assembled an impressive list of cuts, but the package lacked a coherent theme and rationale for why so many programs should be reduced. So he came up with a set of principles—"illusions" as one OMB official called them—to justify the cuts. The criteria he settled on included: "to eliminate unintended benefits, reduce middle- and upper-income benefits, recover clearly allocatable costs from users, apply sound criteria to economic subsidy programs . . . and impose fiscal restraint on other programs of national interest."

This type of after-the-fact rationalization became a common practice at OMB, although Stockman and company always felt deep down that their free-market religion justified any budget cuts. "To put themes around it after the fact did seem intellectually dishonest," Susan Runne says, admitting a trace of guilt. But Lawrence Kudlow found the whole exercise amusing. "Moran, Stockman and I had a phrase for this, because we figured out what we had to do and then we figured out how to defend it. We called it 'post-hockery.' I don't know who coined that phrase, but we commonly referred to it among the three of us. There were two expressions that we used—'post-hockery' and 'agit-prop' [agitation-propaganda], as in Lenin and Trotsky. Those guys were great with agit-prop. Stockman would look down the table at me, and he would say, 'Kudlow, we need some agit-prop from your shop.' We'd figure out a campaign, we knew what we wanted to do. So now it's a question of selling it. But that agit-prop was for the big issues. You know, like if we wanted to whip up a little deficit scare, we'd need some agit-prop to do it."

In little more than two months since his designation as budget director Stockman had put together the most comprehensive and detailed overhaul of the federal budget ever attempted. Soon he would become a household name and famous face as the "point man" for Reaganomics. The Washington *Post* reported that at a February Cabinet meeting, fittingly Friday the Thirteenth, Stockman had finished a briefing on the budget cuts that would be unveiled the following week, and Reagan quipped: "We won't leave you out there alone, Dave. We'll all come to the hanging." Everyone got a big chuckle out of that. But at the same time, there was some handwriting going on in private. Edwin L. Harper, who had joined OMB as deputy budget director, warned Ed Meese about the large "unidentified savings plug" that had to be inserted into the budget plan at the last minute, and the dimming prospects for balancing the budget.

"I told Ed that even with all the cuts, we still were a long way from a balanced budget and we should be clear about that going in," Harper says. "I explained that it would be very difficult to achieve that objective and we should be going in with our eyes open. You and the President should be prepared for that."

The heroic budget battle that ensued that winter and spring of 1981 truly made David Stockman an overnight celebrity. He was a regular on television news, testifying at hearings, granting interviews or just scurrying from one meeting to another, head down, thick black books under his arm. His face dominated a cover of *Newsweek* magazine next to the words, "Cut, Slash, Chop." He was front-page copy in newspapers. He became an immediate favorite of cartoonists who would embellish his big glasses, pointed nose and prominent adam's apple and portray him as the Grim Reaper, Darth Vader, and Hooded Executioner. He became the villainous target of every group in the country upset with the cuts being proposed. Senator Howard Metzenbaum, a liberal Democrat from Ohio, assailed him as an evil genius. "I think you've been brilliant. But I also think you've been cruel, inhumane and unfair," Metzenbaum thundered as Stockman sat facing him at a Senate Budget Committee hearing on March 12. Metzenbaum was dead serious.

While his enemies were creating the image of Stockman as heartless hatchman, his supporters were creating another as the brilliant budgetmeister who would save the country. And they had a lot to work

338

with. Stockman could do something rarely seen in Washington: he could go before any audience and argue an articulate and statistics-filled case for actually taking something away from voters. He was effective because he spoke from both deep conviction and broad knowledge.

It was true, as his critics charged, that he was seeking reductions in programs benefitting the poor, the disabled and the unemployed. Medicaid payments to states would be capped. Social Security minimum benefits would be eliminated and student benefits and disability insurance would be restricted. Extended unemployment insurance would be limited. Trade Adjustment Assistance for workers idled by foreign competition would be sharply curtailed. Eligibility requirements for food stamps and general welfare (Aid to Families with Dependent Children) would be tightened. Public service jobs under the Comprehensive Employment and Training Act would be phased out. Legal services for the poor would be eliminated. And the list went on. He argued that the "truly needy" would not be hurt; that for many of these programs, spending would still increase but at a lower rate; that those most affected would be the people who were not really supposed to qualify in the first place: and that even if some deserving low-income people were to suffer a loss of benefits (which later studies proved to be true), they would be better off on balance because of the improved economic conditions the program would bring, namely lower inflation and more jobs. Ever since his boyhood visits to Benton Harbor, Stockman felt convinced that the answer to the problems of the poor involved three elements: the federal government had to provide an equal opportunity for economic advancement, the individual had to provide the personal incentive to work for it, and the local community had a primary responsibility for helping those who could not escape. A government handout fulfilled none of those conditions and government efforts to mandate equality was totalitarianism. He felt strongly about this, and so long as he kept his mind on the abstract overview without focusing on any individual victims, he could withstand the barrage of attacks without feeling guilty.

If he sounded righteous, it was because he felt he had balanced cuts in programs for the poor with cuts in programs benefitting middle-income, high-income and business groups. Upper-income families would be barred from receiving subsidized school lunches and low-interest student loans. The budget for underwriting the arts and humanities would be cut. Postal Service subsidies would be eliminated. Low-interest loans for foreign customers of major exporting corporations would be cut back. Synthetic fuel demonstration projects would be scrapped. Lending programs to farmers would be curbed. Subsidies for electric utilities and water-treatment plants would be reduced. Stockman was proud of these program cuts because they represented in his mind all the worst offenders in the Social Pork Barrel. That is, except for the Pentagon. But the President had insisted on doubling the military budget over the next five years, and Stockman went along without questioning it.

Although Stockman was able to include many previous untouchables among his domestic budget

cuts, he had to accept a few select political considerations and pass over some programs that he had
opposed as a member of Congress. The most conspicuous of these was his proposal to continue funding
the Clinch River Breeder Reactor in Tennessee. The
new Senate Majority Leader, Howard Baker of Tennessee, liked the project for obvious reasons, and
Stockman knew that without Baker's support his
budget would be headed for the bottom of the Clinch
River.

Stockman, as mentioned, may not have been a very
effective practitioner of politics himself, but he had a
thorough understanding of how the political process
worked regarding the budget—certainly more than
any senior member of the Administration—and that
knowledge gave him enormous power during the first
half of 1981. In prior administrations the President
would send his budget proposals to Congress and
then essentially abandon them to the legislative
branch, where all the powers to tax and spend reside.
Stockman appreciated the constitutional separation
of powers. He knew that the President may be
Commander-in-Chief of the armed forces, but he was
a powerless chief over the budget. To get his sweeping
reforms through, Stockman began working on a daily
basis with Republican leaders in Congress. A budget
director had never gotten so involved in the congressional process before. It was as if he were trying to
create an ad hoc parliamentary system under which
the ruling party both administered and legislated. For
months Stockman operated literally as a one-man
link between the two branches of government. Had
he not played that role, the Reagan budget would

341

never have become law.

Predictably, the Democrats who controlled the House lambasted the plan as both an attack on the poor and a phony balanced budget plan based on absurd economic assumptions. Senate Democrats said the same thing, and the nonpartisan Congressional Budget Office reported that the Administration had underestimated the 1982 deficit by $20 billion to $25 billion—a mistake that Stockman later wished were only that small. The Republicans who controlled the Senate grudgingly went along with Stockman's budget forecast even though many of them were privately saying that it was pure fantasy; they simply had nowhere else to go. Stockman's strategy from the outset was to tie all the cuts together in one package, rush it through the Senate and pick up enough conservative Democrats in the House to ram it past the Democratic leadership, which was certain to oppose the plan. The package had to be kept intact as much as possible to prevent each parochial interest from picking it apart until there was nothing left. It also was vital that the program be enacted very quickly while the Republicans were still feeling the mandate of the 1980 election. In one of those strange twists of fate, the assassination attempt on Reagan's life on March 30 gave the Administration a surge of popularity at a critical moment and may have provided Stockman the edge he needed to squeeze through the House three months later.

Stockman's guardian angel during this period— and his chief congressional ally for the next four years—was Senator Pete Domenici, a Republican from New Mexico who had become chairman of the

Senate Budget Committee. Domenici and Stockman saw eye to eye on just about every budget issue except synthetic fuel research subsidies, a program Domenici had helped create and Stockman had always attacked. As personalities, they made a strange team. Domenici, outgoing and sociable, was always trying to get Stockman to slow down and share some pizza and beer with him in his Senate office. Stockman was always the whirling dervish, too wound up to relax.

"I think the first time Domenici put his arm around him, I thought Stockman was going to crawl back into his shell," says Steve Bell, staff director of Domenici's committee. "But to Stockman's credit, although those visits may have been painful at first, I think they became very comfortable at the end. At the beginning Stockman said to himself, 'This is a person I probably wouldn't choose to deal with in a perfect world, but I will drink this guy's beer and have a sip of white wine.' And I think the thing that broke the ice with Stockman was that Domenici was willing to spend more time on details and numbers than almost any other senator you could imagine. Then Domenici would take the numbers to other senators and, in his inimitable fashion, say, 'We got to do this cause it's the right thing to do and, goddammit, here are the numbers. Now, aren't these the numbers? You go back and ask your staff if these aren't the numbers. We got to do something.' "

Domenici and Bell worked in close partnership with Stockman and gave him some key advice. It was Bell, for example, who had suggested in late December of 1980 that Stockman package the budget cuts using "reconciliation," an arcane legislative rule that had been employed only once before on a far more limited scale. Basically, reconciliation was an enforcement mechanism that required congressional committees to comply with spending ceilings.

Stockman also had a secret weapon in his mastery of the budget numbers, a skill members of Congress had seen in some lower-level OMB examiners and congressional staff assistants but not in a Cabinet level officer with Stockman's power. Indeed, Stockman functioned like a budget examiner or staff assistant. He wrote his own speeches and testimony, compiled his own statistical tables, prepared his own graphics, and consulted directly with his examiners and congressional staffers. He did not bother with the customary practice of dealing only with other department "heads" or members of Congress befitting his status. Never willing to abandon the academic lifestyle, Stockman would spend hours alone at his desk in the old Executive Office Building preparing lengthy briefing papers and books that provided political and economic justifications for his budget cuts. His large second-floor office, with its high ceilings, sculptured moldings, parquet floors and unused fireplace, had the appearance of a professor's study, with shelves of black binders covering the walls, papers and books scattered everywhere and legal-size pads with his scribblings littered about his work table. In his oral presentations Stockman rattled off one statistic after another. "That absolutely snows senators," said Steve Bell. It also snowed members of the House, Reagan, the senior White House staff and most of the Cabinet, although the tactic wore a little thin after a while.

Stockman was quite conscious of this ability of his and he used it well. Most of his high-level counterparts depended on their staffs for details, and Stockman knew he could easily intimidate a department head with his statistical barrages. A kind of mythology grew up that he was literally a walking computer of budget numbers. Actually he sometimes faked it when the real numbers failed him or when he needed an example to make a case that he had not anticipated. "He could be very glib with numbers," says Alice Rivlin, former director of the Congressional Budget Office. Rivlin is a great admirer of Stockman, yet she discovered that "he's not quite as good as he's cracked up to be. People get bowled over easily with numbers, and he knew that. But if you question him, you find out that the numbers did not always add up." A former White House official who was a bitter rival of Stockman notes: "I always suspected he made some things up because he knew his audiences generally didn't know squat and he could get away with it. But you could catch him at meetings and he'd laugh and say, 'Okay. Okay.' He was the charming rogue." Paul Gilman, Domenici's administrative assistant, recalls attending a meeting with Republican senators at which Stockman was hurling numbers about the synthetic fuels program with such rhetorical force that Senator James McClure, a Republican from Idaho, appeared to lean back in his seat to escape the onslaught. But when Stockman tried to blame the Carter administration for a program funded under Reagan, Gilman interrupted him and said, "That's not correct." Stockman said nothing in reply. "He would never say, 'You're right' or 'I was wrong,' " says

Gilman.

If Stockman occasionally faked some numbers in those first months, he could rationalize it away as a small price to pay for a giant cause to which he was dedicating his life. Continually operating in high gear, which seemed to be his only speed, he worked eighteen to twenty hours a day, every day, and survived on fast-food cheeseburgers, potfuls of coffee and cigarettes. He would be up at four or five o'clock in the morning, just like he was back on the farm, to do some reading or start writing a speech. Breakfast was in the OMB conference room, where his senior staff would meet each morning at 7:30 for coffee and "Doughnuts with Dave." After that it was an endless day and night of shuttling back and forth from his office to the White House to Capitol Hill. "We lived on cheeseburgers and barbecue potato chips," says former legislative aide J. L. Cullen, who clung to his side throughout those early months. "One time, when we were driving back from the Hill, both of our stomachs growled at the same time. We couldn't remember the last time we had eaten, and we broke up laughing."

By April, even as Stockman was making progress converting Congress to his budget cuts, Wall Street was expressing a lack of faith in his plan. On April 22 Henry Kaufman, the seer of Salomon Brothers, declared the program would result in huge deficits, not a balanced budget. The result, Kaufman said, would be a continuation of high inflation and a rise in interest rates along a "rocket trajectory." The next day Stockman — who would much later become Kaufman's colleague at Salomon — tried to rebut the widely followed economist. But investors listened to Kaufman. The stock and bond markets fell and interest rates rose. So much for the "rational expectations" turnaround theory on which Stockman's entire budget plan had been premised. The rational expectation that moved Wall Street in the spring of 1981 was that the deficit would get bigger, not smaller, and that belief became a self-fulfilling prophecy through worsening economic conditions.

Privately, Stockman must have known Kaufman was right about the deficit forecast. Internal estimates prepared by the Senate Budget Committee were showing a 1982 deficit running nearly double Stockman's official target of $45 billion. Starting April 1, at Domenici's instructions Steve Bell would have his staff prepare a deficit update every month for the Senate Republican leadership. "And every month," Bell says, "I had to walk into Howard Baker's office and sit down and say, 'Hello, Mr. Leader.' And he'd say, 'Hello, Steve. What's the deficit?' I'd say, 'Well, sir, I believe right now our forecast is that it will be at least $80 billion.' And after a couple of months, Mr. Baker would say, 'Steve, how come every time I see you it's bad news?' I'd say, I don't know, Mr. Leader.' "

The Budget Committee's rising deficit estimate was, in fact, on the optimistic side, assuming as it did passage of all the Reagan budget cuts. By May, Bell recalls, "Domenici would call up Stockman and say, 'Jesus Christ, David, these numbers are getting out of control.' And Stockman would say, 'Yes, I know.' " So Stockman came up with two solutions: scale back the size of the tax cut and cut Social Security out of

347

the Safety Net. Both attempts failed, and the Social Security episode turned into the biggest political fiasco of Reagan's first term.

Ever since February 1981, when he came up so short of the savings he needed to balance the budget, Stockman knew that the only way to get the big bucks he needed was to go after the big programs in the Safety Net. Social Security, which accounted for 20 percent of the entire budget, was the obvious candidate. There even was some bipartisan support on the Senate Budget Committee in March 1981 to freeze the cost-of-living increase in Social Security and other federal pension programs for one year, a move that would have saved nearly $4 billion in the first year. But Reagan was adamantly opposed because of his campaign pledge. Congressional Budget Office chief Alice Rivlin had made the same point to Stockman at the time. "I called him up and said, 'You're really missing a chance here. You've got to get Social Security COLAs [cost-of-living allowances] into your package.' He sort of agreed in principle but said it wouldn't be necessary because once they got inflation down rapidly, it wouldn't save much. I said, 'Dave, you don't really believe that,' and he said, yes, he did, and he also noted the President's commitment." What Rivlin didn't know was that he had a much bigger plan in mind for Social Security.

Apart from his work on the budget in early 1981, Stockman was involved in an administration group studying ways to restructure the giant retirement system, which was becoming insolvent. Democratic

Congressman J. J. Pickle of Texas, chairman of a House Social Security subcommittee, was seeking to bail the system out temporarily by using general revenues and raising the full retirement age from sixty-five to sixty-eight. But Pickle also had assured the administration he would give a responsible alternate plan a fair hearing if the President produced it soon. Richard Schweiker, Secretary of Health and Human Services, interpreted that as being a Democratic pledge to work in a bipartisan manner with the administration, and not to exploit it for political gain. With that assurance Schweiker, Stockman, Meese, Marty Anderson and John A. Svahn, then the Commissioner of Social Security, headed up a task force that would produce an alternative. Although the ostensible objective was to make the plan self-sufficient again, Stockman made it clear to the group that he saw Social Security's problems as an opportunity to achieve major budget savings.

As Social Security experts briefed the group on the various trend lines and statistics, one particular trend jumped out at Stockman — two out of three recipients were taking early retirement rather than waiting until age sixty-five. Far above any other factor, this development was throwing the system into the red. Stockman and the others agreed that the trend represented a de facto cut in the retirement age to sixty-two, against the intentions of Congress, and which had allowed benefits to be paid out before age sixty-five at only a slightly reduced level. If early retirement benefits were cut back more, fewer people would retire early and the regular retirement age of sixty-five would be restored. The cutbacks also would produce enormous savings. So the group agreed to reduce early retirement pensions from 80 percent of full benefits under the current law to 55 percent. That would mean a cut in monthly benefits from about $470 to $311, and it would take immediate effect because Stockman wanted the savings right away. That change became the centerpiece of a Social Security reform package that included a reduction in the payroll tax, a three-month delay in payment of cost-of-living increases and a phaseout of benefit limits imposed on retirees with outside income. The obvious flaw in the proposal was the immediate cut in early retirement benefits. It was considered unfair to change the rules abruptly, to tell someone who was sixty-one and preparing to retire the next year that the benefits he or she had planned on would be sliced by $160 a month. In retrospect, top administration officials acknowledge that they blundered badly in not sufficiently recognizing that inequity.

But Martin Anderson went along: "We thought if we could have a chance to explain it, it would sound reasonable. We would point out how we were making the system sound and reducing taxes a teeny-weeny bit." Svahn and Meese went along too. So did Schweiker, although he later claims he raised a red flag, a warning the others do not recall. "I argued several times that it was too abrupt and severe but I didn't push it," says Schweiker, who left the Cabinet in 1983 to become head of the American Council of Life Insurance. "In retrospect, I should have pursued it. We should have done it over time to cushion people, but Stockman was really adamant because of the budget. He wanted to do it at once. He wouldn't have it phased in over five, ten years because he wanted the savings." Indeed, the benefit reductions would total as estimated $46 billion over five years.

So they all agreed to it.

The political and public relations operators in the White House—namely Jim Baker and Mike Deaver— knew the Social Security task force was meeting but did not pay much attention—which they would deeply regret. "We invited them early on to sit in on the discussions but they glossed over it," Schweiker says. "Baker was always too busy to come. But .we always informed him and invited him through the final process. . . . I wish those people had sat in on our meetings."

Jim Baker finally focused on the plan on Saturday, May 9, 1981, three days before the proposed announcement. Baker, who thought all five members of the task force were politically inept, couldn't believe what they were telling him. Stockman and Schweiker were arguing that they had adequate "political coverage" because Pickle had asked for a proposal. "I think you guys have been smoking dope if you think this is going to fly," Baker replied. But Stockman and Schweiker insisted that they had been up to the Hill and felt confident the Democrats would not "demagogue" them on the issue. Marty Anderson, Schweiker, Stockman and David Gergen, the White House director of communications, then made the case that it was essential for the Great Communicatora, Ronald Reagan, to sell it personally with one or more major television speeches. Otherwise, Stockman and Schweiker warned, the proposal would be a "big turkey." But Baker and Deaver said there was no way they would let Reagan near the package. Baker reluctantly agreed to go ahead and put the proposals out only because they had gone this far, but he said Schweiker would have to be the front man and Reagan would be kept a safe distance away.

The President first learned of the plan on Monday morning, May 11, during a twenty-minute briefing. Schweiker said that was standard operating procedure. "Reagan wouldn't get briefed until a day or two before something was released," he said. Baker and Deaver warned Reagan that they did not think the proposal would fly, but his reaction, according to one eyewitness, was, "Well, gosh, fellows. It was a unanimous recommendation." So on Tuesday, May 12, Schweiker, feeling a little like Marie Antoinette on the way to the guillotine, publicly unveiled the plan. To no one's surprise, it bombed with the political force of a hydrogen blast. Pickle was restrained in his criticism and promised to look at the plan. It was just as Stockman and Schweiker had said, but they forgot about all the other Democrats, who howled with outrage. House Speaker Thomas P.. O'Neill, Jr., of Massachusetts called it "a rotten thing to do" and vowed to fight it "every inch of the way." A week later the Senate adopted a resolution by a unanimous 96-0 vote promising not to "precipitously and unfairly penalize early retirees." Svahn says he got a telephone call late one night from a sixty-two-year-old man in California who was just getting ready to retire and would be caught in the proposed change: "He called me every name in the book, said I was a goddammed bureaucrat, and said he might even change his name. Then he said, 'No, you change yours.' And I said,

'But, Dad . . .' "

The proposal died quickly and Reagan would forever afterward be loath to touch Social Security except with prior bipartisan agreement. That fall he publicly disowned any intention of cutting retirees' benefits and even backed down from his earlier proposal to eliminate minimum Social Security benefits, one of the cuts in Stockman's original package. To solve the system's financial woes, Reagan appointed a bipartisan commission that proposed correcting the problem mainly by raising payroll taxes. In 1983 the recommendations were approved by Congress and signed by Reagan. But the original experience left everyone in the White House deathly afraid of Social Security, except Stockman. "Jim Baker became almost catatonic on the subject," says Don Moran. Steve Bell added wryly: "It sort of became like high-level radioactive waste. You touch it and you glow and you die."

Over the next four years Stockman would try again and again to cut Social Security, and fail. "There were at least three or four other instances where he argued we should do something about it, and we would say no dice," says one former top White House official. "And I'm sure he feels strongly that we were wrong." Another Administration official notes, "On Social Security, David Stockman has a blind spot."

The Social Security incident revealed a fundamental mistake in strategy that Stockman would repeat throughout his tenure at OMB. By playing the revolutionary instead of the gradualist, he only set back his cause. In his obsessive drive to reduce the deficit, he gambled on a bold course that wound up oversensitizing Reagan to Social Security and discouraging him from doing anything in the future. Had Stockman pursued a more cautious course in the short term, he might have achieved greater Social Security savings in the long run. In later years he would admit that he should have gone after the cost-of-living allowances, as Alice Rivlin had suggested, but he still failed to see why he had not done so. "That should have been done in the original package," he said in a 1984 interview with the author. "I can't remember why we didn't. It just doesn't make sense now."

After the Social Security firestorm, Stockman realized further deficit reductions on the spending side of the budget had been closed off. "When that thing blew up, I really panicked," he admitted. He was not at all elated by the Administration's first-round victory for its budget cuts in the House just the week before, on May 7. Reagan had declared the House vote a "resounding victory" over Democratic leaders. But Stockman knew that the $42 billion in budget savings that had been approved for 1982 were not nearly enough. He could go after some of the other programs in the Safety Net, but that still wouldn't do the trick. His only remaining hope was to limit the tax cut.

On May 14, 1981, just two days after the Social Security blowup, the New York *Times* carried a story in which an unnamed "senior White House official" said the President was worried about the drop in financial markets and therefore was prepared to accept a scaled-back tax cut if Democrats in Congress would make the first move toward compromise. That was news to the President. It also was news to Treasury Secretary Donald Regan and his supply-side assistants who were in charge of shepherding the President's tax plan through Congress. Regan was enraged and suspected immediately that the "official" who had put out that word was Stockman. His hunch was right. Stockman later admitted he had talked to the *Times* reporter, although he claimed the reporter had only asked him to confirm the story, which allegedly had been obtained from someone else first. Regan, who was supposed to be the administration's chief economics spokesman, disliked Stockman — so young, so sure of himself — and he resented the way the budget director had upstaged him in the news media. Regan was amazed that Stockman could be so brazen as to float a trial balloon on his own when the orders from the White House were to get the President's tax bill through Congress without compromise.

Unlike spending cuts, which take something away, tax cuts are easy to get through Congress because they give something away. Stockman knew a tax bill would pass that summer; the only question in his mind was, how big and how damaging to the deficit? The Democrats were talking about a similar but smaller tax cut, and Stockman worked behind the scenes to get the White House to compromise on a bipartisan bill with Congressman Dan Rostenkowski, an Illinois Democrat and chairman of the House Ways and Means Committee. He knew that many of the traditional Republicans who had leadership positions in the Senate, such as Domenici and Finance Committee Chairman Bob Dole of Kansas, shared his concern about the deficit and favored a scaled-down version of Reagan's tax cut. But Ronald Reagan, Jim Baker, Ed Meese and Mike Deaver were feeling their oats. They sensed political momentum on their side. They wanted to go for an all-out victory on their terms and stick it to the Democrats in the House. "It became a pure macho thing for those guys," says one White House official involved in the tax strategy discussions. "They felt the Democrats were disorganized and they wanted to win." The president wanted his three-year tax cut.

So in early June, to Stockman's dismay, the White House put together the same majority coalition of House Republicans and conservative "Boll Weevil" Democrats that had supported Reagan's spending cuts. But to win the Boll Weevil's support the White House had to modify the bill slightly. Instead of a 30 percent cut in individual tax rates over three years, beginning in July, Reagan agreed to a 25 percent cut in rates spread over thirty-three months, beginning in October. In addition, tax breaks for businesses were reduced somewhat. The conservative Democrats had pressed for a smaller tax cut because they, too, were worried about the effect on the deficit. Stockman was pleased with the smaller tax cut, but he would have been happier had the White House gone along with House Democratic leaders, who had countered with a 15 percent tax-rate cut over two years. His hope was that the Democrats would save Reagan from himself. Meanwhile, at the Treasury Department, Don Regan and his team were steaming over reports they kept getting from Capitol Hill that Stockman was maneuvering behind the scenes on behalf of the Democratic tax bill. It was bad enough that he was poaching on their territory, but that he had the audacity to pursue his own policy agenda instead of the president's left Regan, the consummate team player, flabbergasted.

In late June Stockman had to forget about the tax bill for a while to concentrate on guiding the budget cuts through Congress. Congress had approved the cuts in theory, under the budget resolution it passed in May, but it still had to pass a law that implemented the savings. The enforcing bill was dubbed "Gramm-Latta II," after its House sponsors, Texas Democrat Phil Gramm and Ohio Republican Delbert Latta. The measure passed the Senate easily, but the fight in the House was ferocious, and Stockman, in a last-minute flurry of negotiations, had to oil a few squeaking wheels. Moderate and liberal Republicans from the northeast—the "Gypsy Moths"—won some extra money for Conrail, student loans, Medicaid and mass transit operating subsidies as the price for their support. The Clinch River Breeder Reactor got some more money to win over Tennessee congressmen. And to sweeten the pot for some Southern congressmen, Stockman had to go against his free-market principles and cut a deal on a new price-support program for sugar. The congressmen said Reagan had personally promised them the sugar program. Out of that frenetic trading session came a classic quote from Congressman John Breaux, a Democrat from Louisiana. When asked if his vote was bought with sugar price supports, he said: "I can't be bought, but I can be rented."

As a result of these last-minute changes, the budget cuts became more heavily targeted on programs for the poor—the weakest of the special interests. That imbalance, together with tax cuts that gave the largest breaks to upper-income groups, gave rise to the "fairness issue"—charges that the Administration's policies unfairly benefited the rich at the expense of the poor. Several studies confirmed this argument statistically. The accusation troubled Stockman, who saw fairness as one of his guiding principles. And so for the next four years Stockman would crusade for tax increases and spending cuts which would hit middle- and upper-income groups. Most of the time, he would fail. ·

The final vote in the House on June 26 was a cliffhanger. Reagan was on the phone lobbying wavering members, and Democratic leaders were warning that members did not even know what they were voting on. As evidence, they pointed to a copy of the two-inch-thick book containing the bill's provisions. Normally, bills are neatly printed and organized for careful consideration, but Gramm-Latta II was a mess. It had been put together in the wrong order. Pages were heavily edited with handwritten insertions. Numbers were crossed out and replaced with handwritten ones. Paragraphs were crossed out or scribbled over. On one crossed-out page was typed "Source: CBO, Rita Seymour, June 5, 1981, 225-4844." It was the first time the telephone number of a Congressional Budget Office analyst had made it into a major piece of legislation. House Republicans blamed the sorry condition of the bill on Democrats who had requested to look at the amended version the night before. The Republicans said the Democrats mixed up all the provisions and got the bill to the government printing office too late for it to be printed properly. So it had to be reproduced by photo offset, which left in all the mistakes. The bill, messy appearance and all, squeaked through the House by a vote of 217 to 211. Twenty-nine Democrats joined the Republicans to pass the measure, which Stockman estimated would save about $38 billion in 1982. Ironically, the final printed version of the bill that went to Reagan for his signature inadvertently had left out the pro forma line that would put it into effect: "Therefore, be it enacted." But the Republicans, when they later caught the technical slip, kept their mouths shut. Why invite trouble?

Stockman should have been elated with passage of Gram-Latta II. It was an unprecedented political achievement; no one had successfully cut back the social pork barrel before. He was potent. His longtime friend Richard Straus was so impressed that even he started to look in awe at Stockman. But Stockman did not have the time to become impressed with himself. He knew the budget cuts were not nearly large enough to solve his problems, and he continued to hope that the Reagan tax cut would be scaled back.

One opportunity to reduce the tax cut came and went in June. By law, OMB was required to issue a new budget outlook in mid-July based on updated economic forecasts. Stockman's economist, Larry Kudlow, had turned bearish about the economy and wanted to replace Rosy Scenario with a gloomier forecast. But that would have meant that, instead of predicting a balanced budget at the end of the rainbow, the administration would be predicting record deficits — exceeding $100 billion by 1984. If such a forecast came out just before final congressional action on the tax bill, Congress would be so alarmed it would scale back the tax cut, perhaps even drop it. Not surprisingly, the supply-siders at Treasury were adamant in their opposition to Kudlow's forecast. They were still bullish and, if anything, wanted to make the forecast rosier. Kudlow remembers a June meeting of economic advisers and White House officials in Jim Baker's office at which he and Jerry Jordan, a member of the Council of Economic Advisers, made the same argument: "Number one, we were heading for a recession. Number two, the whole foundation of deficit projections was going to be knocked out from under us. Number three, we'd better deal with that. And we lost. We lost because we would have lost the tax bill. That's why we were defeated. Treasury won. Treasury was predicting a strong recovery in '81."

In our 1984 interview, Stockman said of that battle:

"I think we can be forgiven the February forecast, because it wasn't much different than CBO [congressional budget office]. But the July one we can't. We should have started signaling right then and there that these numbers from the outset were very bad, and I wanted a much lower, much less optimistic economy. So did Murray Weidenbaum. But that is where Don Regan asserted himself for the first time, prodded along by Craig Roberts [assistant Treasury secretary and a supply-sider], and we put out a forecast in July that was identical to what we had in February. So the deficit numbers didn't move. If you had come up in July with a big deterioration in the numbers, things might have turned out a little differently at the end of the month, when the tax bill was passed. If you want a real turning point, if we had put out a forecast in July that reflected what conventional economists were predicting for the next two or three years for the economy at that time, you would have had such big deficits suddenly appearing out of nowhere in '82, '83 and '84 that you would have probably gotten a different outcome from the tax law. It would have been less fat."

What Stockman was saying, and everyone in Washington knew, is that administration budget plans are marketing strategies for their political objectives. The White House had to promise a balanced budget not only to win the tax cut but to win the spending cuts too. Congress needed to offer constituents a salve for the pain it was inflicting on them in the form of budget reductions; the tax cut and the promise of a balanced budget provided the medicinal relief. Without a balanced budget in prospect, many members of Congress would have figured the spending cuts were not worth the political trouble. In fact, that became the congressional attitude over the next four years, when it was clear that a balanced budget was not obtainable. What made Reagan's budget unique from those of prior administrations was not the political deception itself but the enormous discrepancy between what was promised and what actually happened.

White House officials said that they stuck with the forecast for both the obvious political reason and because there was such a divergence of opinions among economic advisers over the course of the economy. By late June, no one knew for sure that a recession was coming. A month later, after the tax cut passed, they knew for sure.

On July 15, 1981, OMB published its "Mid-session Review of the 1982 Budget." It predicted that the Reagan economic plan would produce robust economic growth, lower inflation, falling interest rates, a drop in unemployment, a balanced budget by 1984 and a $28 billion surplus by 1986. It even predicted a slightly lower deficit for 1982 — $42.5 billion rather than the $45 billion figure published in the original plan. The OMB forecast gave Congress the green light to go ahead and cut taxes. Congress went at it with a frenzy.

What emerged was a bidding war between the administration and House Democratic leaders for votes. Each side was willing to add on special, narrow-interest tax breaks sought by members as the price for their support. In the process, the tax cuts got larger and larger. For Stockman, that meant less and less revenue. But that was *his* problem: the Treasury Secretary had a different objective.

"My task was to identify which of those things we could accept [that] would be good for the economy, and nobody in the White House wanted to hear what the drain on the revenue was," Donald Regan said in a 1984 interview. "It was that 'The President has to win. This is his first big test, and it's us against them.' We had to have the Boll Weevils, who were extracting things. I remember one saying, 'Oh, you've got to do this for the oil people.' We had other things in there for cotton farmers. God, what we didn't put into that bill . . . On the face of it, each proposition was a good one. But it just became a real grab-bag, everybody seeking his own little package and finally the thing got to where we had enough votes to buy it. So we bought it. The President could look at the list . . . and see most of them were in the Republican platform of 1980. So therefore, he could accept them.

"But it was an awful big apple that we swallowed whole. All I knew was that it was a wonderful party and some day there was going to be a hangover. But who cared? I mean, you're in the middle of a party. Everybody's enjoying it. My job was to win." But within a few weeks, Regan added ruefully, "people began to realize that the party's over."

The Reagan tax bill cleared both houses of Congress on July 29. The final version, the biggest tax cut in history, was estimated to cut revenue by about $750 billion over the next five years. That was "only" $50 billion higher than Reagan had proposed in February. But in two other ways it proved to be a much larger tax cut. One late addition was a provision that automatically indexed tax rates to inflation, starting in 1985, so that people would not be pushed into higher tax rates simply because inflation swelled their income. Indexing, in effect, became a permanent tax cut that would grow in size each year. The other difference was that the tax cut proved to be larger than planned relative to the size of the economy. The original program was intended to reduce taxes to just below 20 percent of the gross national product (GNP). Instead, taxes fell below 19 percent of GNP.

With the passage of the tax bill Stockman's worst fears were confirmed by Kudlow, who was running new deficit estimates through the OMB computer

363

based on indications of a coming recession. "The numbers started coming out that we were looking at deficits of $100 billion, $125 billion, up to $150 billion by 1982," says Kudlow. "In other works, the deficit wasn't going to come down from $60 billion to $40 billion, it was going up to $150 billion. Stockman's reaction was horror and then belief. He just looked at me and said, 'It's this bad?' And I said, Given the assumption of a recession, it's this bad.' Then we had meetings. The question was, how deep is the recession going to be? It was clear it was going to be worse than we thought it was going to be."

While the boys at the White House were whooping it up over their stunning political victories, Stockman was feeling depressed. Not only was his budget plan suffering from too few spending cuts and too big a tax cut, but the whole program was about to be clobbered by what would prove to be the worst recession since the 1930s, when FDR launched the New Deal to counter the Great Depression. Stockman and the rest of the Administration had paid too little attention to what was going on at the Federal Reserve Board. Chairman Paul Volcker, alarmed by the enormous deficits he saw in Reagan's original budget plan, decided the nation's central bank would have to fight inflation by itself. So he slammed down the credit brakes, drove interest rates up and forced the economy to grind to a halt. Instead of the sunny skies promised by Rosy Scenario, Volcker produced a cloudburst.

Until the tax cuts passed Congress Stockman, by his own admission, refused to believe the obvious. Tip O'Neill, Henry Kaufman and Pete Domenici had been warning all along that the big tax cut would cause a huge deficit. Yet Stockman kept convincing himself that somehow he would find a way to overcome his budgetary problems and things would work out in the end. He was not one to back away from a tough challenge. Now there was no way to avoid the fact that the government was headed for the biggest deficit in the country's history, and Stockman felt responsible. "Dave became more and more concerned with the deficit," says former White House Official David Gergen. "In a sense, it became a cross to bear."

During the first week of August, just before Reagan headed for a long summer vacation at his California ranch, where he would sign the tax and budget cuts into law, Stockman broke the bad news at a White House meeting. As he remembered it:

"We had a briefing which was ostensibly the introductory briefing for the fall decision process on the '82 budget. I shocked everybody and said that we were looking at $70-80 billion deficits and that we're going to have to do far more draconian things than we've done already, and everybody screamed. The President had won his tax battle, was getting ready for vacation, and I laid this thing on him. I think you may have observed a reaction of general shock [in Reagan] to the same degree as Meese or Baker or anybody else who was paying attention. Then I went through it all. I said we are going to have to think about three choices for next fall. Do we slow down our defense buildup? Do we take back some of our tax cuts? Or do we forget a balanced budget in 1984? I even had a little scenario where you can get it balanced in '86. They said no. They didn't say what to do. They just said, 'No. We're not giving up on a balanced budget. No way can we give up on a balanced budget in '84.' That was the one firm thing that came out of it. The President said, 'You guys go to work.' "

Stockman interpreted that as a signal to look for cuts in the Defense Department budget and new sources of revenue.

One other thing that Reagan said at the meeting stuck out in Stockman's mind:

"The only time I ever heard him doubt the program was a statement he made after I finished that briefing. He said, 'If all this was true, maybe Tip O'Neill was right.' "

CHAPTER 10

FALL FROM
GRACE

November 10, 1981: the day David Stockman reached his biblical half-life was filled with surprises.

The first came that Tuesday morning during his weekly breakfast at the Treasury Department. Donald Regan surprised him with a birthday cake decorated with thirty-five pink plastic hatchets. Regan also gave him a green T-shirt with white letters that proclaimed "I AM A TEAM PLAYER" on the front and "TREASURY DEPARTMENT SUPPLY-SIDERS" on the back. Within twenty-four hours Regan would see a terrible irony in his gift, but that morning the Treasury secretary was thinking about repairing the strained relationship that had developed between him and the budget director during their fight over the tax cut the previous summer. Regan, a sociable type who frequently wrote thoughtful notes or sent gifts to Administration officials and their families, detected some embarrassment creeping over Stockman's face. Perhaps it was because the budget director realized how thoughtless he was when it came to little personal touches. In Regan's eyes Stockman should have felt ashamed for the way he knifed the Treasury Secretary during the tax battle.

The next surprise came that afternoon when CBS White House correspondent Lesley Stahl called Stockman's public affairs director, Ed Dale.

"I have to talk to Stockman. Do you know about the *Atlantic Monthly*?" she said.

"Oh, God! Is it out?" Dale replied.

"Yes, and I need some comment from him."

Dale said he had not seen it and would have to get it. Actually, a copy of the magazine had arrived at Stockman's office earlier that day and was sitting in the middle of a thick stack of mail, but no one knew it at the time. Dale rushed across the hall to the director's office.

"The *Atlantic Monthly*'s out," he said.

"Well, get it," Stockman told him.

Dale called the Washington *Post* to obtain a copy of the magazine from assistant managing editor William Greider. Stockman had confided to Dale in September that Greider was writing an article about the year's budget battle's, but Stockman did not know exactly when it would be coming out. Dale remembered Stockman expressing concern about the contents of the piece, but that was the last time they had discussed it until now. Greider had told Stockman that the article would be published in December and had promised to send galley proofs to the budget director before publication. He did not know mail subscribers began receiving their copies so soon.

Greider, who had just received the galleys himself, rushed a set off to OMB late that afternoon while Stockman was at the White House for a meeting. In a cover letter accompanying the galleys, Greider wrote, "I'm sorry I didn't get these to you sooner. I didn't know the subscriptions would go out so quickly." Margaret Suzor, one of Stockman's personal assistants, started flipping through the article and immediately knew trouble was brewing. She gave it to David Gerson. He paled while glancing through it, and then rushed off to make photo-copies, a job he normally would delegate to an assistant.

Stockman had another surprise waiting for him when he returned from the White House. His staff had arranged a little surprise birthday party for him and a clown, provided courtesy of Republican Congressman Gene Johnston of North Carolina, was nervously hiding in the budget director's personal bathroom awaiting Stockman's return.

When he got back, Stockman conferred briefly with Gerson and the rest of his inner circle to warn them that the article was coming out. He then walked into his office to shouts of surprise from his colleagues. Suzor remembers him looking pale as a ghost as the clown placed a huge pair of plastic glasses on his face, covered him with streamers and gave him a large pair of blue plastic scissors. The clown and Dale read some amusing limericks and everybody laughed, but the lightheartedness barely masked the anxiety within Stockman's inner circle. Fred Upton recalls Stockman giving a little speech thanking everyone for being "truthful and helpful." Then Stockman said, "You know, we're all survivors." Suzor thought Stockman looked frightened as he spoke.

The party did not last very long. Stockman and Dale each grabbed a copy of the twenty-three page article and spent nearly an hour in their respective offices reading it. Based on a long series of interviews with Stockman between December 1980 and September 1981, Greider had written a stunning and naked account of how the Reagan Revolution had gone wrong as seen through Stockman's perceptive and critical eyes. The article was littered with candid revelations of mistakes and duplicity, personal misgivings and self-criticisms, snide assessments of people in the Administration of Congress, and Stockman's favorite attention-grabbing phrases. It was a refreshingly honest account by an insider who confirmed what had become obvious to outsiders months before. But in Washington, members of the inner court are not the ones to declare that the emperor is wearing no clothes.

Dale underlined passages that he thought would be particularly troublesome. There were plenty of them. Then he returned to Stockman's office to give the budget director his biggest surprise of the day: a literal midlife crisis.

"This isn't so bad," Stockman said hopefully.

"Oh, yes it is," Dale replied glumly.

Meanwhile at the White House, Communications director David Gergen was also trying to determine what was in the *Atlantic Monthly*, and he called OMB to find out what was up. Dale said he was still trying to get a copy of the magazine. Gergen became interested in the magazine after Lesley Stahl had waved a copy of it in front of President's Reagan's face at the end of an afternoon news conference. "What do you think of what your budget director said in the *Atlantic Monthly*?" she called out to Reagan as he was making his exit through a crowd of reporters. "I haven't read it yet," he replied with a shrug. Earlier in the day Stahl had been talking to a friend on the telephone and had asked casually what she should ask Reagan at his news conference. The friend said he had read a fascinating article about Stockman in the *Atlantic Monthly*, which had arrived at his house the day before, and suggested she raise that with Reagan. Stahl did that after making numerous calls around town and finding someone who had a copy available.

At his news conference Reagan was asked a lot of questions about the deteriorating economy and worsening budget outlook. He acknowledged that the economy was headed for "hard times" for a few months and that his goal of a balanced budget in 1984 was unlikely. But he defended his economic program as being sound and said he would keep pushing for additional domestic spending cuts because what he got from Congress during the summer was not enough. When someone asked about his recent warning to his national security advisers to stop feuding in public, he replied: "There seems to be too much just loose talk going around, but it has been exaggerated out of all reality. There's no animus, personal animus, and there is no bickering or backstabbing going on. We're a very happy group." Reagan soon would find those words as ironic as Regan's T-shirt.

By early evening Stockman was trying to assess what political trouble the article might cause. He called his friend George Will, the *Newsweek* columnist, at home and said he was sending a copy over for Will's reaction. "He was nervous," recalls Will. After

371

reading it, Will called back and said, "I don't think there's a second bounce in this thing." Will says his initial reaction was, "This is hardly shocking except compared to the blandness machine in Washington . . . This wasn't scandal." By Wednesday, Will had realized he was wrong. "I was in Detroit the next day and saw that the Detroit newspapers were playing it up. It became very clear that it was going to be a big deal."

Stockman also went into the office of his deputy, Ed Harper, where several top OMB aides had already gathered to watch the evening network news shows. "Oh, boy, I've got to watch this," he told Harper. "This could really be a big problem." His little remaining color drained from his face as he watched CBS lead its broadcast with a report by Lesley Stahl that combined Reagan's comments at his news conference with Stockman's confessions in *Atlantic Monthly*:

"While the President was speaking confidently of his program, his budget director, David Stockman, in a series of interviews in the *Atlantic Monthly*, expressed great disillusionment. Conceding that, quote, 'there was a certain dimension of our theory that was unrealistic,' Stockman told the *Atlantic* that his initial budget numbers were constructed on shaky premises, saying, 'None of us really understands what's going on with all these numbers.' He said the defense numbers got out of control. 'We didn't know where we were ending up for sure.' And on the entire package, he said, 'The pieces were moving on independent tracks—the tax program, where we were going on spending and the defense program, which was just a bunch of numbers written on a piece of paper. They didn't quite mesh. But, you see, for about a month and a half we got away with that because of the novelty of all these budget reductions.' The *Atlantic* said that Mr. Reagan's policymakers knew their plans were wrong, or at least inadequate in some respects, but the President went ahead and conveyed the opposite impression to the American people. President Reagan said he had not read the article yet. Stockman had no comment. Lesley Stahl, CBS News, the White House."

The OMB group sat in silence for a few moments. "Everybody was stunned," Ed Harper says. "Dave's face was flushed and he obviously was very concerned. He said, 'I'll have to talk to the President about this.' Then he left and I thought this would be very troublesome. It would put him in a very difficult situation with people on the Hill and in the White House. He expressed some remarks that would dilute his effectiveness. And there was some naiveté in what he said."

Stockman and Dale then went over to the White House, where they conferred with Jim Baker; his deputy, Richard Darman; Gergen; and Craig Fuller, another top White House official who coordinated policy actions with the Cabinet. The White House group also had seen the news report and were trying to figure out an appropriate response to what Gergen initially had described to Baker as "a little problem." At that point, Darman was the only one from the White House group who had actually read the article.

373

According to one participant's recollection, Stockman conceded he had made a mistake in saying some of the things he had but he thought the article would not appear until a later date. "Our immediate instinct was to rally around him," the official has said. "We felt it would be an embarrassment to Ronald Reagan but we also felt we needed Stockman." So after nearly an hour of debate the group finally decided on a short statement that was put out by Dale that night: "The *Atlantic* article creates an impression that is wrong and grossly misleading. From the beginning, Mr. Stockman and others in the administration have been dealing with a series of problems, numbers and economic assumptions that have been open for all to see. Although problems and challenges remain, Mr. Stockman is convinced that the program set forward by the President is sound and that it will work."

The statement was untrue on two counts. The article had not created a wrong or misleading impression. Subsequent news reports about the article might have given a distorted view because of their brevity. But except for one significant mistake, Greider's lengthy article, when read in its entirety, created an accurate impression of what Stockman had been conveying over the course of eighteen Saturday breakfast meetings with the *Post* editor. When the interviews began in December both men assumed that Greider would chronicle for posterity Stockman's history-making attack on the federal budget. But as things started to go awry the budget director bared his doubts and worries to Greider and his running tape recorder. Initially Stockman sounded naive, idealistic and confident, but he soon began admitting his own errors and revealing his contempt for everyone in the political process who threw up roadblocks to his objectives. And he would embellish his points with metaphors that were part of his stock vocabulary, such as "pigs feeding at the trough" and "Trojan horse." Greider had correctly perceived the material he had collected as a long confessional of all the structural flaws in Reagan's economic program from its master builder. Greider's major mistake was to write that Stockman "changed the OMB computer" so it would show a balanced budget on paper. That tended to give the impression that Stockman had fed a fake program or phony numbers into the computer, when all he had done was revise an economic forecast, a legitimate and standard practice, and that change produced different budget numbers.

The claim in the Tuesday night statement that Stockman believed Reagan's program to be sound also was not true. John Anderson was right. Reagan could not cut taxes, boost defense spending, lower inflation painlessly, and balance the budget all at the same time. But now Stockman would repeat those very claims over and over again during the next forty-eight hours with his job in the balance. Once again, Stockman would veer between the extremes of lofty idealism and less noble self interest.

While Dale was handling the press, Stockman did some damage control among political friends he had hit hard in the article. One was Jack Kemp. Stockman had described Kemp's across-the-board tax cut as a "Trojan horse" to lower the top tax rate, and said

375

supply-side economics was really a "trickle-down theory" of giving tax breaks to the rich so they would create wealth that flows down through the society. "He called me the night it came out," Kemp says. "I guess he called a couple of people and said it was coming, and I wrote it off as naiveté."

Stockman also called Caspar Weinberger, whose Defense Department had been lambasted by the budget director for being a multi-billion-dollar "swamp" of waste and "so goddamned greedy that they got themselves strung way out there on a limb." Weingberger remembers that Stockman "telephoned me to tell me there had been some injudicious things said in that interview and not to believe them and that he shouldn't have said some of the things he did, but that they didn't represent his viewpoint. I hadn't read it at the time and I remember the call came into the White House just before I was going to a meeting. I said, I understand it, I appreciate your calling and letting me know so that when I read it I'll have a proper perspective.' " When Weinberger got around to reading the article he was startled. "It seemed to attack the entire philosophy and beliefs of the President and the policies that we had been pursuing up to that time. So I was quite surprised at it, but I had in mind his phone call so I didn't take it quite as seriously as some did."

Around eight o'clock that night, Stockman and Jennifer Blei went to Le Lion d'Or, a posh French restaurant in downtown Washington. They had planned the dinner as a birthday celebration but he was not in a very celebratory mood. Later that night Vice-President Bush called Stockman at home. Bush expressed some concern about the article and asked, "Is there anything else we should know about?"

On Capitol Hill Tuesday night, Democrats were overjoyed with the article, feeling that it confirmed everything they had been saying about Reagan's program, only this was Reagan's own budgetmeister making the accusations. J. L. Cullen, Stockman's legislative aide, got a telephone call shortly after midnight Tuesday from a friend who reported something fishy was happening up on the Hill because twenty-five copies of the *Atlantic Monthly* had been delivered to the Democratic cloakroom that night.

Among top White House officials, who finally got around to reading the article in full Tuesday night or Wednesday morning, the initial reaction was mixed. Those who had worked closely with Stockman on the budget over the previous months — Baker, Darman, Fuller and Gergen — had heard him say the same things expressed in the article to them in person. Vice-President Bush also was supportive. What shocked the group was that he would allow such impolitic remarks to get into print. At the same time, although these were his allies, they wondered whether he was not more manipulative than they had thought. Had he, perhaps, intentionally gone on the record so that if — when — the program failed he wouldn't be blamed? "I remember as I looked at some of the proofs I thought, 'What in the world is he doing?' says one of his close allies high up in the White House hierarchy. "I've got to say it made me wonder a little bit about him, whether he was more than just an extremely hard-working, bright, diligent budget director. I had to wonder whether he was, to some extent, a sharp operator as well."

Other White House officials who were not as close to Stockman and had not heard him express similar feelings in private were enraged and wanted him fired, including such long-time Reaganites from California as Michael Deaver, political adviser Lyn Nofziger and personnel assistant Helene Von Damm. Ed Meese also was upset by the article but straddled the fence on the question of firing Stockman. Several officials recall him taking both positions at different times which, they added, was typical of Meese. Treasury Secretary Donald Regan did not vacillate at all. He was horrified by the article, thought Stockman had double-crossed Reagan and urged the President to fire him for gross disloyalty.

Nevertheless, Regan did not reveal his animus toward Stockman on Wednesday as he joined the other members of the White House Legislative Strategy Group, of which Stockman also was a member, in making light of the article. Baker, Meese, Regan, Darman, Fuller and Kenneth Duberstein, a legislative affairs official, had given Stockman a signed plaque that said: "This award for the best cover story in the December 1981 *Atlantic Monthly* presented to David A. Stockman by the Legislative Strategy Group." Darman had written the gag award as a way to break the tension over the controversy.

Initial press coverage of the article on Wednesday was as mixed as the reactions at the White House. The Washington *Post* carried a story but it did not put it on the front page, because Greider had been feeding the newspaper stories from his interviews for months. Much of what appeared in *Atlantic Monthly* already had been in the *Post*, but often without direct attribution to Stockman and without the colorful metaphors. The New York *Times*, which also had carried similar stories over the months by referring to Stockman only as an unnamed administration official, carried just four paragraphs from an Associated Press story buried inside the business section. But the story was major news in all the major newspapers elsewhere in the country. Like the White House officials, editors familiar with Stockman's views were not especially impressed, but those who were not as close to the story found it sensational.

First reactions from the public varied as well. Messages coming into Stockman's office included hate-callers who branded Stockman a "draft dodger" and accused him of betraying the President. But a greater number of calls were from people who wanted to salute what they saw as his honesty.

In Congress virtually everyone was stunned by what Stockman had said and the fact of his saying it publicly. The Democrats were ecstatic because they knew they had a great issue, and the Republicans were horrified that Stockman had marched them onto a leaky ship, directed them out to the middle of the ocean and then jumped ship just as it was sinking.

Reagan also had mixed reactions after reading the article. At first he was upset and angry by what he had read. "He was hot. And he should have been," says Senator Paul Laxalt of Nevada, a long-time Reagan confidant. One senior White House official has said Reagan "wasn't too pleased with it because there was some stuff that ran directly counter to his beliefs."

Michael Deaver recalls that on Wednesday morning he, Reagan, Bush, Baker and Meese sat in the Oval Office spending "ten minutes or so" reading the article and then talking about what to do. "Everybody was shocked, upset, trying to figure out what to do about it," he says. "I was arguing that we ought to fire him, but no one else took that position. The others were outraged but nobody was coming down on a hard position right away . . . I thought his statements were outrageous. I could not believe that anybody who had been dealing with the press in this town to the extent that he had could have been taken. He just wasn't that dumb, and if he was that dumb he ought to leave."

Reagan, however, was inclined to conclude that Stockman had been betrayed by a reporter and now was being victimized by a press corps that was blowing the whole thing out of proportion. "He generally believed that the reporter was at fault, not Dave," Deaver adds. "I think the President tended to believe he was misquoted, things were taken out of context, he was talking off the record." Stockman was not going to dispel that impression in Reagan's mind. Fred Khedouri's recollection of that stormy period is that "the people who actually read the whole article did not have the extreme reaction that others had. They thought that he had said some stupid things but they didn't think that he had some horribly deficient character. I think the President was in that group. My impression was that he thought Dave had created a terrible problem and that it was stupid and unfortunate but not a fatal act, that it was outweighed by his obvious dedication to the effort and his obvious capabilities."

Stockman also had very strong allies in Bush and Baker and Darman. They felt Stockman, with his knowledge of the budget, was indispensible to keep the Reagan Revolution moving. Bush felt that Stockman could be forgiven one stupid mistake so long as he didn't repeat it. Stockman's backers also were angry that some of Stockman's most vociferous critics in the White House were people who had done little or nothing to get Reagan's budget and tax cuts through Congress. "You had these true-blue Reaganauts, like Nofziger and Von Damm, saying he should go when they hadn't lifted a goddamn finger to enact the Reagan Revolution. And he [Stockman], more than practically any single person in America, had been responsible for giving meaning to the Reagan Revolution," says one close friend in the White House.

The controversy over the article grew steadily on Wednesday, with most of the flames being fanned by the Reaganauts in the White House and furious Republicans in Congress. They wanted Stockman's head on a platter and forced Reagan to meet with his senior advisers again on Thursday morning to consider the political damage he might sustain by keeping Stockman. Finally he agreed to confront his budget director one-on-one at a private lunch that Stockman arranged through Bush, who agreed to cancel his own regular Thursday lunch with Reagan.

By now rumors were sweeping through Washington that the "boy wonder of the budget" was on his way out. But that was not the impression Reagan gave during a White House meeting with Republican leaders from Congress. J. L. Cullen, who says she never read the *Atlantic Monthly* article, recalls Stockman asking her to walk over to the meeting with him. First he met with Reagan in the Oval Office for about five minutes. Then they both joined the congressional Republicans. Cullen says Reagan started the meeting by saying, "Dave has something he wants to say to you." Stockman then stood up and apologized profusely. Cullen recalls Reagan responding, "Dave, I know how these things happen with the press. It happened to me when I was president of the Screen Actors Guild." Reagan then related a story about how guild officials had held a strategy meeting and swore each other to secrecy, but their discussions showed up in a newspaper the next morning. Reagan said it turned out that the man who leaked the story had been standing by the door and said he did not feel bound by the pledge to secrecy because he was not sitting at the table. "So, Dave, I can understand and we have more important things to do." Cullen says Reagan then dropped the matter. That episode, she says, convinced her that Stockman was not in big trouble with the President.

Jim Baker, it seems, was not quite as confident. He advised Stockman that his only chance to survive was to go in to his private meeting with Reagan, offer his resignation, act as humble and contrite as possible and swear his allegiance to the President's program. "What the President really wanted was to hear from Dave that this was a stupid mistake and it didn't represent a fundamental difference in belief or philosophy," said one close presidential assistant.

Stockman later told friends and colleagues that he

followed Baker's advice and it worked. The President was forgiving and declined Stockman's resignation during their forty-five-minute meeting. Stockman also said Reagan did not act like he was very upset with him. "Dave said the President couldn't have been nicer," Ed Dale recalls. A top White House official adds that Reagan was polite and calm toward Stockman because of a conscious decision within his inner circle to "do a good cop-bad cop routine" on the budget director. Reagan, naturally, played the good cop, and in so doing displayed a capacity for loyalty and compassion that many argued Stockman lacked. "The President was impressed with Dave's sincerity," Paul Laxalt says. "He felt Dave was talented and had been trapped by a reporter." One official said Reagan repeated his story about the leak of the Screen Actors Guild meeting to Stockman during their lunch.

"I don't think the President was upset," Jennifer Stockman concludes after many years of discussions with her husband on the painful subject. "I think initially he was. You know, the President was as upset as his staff. He goes purely on staff briefings. And I think he listened to Deaver, and Deaver said, yes, we should get rid of him. And he listened to Baker, and Baker said we should give him another chance; maybe it wasn't as bad as the press is making it out to be. And the President said to David that he read the article, he didn't think it was so bad, he thought it was blown out of proportion and he himself understands how the press blows things out of proportion. So in a way he empathized. He never doubted David's loyalty, to my knowledge."

Jennifer Stockman paused for a few seconds, recalling the episode in her mind. Then she added: "It's really amazing that he defended David the way he did when you think of the magnitude of what David did and what he was saying."

As Stockman was leaving the Oval Office, according to Deaver, Reagan told him and Baker that the budget director had been very contrite and wanted to go before the press. "You better be one humble son of a bitch," Deaver recalls telling Stockman. "Oh, I will," an apparently chastened Stockman replied. Stockman then conferred with Baker, Darman and Gergen about what he should say at his news conference. It would not do to say how gracious and understanding the President had been. That would never have satisfied the angry Reaganauts and congressional Republicans who wanted blood. So they agreed that Stockman would create the impression that he had been severely rebuked by Reagan. It wouldn't be too hard to do since Stockman looked ashen and more visibly upset than anyone had ever seen him. "He looked liked a scared little boy," said one close assistant.

Stockman walked back to his office in the Old Executive Office Building to write his statement. "He looked like death warmed over," says Larry Kudlow. "He was writing his press statement when I walked into his office. I just kind of looked at him and said, 'Is there anything I can do for you?' He said, 'No, just come to the press room later.' I told him, 'Well, what I can do now is tell you that I'll always stand by you.' And he got a little teary, so I said, 'I'll leave you to finish your document.' Then Ed Dale and a few of us went down to the press room with him and just watched the vultures pick the carcass."

Stockman stepped to the podium in the White House press room to confront a crush of reporters and a live television audience. The man who always had his emotions in control was obviously upset and paused occasionally to maintain his composure. In his opening statement, Stockman ate humble pie:

"I tendered my resignation . . . because my poor judgement and loose talk have done him [Reagan] and his program a disservice. Worse, they have spread an impression that is utterly false. . . . Never, ever has he attempted to mislead the Congress or the American people, or say things which weren't true. To the extent that my quoted words suggest or have been construed to imply otherwise, I take full responsibility and blame. In our meeting I told the President that I would not permit my careless rambling to a reporter stand in the way of the success of his Presidency or the credibility of his program. At the end of the meeting the President asked me to stay on the team. But let me be clear on my own account: I would not be here now—nor would I have worked sixteen hours per day for nearly a year—if I did not believe in the President and his policies. Honest people may worry about how best to advance our visions for getting the messed-up economy we inherited back on track and the overgrown budget under control. I have worried, but too publicly, and deeply regret any harm that has been done. I am staying on because I believe even more deeply that the President has charted a sound, constructive course. I am grateful to the President for this second chance . . ."

The White House also put out a statement that

said, "Mr. Stockman acknowledged that he had made a mistake and apologized for what he has now come to recognize as a grievous error. The President expressed his grave concern and disappointment about the issues raised by the article. He expressed particular dismay at the possible suggestion that his Administration — or any members of his Administration — might seek to mislead the American public. He stated unequivocally that he would not tolerate any such behavior; that the policies of this Administration were being pursued — and must continue to be pursued — in good faith, on the basis of the best evidence and judgement available. Mr. Stockman stated that he shared the President's concern and disappointment . . ."

During the tough questioning from reporters that followed, Stockman defended most of what he said in the article as being consistent with positions he had taken in the past. That was something of an exaggeration, since he never had been so explicit in public before about his despair and criticisms. But this was no time for the candor that had brought him here in the first place. Stockman also took back some of his more provocative throw-away lines:

Question: What did you mean by saying the tax cuts were a Trojan horse, which is a symbol of betrayal?

Answer: "A Trojan horse is a wooden beast without a brain, and had I recalled that, I never would have used that metaphor. . . . I can only say that it was a rotten, horrible, unfortunate metaphor."

Question: Did you actually make up numbers?

Answer: "No, I didn't make up numbers. I didn't invent numbers."

Question: Can you be a credible spokesman for the President on Capitol Hill?

Answer: "I can't judge that, but I would only say that almost anything other than maybe an indiscreet quotation or expression or metaphor that's contained in the article basically reflects things that I had been saying in our private deliberations as well as in public comments over the last nine months."

Question: Do you stand by your statement that Reagan's program is nothing more than the old GOP trickle-down theory of economics?

Answer: "Well, I'm not certain what trickle down means . . . Rather than argue the case any longer with Bill Greider . . . I simply conceded his point, if that's the terminology and the political characterization that he wanted to use."

After flaying himself for his use of certain metaphors, Stockman invented his most memorable one in response to a question about how Reagan took it: "I hesitate to use metaphors after the bad luck that I've had in recent days. But I grew up on a farm, and I might say, therefore, that my visit to the Oval Office for lunch with the President was more in the nature of a visit to the woodshed after supper."

The "woodshed." That was the metaphor that would stick in the mind of the press and the public. And it seemed to fit perfectly. The little boy had been bad and his father had given him a spanking. Now all was forgiven. And it satisfied those who wanted Stockman punished. Yet Stockman never seemed to

387

have learned his full lesson. After several months of isolation from the press, he would start telling tales out of school again, repeating the same kinds of remarks that got him in trouble in the *Atlantic Monthly*. Where he had grown wiser was in being more careful that he was not quoted on the record. In later years he would even tell people that his fabled visit to Reagan's "woodshed" was just that — a fable.

But Stockman had, in fact, been taken to a woodshed and thrashed in a far more painful way than any punishment that might have been meted out in the privacy of the White House. He had been subjected to a public humiliation. Rather than stick to his expressed convictions and resign, if need be, he compromised by taking back almost all of what was said in the *Atlantic Monthly*. He also had lost much of the enormous power he had wielded for nearly a year. Overnight he went from being a surrogate President on economic matters to a presidential accountant with questionable influence. It was a long, abrupt fall.

Why did he do it? How could it have happened? Why did he stay? What could possibly have been going through his mind? Was it all a big unfortunate misunderstanding, an innocent arrangement gone amuck, as Stockman would say? Had he fallen victim to his own hubris, playing Peck's bad boy once too often, as friends speculate? Or was this the calculated mark of the Machiavellian operator manipulating the news media to achieve his policy goals and to make himself look good for history, as his political critics would maintain? Years later, many of Stockman's closest friends and political associates are still perplexed by the entire episode, even after lengthy conversations with him. Looking back, one close associate says, "I'm convinced that deep down Dave knew exactly what he was doing with Greider and the possible repercussions."

Whatever, it was surely a unique incident of high political drama with elements of classic Greek tragedy. Some have compared the *Atlantic* flap to Richard Nixon's decision to make and then keep his Watergate tapes. Granted, Stockman only committed candor while Nixon may have committed a felony. But in each case a powerful man brought about his own eventual downfall because he created a record of his private conversations. Each had his reasons: a sense of history, personal vanity—a belief he was clever enough to break the rules and get away with it. And there also was fate: who could have predicted the outcome? Perhaps it was because Nixon saw the parallels that he called the budget director's office while Stockman was under siege to outline a strategy to survive. Nixon telephoned Stockman's deputy, Ed Harper, who had worked in the Nixon Administration, and said Stockman could weather the controversy by dropping out of view—keeping his head down, his mouth shut and the press far away. Which is what Stockman did for several months.

For both Stockman and Greider, the *Atlantic Monthly* saga began innocently. Although they were not friends in a social sense, they liked each other's company on an intellectual level. On economic issues Greider was a hard-core liberal and Stockman was a hard-core conservative, but each admired the other as a bright person interested in new ideas. They also served each other's professional needs. Stockman became a valuable "background" source during the 1980 political campaign, and Greider became Stockman's "pipeline" to Washington's power brokers. Ideas and opinion are the chief products manufactured in the nation's capital, and the Washington *Post* is the principal medium of exchange. Stockman had become visibly successful in large part by courting reporters and getting into the national news media. The *Post*, more than any other paper, had helped make him famous and influential. Greider, who had commissioned many of Stockman's articles as editor of the *Post*'s Sunday opinion section, thought Stockman a very good writer with refreshing ideas and a provocative style. When Greider warned Stockman that his 1979 "Company Town" piece describing one week as a congressman might be a little too provocative, Stockman replied, "What the hell." He was a reporter's dream source.

When Stockman was named budget director it was Greider who proposed that they meet regularly so Greider could chronicle the upcoming budget battle, which both sensed would have historic implications. Stockman immediately agreed but said, "Not for the *Post*." Greider replied, "No, no, for a magazine, like the *New Yorker*." At the time, Greider says, "I thought I'd be doing a sober-sided budget piece: here's how the budget process works. I never thought I would be writing a sensational political story." Neither did Stockman at the time. So they set some basic but vague ground rules. As Greider later remembers the bargain, everything Stockman said would be off the record at first, but then everything would be on the record for a piece to be done when the budget battle was over. Neither specified at the time when that might be. Stockman never disputed Greider's description of the ground rules, but he later has said that he failed to focus clearly on what would or would not be on the record eventually. It was the kind of oversight that would be expected of a man of great confidence. And so they began.

At the start Stockman felt sufficiently comfortable with the arrangement to take Greider home to visit his family farm for Christmas, 1980. "He had Christmas dinner with us, was here when we opened our presents," Carol Stockman says ruefully. To her, Greider became a Judas who betrayed her son. "That's why I didn't invite you to supper," she said in explaining why she scheduled an after-dinner time to be interviewed for this book.

In Washington they settled on a routine. Approximately every other week for nine months they would have breakfast for an hour to an hour and a half at the Hay-Adams Hotel, a favorite of Administration officials with its elegant but masculine decor and its proximity to the White House—some 100 yards directly across Lafayette Park. After a while the waiters would turn down the Musak in the background so that they would not drown out Stockman's words as he spoke into Greider's tape recorder. But Greider did not have unique access to Stockman. The budget director was making the rounds with all the major opinion-shapers in town, particularly the widely followed syndicated columnists—ultraconservatives such as Robert Novak (of Evans and Novak); moderate-conservatives such as George Will, and liberal-moderates such as the late Joseph Kraft. Occasionally Greider had to wait in line to have breakfast with Stockman.

Early on, Stockman told friends within the Administration that he had established an important pipeline to the liberal *Post*. His apparent strategy was to convince the political opposition that his views were credible and correct. "Dave is always trying to persuade the press. That's his Achilles' heel," says one close friend. "David always liked trying to persuade people of different views, and he was very challenged by the prospect of converting them," says Jennifer Stockman. "He was big on converting liberals who didn't see things his way. It also was a way of testing his own views, I think. If he could convince somebody smart like Greider, then that just gave his views more credibility. He also respected Greider. He knew he was a liberal, but a smart liberal. He was very intellectual. If David could convince Greider that this new revolution made sense, then it really must be sound. But he never did convince Greider." Ironically, she suggests, it was Greider who convinced Stockman that the revolution was not sound. "Greider asked all the hard questions."

Greider's saga began with a summary of Stockman's background and a picture of a cocky young man convinced he could make Reagan's program work. But almost immediately he had encountered problems, and began sharing them with Greider, such as the need to use new economic assumptions to show a balanced budget. And he gave out some throwaway lines that would come back to haunt him: "Laffer sold us a bill of goods . . . Laffer wasn't wrong—he didn't go far enough." He talked about how he worked the Cabinet to get the spending cuts he needed, about how he would go after the "swamp" of waste in the Pentagon after the first round of cuts to deal with its "blatant inefficiency, poor deployment of manpower, contracting idiocy." He described how Reagan had turned down his proposals to close tax loopholes for big business and the rich, how he failed to come up with enough spending cuts to achieve a balanced budget. "None of us really understood what's going on with all these numbers," he declared at one point. Honest, but also politically damaging.

By spring of 1981, Stockman was confiding his worries about the vote of no-confidence that the program was receiving from the stock market, which was slumping. And as economic conditions moved in the opposite direction of his forecast, he began acknowledging that the spending, tax and defense portions of the budget never really meshed. He blamed part of the problem on the greedy generals at the Pentagon. "They got a blank check," he fumed. He blamed another part on Congress for refusing to go along with as many spending cuts as he wanted: "there are no REAL conservatives in Congress." He became a skeptic about the tax cut as well: "I've never believed that just cutting taxes alone will cause output and employment to expand."

As spring turned to summer, Stockman was unloading to Greider on the tax cut: "The hard part of the supply-side tax cut is dropping the top rate from 70 to 50 percent—the rest of it is a secondary matter.

The original argument was that the top bracket was too high, and that's having the most devastating effect on the economy. Then the general argument was that, in order to make this palatable as a political matter, you had to bring down all the brackets. But, I mean, Kemp-Roth was always a Trojan horse to bring down the top rate . . . . It's kind of hard to sell 'trickle-down,' so the supply-side formula was the only way to get a tax policy that was really trickle-down. Supply-side is 'trickle-down' theory."

This was another damning statement, sounding as it did like an accusation of duplicity. Yet Stockman was correct in his analysis. Supply-side economics *is* based on increasing capital formation, and wealthy people are the ones who form most of the new capitol. "To be totally blunt about it," says Jack Kemp, "you can't cut the rates at the top without cutting the rates at the bottom. I mean, that's just good politics. So if that's what he meant, then I give him credit for an honest political statement." Treasury Secretary Donald Regan had made a similar point in explaining his opposition to an attempt by House Democrats to limit the third installment of the President's tax cut to incomes of $50,000 or less. Although the Administration publicly opposed the tax-cut cap on the grounds that it hurt two-income, middle-class families, Regan confided in an aside to a reporter that from an economic standpoint there would be no purpose in a tax cut unless it went to people making more than $50,000 a year, because they are the ones who create jobs and wealth in the country. But from a marketing standpoint the Administration did not like to play up its vision of wealth "trickling down" from the top, because that was how the Democrats had been criticizing Republican economic policy for fifty years.

As Stockman described the last-minute deals he made to win votes on the budget cuts, he complained about the "piranhas" in Congress, and after the package passed he minimized the accomplishment by suggesting that he had exaggerated the savings all along: "There was less than met the eye . . . Let's say that you and I walked outside and I waved a wand and said, 'I've just lowered the temperature from 110 to 78.' Would you believe me?" And on the bidding war over the tax cut, he said: "Do you realize the greed that came to the forefront? The hogs were really feeding. The greed level, the level of opportunism, just got out of control."

By early August, Stockman was expressing his concern about the budget deficit to Greider over the breakfast table, and to Reagan over the Cabinet table. It was at this point that Greider assumed the budget battles were over and figured it was time to tell the story. But Stockman still had an internal battle to wage.

After he had shocked Reagan with his briefing about the growing deficit and Reagan had told him he still wanted to balance the budget by 1984, Stockman began working on a new master plan: he would go back to Congress with a midcourse correction—a "fall offensive" that would mean additional domestic spending cuts, some tax loophole closings to raise some revenue, and a big whack at defense. Defense was his biggest target.

Stockman had made the mistake of ignoring the

Pentagon in February, when Weinberger locked the President into a far more ambitious military buildup plan than Stockman had ever imagined. Defense spending would more than double between 1981 to 1986, from $162 billion to $343 billion, and the share of each federal dollar sent to the generals would grow from a quarter to thirty-eight cents. Stockman felt that Weinberger had failed to implement the cost controls that had earned him the nickname "Cap the Knife" as Nixon's budget director, so Stockman prepared a detailed case for stretching out purchases of some weapon programs, eliminating some weapon development projects and cutting other military costs to save between $10 billion and $20 billion a year. He and Jim Baker had leaked word to the press that Reagan would approve a military retrenchment of about that magnitude. They were wrong.

Stockman's first defeat came in August, when Reagan interrupted his vacation to meet with his top staff, at the Century Plaza Hotel in Los Angeles, to review Stockman's revised budget plans. As always, Stockman was armed to the teeth with briefing papers, charts, numbers, arguments and confidence. Ed Harper remembers Stockman carefully laying out his case, which included scrapping plans for the Sergeant York division air defense gun and the Bradley troop carrier on the grounds that they were costly and poorly designed. But Weinberger argued in favor of both weapons and emphasized the need to build a 600-ship Navy. (Four years later, Weinberger scrapped the Sergeant York program for the same reasons Stockman cited in 1981. And the Bradley carrier could be headed for the same fate.) Harper also recalls being amused watching Stockman explain the defense buildup with a set of numbers adjusted for inflation that confused Weinberger and threw him off guard because he didn't have a comparable set of numbers. But Weinberger—backed up by Secretary of State Alexander Haig, CIA Director William Casey and National Security Adviser Richard Allen—countered Stockman's numerical barrage with a rhetorical barrage that Reagan could understand easily: the nation's security was at stake, and any weakening of resolve to rebuild U.S. defenses would send the wrong signal to the Soviet Union. Reagan deferred a decision, hoping Weinberger and Stockman could find some middle ground. But OMB economist Kudlow, who sat in at the meeting, relates some telling social interactions that convinced him Weinberger would prevail:

"After the meeting we had lunch. There were about twenty of us sitting at two long tables next to each other. Reagan was in the middle of one table with Stockman on his left and Don Regan on his right. And sitting directly across from Reagan in the middle of the other long table was Weinberger, with Haig on one side and Ed Meese on the other. Now, throughout the lunch Stockman was trying to whisper to Reagan's ear to score points in classic politico-bureaucratic gamesmanship. But Reagan had no response, no response. Also, throughout the lunch Al Haig was trying to make statements about the foreign situation to show how important he is and to get Reagan's attention. Reagan never responded to Haig, either. What happened instead was that Reagan started telling Sacramento stories from back in the sixties, with Meese and Weinberger. Remember now, Meese is an old Reagan guy and Weinberger goes way back with Reagan. And they're telling these yarns back and forth. And I'm sitting at the far end with the little peewees but I could see this.

"I know about social things. I know what happens at dinner parties. So I walk out later with Stockman, Harper and Murray Weidenbaum, and we get into a car on the way back to the plane. And I said, 'We're finished. Did you see what I saw at lunch?' Murray didn't see it, but Harper did because he had a lot of corporate experience and knows how business gets done. And I'm saying, 'We are finito. It's over as far as I'm concerned. I should be going back to Bear Stearns.' And all the way back on the plane I told it to Dave. He said, 'No, no. Baker tells me we'll win.' Baker believed that he was going to win this thing. Wrong."

After Labor Day Stockman knew he had lost and he was furious. Everyone was back in Washington now, and Stockman had just been rolled by Weinberger in the Cabinet Room. Cap had his own show-and-tell charts this time. One showed the result of the Pentagon's military buildup—a tall, clear-eyed and resolute infantryman proudly holding his rifle. Another chart depicted the consequences of the OMB cutbacks—a hunched-over, frightened soldier without a rifle. Reagan got a chuckle out of it. He also got the picture. He agreed to nick the defense budget, but no more. Stockman would get about $5 billion a year in savings. Weinberger had outcharted David Stockman: "Our best counter to the soldiers was a chart showing how Defense was increasing car purchases from one hundred sedans a year to several thousand," Harper says, laughing. "So we made these little cutouts of Chevrolets and stacked them up."

Stockman took what little savings Weinberger gave up and went ahead with his fall offensive. It included cuts in two Safety Net items (Medicare and veterans benefits), further cuts in food stamps, and a 12 percent across-the-board cut in most other domestic programs. It also included a small package of tax increases. Since Reagan did not want to have to admit he was raising any taxes, Larry Kudlow coined the euphemism, "revenue enhancements," to market the tax package as something other than what it was—a tax hike.

Stockman, urged on by Senator Pete Domenici to do something about the deficit, persuaded Reagan to propose the deficit-reduction package to Congress on September 24. It flopped nearly as badly as the Social Security package had. Republican members of Congress were furious at Stockman. They had left for a long summer recess believing that all the politically painful budget cuts they had approved little more than two months before would balance the budget. Now they were being told they would have to cut some more and the budget still would not be balanced. Many felt Stockman had deceived them. Others felt he had gone back on his word to them. Not surprisingly, the proposals died a quick death in Congress. Stockman's fall offensive against the deficit had been routed.

Greider had stopped interviewing Stockman just before the fall offensive, but the ending to his saga provided by Stockman was just as gloomy: "We were working in a twenty- or twenty-five-day time frame and we didn't add up all the numbers." And in a parting shot, Stockman said: "Some of the naive supply-siders just missed this whole dimension. You don't stop inflation without some kind of dislocation." Whether he realized it or not, Stockman had been one of those "naive supply-siders" he was now criticizing. But then, Stockman had learned so much so quickly that he may have forgotten what he thought just a year before. The last nine months had truly been "The Education of David Stockman," as Greider would title this article.

It was in August, after the budget and tax cuts had passed Congress, that Greider had first broached the subject of writing the magazine article. It seemed like a logical time. Besides, Greider had been steadily feeding Stockman's comments to other *Post* reporters, who had written stories about the budget battles that either quoted Stockman by name or anonymously as a "senior Administration official." *Post* political columnist David Broder recalls Greider saying he was worried that he had fed so much of his interviews to the newspaper that he had nothing special left for his magazine article. Greider also had recognized Stockman's anonymous laments in other newspaper stories or columns. So at one August breakfast, Greider remembers telling Stockman the saga had ended: "I said, 'I'm ready to write.' And he agreed without any discussion." Greider raised it again at their last meeting in September, shortly after Stockman had lost to Weinberger on the defense numbers. "I said, 'I'm going ahead. Okay?' He said, 'Yeah, it's fair.' " Greider adds that he always assumed that Stockman had the final say on when the article would be written. "If he had said no, no, no, I would have had to reconsider." But Greider does not recall Stockman expressing the slightest reservation at the time.

Stockman, however, clearly was worried. After that last conversation with Greider, he disclosed their arrangement for the first time to Ed Dale. Dale had known that the two were meeting regularly but he did not know why. He remembers Stockman appearing quite nervous when he finally told him: "Greider tells me that under the ground rules, he is now free to publish. I thought it was all off the record. Is there anything we can do about it?" But after Stockman explained the situation, Dale told him that under their hazy rules, Greider was within his rights to write the article.

Greider and Stockman did not talk again until Greider called in October to help arrange for a photographer to take pictures. Stockman agreed to let someone follow him around for a day. J. L. Cullen recalls that she was with Stockman on Capitol Hill when she spotted a photographer taking pictures of them. When she asked him what the photographer was doing, he told her Greider was writing a piece about him for *Atlantic Monthly*, "but it was no big deal."

At first, as Greider went through his long transcripts, he did not think he had much of a story. But then he detected the essence: Stockman's triumphant march up the mountain and his despairing climb down. The same thought occurred simultaneously to Stockman. He knew how he liked to throw colorful quotations around freely, and was worried that Greider might have too good a story. As Greider recalls, Stockman telephoned to ask about the use of direct quotations. "I told him the article would rattle some windows, and he worried about ad hominem attacks on people. I agreed that any personal insults against specific people would be off the record, and he said 'all the other stuff is fine because people know my views.'" Stockman later told friends that he thought Greider would clear quotes with him, and when Greider said he wouldn't, "I panicked." Later he told his assistant, David Gerson, that the article "would blow sky high." One close friend in the White House said Stockman told him in advance that he was worried about the article because "Greider was going to use some material that he thought would not be used, and he said, 'You might have a problem.' He seemed moderately concerned but not terribly concerned about it."

Jennifer Stockman, however, does not recall him confiding any concerns in advance. "The whole incident was very bizarre," she says. "I'm not sure David ever really focused on what this all meant and never thought that much about the timing," she said. "So he didn't confide that much to me because he didn't have that much to confide. It wasn't that big of an event as it was happening. He didn't think of it as a big deal. He never said to me, 'I'm talking to this guy every Saturday and I really want this article.' It just happened. Then all of a sudden when it happened, my God, he was scared to death. I mean it really, really shook him. There's no question about that."

After the storm broke, Stockman told reporters

that he had no objection to Greider's writing the article but thought verbatim quotations would not be used. Greider firmly disputes that interpretation, noting that his transcripts of their conversations are filled with caveats by Stockman such as, "Now, this is for use later," or "turn off your machine, this is completely off the record." In Greider's mind there was no misunderstanding. But that is what Stockman would plead and that, ultimately, is what saved him with Reagan.

"I was somewhat shocked to find that this gross misunderstanding had gone on unspoken for about nine months," he said at the news conference that followed his lunch with Reagan, "but that's where we are now and I don't take issue with him or fault him for doing what he did. That was his understanding."

"Sometimes," he added ruefully before the crowd of reporters, "large misunderstandings occur in life with very unfortunate and tragic effects. And I think this is one of them."

The *Atlantic Monthly* article proved to be a critical turning point for both Stockman and the Reagan Revolution. His power was diluted and Reagan's assault on the federal budget stopped dead in its tracks. Although Stockman was still the brightest, most knowledgeable and hardest working member of the senior team, his effectiveness plummeted; he would never again repeat his success at reordering budget priorities on a massive scale as he had during that first round.

Some of his former friends-turned-critics contend

that if he truly were a man of his convictions, he would have resigned on the spot; by staying, according to them, he revealed that he was motivated mainly by ambition. "He missed a golden opportunity," charges Keke Anderson. "Had he resigned, he would have been a hero to the country. But he made a fatal mistake. The little dummy liked the trappings of his office." David Broder criticized Stockman for thinking he could play by a different set of rules: "I felt he was duplicitous . . . It's one thing to argue on the inside and cultivate a public debate, but it's something different to do what he has done—to be both Mr. Insider and Mr. Outsider, like Henry Kissinger. He did not want to forsake Bill Greider or Meg Greenfield, so he let it be known that he was dealing with zealots and idiots but he never denounced the policies at the time. That is a moral failing."

Stockman has given friends a simple explanation for why he stayed: "I felt a good part responsible for letting things get off the beaten path. I felt responsibility for why we made such a large error and I wanted to be there to fix it up. And I thought we would."

By staying, Stockman became the darling of the other side overnight. The Democrats and other Reagan Administration critics who had been depicting him as Mr. Evil were now hailing him as Mr. Righteous, for having the courage to tell the truth. He became a favorite of the press corps, which relishes those few unvarnished occasions when a politician says what is really on his or her mind. And he became a symbol of honesty and integrity to much of the general public. At the same time, Stockman had become a symbol of trickery and betrayal to his fellow Republicans. He was the Administration's Trojan horse and had lost forever much of his credibility with Reagan, senior members of the White House staff, the Cabinet and Republicans in Congress. "In that first year, everything basically functioned through OMB," said one Stockman associate. "But after the *Atlantic*, I said to Dave, 'You will never have the final say any more.' "

Although Reagan had decided to keep Stockman on, it was not at all certain in those first weeks after the episode whether he would be able to stay. Many Congressional Republicans were still in a rage, and they saw Stockman as too big a political liability. On Saturday, November 14, two days after his visit to the "woodshed," Stockman discussed the possibility of resigning over a long lunch with Richard Darman. But Darman considered Stockman far too valuable to leave and Stockman dropped the idea.

Many Republicans in Congress did not share Darman's confidence in Stockman, whom they now considered to be either a fool or a turncoat. After the article came out, Stockman's legislative assistants and a few friendly senators circulated a letter of support that was signed by thirty-two of the fifty-three Republican senators. Significantly, among those who did not sign the letter were Majority Leader Howard Baker, who was not responsive to Stockman's personal entreaties, and Paul Laxalt. Fred Upton says Baker's staff aides had been "gleeful" about rumors of Stockman's imminent resignation. Laxalt said, "I couldn't understand how he could be so naive to trust a reporter the way he did. I have no problem about him citing his historical reservations, but to let it leak?" A close aide to Republican leaders added: "The Republicans had bought this program hook, line and sinker, and the *Atlantic* article was devastating. They had gotten bad feedback from people back home during the August 1981 recess and then the architect of the whole program dumps on it and walks away from it. People really felt betrayed."

Steve Bell of the Senate Budget Committee recalls a sense of bewilderment on the Hill. "I think Howard Baker's reaction summed it up: 'How could somebody that smart be that dumb?' There also was some glee on the part of people whose programs David had helped cut, and they're saying, 'Oh, good. That son of a bitch. He deserved it.' You must realize there are many people in the world—I'm not one—but there are many people in the world who think he's extremely arrogant and they were happy to see one of their enemies discomfitted in this way. And I'm talking about Republicans now. The Democratic side showed a combination of glee that it would embarrass the Administration and absolute astonishment that such good fortune could have happened. Most people, by the way, attributed it to arrogance. They figured David was just so goddamn cocksure of his position and so arrogant that he could get away with anything."

Jack Kemp's reaction seems to have been more one of disappointment than anger or a sense of betrayal: "Some have speculated that he just wanted to cover his own hide. I think that is more pejorative than I would interpret it." Kemp says he would be inclined to assume the best, that Stockman "had a desire to keep this in a historical perspective . . . But Dave really did a horrible job of explaining what incentive-oriented Reagan economics was all about. I mean, just from his own standpoint. That was my disappointment. I didn't have any personal problem with him saying anything. I'm used to that. My disappointment was not, 'Why did you take a shot at me?' It was more that I had expected a better intellectual approach to what supply-side tax policy was all about. It was really poor. I mean, just outright poor, notwithstanding the fact that it was wrong."

The other half of the Kemp-Roth tax-cut team, Senator William Roth, chose to assume the worst rather than the best. On the day of Stockman's lunch with Reagan, Roth's office issued a wickedly sarcastic news release inviting Stockman to the senator's Delaware home for Thanksgiving dinner that would include "Trojan horse pâté . . . trickle-down consommé, Atlantic (Monthly) wide-mouth bass, foot-in-mouth filet, stuffed crow, half-baked potatoes au Stockman, humble pie with scapegoat cheese . . . and sour grapes." The release ended: "Following dinner, Mr. Stockman will be offered a blindfold and a cigarette. (P.S.: This news release is off the record.)"

A former friend of Stockman's from their congressional days, Republican Congressman Newt Gingrich of Georgia, denounced the article as "a classical sense of hubris. He was so bright, he never had to be wise. He had all the answers." Senator Phil Gramm, who is still a friend, shrugged off the article as "a lot of self-justification . . . I sort of felt that maybe David was getting this down as a way to cover his ass. I was prepared to go down with the ship." Looking back,

Gramm speculates that part of the uproar was created by "people who wanted to attack Reagan but couldn't, so they attacked Stockman. He was the most powerful person in the country at the time—that is, other than the President." Others attributed some religious significance to the entire episode: Stockman was confessing his sins to Greider.

Stockman took an enormous amount of flak from Congress, but one week after it all broke he received a bit of cheer from Gene Johnston, the congressman who had hired the clown for his birthday. Johnston sent a clipping from the November 17 New York *Times*, which had written a profile on Odessa Ferguson who had spent thirty years serving up breakfast to congressmen in the Longworth Office Building's cafeteria. The article said, "Through the years she has had her favorites. One was David Stockman . . ." Johnston attached a note that read: "Well, at least you got one friend on the Hill."

Strong negative feelings about the *Atlantic* episode also persisted among Administration officials despite Reagan's decision to keep Stockman. "Hubris is a polite term," groused one Meese associate. "It was grossly disloyal, showed a disdain for the President, and if I were the President, I would have fired him." Former White House economist Murray Weidenbaum says, "I never heard the things expressed in the *Atlantic Monthly*. Someone who cuts up the Administration like that should be fired." Martin Anderson, Reagan's former domestic policy adviser, says, "I was appalled. Stockman had never said some of those things to me. That article set back Ronald Reagan's economic policy six months to a year. It stopped the momentum dead. There were some things in it that were not true; it was an incorrect view and presented a picture to the country that was at odds with what was going on . . . Why was Dave doing this? The only answer I have was that he wanted to give his views to history . . . He had a basic character flaw—to make himself look important." Anderson's wife, Annelise, who worked with Stockman as an assistant OMB director, says she was "stunned" by the article. "One can comprehend him wanting to record history as it occurs and to establish himself as a hero, but instead of keeping a diary, he chose to speak to somebody at a time when things weren't coming out the way we predicted . . . He was quite young for responsibilities of that type, and he damaged the President. He placed his own objectives ahead of the damage it might do to the Administration. And he did a lot of damage, mainly to himself. He damaged his own ability to be an advocate within the Administration and with Congress."

Part of the damage was his de facto demotion from chief presidential budget cutter to budget technician. Larry Kudlow claims that Stockman managed to stay in his OMB post in large measure by creating an "illusion" that he was irreplaceable because no one else understood the budget numbers. "He went through this period where he wanted to be the best technician in Washington," Kudlow adds. "He adopted this new role for himself as the inside guy with the numbers. That's when all the talk surfaced about Stockman being the best numbers guy in town. That's when there were still rumors that he'd be fired. And his Republican friends on the Hill—Pete Domenici, [Senate Finance Committee Chairman] Bob Dole, [House Republican Leader] Bob Michel — all defended him by saying, 'We need him because nobody knows the numbers the way he does.' Now that, of course, is totally untrue. I mean, it's almost a silly assertion. But Dave managed to create this illusion that he and only he knew the numbers. He worked very hard at creating this illusion — very, very hard. He spread the word among the press and he carried his calculator around and he got very heavily involved in quantitative and statistical analysis . . . And the non-supply-side Republicans in Congress played along because they were scared to death of who would replace him. They figured that the White House would appoint some deficits-don't-matter type guy, like a supply-sider."

More damage was a loss of trust in him that translated into lost influence with Reagan and, therefore, lost clout in Washington. "Dave's credibility was hurt," says Michael Deaver. "I don't think Dave ever really understood the President . . . By being devious, he would just hurt his own positions." For example, Deaver recalls, "I heard the President on one occasion question Dave's position and figures." Other senior officials close to Reagan, including Baker and Regan, also saw a gap develop between the President and his budget director. "Dave clearly planted seeds of doubt in the President's mind," said one high official. And another: "I think in retrospect, after a couple years, the President may have had a change of heart about his decision to keep Dave." A third added: "I don't think he ever again had the President's confidence, though the President wasn't angry with him. You could tell in the body language. The main difference was this: before the incident, Stockman could be confident that if he presented something to the President, there was a 99 percent chance it would be rubber-stamped. Afterward it was a 99 percent chance that it would have been looked over pretty carefully."

Perhaps the heaviest price Stockman paid to keep his job was having to withstand the insults and attacks from his fellow Republicans in Congress, who would exploit his new vulnerability for political gain. If they opposed his budget proposals, rather than argue the merits of the issue, they would question the reliability of the numbers he was providing. "Everyone on the Hill knew they could stick the knife in," says one former White House official who worked closely with Stockman in his congressional dealings. "For instance, Mark Hatfield [chairman of the Senate Appropriations Committee] would say, 'Dave, you're not being square with the President.' I remember one rancorous meeting in Howard Baker's office. Hatfield and Stockman really went at each other, and Hatfield turned away from Dave and looked right at me and said, 'I want the President to know that the baseline and the numbers are incorrect. They're phony.' " A senior Senate leadership aide tells of a similar incident involving Senator Warren Rudman of New Hampshire: "Rudman asked me once how we were coming along on a CR [continuing spending resolution], and I said, 'David Stockman doesn't think we've estimated enough outlays.' And Rudman said, 'Who gives a shit what David Stockman thinks. How can we believe him?' "

The animosity was so great during the first few months after the *Atlantic* article that Stockman could not go to the Hill alone. He always had to be accompanied by Jim Baker or Dick Darman because many members would not accept Stockman's word. By January 1982, the Senate Budget Committee was wondering whether Stockman would even be able to testify on the Administration's new budget as was customary for budget directors. Domenici telephoned Bell and asked: "Do you think we should have David up?"

"Who in the hell else? Nobody else down there knows anything about the budget," Bell replied.

"Do you think they'll let him?" Domenici asked.

"Well, I don't think they'll fire him because no one else can do his job, at least no one Jim Baker could depend on."

Bell then called Stockman. "Well, are you going to come up and defend the budget?"

"Yes, I guess I am unless they tell me not to." Stockman replied.

He came up.

Besides the lingering political effects, the *Atlantic Monthly* article seems to have taken its psychological toll on both Stockman and William Greider. Without question, "The Education of David Stockman" was the most powerful piece of political writing of Reagan's first term, and it may well be enshrined as a journalistic classic. Earlier events already had slowed the Reagan Revolution and it may have halted on its own by the fall of 1981, but Greider's article made sure of that. Nevertheless, Greider has been dogged by a lingering impression that he betrayed an old friend and perhaps broke some basic rules of journalism. "Greider seemed real nice, very charming, but he pulled the wool over our eyes," said brother Dan, who met the journalist that Christmas. "Dave doesn't have much to say about him now. He thought a lot of that stuff should have been off the record." Perhaps the harshest attack against Greider came from Ronald Reagan who, in a December 1981 interview in *People* magazine, actually compared Greider to Reagan's would-be assassin, John W. Hinckley, Jr. Both Greider and Stockman deny emphatically that Greider did anything wrong, but the belief persists and it has anguished Greider considerably.

When the article first appeared, Greider also was accused of scooping his own newspaper, and some colleagues questioned his loyalty to the *Post*. Although he had informed his superiors of the arrangement and had faithfully fed material to the news pages of the *Post* from the outset, there were rumors when the article was published that *Post* Chairman Katherine Graham was upset. In 1982 Greider voluntarily left the *Post* to take what he described as a more attractive position as national correspondent and editor for *Rolling Stone* magazine. Yet many believe, incorrectly, that he had been forced out by the *Post* as a result of the *Atlantic* article. Greider, who still talks with Stockman occasionally, also has tried in later years to avoid being identified as a "Stockman expert." He says he turned down numerous invitations to appear on television shows about Stockman for that very reason. Greider also has refused to make public the complete transcripts of his conversations with Stockman despite pressures to do so, particularly after the article came out. To do so, he says, would be a violation of his agreement with Stockman.

For Stockman, the pain obviously has been deeper. At first he was hurt. "Then he became angry," says Jennifer Stockman, "at the press, at the superficial way they would take all these quotes without any substance and blow them out of proportion. He was angry at the politics in the White House. Here he was working like a dog, trying to make this thing work, and just like that — all because of misinterpretations. So at first, after he got over the shock and feeling bad that he shouldn't have done this, I think it turned into anger. And I think that's what enabled him to handle it so stoically."

It took months for the furor created by the *Atlantic Monthly* to die down and nearly a year before Stockman felt rehabilitated enough to emerge from hiding. But rumors of his imminent departure persisted throughout his tenure, and searing memories of the episode will stay with him permanently.

"It was very painful, and he knows he will have to spend the rest of his life handling it," says friend Richard Straus. "And I think a major motivation for his staying on as long as he did was so that when David Stockman finally left, the first line of the article wouldn't be, 'The man who lost his clout after the *Atlantic* article has finally disappeared from the Administration,' or 'has been let go finally.' I think he spent an enormous amount of time and effort to create something in the post-*Atlantic* era that would make his political obituary — and perhaps even, in his own mind, his eventual obituary — something other than that of a man whose potential was realized the day before the *Atlantic* article was published."

Stockman's big push in 1985 to cut middle-class programs was part of his effort to escape the shadow of the *Atlantic*, according to Straus. Although Stockman lost that battle before resigning, he showed "he was somebody who was devoted to a healthy, sensible economic policy, and somebody who was determined to fight the good fight until the last drop of blood. And I think that by showing that he did all that he could do, nobody could whisper that he was being pushed out. He was going a very far distance in erasing the whole image of somebody who was crippled, fatally undermined by the *Atlantic* article. And I think that gave him a tremendous amount of satisfaction."

And yet there is an irony to his departure. Stockman lost his last budget battle in large measure because of the *Atlantic* article. His candid admissions of earlier misrepresentations about the budget only stiffened congressional resistance to spending cuts and made his later forays against spending that much less effective. As in the case of his attempt to cut Social Security benefits in May 1981, Stockman appeared to be his own worst enemy. Repeatedly, his short-term maneuverings would work against his high-minded long-term goals. His means ultimately tended to frustrate his ends.

CHAPTER 11

STOCKMAN
AGAINST
THE WORLD

Most mortals would have been devastated by the *Atlantic Monthly* ordeal and would have dragged themselves off for a lengthy recuperation to let their shattered psyches heal. But not David Stockman. He had created the budgetary mess and, by God, he was going to set things right. So he picked himself up off the floor, dusted himself off, rolled up his sleeves and went back to work. For Stockman, the *Atlantic Monthly* controversy was a momentary personal distraction from a far more important national concern: what to do about a federal budget deficit that was now skyrocketing to once unimaginable heights— $100 billion, $150 billion, $200 billion. Even close friends were amazed that he bounced back as he did, not comprehending, apparently, that resiliency was basic to the Stockman nature. "He doesn't dwell on the past," says his mother, Carol. "That's probably part of his upbringing. We never dwelled on things. If they happened, they happened. You go from there."

The deficit gave Stockman something else to concentrate on. It consumed him. Reducing it became his exclusive policy objective, and in the process he seemed to lose touch with the real world "out there."

"He's the only guy who walks in here every day and never says hello," said one of the security guards stationed at the entrance to the old Executive Office Building. "He never said hello to anyone," explained a former aide. "It wasn't rudeness. It's just that he's shy and was totally obsessed with what he was doing. I remember he would always look down at the floor as he walked and once he bumped into a desk in the vice-president's office." But many other lower-level assistants were put off, never having seen the caring, unpretentious and occasionally even silly side that "Dave" would share with only his close friends. "I was pregnant twice while working for him and he never once said anything to me," says one aide. "I never met anyone with more brainpower. You could hold your hands out and feel the warmth of his intellect, but I could never understand how he got elected to Congress." Another aide complained that he could be insensitive to those around him: "He wanted his staff at his beck and call and he'd keep his driver waiting an hour."

His cause was too great for niceties.

Despite the ardor with which he launched his crusade, few members of the political establishment were willing to join. Most of them were infidels. Donald Regan fought his efforts to raise taxes, Cap Weinberger drove back his attacks on the Defense Budget, virtually every member of the Cabinet and most members of Congress threw up defenses to protect domestic programs from assault. Ronald Reagan agreed big deficits were bad but he didn't want to raise taxes or cut defense or risk an all-out drive against politically popular domestic programs.

Undeterred, Stockman waged his war, with the help of a few friends, year after year after year, from the end of 1981 until the summer of 1985. And when he finally left, at least no one could say he didn't try.

During those battles Stockman's already well-known reputation as an ideological zealot, budgetary wizard and round-the-clock worker took on a different cast. Many Administration officials and congressional leaders who had once admired or feared those traits now were suspicious of them and challenged them. In their minds Stockman was turning into an uncompromising fanatic on cutting the deficit who was willing to play devious games with his numbers to achieve his objectives.

"I was always impressed by his mind, his organization; he always came prepared with a piece of paper in front of him. And he was always one jump ahead of everybody else," says Michael Deaver, Reagan's former deputy chief of staff now turned private political consultant. "There is no question that technique wore thin. I think Dave got the reputation of using figures and statistics to prove his point whether they were right or wrong. By the last year his credibility was not what it was when he began. And I think any time you had to come in and lead the fight against every member of the Cabinet fours years in a row, pretty soon you lose some of that credibility. People are constantly shooting you down, poking holes in your arguments, going separately to the President or someone else and saying, 'Dave's wrong. His figures don't jibe.' Well, when it came to the need for taxes or what the growth in the economy was going to be, the President chose not to go with Dave's forecasts." Clearly Stockman's view of the world was too gloomy for the ebullient Reagan.

Stockman acknowledged that he played loose with numbers on occasion, but he could always rationalize his actions. Often he was forced to use numbers to disguise irrational policies, such as Reagan's desire to show a declining deficit without doing something real that would eliminate red ink. Other times Stockman would stretch the facts for the sake of closing a deal on a budget change that he felt was absolutely the right thing to do.

"Dave was an amazing mix between true believer and politician. He was like Jekyll and Hyde," says OMB public affairs director Ed Dale. "He was completely capable of being disingenuous, but he was not a liar." Steve Bell, who left his job as head of the Senate Budget Committee Staff in early 1986 to follow Stockman to Salomon Brothers, says he greatly admired the budget director both personally and professionally, yet "I used to get so mad at the damn budgets he'd send up here. I'd say to Domenici that this is absolute crap. The savings are exaggerated, it's the wrong baseline. What the hell is he doing? And Domenici would say very simply, 'Well, the President told him to produce a budget of a certain kind and he did the best he could do.' That was Domenici's exact answer. It's also the right answer."

Bob Dole of Kansas, who was chairman of the Senate Finance Committee until becoming Senate Majority Leader in 1985, praises Stockman for being "the best numbers guy in town." Although Dole was a major ally in Stockman's fight to reduce the deficit and credits him for doing a "masterful job" overall, even he had his reservations about how the budget director added up his numbers: "He had this enormous ability to put things together. At times, we weren't quite certain what we had when we finished. I mean, you never knew whether you had an elephant or a rat . . . Knowledge is power around here and he just had more than anybody else. And even if he didn't have it, you didn't know he didn't have it because you didn't know what the numbers were."

Dole also came to recognize that Stockman would use a variety of means to justify his own or someone else's ends: "Dave is the kind of guy that you never really were certain where he was coming from. You knew where he wanted to go, but you weren't certain how you were going to get there. There was always a little mystery about him . . . You always knew he was the brightest person around the table and you had to stand back and take a look at Dave's work to see what it really was. I'm not a numbers guy. I wanted to see where we were going. Do I want to be on this train or not? It might be going over a cliff."

Dole and other members of Congress could check out Stockman's numbers with their own staff experts, whose job it is to question and verify budget numbers provided by the executive branch. And over the years conflicts between Stockman's numbers and those estimated by congressional staffers precipitated numerous and bitter fights. The Administration, however, had no comparable check on Stockman. OMB was the final arbiter on numbers, and that became a major reservoir of Stockman's influence. Even though Cabinet secretaries and other agency heads became distrustful of his numbers at times, they were not equipped to challenge him on his terms at high-level meetings. During their fights over taxes Donald Regan tried to challenge Stockman on the spending side, but it was an impossible task and he eventually gave up. The Cabinet members had to count on political, philosophical or personal arguments to rebut his statistics, which they did with increasing success over the years. But when he kept the debate on his turf, he could be devastating.

People who were themselves comfortable with statistics tended to find his image as a numbers wizard somewhat overblown. Federal Reserve Chairman Paul Volcker, for example, cannot figure out why Stockman had such a reputation since Volcker has worked with other budget directors who, he feels, have been equally good or better figures men. Assistant OMB Director Carey P. Modlin, a thirty-five-year veteran of the agency and its highest ranking non-political appointee, says he has known budget directors equally as knowledgeable in the details, such as Charles L. Schultze, budget director under Lyndon Johnson and chief economic adviser to Jimmy Carter. What made Stockman different, however, was the extraordinary amount of time he would spend memorizing budget numbers to use them in arguments for cutting programs and as a debating ploy to intimidate his adversaries. No predecessor put in the hours he did preparing his rationales, writing briefing papers and drawing charts on his ubiquitous yellow legal pads. And no predecessor ever worked both ends of Pennsylvania Avenue the way he did, shuttling between Congress and the White House.

Colleagues are filled with stories about his obsession with numbers. One aide remembers him sitting in his chauffeured car en route to Capitol Hill scanning some lengthy testimony he was about to deliver. Suddenly spotting a small error, he got on the car telephone and the examiner confirmed that the number was, indeed, in error. Treasury Department officials tell a story about an early 1981 meeting with Stockman at which he was trying to persuade them to increase their tax revenue estimates by a few billion dollars. "Look at this," he told them as they gathered around his hand-held calculator. The display showed a number that was supposed to stand for $3 billion. Then Stockman punched in a series of numbers and help up the display, which showed a zero. "See," he said with a mischievous grin, "it's all in the rounding."

Joe Wright, Jr., deputy director at OMB, said Stockman simply became "the best budget examiner we had, and I'm talking from a technical standpoint. Dave would sit down by himself with budget books and develop an entire analysis." Wright tells the following story to illustrate:

"It was on July Fourth weekend, maybe 1983, and you know what July Fourth is like in Washington. It's hot, muggy and nobody's here. In those days when it was a holiday the only people around anywhere in the buildings were the senior people in OMB. So I walk into Dave's office and Dave had a table in there you could land a 747 on. I mean, this was one of the longest damn things you ever saw. He had it covered with budget books. He was dressed in blue jeans, tennis shoes and a T-shirt and had a little calculator and a large yellow pad. I walked up and said, 'Dave, what are you doing?' He said, 'I'm reformatting the budget,' I said, 'What budget?' He said, 'THE budget — budget of the United States.' So I said, 'David, we've got like about two hundred people I can bring in here on Tuesday to do this for you.' He said, 'No, I want to do it myself.' I said, 'Fine.' So, you know, as far as I was concerned, he had finally flipped. I said, 'I'll talk to you later.'

"I came back about eight hours later — it was like five in the afternoon. He hadn't moved. There was a half-eaten McDonald's hamburger there, right? Which is all he ever ate. And some french fries. And he's still jumping up and down around the table, working from budget book to budget book, putting together these tables on these yellow pads with a calculator. I sat down next to him and said, 'You're really going to do this?' He said, 'Yeah.' I said, 'You're going back seven years, forward five years?' He said, 'Right.' I said, 'All accounts, the entire account structure?' He said, 'The entire account structure.' I said, 'Why?' He said something like this: 'First of all, we can do no trend analysis because they change the rules every year, so we've got to establish a baseline of these trends and then put it in the computer where we can adjust it every single year.' Which is true, we hadn't had that before. 'Second, it doesn't make any sense any more and the account structure is just totally out of whack. It's been thirty years in disrepair.' Which is true. He said, 'Third, if we do this, the CBO [Congressional Budget Office] and the Congress will probably use our format, 'cause nobody else has done it, and fourth, everything I write down I memorize. And I'll know more about the budget than anybody else.' I said, 'Dave, you already do.' He said, 'Yeah, but I'll know more.' That's what he said. And, by the way, for the most part, I think he did memorize, because he had a phenomenal memory.

"So he stayed in his office for like two weeks doing this and then he brought in the programmers, spent like two days with them explaining what he had done. He personally wrote up all the account structure and personally reformatted the budget of the United States government."

Wright's account of what Stockman accomplished is a slight exaggeration. Actually, Stockman reclassified budget programs by groupings that cut across departments, such as all low-income programs, all agricultural programs, all individual "entitlement" programs. Officially known as PBBCAS ("pibcus"), for Program-Based Budget Classification and Analysis System, it regroups program-spending levels since 1962. It was designed for his personal use in developing policies, and now that he is gone, OMB is thinking about scrapping it.

The fanaticism with which he designed that computer program spilled over into his preparations for Cabinet debates. "He would have thirty arguments ready to go when in many cases he only needed ten to win," says Wright. "It's like having all six cylinders of a revolver ready to shoot when you're a good enough shot just to need one. He did overkill sometimes . . . He would have an hour's worth of material for a half-hour presentation. And he would be preparing up to the last minute, with everyone here going crazy trying to put his material together. Normally we'd deliver the material after he began his presentation at a meeting.

"At the meetings Dave would sit back in his chair smoking a cigarette while waiting his turn, looking bored if the subject didn't interest him. Then, with a minute before it was his turn, he'd sit up straight. Thirty seconds to go, the cigarette is put out. At about ten seconds to go he would sit up on the front of his chair and his feet would literally start moving. And then they'd say, 'Okay, Dave,' and he would put his stomach right against the table and start talking with his hands as if he was pushing the people sitting across from him back in their seats. He would come across with such intensity at the beginning of a Cabinet meeting, just like a wild horse coming out of a chute at the rodeo. I would sit behind him and I used to love to watch it because he went through this routine every single time."

Other Administration officials respected his awesome competitiveness in policy debates but they also despised his instincts for overkill and his preference for hand-to-hand combat over gentlemanly compromise. But his style paid off — sometimes. One Administration official who has spent more than a decade observing government policy made at high levels says the high point of his career came on a day in 1983 when he watched Stockman argue a case he had spent three days preparing for a Cabinet-level meeting to contest the Environmental Protection Agency's proposed program to clean up acid rain:

"You had these intellectual gladiators. Ten thousand EPA bureaucrats versus Stockman and OMB.

[EPA head William] Ruckelshaus conceded Stockman's numbers that the program would cost between $20 billion and $220 billion over the next twenty years, depending on the scope of the cleanup, but he argued that the question was not the money but political leadership. 'What cost do you put on that?' he asked rhetorically. Ruckelshaus had expected Stockman would be vulnerable on the political argument. But Stockman had considered the whole question and decided that the numbers were there, and he argued the environmental case brilliantly and in a way no one expected. He began by quantifying the problem, how many lakes we were talking about, how many acres they covered, how many of them are believed to be affected by acid rain, the number of fish per acre of polluted lake. And he took people carefully through this exercise with this twenty-page document that even had little pictures of fish, some with X's through them. You could see people starting to smirk and smile at each other because they knew this was vintage Stockman; he was leading down a path no one had anticipated. And then he concluded, 'If we go ahead with this it will cost the public between $6,000 and $66,000 for each pound of fish we save.' Then after a short pause for dramatic effect, he added, 'Gentlemen, this would be the most outrageous budget decision in the history of the United States.' There was total silence in the room for what seemed like two or three minutes. Finally someone spoke up and said, 'Well, we'll talk about this later.' But Stockman had been so devastating that everyone in the room knew that acid rain controls were dead from the moment he stopped speaking."

Indeed, the Administration did not support a major acid rain clean-up program while Stockman was at OMB. After his departure, the administration announced it was launching a multi-billion-dollar acid rain control program.

Stockman's style, although effective in cases such as this, could also be counterproductive. By the nature of their jobs, budget directors are not going to win popularity contests, and Stockman's budget-cutting blitz during his first months made him especially unpopular with Cabinet members who had been shown up by this young ex-congressman while they were still trying to find their way out of their executive suites. But his personality grated on many Cabinet members, half of whom were old enough to be his father. Nearly all were traditional white males from the World War II generation who had made personal fortunes in business, traveled in elite social circles and were perfectly happy with a status quo that had made them enormously successful. Many of them could match him in arrogance. But they were not as intense, as abrasive, as rigid in philosophy, or as competitive. This was not the proper style for the laid-back ambience of Reagan's White House. Some old Reagan friends from California in particular, such as Attorney General William French Smith and Interior Secretary William P. Clark, were lazy and rarely prepared, according to their colleagues. Although the Cabinet members viewed themselves as conservatives, they thought their years of experience had taught them wisdom, pragmatism and respect for others' opinions, qualities they saw lacking in Stockman. "Dave would sit back in a Cabinet meeting, cross his legs, smoke his cigarettes and reveal this look that said, 'I can't believe you're saying this dumb thing,' " said Wright. But a few of the Cabinet members—particularly Regan, Weinberger, Secretary of State Alexander Haig, Energy Secretary James Edwards, Education Secretary Terrel Bell and Interior Secretary William P. Clark—picked up those subtle betrayals of contempt and developed a personal animosity toward him. Their hostile feelings often manifested themselves in policy disputes that ultimately frustrated Stockman's goal of reducing the deficit. Many of his own colleagues conceded that had he spent more time trying to cultivate better personal relationships with the Cabinet members, especially with Donald Regan, he would have achieved greater policy successes.

Stockman, however, was not interested in becoming part of the millionaire social set in which his Cabinet colleagues traveled. He was working on policy while they spent evenings at exclusive dinner parties. He was working while they spent weekends golfing at exclusive country clubs. He was still the sixties radical, although now a radical of the Right, who was impatient for change. And the Cabinet members would regard him condescendingly as an inexperienced impetuous kid. "Remember, he never ran anything. He was the technocrat personified—a very bright guy who worked long hours," says former chief White House economist Murray Weidenbaum. "But he could be very cocky, very ambitious, very competitive, brusque and preoccupied. He would correct members of the Cabinet and upstage them. At the same time you could not always trust Dave. He could be a lovable rogue." Weidenbaum says the President seemed to treat him like a son, but Donald Regan never saw any closeness; Regan thought the President treated Stockman more like an able technocrat. Former domestic policy adviser Martin Anderson describes Stockman as "the smart kid with the numbers, but he was not Ronald Reagan's man. When Bert Lance put his arm around a Cabinet secretary, you felt Jimmy Carter's embrace. Stockman had to fight for everything and he could get rolled a lot by the senior guys—Cap, Regan, [Secretary of State George] Shultz." Larry Kudlow recalls a meeting at which "Haig really condescended to Dave like he did to everybody. I think it was a Cabinet meeting on the military budget and Haig said something like, 'My dear boy, when you get older and gain more experience you'll understand this.' And Dave really held that against him."

Stockman's youthful arrogance stemmed from his shock that so few members of the Administration understood the gravity of the deficit problem as he did. And if they did, they did not want to do anything but wring their hands. Of everyone in the Cabinet, he felt Reagan and Meese understood the problem the least. Although Stockman thought Meese was nice enough personally, he became infuriated with what he viewed as Meese's limited intelligence, ignorance, incompetence and interference on budget issues. It was Meese who was always whispering in the President's ear and persuading him to reverse one of Stockman's budget cuts on political grounds. It was Meese who talked about eliminating waste and fraud, which Stockman considered idiocy. And worst of all, it was Meese who would poach on Stockman's jealously guarded territory. Reagan and Meese took great interest in the budget savings recommended by the Grace Commission, a group of corporate executives headed by multimillionaire businessman J. Peter Grace. The commission claimed to have found hundreds of billions of dollars that could be saved, largely through better government management and efficiency. Stockman thought the findings were "a pile of crap," Ed Dale has said. But under direct orders from the President, he was forced to consider them and incorporate as many as possible into his budgets. So he passed the whole thing off to his deputy. "I don't think he ever opened the commission's report," says one close aide. "Some still think there are vast pockets of fraud, waste and abuse out there," Stockman said in an interview published by *Fortune* magazine in February 1984. "In fact, nearly every stone has been turned over." The message was intended for Reagan and Meese, but he never got through to them, he later said.

Stockman also became upset after the 1984 election when Meese began working on his own set of budget proposals, based on suggestions he was getting from conservative think tanks. Stockman insisted that Baker get Meese to stop, which he eventually did. "That just brought back a lot of bad memories Stockman had about Meese, because they used to tangle on a lot of things," says Larry Kudlow. Stockman did not have much patience with people he considered to be intellectual lightweights, Kudlow says, adding, "but he also didn't have much patience with people who disagreed with him. There's a certain hubris there. In other words, Dave was sometimes unable to see through the veil of a disagreement and recognize the merits of somebody else's argument. He was very bull-headed about this."

That was the side of Stockman that most of the Cabinet saw, although Kudlow and other associates note that he was always very open to new ideas from people whose intellects he respected. He just didn't find very many of them in the top echelons of the Reagan Administration. From the Cabinet's standpoint, he was letting his ideological purity and radical spirit get in the way of sounder and more pragmatic political judgements. Although the Cabinet members agreed with Stockman's free-market views in principle, they would argue that his extreme solutions would get him nothing, whereas a middle course might succeed.

Commerce Secretary Malcolm Baldrige, who supported most of Stockman's budget cuts, fought one attempt by the budget director to eliminate most of the department's export-promotion activities. Baldrige was stunned that Stockman would take an ideological approach that was not tempered by business experience. Baldrige argued that Stockman was right in principle but that a unilateral move by the United States to eliminate export subsidies would give a distinct advantage to foreign competitors, because their governments would continue subsidizing exports. In Baldrige's mind, Stockman was jousting at windmills without considering the practical effects. Baldrige won that fight.

Samuel R. Pierce, Jr., secretary of Housing and Urban Development, claims to have had a friendly relationship with Stockman. The only issue on which they would regularly fight was continuation of the Urban Development Action Grants (UDAG) program. Stockman was always trying to eliminate UDAG, a grant program that combines federal, private and state or local funds to promote economic development in distressed areas. Stockman argued that the funds were not really reaching poverty areas and that cities were misusing the money. "From the day I got here, David Stockman did not like UDAG," says Pierce. "David argued well, but I didn't buy it.-I said when you have a program that big, it can't be 100 percent perfect, but the vast majority was good. I argued that it was the kind of Republican program that the President liked because it was a public-private partnership." Stockman lost the first few rounds with Reagan. "I wanted to get rid of that entirely," he said in a 1984 interview with the author. "That is the worst kind of thing, where you're just spreading money around, moving investment and jobs from one city to another. But Meese got convinced by somebody that this was a Republican kind of program because it mobilized private capital, which is what they always say for any federal spending program, and I lost." Obviously, Meese got convinced by Pierce. Stockman finally persuaded Reagan to propose an end to UDAG in his 1986 budget. Congress, however, did not go along.

Pierce says Stockman also tried unsuccessfully to phase out the Federal Housing Administration (FHA) loan program and to turn the Government National Mortgage Association over to the private sector. "But I will tell you that Dave hit my heart in one area," says Pierce, who is black. "He was very good protecting programs aimed at getting rid of discrimination. He never tried to cut our budget for fair housing and equal opportunity enforcement. He was fair in this regard. His heart was in the right place."

Interior Secretary James Watt was among the few Cabinet officials who had no major policy differences with Stockman, because he was as ideologically extreme as the budget director. Where they differed was over who should be calling the shots. Watt settled that dispute at one Cabinet meeting, according to one former White House official, who quoted Watt as stating, "Mr. President, I thought I ran the Interior Department. If you want Dave to, I'll resign. Otherwise, I'll decide on the cuts." Added the official, "After that, Stockman didn't want to go to the mat with Watt. Watt knew his stuff."

On the other hand, one of Stockman's most vociferous opponents on policy was Harry N. Walters, head of the Veterans Administration. "Dave would get furious when Harry would turn Meese around on the VA," says one White House official. John Cogan, who worked as an associate OMB director from 1983 to 1985, recalls Stockman having a particularly difficult session with Walters in the winter of 1984-85. "It got downright nasty in tone." Cogan said Stockman had won Administration backing for a change in VA insurance coverage that would slow down rising costs, but the measure ultimately died in Congress in 1985.

It was well known that one of Stockman's favorite tactics in his policy battles with the Cabinet was the element of surprise. But he outdid himself in early December 1984, when Reagan held a special Cabinet meeting for Stockman to review the budget cuts he had been preparing in secret during Reagan's campaign for reelection. Stockman's list of draconian budget cuts was so sensitive that even Cabinet heads were not told before the election, lest it leak out and damage Reagan, whose campaign was based on feel-good themes, such as his claim that the economy would grow its way out of the deficits. Now with the election over, it was safe to go back on that pledge. James C. Sanders, head of the Small Business Administration, recalls having to cut short a meeting with SBA regional managers in California and catch a red-eye flight back to Washington for a 10:00 A.M. Cabinet meeting for all department and independent agency heads, the President and the Vice-President.

When Sanders first looked at a summary of the 1986 budget plan that Stockman had passed out, he thought he must have been punchy from his overnight flight. "I looked for a line on SBA and it was pretty obvious there was not going to be an agency there," he says. "It was to be phased out on December 31, 1986." Sanders was not the only one surprised. William H. Draper, chairman of the Export-Import Bank, discovered that the bank's direct-lending programs were to be eliminated. Pierce discovered cuts in subsidized housing. Margaret Heckler, Secretary of Health and Human Services, discovered that some Social Security offices were to be closed. Transportation Secretary Elizabeth Dole discovered that subsidies for Amtrak were being eliminated. "By doing this in front of the President, it had a great psychological effect, like a fait accompli," says Sanders, who appealed the termination of his agency during a forty-five-minute meeting with Reagan on December 20, 1985.

"I argued that it was not a very good strategy to eliminate an entire agency, that we could eliminate 75 percent of the cost without eliminating the independence of the agency, which was a creation of Congress and a symbol to small businesses. I warned that we'll lose other fights and lose credibility with Congress. Stockman argued that the agency was badly perceived and benefitted only a small minority of businesses. I said we were using market interest rates and he was exaggerating his arguments. He claimed most of our loans went to new restaurants and bars, and I said Americans like restaurants and bars. They're not un-American. I said we weren't into industrial policy, where we decided which industries should get loans. And I said that, frankly, the only effect I could see that OMB has had on us was to put us back more deeply into farm lending. After the President left, Stockman said that last comment was unfair. I said it was a fact." Sanders lost the appeal, and the administration proposed transferring SBA into the Commerce Department under a new office of economic opportunity. Ultimately the SBA was saved by Congress, but Sanders says it was for all the wrong reasons and without achieving any cost reductions that he could have won. The episode also created lingering personal animosity. Stockman publicly had described the SBA as "a billion-dollar rathole." Sanders publicly criticized Stockman as an "embarrassment" to the Administration because of his abrasive and confrontational style, and he said Stockman's budget-cutting assistants were "fanatics with no real-life experience," "zombies," and "mechanical prostitutes."

Richard Schweiker, Heckler's predecessor as Secretary of Health and Human Services, supported most of Stockman's cuts in his agency but occasionally felt Stockman was overzealous in finding small savings in programs that were popular and effective. Because Schweiker knew about his budget as a result of his years as a U.S. senator from Pennsylvania, he and Stockman worked cooperatively during the first round of budget cuts in 1981. Where they had their biggest clash was in the winter of 1982-83:

"My department had reduced growth by about ten to eleven billion dollars and I thought our budget was in pretty good shape for the new fiscal year. But Stockman comes back with about 250 million dollars of Mickey Mouse items that I couldn't conceive of us doing. There were about fifty items in all. One was to eliminate an Indian health service program that provided medical care. Another included measles vaccinations. I thought that was ridiculous because we were just on the verge of eliminating the measles epidemic. I thought it would be foolish to fight and shed blood on these. It violated the Safety Net, it was political suicide and it would never pass the Hill.

"So I went through the appeals process and just Meese and Stockman were there. I started, 'Okay, I'm going to pretend I'm the producer for CBS news. Let's bring cameras into an Indian reservation and have them grind away while doctors pack their things and leave. And the reporter explains how these people living in abject poverty will get no medical help whatsoever because Ronald Reagan is making doctors and nurses leave. The next day the cameras visit a measles clinic where doctors are closing things up, and CBS speculates about what will happen. Will there be a Reagan measles epidemic? I feel strongly enough about these issues that Reagan should understand who is responsible for putting him on the evening news.' At that, Stockman pulled out a white handkerchief and started to wave it. It never got to the President and I got fifty cuts back. Meese said I got the academy award for the best dramatic presentation by a Cabinet officer."

A senior White House official said Stockman won high marks for his dedication in trying to reduce domestic spending, but he became so obsessed with cutting costs that he failed to see merit in any programs: "He originally wanted to get rid of the space shuttle and curtail NASA dramatically," said the official. "He argued we should let private business do it. Well, the funding went in the other direction and he would crack, 'You guys and your space program.' We saw it as important and a symbol of a vision for the future. The Cabinet came to appreciate there were some things worth funding. Sometimes Dave lacked a breadth on these. For example, Ruckelshaus once argued that the EPA needed a program to remove carcinogens from public drinking water. Dave was against it, and we said, 'Come on, Dave, what is the President supposed to do? Come out for cancer-causing chemicals in water?"

It was always a battle between politics and ideology, and in Stockman's mind, the wrong side kept winning.

437

Of all the fights Stockman would wage over domestic spending, none consumed as much of his time and passion as farm programs. Because he grew up on a farm that did not depend on government subsidies, he felt he had real-world experience to support his free-market principles. He could not make that claim about other programs, since he had never worked in the private sector during his adult years. His attitude toward farm subsidy and crop marketing programs was simple and straightforward: they should be eliminated to let the marketplace determine price and supply. That position put him in constant conflict with Agriculture Secretary John Block and Deputy Secretary Richard E. Lyng, who succeeded Block in 1986.

Lyng knew a lot about farm programs, having worked at the Agriculture Department of four years during the Nixon Administration, but Block, a former head of Illinois agriculture department, knew very little about the federal programs. On the other hand, Stockman and his assistant Fred Khedouri were extremely knowledgeable and took the lead in setting farm policies for the administration. On Capitol Hill Stockman was regarded as the real secretary of agriculture, and Block was viewed as a likeable yokel who took his orders like a good soldier. Stockman quickly wrote Block off as a lightweight and treated him disrespectfully. Aides to the OMB director recall that during Block's frequent visits to OMB, Stockman would make him wait in his outer office for ten minutes or so, and he would make fun of how easy it was to defeat Block on policy disputes. "Once I went over to David's office and saw Block waiting in the anteroom, and I'd go in and Block was still waiting outside. "I was astonished," says one close friend. "I walked up to David's secretary and said, 'Isn't that the Secretary of Ag?' And she said, 'Yes, he's here all the time.'" A close aide of Stockman's remembers a meeting in the OMB conference room in 1981 to discuss pending farm legislation: "John Block strolled into the room, no material, no staff. Stockman naturally had thick sheafs of paper and proceeded to trash Block's arguments on the bill and legislative strategy. Dave went on for thirty minutes and it was embarrassing to watch Block just sit there. Finally he said, 'Now, Dave, just a minute,' and he fumbles around in his chair. 'I'm not sure all this is true.' God, how ill-prepared he was."

Over the years Block would loyally trek up Capitol Hill to sell Stockman's radical farm program cuts to Congress, only to lose over and over again. In the end, both Block and Lyng contend, Stockman's fanaticism proved counterproductive; the Administration would have gotten a lot further in the farm area by going a lot slower.

Lyng, a modest and plain-talking Californian who respected Stockman's abilities and liked him for being "an independent cuss," vividly remembers the first time he and Block met the new budget director in his office in early 1981. "We walked out shaking our heads in wonder—not dismay or concern, but just wonder—at this guy who knew more about the budget at the Department of Agriculture than we did," says Lyng. Although Lyng considers himself an economic conservative, as does Block, neither were prepared for the hard line Stockman took at that first meeting. As Lyng recalls:

"He said, 'We want to do away with the dairy [price] support programs.' And I said, 'No, you can't do that, you'd have a shortage of milk.' He said, 'You can't have a shortage of milk because the price would get higher and some people would stop buying milk. But the market would adjust to that. I believe in the market system.' And I said, 'But we also believe that every poor child should have access to milk. Milk is different than other things.' I don't think he had thought about that side of it. I don't say that we totally disagreed on that but he pointed to a picture on the wall and said, 'Do you see that farm there? I milked cows on that farm until I was fifteen. There're a lot of people that have gone out of the dairy business like my family and there are better things for people to do than milk cows.'" In recalling that conversation in later years, Stockman said he was trying to explain that his parents got out of the dairy business because they couldn't make a profit. But his parents say the business had been profitable. They got out because they would have had to expand the operation to keep it profitable, and their sons were too busy with sports and other high school activities to help run a bigger dairy.

In late 1983 Reagan signed a new dairy price-support bill into law over Stockman's vehement objections. Stockman later complained that Reagan opposed the bill on principle but signed it at the urging of Ed Meese and ultraconservative Senator Jesse Helms of North Carolina, who attached a tobacco price-support bill to the legislation. Stockman complained that Helms had mobilized the New Right network to lobby Meese and Reagan. "It was a rotten bill and it should have been vetoed," Lyng concedes, except for a very major political consideration: the old law called for an increase in the support price on October 1, 1984, a month before the presidential election. The new bill had a different schedule, so milk prices would not rise just before the election. Lyng also recalls that the new bill had strong bipartisan support and that the tobacco bill attached by Helms actually lowered support prices. "So the President signed it and Dave was just livid. He was mad at me. At a Cabinet meeting the next morning, he said, 'I hope you're satisfied you got that rotten bill signed.' "

Block was always impressed with Stockman's intelligence, but he became distressed with the budget director's philosophy: it's not how you play the game, but whether you win or lose. Before a meeting with the President, Block would check with other Cabinet members on issues where they might be in conflict to "be sure that we were pretty much in sync," but Stockman would never reveal his position. "I'd go over and see him and say, 'David, for Chrissakes, let's work together to try to carry a united front. Maybe we could work out the differences and then go together.' . . . But Dave's strategy was to never tell you anything — or to tell you very little — about where he stood on the issue, and he'd always come to the meeting prepared to throw out a surprise paper or new surprising statistics, whether they could be documented at the time or not, and there's never time to launch a counterattack on that occasion. And I always felt that that was a devious approach . . . That was his way of winning and I think that's fine. I think you should try to win. But I think there are rules that you go by, because the truth is, we're all here to serve the President . . . I just don't think Dave appreciated the importance of fair play. The importance of winning overrode the necessity to engage in fair play."

Both Lyng and Block also complain that Stockman's radical approach to cutting farm programs cost him more money in the long run. One example Block cited came in the spring of 1983 when Stockman was trying to get Reagan to change Agriculture Department marketing orders, which prop up prices of certain fruits, nuts and vegetables through regulations that limit supplies. Stockman, knowing Reagan's weakness for visual images and for heroes, sent him a blown-up magazine photograph showing a huge supply of oranges rotting on a hill. Attached to the photo was a letter and a brief memo that said:

1. On complex economic arguments, sometimes a picture is worth a thousand words! The attached shows thousands of tons of oranges rotting because the federal marketing order made it illegal for growers to sell them.
2. Please read the attached letter from a World War II veteran and German prisoner of war—who is being financially ruined by the USDA spearmint marketing order. It tells the whole story.
3. I strongly urge that you approve Option 2 and get rid of this forty-five-year-old relic from Henry Wallace's so-called 'New Deal'

farm program.

Stockman also showed the pictures to Reagan during a Cabinet meeting at which Stockman argued that the government was interfering in the marketplace at the expense of higher prices to consumers. Stockman had gotten Block to go along, and Reagan initially went along too. Then politics intervened in a big way. It turned out that many large-scale growers in California liked the marketing order the way it was, and they raised hell with Meese, "who turned that around and blew Stockman out the door," says Block. "I think California came down real hard on the White House and they had to back off." Not only that, but Congress became so infuriated with Stockman's meddling that it passed a law later that year that barred OMB from having any input in marketing orders.

Block and Lyng were also upset that Stockman ignored their recommendations for a new farm bill in 1985, a bill that they had drafted after a year's study. Instead, Stockman and Fred Khedouri put together a bill that cut back farm programs severely—and was dead on arrival at the Congress. The Congress then wrote its own bill without paying any attention to the Administration. As a result, instead of the $8 billion farm bill Stockman had proposed at the start of 1985, Reagan wound up signing a bill later in the year that was estimated to cost more than $50 billion. "His approach was always so severe and harsh, you lose your credibility with Congress," says Block. "If you're just way too far out, they just kind of ignore you. But he felt he knew better how to do what was to be done than the secretary."

Adds Lyng: "His was a radical approach, ours was a gradual one. That was the major difference, and I think that his radical approach failed to understand the politics that frustrated him so badly and, as a result, he accomplished very little . . . He was a fellow who would work himself right down to the nib. He had to be a young, strong guy—he didn't look very strong—but he had to be very strong because he worked all hours, you know. He would study the Defense budget or the budget at Health and Human Services or Agriculture, and he was so bright he would absorb all this stuff. But in forming the conclusions he just didn't have time to compare with some of us who might not have been nearly as smart but had one segment of knowledge. He didn't even have time to listen to us in great detail . . . I would have liked to have seen him go into a little less detail and be a little more political and try to get some results rather than go down in flames, as he did too often."

Stockman's final crash-landing on the subject of farming came February 5, 1985, as he testified before the Senate Budget Committee on the President's new budget proposals. When Republican Senator Robert Kasten of Wisconsin asked when the Administration would propose legislation dealing with the farm-credit crisis, Stockman let loose:

> We built our way brick by brick to a trillion-dollar budget, brick by brick to a quarter of a trillion-dollar deficit by responding to desperate needs, emergency crises, without any explanation or reason as to why it was the federal

government's responsibility in the first place.

For the life of me, I cannot figure out why the taxpayers of this country have the responsibility to go in and refinance bad debt that was willingly incurred by consenting adults who went out and bought farmland when the price was going up and thought they could get rich, or who went out and bought machinery and production assets because they made a business judgement that they could make some money.

Why do the taxpayers have the responsibility to bail out through loan guarantees, which will create costs down the road, that kind of speculation. If that had been caused in the first place by New York banks and other city slickers who tempted those farmers with money to buy land, it would be one thing. But I can prove to you that the entire land boom from 1977 to 1981 was financed by the farm credit administrations, particularly the land banks, which are owned and controlled by the farmers, who made loans to each other to buy each other's land. And now that has all gone sour, because it was based on unsound economics and because it was propped up with federal price supports and cheap credit which could not be justified.

I do not see why we have the responsibility to step in, why it is any different than small businesses, the hundreds of thousands of them that go out of business each year, the 1,000 savings and loans that have closed since 1980, the hundreds of thousands of people who have lost their jobs in the auto industry. . .

We are probably going to have to do something, because the drumbeat of political demand is so great and because, basically, we are threatened with a kind of blackmail situation . . . I think it is a sad day that those kinds of threats are being made, but frankly they are, and so we will end up probably having to do something. But it is sure a bad way to start the process of trying to get our fiscal house in order where . . . the one group that has had the greatest budget excess in the last five years, $60 billion in farm subsidies, starts the log rolling by demanding more. That is a little bit discouraging.

It was vintage Stockman. Once again he demonstrated his brilliant analysis, his powerful articulation of the case for a free-market economy, his total honesty at the expense of political trouble and a complete blind spot when it comes to the human part of the equation. What he said was true. Block knew it. So did Lyng. So did some of the farmers who are going under. But that didn't make the fear and desperation go away. "Even those that agree with him resent it when he says it. That's the funny thing, see?" says Lyng. "I even kind of agree with what he said, but . . . you got a bunch of broke farmers faced with a strong dollar, change in inflation, falling land values, people committing suicide. People in the top level of government positions should show a little compassion for this sort of thing. Dave showed none."

It was just another one of those ironies about him. A farm boy made good who does not accept the national political consensus in the country that family farms should be exempt from the normal rules of the free market and be given preferential treatment — a view that perhaps derives from the country's roots as an agrarian society made great by the sweat of those who worked the land. These were David Stockman's roots too, and yet he became known as the Reagan budget-cutter who hated farmers.

"He's very bright but flippant at times. Who else could say that the farmer is responsible for his own plight, which is ludicrous," says Jack Kemp. "I mean, given the fact that we've gone from a rapid inflation to a rapid deflation, only David Stockman could then say that fault lies with the farmer when demonstrably the fault is with the government." Phil Gramm adds wryly, "Truth is like a powerful drug, to be used sparingly. Stockman knew he was leaving."

That latest example of Stockman's ideological fanaticism stirred up such a ruckus that even his mother was portrayed as disowning his comments, although her criticism was based on a misunderstanding of what he had said. A reporter from radio station WHO, in Des Moines, Iowa, where Ronald Reagan once worked as a sports announcer, had asked Carol Stockman to comment on her son's claim that there were too many farmers in the country. After the reporter said the comments "didn't sit well with Iowa's farmers," she said, "I don't think it will set too well with me either. I think he doesn't realize that there's not many young farmers getting into it anymore. They just can't afford it anymore." She added, "I know there are people that are really hurting. When I looked at our books last week and found out how much money we lost, I was awed, really." Later, interviewed by a Benton Harbor radio station, she said, "There might be too many corporate farms, but there can never be enough young farmers." The interview became big news around the country, prompting a telephone call home from a very displeased son. He said his comments were misinterpreted: she said *her* comments were misinterpreted and stressed that she had agreed with his basic argument that farmers should not rely on the government to solve their problems. Looking back at the flap, Al Stockman says: "If he had talked about too many farmers as individuals, then he was wrong, because if an individual goes out of farming, somebody else picks up his land and farms it anyway. So you're still going to have the surplus." But in the folklore about Ronald Reagan's young budget-slasher, it will always be remembered that even his mother thought he could be heartless.

Like his inability to find a solution to the poverty in Benton Harbor and his opposition to loan guarantees for Chrysler, Stockman's attack on the farm crisis reinforced the impression that he is incapable of feeling compassion for those in trouble.

"I remember when [former Defense Secretary] Robert McNamara was here in the early sixties, and I think McNamara and Stockman are very much alike," says one former Reagan Cabinet secretary. "Both were brilliant, had great analytical minds, were incredibly knowledgeable, but they never cranked the human equation into the figures. McNamara didn't take that into account as a factor during the Vietnam war, and Stockman had the same problem with the impact of the human factor on the budget. Really, when you think of it, both of them had these computerlike minds that didn't give the same weight to human input as they did to numerical imput. It was always the body count and the budget. Now, McNamara has mellowed since then, and perhaps Stockman is in the process of doing that too."

Stockman's wife argues that he gets a bad rap on the compassion question. Jennifer Stockman says he feels it, he just does not express it; he is a caring person who feels anguished when he sees the homeless on the street but he separates his personal feelings from his work. "He can't even stand to look at them when he'd walk down the street when they're sitting on the grates, but he doesn't feel it's a federal responsibility," she says. "He does believe in giving to charities. He believes in doing what he can personally. It's not that he doesn't want to do anything. He's very generous."

It is true, she says, that he can be ideologically rigid, as so many former colleagues in the White House and at the Cabinet table found. But now that he is a new father, his wife points out, David Stockman is starting to consider the human part of the equation:

"It's funny. Now we have a baby and I look at the Consumer Product Safety Commission, which he wanted to abolish. I remember we bought a Johnny Jumper, and they're a little frightening. You attach them to a door and if they fall, my God, the baby could be seriously hurt. But it had the CPSC seal of approval. And I said to him, kind of tongue in cheek, 'Aren't you happy that we have a government commission to tell us the product's okay?' He couldn't disagree with me, and you know what he thinks about the commission. But he was relieved that at least he wouldn't have to learn the hard way. His first reaction was to say, 'Well, if they really hurt babies, then obviously they wouldn't sell any more. The market would make it an unmarketable product because it would deem the product unsafe.' But I said, 'Aren't you glad that we don't have to be one of the test cases?' Well, he understood. I mean, he agreed in a way. But he doesn't like to agree because it's much easier to see things as black and white. It's much easier to be consistent and he's been very consistent."

Stockman's fights with the Cabinet over domestic cuts were skirmishes compared to his ferocious battles with Reagan over taxes and with Weinberger over defense spending. It was obvious that the deficit could not be closed just by cutting domestic programs. All the politicians in Congress, the Cabinet and the Oval Office made that clear. Defense and taxes were the two other legs of the three-legged stool Stockman wanted to build to narrow the deficit, but his senior Cabinet colleagues did not want to sit on that stool. As it turned out, neither did Ronald Reagan.

Of all Stockman's feuds within the administration, none took on the bitter personal dimension that characterized his long-running arguments with Donald Regan. Not only did they have fundamental disagreement over economic policy, but they developed considerable contempt for each other. Regan comes from Ronald Reagan's generation and has almost nothing in common with Stockman in terms of background, personality and the social sets in which they travel. Twenty-eight years older than the budget director, Regan was born in 1918 to Irish-Catholic parents in Cambridge, Mass., went to Harvard, where he became a Republican for life, and saw combat as a Marine officer during World War II. After the war he spent thirty-four years on Wall Street, where he climbed to the top of the world's largest brokerage firm, Merrill Lynch and Company, and amassed a multimillion-dollar fortune along the way. Regan has the charm and social grace of a supersalesman, but he also is a fearsome, demanding boss with a quick temper. When he came to Washington he had no political experience but he knew plenty about the wheeling and dealing in the corporate world, where total team play and loyalty to one's organization are demanded. Like Stockman, Regan has a very large ego and boundless ambition to acquire power. But whereas Stockman never seemed to be conscious of his own ego drives, which gave him a certain unpretentious charm, Regan was very much in touch with his and struck many people as a vain peacock. Regan also has as strong a competitive drive as Stockman, a trait the budget director had underestimated in his rival, to his later regret. Stockman proved to be the hare and Regan turned out to be the tortoise.

When he was named Secretary of the Treasury, Regan was told he would be chief economic spokesman for the Administration, but it was clear that Stockman had usurped that role for himself at the outset. He was the one with all the answers and the one getting the media attention, while Regan stood uncomfortable in the younger man's shadow. That did not go down well with Regan. "The publicity factor was a very important factor," says John "Buck" Chapoton, an attorney who served as an assistant treasury secretary for tax policy during Regan's first term. "It grated on Don because it gave Stockman more power." Stockman aggravated the strain by dismissing Regan as a vain, rich Wall Streeter who was not particularly intelligent, had no knowledge about the federal budget and was ignorant in the ways of politics. Regan picked up on those feelings. He sensed that Stockman disdained his skill in running a large organization and making a lot of money for himself and his clients. In return, Regan thought of Stockman as the smart kid in school who always raises his hand first when the teacher asks a question. In Regan's eyes Stockman was a walking encyclopedia on the budget but a cold fish when it came to personality and a little too slick when it came to tactics. He assumed early on that Stockman could not be trusted and would use numbers to overwhelm his opponents in the Administration. What Donald Regan, the loyal team player, found most surprising about Stockman was the budget director's determination to place his own desire to balance the budget above the President's desire to cut taxes.

The two men began clashing over policy as early as the spring of 1981. Regan would hit the roof over leaks in the newspapers or reports from friends in Congress indicating that Stockman was trying to negotiate his own deal on a tax cut, which was supposed to be Regan's show. "Goddamn it! Stock-man isn't even a part of these meetings. I'm doing the negotiating," Regan would yell at his staff. Once, after reading a newspaper story quoting a senior Administration official about a possible tax compromise, he exploded with: "That son of a bitch Dave leaked another story." After the tax cut passed and Stockman began lobbying behind the scenes for tax increases, Regan would counter by arguing that there still were plenty of budget cuts to go after first, and that the deficit was not as terrible a threat to the economy as conventional wisdom suggested. Privately, Stockman would ridicule Regan's views and say he was a fool to think that way. "Regan just doesn't understand the budget," he would say, sometimes referring to him as the "chancellor."

Initially Stockman's biggest mistake was to ignore Regan rather than to try to cultivate a personal relationship and discuss budget-cutting with him. Had he done so he might well have had a powerful ally instead of a resentful enemy. But it apparently never occurred to him. Stockman thought strictly in terms of policy and numbers, not personal alliances. "Regan became very frustrated and angry with Dave," says J. Gregory Ballentine, who worked for both men, first as a deputy assistant treasury secretary for tax analysis and then as chief OMB economist. "Every time he [Regan] would say 'just cut 5 percent across the board,' Stockman would wave sheafs of paper at him, saying, 'No, you can't,' and it would drive Regan up the wall. Stockman would not take the time to educate Regan about the numbers and Regan did not trust Stockman. He didn't think Stockman should be a big decision-maker; he thought Stockman should be a staff man kept on a short leash."

Chapoton recalls Regan coming back from White House meetings furious with Stockman. "He would castigate Dave for making up presentations that were pushing the President in the direction of taxes," said Chapoton, who sided with Stockman despite working for Donald Regan. "When Dave talked about the danger of deficits, we came out with this deficits-don't-matter line. Dennis [Thomas, a Regan deputy] argued that we needed to take the emphasis off deficits. I thought that was one of the dumbest ideas."

During his first year at the Treasury, Regan's inner circle readied him like a prizefighter. Most of them were supply-siders or just generally anti-tax, and they would prep him with statistics and talking points, stiffen his resolve and send him out to square off with the quick-footed Stockman. Regan would come back bruised, battered and discouraged. Stockman was too knowledgeable and clever; he did not need to depend on written briefings prepared by his staff, as did Regan. So the Treasury team would clean him up, give him another pep talk and send him in again. At one Treasury meeting Regan's aides were urging him to oppose Stockman's plan for "revenue enhancements," which the budget director claimed were not really tax increases. Ann Dore McLaughlin, Regan's assistant secretary for public affairs, put a wind-up duck labeled "tax increase" on the conference table during a senior staff meeting. The message: "if it walks like a duck . . ."

After the *Atlantic Monthly* furor Regan eclipsed

Stockman as the unchallenged chief economic spokesman for the President. And he ingratiated himself with Reagan by drawing a sharp contrast between Stockman's apparent disloyalty and his own devotion to the Reagan agenda. And whereas Stockman was the chronic pessimist about the economy, Regan was the constant optimist—a viewpoint with which the President cheerfully identified. When Stockman survived the *Atlantic* controversy, in spite of Regan's recommendation to the contrary, the treasury secretary predicted to aides that Stockman would turn into a mere "numbers cruncher." But Stockman still could wield influence through his patron Jim Baker, much to Regan's displeasure. In late 1982 Regan arranged a secret weekend meeting with the President and Secretary of State George Schultz to show them a plan his staff had written for the upcoming budget. According to one former Regan aide, the President approved the plan in principle: but when word reached Stockman, who had been excluded from the meeting, he became furious and got Baker to ease the President away from it. Yet even though Stockman managed to reassert his role as budget chief, he had to defer to Regan on broad economic policy questions. If Stockman wanted to get Ronald Reagan to raise taxes or cut defense spending, he had to persuade Donald Regan first.

When Regan became White House chief of staff in early 1985 it was clear that Stockman would not stay long. Regan did not want Stockman around, and the budget director was not interested in staying. Stockman had been thinking seriously of leaving since 1984, but Regan's move to the White House reinforced his feeling and he notified the new chief of staff in February 1985 that he would leave at a suitable time. Regan did not encourage Stockman to change his mind, and both agreed that the summer was the right time for a leave-taking. Now that Regan had settled into Stockman's turf, Stockman would try his luck in Regan's old stomping grounds — Wall Street.

One Cabinet-level official, who is close to Stockman but has worked closely with Regan as well, contends that the source of their friction was more personality than policy:

"The problem with Regan is his own personality and David's command of the media. As we've seen in his current job, Regan wants to be Numero Uno so much that he has to surround himself with mice so that there's not a remote possibility of anyone being in competition for attention, for power, for anything. Regan was supposed to be Numero Uno for the economy, that's what he thought he was here for. And what he discovered was David on the cover of *Newsweek*. Stockman was unquestionably viewed as Number One in economic policy-making. And I think that it was fundamentally *that* that bothered Regan. It wouldn't have made any difference if they'd agreed on policy. The policy disagreements became an excuse, an opportunity for Regan to try to do Dave in. He saw his way to becoming a true-blue Reaganaut when he saw that Dave was deviating. Regan could be more Catholic than the Pope, appeal to the President and dump on this upstart kid."

Stockman's feud with Regan did not end with his departure. If anything, from what he told friends, he planned to intensify the fight by making Regan one of the principal heavies in his memoirs on his Administration experiences. Stockman told Regan about his plans to write a book on the day he announced his formal resignation. The conversation he relayed to friends went like this:

Regan: "Well, if I were you, I'd go out and write a book."

Stockman: "Funny you should mention that, Don. . . ."

Regan: "Now, don't burn your bridges. Your worth to Salomon Brothers is mainly dependent on me and the President."

Although Regan later contended to associates that he was quoted out of context, Stockman said Regan added: "You know, you're making a big mistake going to Salomon Brothers. You'll never get ahead there. You're not Jewish."

Stockman's battles with Weinberger over defense spending took on a pattern similar to his fights with Regan, except that Stockman always respected Cap's tenacity as a turf-fighter, a talent learned from decades of government experience. "David once said that if he were ever sent up death row, he would want Weinberger as his defense attorney because he's so indefatigable," says a friend. "He could never beat him." Tempted with that prospect Weinberger, one suspects, might give up on the final appeal.

Weinberger, twenty-nine years Stockman's senior, is a native Californian who earned a law degree from Harvard and won a Decorated Bronze Star during

World War II, during which he rose from the rank of private to captain in the infantry. When Ronald Reagan was governor of California Weinberger served as state finance director for two years. In 1970 he came to Washington, where he spent the next five years as chairman of the Federal Trade Commission, OMB director and Secretary of Health, Education and Welfare. "Cap the Knife" was a hero to Stockman when the younger man first moved to Washington. But when Stockman became budget director, he soon became disillusioned with Weinberger's refusal to scale back a defense buildup that Stockman insists grew much larger than originally intended. It wasn't long before Stockman would ridicule Cap in private — as he did nearly ever other senior Administration official.

Stockman and his inner circle at OMB would joke about how Weinberger and Secretary of State George Schultz had presided over "Great Society II" during their years running economic policy for Nixon. Schultz preceded Weinberger at OMB and also served as Secretary of Labor and Treasury. Stockman complained that while the excesses of the social-welfare state began under Lyndon Johnson, they accelerated under Nixon. Stockman blamed the trend on both politics and incompetence: Johnson's Great Society programs were meant to aid the poor; Nixon would buy votes in the form of benefit programs aimed at the middle-class. And in the case of programs he opposed, Nixon's administration lacked the legislative skills to stop the Democratic Congress from expanding them. To Stockman, the Democrats made fools of Nixon's men on domestic policy. Once as an internal gag Stockman and his crew drew a chart that showed the steep rise in federal spending in every agency that Weinberger ever headed, from the FTC to the Pentagon. The more Cap won the defense fight with Reagan, the more Stockman would reveal his contempt. "Dave used to think Cap was stubborn, but now he thinks he's just plain dumb," one OMB aide confided in 1985.

Stockman's disagreement with Weinberger on defense derived from the original set of of numbers they agreed to put into the February 1981 budget plan. Stockman insists that they agreed on an arbitrary rate of growth for the defense budget — 7 percent a year after discounting inflation — and then Stockman used a calculator to determine the figures for each year. But the figures were never backed up by a precise accounting of actual military needs. Stockman would say that an unexpected drop in inflation, and his mistake in using a larger base than he should have for calculating the annual rate of increase, allowed the Pentagon budget to balloon much faster than planned — an average 10 percent a year after adjusting for inflation. "The numbers were pulled out of thin air and then became a Rock of Gibraltar," Stockman later declared.

But Weinberger insists that there was no miscalculation, that the growth path of the defense budget was intentional and based on military needs, not a numerical rule of thumb. And so he would refuse to make more than token cuts at the edges, and Reagan went along.

This became the basis of their dispute, and they would argue it over and over and over, even after

Stockman was gone. "We reached an agreement on a high plane of increases," says Weinberger. "And, of course, there's some theory around that we picked a number out of the air and then asked all the services what they wanted to fill out that number, which I can assure you is totally wrong . . . If that is his charge, he's simply condemning himself, because he was over here during the process and he knows that was not the case . . . What we considered was a number of requests — army, navy, air force, marine corps — things that they felt they had needed and had been, in effect, deprived of over the years . . . But we emphatically did not pick a number out of the air and then work to fill it up. We worked exactly the reverse."

Weinberger says Stockman's fervor to cut defense was that of a bookkeeper "trying to get a tidy and better looking balance sheet — that is to say, a lower deficit. And he felt politically that it's a lot easier to get Congress to cut defense than domestic spending requests." Weinberger also claims that after Stockman lost his debate within the Administration he would lobby for those defense cuts in Congress. "Some of the senators, friends of mine, would show me charts that he had left with them that he had used in losing presentations . . . as to reasons why they didn't have to support particular items in the budget, and I found that very disquieting." Senator Pete Domenici, a leading critic of Weinberger's budgets, disputes that charge: "If he was running up here to undermine the defense budget he would have done a much better job." Domenici also believes the defense numbers were invented and not based on military needs. Why else, he asks, did the army, navy and air force each come in with initial budgets of nearly identical size?

Ironically, one of Stockman's chief arguments against Weinberger's budget was the same one he ignored when Agriculture Secretary John Block used it on him: If you go in with too extreme a position, Congress will deal you out and write its own budget. That, ultimately, is what happened to Weinberger.

Stockman prepared his arguments and briefing materials carefully for his battles with Weinberger. He would point to the deficit, he would show how weapons purchases could be stretched out without hurting national security. He would contend that Weinberger was making it easy for Congress to shift money from the military to domestic programs without producing any net budget savings. But he was destined to lose, as he suspected early on. "When Cap brought his chart with the little soldiers and no guns, it was no longer a matter of fiscal policy. It was a matter of national security. So that got lost," he said in 1984. "I keep saying we can't afford it, but Cap never responded to that argument."

If Stockman thought he was the clever young man, Weinberger showed that he was the clever old dog. One White House official recalls that during one round of budget appeals with a Cabinet officer, Weinberger would sit on Reagan's left and arrange for the department head to sit across the table, but Weinberger showed up early for his session and took the seat on the President's left, forcing Stockman to be the one sitting across the table. Weinberger also would be patronizing toward Stockman in meetings with the President. "I know how hard a job you have but this is not an accounting issue," he would say, or "I feel obliged to tell you these are only paper savings." On one occasion he challenged Stockman's five-year estimates as being unreliable, knowing Reagan's distrust of long-range forecasts. "Come on, Cap, I'm doing it the same way you used to," Stockman protested. "I know," Weinberger replied with a sly grin. "That's why I don't trust them."

"Dave felt that Cap and Reagan were captured by the generals," says Larry Kudlow. "He could never understand how Reagan could rail on at meetings about the inefficiencies of government spending in the domestic area but not apply that to the defense area." A White House official who observed the debates says they always followed the same basic pattern:

"Stockman would put hours and hours and hours into these substantive analyses of his alternative defense budget, intended to achieve the same bang for less bucks. And Weinberger would come in and make a little speech about the Soviet threat and then basically say: 'Do you believe the Soviet Union is a threat? If yes, accept our budget.' It had nothing to do with what David was talking about, and the President was consistently responsive to Weinberger. Cap also had the President's complete confidence and occasionally, when he would lose his temper, privately referred to Dave as a 'little draft dodger.' I think I heard him do it once in front of the President." Weinberger denies ever using the term, but the official stands by his claim, adding that Stockman knew about such whispers behind his back and found it unsettling. "Dave was very insecure about all the talk behind his back, very insecure," says a friend. "At OMB, the subject of his antiwar days was absolutely verboten."

"Frankly," says former presidential economist Murray Weidenbaum, "when it came to domestic budget presentations, Stockman made his case like a man. But when he gave military spending presentations, he was a boy."

Stockman's years of frustration over the defense budget exploded to the surface in February 1985 during the same Senate Budget Committee hearing where only minutes before he had assailed emergency aid for farmers who were heavily in debt. Stockman had been playing the good soldier, dutifully defending in public a new defense budget he had opposed in private, and he said as much to the senators. But after J. Bennett Johnston, a Louisiana Democrat, goaded him — "Do you and Cap Weinberger really agree on defense?" — Stockman finally let it rip:

"I have not been able to get anything done on military retirement downtown. It is a scandal. It is an outrage. The institutional forces in the military are more concerned about protecting their retirement benefits than they are about protecting the security of the American people. And when push comes to shove, they will give up on security before they give up on retirement. Now, that is another true fact of life and I will probably be in hot water saying it, but I am going to say it because it is about time it was said. And I hope some of you up here who think the military budget is too big will call in the Joint Chiefs of Staff and ask them what they are going to put in the kitty by supporting a reasonable and moderate retirement reform plan to go along with what we need to do on the civilian side."

When he had finished, committee staff director Steve Bell, who was sitting behind Pete Domenici, leaned forward and whispered in the chairman's ear, "That's the voice of a man who has decided to leave."

At OMB, meanwhile, Alton G. Keel, Jr., the associate director who specializes in defense and national security budgets, was watching the hearing on television in his office. As soon as Stockman said it, he gasped. Keel, a former Assistant Secretary of the Air Force, agreed with what Stockman had said. Military pensions had gotten too generous in guaranteeing half pay after twenty years. But Keel also knew Stockman should not have said it. Quickly, Keel called Robert McFarlane, the President's national security adviser and a former Marine officer, but McFarlane wasn't upset. Then Keel called Deputy Defense Secretary William Taft, but Taft wasn't upset. "Should we put troops on Defcon I [Defense Condition One—the final alert before a nuclear attack]?" Taft joked. When Stockman got back from the Hill he came to see Keel.

"Am I in trouble?" he asked.

"In trouble? You mean you have nothing else lined up on the outside?" Keel ribbed him. "You shouldn't have said it."

"They trapped me," Stockman replied.

Which was not completely true; Johnston's question was just too tempting to pass up. Stockman then called around to the top military brass and found, surprisingly, that they were not upset. But the brass one level down, the one-star generals and the colonels, were outraged and felt he had questioned their patriotism.

Veterans groups also squawked and raised Stockman's past as an alleged draft-dodget. The President personally disowned the remarks. Barry Goldwater, chairman of the Senate Armed Services and a retired air force officer, called Stockman's statement a "about as distasteful as anything I've heard coming out of this Administration or any other." Calls flooded into OMB, some negative, but most of them positive. Many of the supporters were veterans who saluted him for having the guts to tell the truth.

Several of Stockman's advisers argued that he should issue a public apology, but he was very reluctant to do that. "He felt he had not insulted anyone and that he was right," says one close aide. "Dave didn't want to apologize publicly again. He had done so over the *Atlantic*. He had been called on the carpet once before, and he didn't want to repeat it." Finally he agreed to let Ed Dale issue a "clarification" that said the budget director "in no way intended to impugn the patriotism or devotion of our men and women in uniform, but was expressing personal frustration with bureaucratic resistance—not peculiar to the Department of Defense—to reform."

As a parting gift for him in July 1985, the Joint Chiefs of Staff sent Stockman a signed photograph of all of them sitting together during Reagan's 1985 State of the Union Address to Congress, which he delivered the day after Stockman's blast at military pensions. Stockman was sitting in front of the chiefs, and the picture showed him turning around and saying something that must have been funny, because they were all laughing. An inscription at the bottom of the picture said: "The only retirement we put above national security is YOURS."

At a farewell party thrown for him at OMB, Stockman received from his staff an alleged replica of the scandalous $640 toilet seat that the Pentagon had purchased for its aircraft. When he lifted the cover, he found an official portrait of a smiling Cap Weinberger.

As his parting shot to the military, Stockman recommended Keel as his successor on the grounds that defense would be the main budget game in town during the remainder of Reagan's term and Keel was OMB's leading expert on the military budget. But Keel did not get the job.

Stockman was finished with the Pentagon for now, but not forever. Should he ever return to government service, he has told friends, he has his dream job all picked out: Defense Secretary.

Was there anyone else left in town to fight? Stockman found 535 of them on Capitol Hill. He didn't fight with all of them all the time, and there were some he rarely fought with, such as Pete Domenici. But one group clashed with him constantly—the Republican members of the Senate Appropriations Committee. These were the people—along with their Democratic counterparts in the House—who literally held the nation's pursestrings. The historical budget reductions Stockman won in 1981 meant nothing until the savings were translated by these committees into bills that actually appropriated money. Like estimating budgets, determining savings for the purpose of appropriations bills is an art, not a science, and the committee staff members who did the computations were as knowledgeable about the budget numbers as Stockman. The principal question in dispute when calculating savings was over the "base line" from which the savings were determined. As Stockman admitted in the *Atlantic Monthly*, the savings could be easily exaggerated or understated simply by changing the base line, as in his example of lowering the temperature from 110 to 78. The base line rarely existed in fact. Rather, it was an assumption about how much something would cost without any budget changes. So big problems rose up when Stockman challenged the congressional numbers. This was something the appropriators were not accustomed to. Budget directors had not challenged them like this before, and they saw it as a threat to their institutional powers.

Stockman was well aware how easy it is to play games with numbers, having done so himself, and he saw the appropriations process as an escape hatch by which Congress in the fall of 1981 could use sleight-of-hand accounting to avoid some of the budget cuts it had approved that summer. He felt he had to police the appropriators because they could not be trusted. When it came to any budget details he regarded the Congress as ignorant and irrational. He made that obvious in a 1984 interview with the author, when he recalled the 1981 budget and tax cut fight and concluded that Congress did not have the slightest idea what it was doing from a numerical standpoint:

"The whole theory of what we did was: you had to

have the spending cuts first before it was safe to go ahead with the tax cut. That was the down payment. They didn't know how big the spending down payment had to be, but it had to be substantial. So we devised this strategy of creating so much turmoil and noise and shrieks from all the groups that were being hit . . . that that sort of created the visceral sense that we had paid the down payment. Now, it's okay to go ahead with the tax cuts . . . They measure things by the amount of political noise that's created, not by the size of the numbers. They can't remember from one day to the next whether it's $30 billion, or over one year or three years or whatever."

In a similar vein he said one reason the tax cut got so big was because there was a personal competition in the House between traditional Republicans who had long advocated business tax cuts and the new supply-siders preaching individual tax cuts: "It had a lot to do with the latent hostility, frankly, between the Kemp wing and the [former New York Congressman] Barber Conable wing. 'God damn it, if Jack Kemp is going to get his program, I'm going to get mine.' That's what it was."

With that kind of attitude about congressional decision-making on fiscal policy, Stockman was spoiling for a fight on appropriations. And he got it. One of his first head-to-head confrontations was with Utah Republican Jack Garn, chairman of the Appropriations Subcommittee on Housing. Garn's subcommittee had voted out the first appropriations bill of 1981 and Stockman was threatening to urge Reagan to veto it because it exceeded the President's revised budget. "Garn was apopletic," says a committee staff member who attended a meeting Stockman held with Senate Republicans. "Garn felt he had saved several billion dollars and Stockman was arguing over a couple of hundred million." Stockman argued, however, that by his estimate the bill was several billion over budget. "Jake Garn went ballistic," recalls an OMB official who observed the meeting. "I remember him sitting at the table, his lips turning white, his knuckles turning white. I didn't think he would be able to control himself. Then he started yelling at Stockman. How dare Dave threaten to veto the bill and seek to embarrass Garn by getting the President to veto the first bill that comes down the pike. 'I've been loyal to Ronald Reagan,' he shouted. And [Appropriations Committee Chairman] Mark Hatfield started yelling too. He said Stockman was the only OMB director to challenge appropriations numbers. How could this upstart challenge the numbers? It was a direct assault on the process. They were doing it this way for thirty years. Finally Stockman and Garn cut a deal. But Hatfield and Dave never got along." Garn cut a few more billion out and Reagan signed the $60 billion measure into law.

Barely a week after the *Atlantic Monthly* controversy broke, Stockman and Hatfield got into a heated confrontation over a spending bill to finance government operations for the remainder of the fiscal year. Reagan, at Stockman's recommendation, had threatened to veto an initial version of the bill for being a "budget-buster," so congressional appropriators worked around the clock over the weekend of November 20-22, 1981, to produce a new measure that Hatfield thought had Stockman's approval. But

Stockman's aides say it was a misunderstanding because Stockman had only agreed to review the bill. That Monday, Reagan vetoed the bill for being over his budget and ordered a government-wide shutdown. The crisis ended later that day when Congress passed a short-term spending bill to see the government through another four weeks, and Reagan signed it. Hatfield felt Stockman had gone back on his word, and would later refer to the budget director as the President's "bean-counter." The episode deposited a lasting feeling of ill will among Senate Republicans, who were angry at both Stockman and Reagan for creating pure political theater when, by their accounting, they had produced larger budget savings.

The next major clash over appropriations came in September 1982, when Congress overrode Reagan's veto of a $14 billion supplemental spending bill to finance the government through September 30. What really infuriated Senate Republicans this time was that Reagan had called the bill a "budget-buster," referring to the fact that Congress was spending more for domestic programs than he wanted. In fact, it was actually $1.3 billion lower than his request because Congress had made cuts in the money allocated for defense. On September 9, the night before the Senate vote to override the veto, Stockman got into a shouting match with Keith Kennedy, the staff director of the Appropriations Committee. "How come appropriations is the only place you try to save any money?" Kennedy yelled. Stockman replied candidly, "Because you need a majority in both houses to change entitlements [such as Social Security and veterans benefits] but only one-third plus one vote in the House to uphold a veto."

Stockman's last big confrontation with Mark Hatfield came shortly before the 1984 election. Stockman had been fighting the inclusion of funds for some new water projects in a spending bill. Hatfield, who was up for reelection that fall, agreed to take the funds out — except for one project to replace a lock at the Bonneville Dam, in his home state, by the end of the year. Hatfield thought he had a gentleman's agreement: but when the new projects were slipped back into the bill during negotiations with the House, Stockman opposed them all. Hatfield accused him of breaking his word, but Stockman countered that the commitment did not stand in the absence of any other savings. Eventually, all the new projects were dropped. "It got very nasty after that," says one Hatfield aide. "The senator would not talk to Dave again until he finally left."

To Stockman, this was a prime example of parochial politics at work. No wonder the social pork barrel kept growing; there were no real conservative Republicans in Congress when it came to spending. Senator Mark Andrews of North Dakota would blow up at him over cuts in farm programs; Senator Alfonse D'Amato of New York would go into a rage when he talked about shaving mass-transit subsidies; Senator Lowell Weicker of Connecticut would complain over cuts in health and welfare programs. And yet, through it all, he won the admiration and respect of the staff experts who saw a bit of themselves in him — someone who really knew what he was talking about because he studied the numbers.

"I never found Dave to cheat; he just could be very

471

clever and manipulative," said one senior Senate Republican staff chief who had numerous run-ins with him. "And I don't believe he ever broke his word. It was more a case of misunderstandings. He was great at the way he would play members off against one another. I remember one hearing where he was arguing for deep cuts in mass-transit operating subsidies and D'Amato was just livid about the reductions, and when he used up his five-minute limit Dave would say something like, 'Senator, I don't see why taxpayers in North Dakota should have to subsidize subway riders in New York,' and he would look at Andrews while he said that. D'Amato went off the wall and Dave would sit there and smile. One of the reasons we admired Dave so much was that he acted like a staff guy who could get away with jabbing at some of these idiots when they were idiots. And they couldn't do a thing about it."

While Stockman was annoying Senate Republicans by breathing down their necks, he was alienating House Republicans by ignoring them. To him, that was the price they had to pay for being the minority party. "After that first year he took more of a Senate perspective and abandoned his base here," complained one top Republican leadership aide. "He would float things that angered both Democrats and Republicans in the House. He knew it was a difficult row to hoe in the House because of the Democrats, but when he moved over to deal exclusively with Domenici and Bell, he undermined his ability to put together a working coalition here. I think that was a big mistake."

Among the things he floated that most irritated

House Republicans and the White House were proposals to freeze or reduce Social Security cost-of-living increases, a political no-no for everyone but some Senate Republicans and Democrats. Although Reagan had vowed repeatedly not to touch the pension system, the White House sometimes got the feeling that Stockman was off again pursing his own agenda. "It became obvious here that Dave was the instigator—or facilitator—of ideas from the Senate Republicans," says one White House official. "It became a joke. There was this one leadership meeting in the Cabinet room, and Dave is sitting across the table from the President and Domenici, making an argument about Social Security that's contradictory to Reagan's position. This is supposed to be Domenici's idea, right? But then he turns to Stockman and says, 'Dave, isn't that the number we talked about?' And I could see Baker and Regan and Darman shooting these knowing glances back and forth, and I'm looking up at the ceiling."

One reason Stockman did not spend much time working with House Republicans was that he felt he got little but lip service from them in his battle to curb spending. Like all the other so-called conservatives, their budget-cutting fervor was mostly illusion. In the fall of 1983 the White House had adopted a strategy of confrontation with Congress on spending and was threatening to veto appropriation bills that went over the President's budget. Phil Gramm, who had switched to the Republican side by then, began circulating a letter to collect pledges from House members, vowing to uphold a veto until he got the required 146.

"Gramm is always alert. He had his senses in the wind, and he started circulating a letter, 'We the undersigned pledge to veto any appropriations bill that is over the mark,' " Stockman recalled in 1984. "He did get enough signatures and he worked like a dog on it for about two weeks." But to get enough signatures, Stockman recalled, Gramm had to keep cutting back the list of bills and the items that were covered by the pledge. "One by one they knocked off general revenue sharing, railroad retirement, all kinds of things were taken off. Then, rather than using the President's budget as the spending ceiling, he used the President's budget of the 1983 level, whichever was higher. That let them put in the things they wanted, and that is the real reason why we ended up vetoing no appropriations. It was clear to the appropriators that our bark wasn't backed up by any bite whatsoever.

". . . But," Stockman said, "the President had gotten this letter and he went around pulling it out of his pocket, saying, 'I got this letter right here from the House Republicans that they are going to support any veto we make,' not understanding that it was not much of a pledge since the letter was way over our budget. Now, I did try to get that point through to him, but it never sank in."

Faced with resistance at every turn, it was small wonder that Stockman would complain about the political paralysis in Washington. Perhaps the most depressing time for him, professionally, was during the Thanksgiving and Christmas seasons. Traditionally that is when budget directors start wrapping up a new government budget to send to Congress at the start of each year. Since most of the budget battles with Cabinet members are usually resolved by that time, it is opportune to collect all the latest spending estimates from the departments, gather the revenue estimates from the Treasury, crank in the economic assumptions and look at the bottom line the computer produces. Every holiday season during Stockman's tenure the computer spewed out enormous deficit figures, starting at $100 billion and shooting up past $200 billion. Needless to say, Stockman was distressed. Until Ronald Reagan hit town, the deficit had never been higher than $74 billion.

Gamely, Stockman would take the new estimates over to the White House, where the President would tend to discount the bad news as pessimistic forecasting and remind his budget director that he didn't come to Washington to raise taxes and weaken the nation's defenses. Stockman would just have to keep cutting away at domestic spending some more—except for Social Security—to get those deficits down, the President would say. With a heavy sigh, the budget director would trudge back to his office, leak the rising deficits to the news media to create outside pressure for action on the debt, and begin brainstorming. Thus was created "Big Think."

"Big Think" was the name given to the crafty deficit reduction plans that Stockman and his crew would dream up in desperation over the holiday season and sell to Reagan at the last minute so they could avoid publishing a new budget that showed huge and growing deficits. Big Think became an annual ritual, and after a while the OMB staff seemed to look forward to the crisis, almost like a family tradition. The objective was to produce a budget that showed a five-year path of declining deficits. The trick was to find a palatable way to get Reagan to support tax increases and defense cuts. Under the rules a little deception in the name of righteous policy was allowed. In early 1982 Big Think produced "New Federalism." In 1983 the "contingency tax" was born. The election year of 1984 gave rise to the "deficit down payment plan." It was not until 1985, in the afterglow of Ronald Reagan's landslide reelection, that Stockman could abandon Big Think in favor of one last whack at the social pork barrel.

New Federalism was an elaborate scheme Stockman dreamed up to slip a tax increase past Reagan. Stockman knew the President had been interested for years in the idea of turning many federal social programs over to the states, and he also knew that the idea was being studied by other White House advisers. So he came up with a complex strategy, "probably while shaving one morning," jokes Don Moran. His idea was to lump together approximately $40 billion of social programs and take $25 billion in existing revenue. The government then would raise another $15 billion in new taxes and ship the whole package — $40 billion of programs and $40 billion in revenue — to the states, and the federal deficit would come down $15 billion. Stockman figured the President would be attracted immediately to the federalism part and tend to ignore the back-door tax increase, which was in the form of higher excise taxes on liquor, wine, cigarettes, leather goods, boats, airplanes, jewelry, televisions and fur coats. Although for the purposes of his argument Stockman described the revenue proposals as "sin" and "luxury" excise-tax increases, Larry Kudlow concedes that "this was the first step to a broad-based value-added tax."

At a White House meeting on January 20, 1982, the first anniversary of his presidency, Reagan tentatively signed off on Stockman's idea, to the budget director's delight. At least everyone there *thought* he had signed off on it. Stockman and Jim Baker had been pressuring Donald Regan to propose the idea to the President because he had more credibility on the tax issue, and Regan reluctantly agreed despite intense pressure from his Treasury Department aides to oppose a tax hike. But fateful coincidence intervened to bring Big Think down on Stockman's head. Word of the President's tentative approval of the excise-tax increase had been leaked by Treasury officials to a few reporters, and stories about the meeting appeared in the next morning's newspapers. Those stories were read by leaders of the U.S. Chamber of Commerce, who happened to have a meeting scheduled at the White House that morning. The Chamber group marched in to see Reagan and raised hell about the tax idea. The chairman of the Chamber, Paul Thayer, who was then head of LTV Corp, a major defense contractor, argued that raising taxes would be a big mistake, economically and politically. Instead, according to participants at the meeting, Thayer argued that the President could reduce the deficit by cutting a lot of the extravagance out of the Defense budget. As a Pentagon contractor, "I know how much waste there is," he boasted to Reagan. The President agreed and rejected the tax package, saying he had been up the previous night thinking that it was the wrong way to go. (Thayer's little speech about Pentagon extravagance wound up getting him the number two job at the Defense Department at the end of 1982. Three years later he went to jail after pleading guilty to a charge of obstructing justice, in connection with a government investigation into his alleged participation in an insider stock-trading scheme.)

Stockman returned from the meeting in a rage. "He came back screaming obscenities, swinging at everybody because of what happened, yelling about [Cabinet Secretary] Craig Fuller for having scheduled the appointment," recalls Larry Kudlow. "Dave went crazy when he came back to our place." Stockman was upset because Ronald Reagan still wanted to go ahead with New Federalism but without the taxes, which was the whole point to the budget director. He knew the states would never accept a plan that asked them to accept responsibility for programs that were not adequately financed. It was like a dead elephant that had to be buried. But he didn't want to cart it away. So he turned to Don Moran, his chief assistant for social service programs: "Moran," he said. "I'm tired of New Federalism. It's all yours." As he had predicted, the plan was immediately rejected by the states.

But Stockman still had to put out a new budget within two weeks. With the taxes out, he had to find another way to show a reduction in the deficit. Those were his orders from the White House. So he stretched the numbers. "About $45 billion was 'management savings' that we cooked up and put in the budget in January after we pulled the taxes out," he acknowledged in 1984. "When we pulled the taxes out, the deficit went over $100 billion for '83. So they put me to work cooking up all kinds of smoke and mirrors to make it come down under $100 [billion] through management savings." The result was a budget plan that showed a $98.6 billion deficit for 1982 and a $91.5 billion deficit for 1983. In fact, the deficits for the two years were $128 billion, and $208 billion, respectively.

The chief reason for the soaring deficits was that the economy was going through a deeper and longer recession than anticipated. The Federal Reserve was squeezing inflation out, and it hurt. A rise in unemployment and a drop in corporate profits meant less tax revenue for the Treasury and more spending on jobless benefits, food stamps and other social-welfare programs. Donald Regan had predicted publicly in January 1982 that the economy would come "roaring back" in the spring, but he was clearly wrong. Larry Kudlow recalls a meeting of economic advisers with the President in March 1982, at which he and White House economist Jerry Jordan predicted the recession would last at least into the summer and maybe into the fall. "At the end of my talk, Jim Baker turns to Reagan and says, 'Mr. President, I agree here with what Kudlow said. We're in deep shit on the economy.' And the President just gave me one of those 'Gipper' stares."

Stockman's "smoke and mirrors" budget died quickly on Capitol Hill. That led to the "Gang of 17"—bipartisan negotiations on a compromise deficit-reduction package—but it, too, fell apart because

Democrats refused to agree to cuts in Social Security and Medicare as the price for Reagan's support for a tax increase. Finally the Senate Republicans, with help from Stockman, put together their own package of spending reductions and tax increases which passed Congress that summer with Reagan's support. To win Reagan over on a tax increase, however, Stockman and his Senate GOP allies had to resort to some numerical smoke that aided them in the short term but cost them in the long run.

To make it palatable for Reagan and GOP conservatives to embrace a large tax increase just one year after they had slashed tax rates, Stockman, Senators Domenici and Dole, and other supporters of the effort devised a three-year deficit reduction package that purported to reduce spending by $280 billion and raise taxes by $100 billion. (They peddled the taxes as tax "reform, compliance and loophole closing" rather than as actual increases, which they largely were.) Out of this accounting method came the famous 3-for-1 ratio. Reagan was sold the tax increase on the assumption that for every dollar he agreed to give up in taxes, he would get three back in spending cuts. And he agreed. The problem was that the 3-for-1 was a gross exaggeration. "There is a lot of mythology about that," Stockman said in 1984. Of the $280 billion in spending reductions, "one hundred billion dollars was debt savings to us because we had cooked up this convention that if we could pass this package, interest rates would come down and then we'd count that as savings. They actually did come down, so some savings really did occur." He went on to explain that another $45 billion in spending cuts were the

480

"management savings" he had cooked up for the President's budget. That left about $135 billion in real spending cuts. Congress eventually passed about 90 percent of the spending cuts that it had agreed to as part of its deficit-reduction package, according to congressional estimates. So the final ratio proved to be closer to 1-for-1.

But Ronald Reagan thought he had been double-crossed. Based on what Stockman had promised, he expected $3 in spending cuts for every dollar of taxes and he hadn't gotten it. Moreover, he had been told that the package would reduce the deficit: but instead, the deficit got even larger, because of the recession. Reagan's lesson from that episode was that Congress couldn't be trusted to reduce the deficit; if he agreed to a tax increase, Congress would just spend it instead of reducing the deficit. In later years Reagan cited his support for that tax increase as one of his biggest mistakes as President and one of the chief reasons why he would not support new tax-hike proposals. "Later on, after the tax passed," confides one former senior White House official, "everyone was too sheepish to tell the President that the 3-for-1 was being exaggerated." Stockman should appreciate the irony, for it was becoming a common pattern: a little short-term hocus-pocus to win a tax increase in 1982 became a big long-term barrier against winning tax hikes in later years to narrow the deficit. "It was one of our biggest mistakes," admits Ed Dale. "The 3-for-1 was flaky." "It was closer to 1-for-1," says Buck Chapoton, Donald Regan's chief tax man who nonetheless sided with Stockman on policy. "Unquestionably it was manipulation of the President . . . but

I would not fault it for being misleading. If it was misleading, it was no more so than normally goes on."

In the fall of 1982 Stockman tried to convince Reagan and a group of conservative House Republicans critical of Stockman's push for a tax increase that their calls for spending cuts as a solution to the deficit problem was a fantasy. So he gave them a quiz. In Reagan's case, Don Moran says, it was "a do-it-yourself budget deficit kit . . . designed to get some idea of how much mayhem the President was willing to have us create once the mid-term election was over." Stockman had prepared a list of domestic programs that were candidates for cuts and gave three options for each. "Level one was kind of incremental budget cutting," says Moran. "Level two was some pretty heavy smoke but something we thought conservatives probably would be willing to go for if they thought it would do some good. And level three was the outer limits, big medicine—big Medicare cuts, wiping out a couple of education programs." Moran recalls that Reagan's choices left a deficit of between $120 billion and $140 billion five years down the road. The conservative alternatives ranged from fifth-year deficits of $180 billion to zero, with the median in the $130 billion to $160 billion range.

"The purpose of the exercise with the President was to get some explicit guidance on what he actually wanted us to do," Moran explained. For the others it was an educational seminar to show that talking about budget cuts in the abstract does not make the deficit problem go away. In the real world of politics, fewer and fewer cuts are possible with each passing year. Presidential pledges not to cut some program, laws passed by Congress, deals cut in back rooms gradually reduce the list of realistic possibilities.

Stockman personally saw the exercise as an education experience for Reagan too. Although he never fully convinced Reagan on the need for more than domestic spending cuts to reduce the deficit, he and the new chief White House economist, Martin Feldstein, managed to sell him on a new Big Think — a "contingency tax" that was included in the budget at the last minute in early 1983. This was a tax increase that was sold to Reagan on the grounds that it would only go into effect if spending cuts did not reduce the deficit enough. Reagan went along and let Stockman propose it so Stockman could show lower deficits in his budget. But as soon as Reagan started to get the feeling that the tax might be more than an idea on paper and could actually pass Congress, he dropped it like a hot potato and never sent any legislation to the Hill.

In February 1983, while the contingency tax was dropping out of sight almost overnight, Stockman and Jennifer Blei decided to get married. As luck would have it, the city was hit by one of its worst snowstorms ever the night before and eighteen inches of snow lay on the ground on the day of the wedding. The couple was married by a rabbi who was assisted by Congressman Guy Vander Jagt, a graduate of Yale Divinity School and a Presbyterian. The wedding was strictly an affair for family and friends; Reagan and other top government officials were not invited. Of all places, the wedding was held at the scene of Stockman's *Atlantic Monthly* crimes — the Hay-

Adams Hotel.

By the spring of 1983 Stockman had suffered another major credibility loss within the White House. He and Martin Feldstein, insisting on a "realistic" economic outlook for the year, persuaded the White House to issue an official forecast that predicted weak growth and large deficits. Instead, the economy began booming, prompting White House officials to snicker about the "doom and gloom twins." The recovery also gave more credibility to Administration optimist Donald Regan, even though he had his own forecasting problems: he was a full year off with his prediction that the economy would come "roaring back" in the spring, but when the long-awaited recovery finally took off, he looked like a prophet.

Larry Kudlow, who had lobbied unsuccessfully to win Feldstein's job for himself, claims he had argued inside OMB for a more optimistic 1983 forecast, "but this was one of the few times Dave and I really disagreed." Kudlow contends that Stockman favored a more pessimistic forecast for reasons of both policy and status.

"He wanted to force the President into focusing more on the budget and deficit. But it also made Dave Stockman's role more important. Obviously, if you put budget policy on the back burner, so goes the OMB director—onto the back burner. And Dave was having a comeback in the White House with respect to his importance at the time. He had kept out of the public view for a year. The fire-Stockman type stuff had died down. Pretty much everyone agreed that Stockman would be around for a while. And Dave wanted to be sure of his primacy; he wanted an economic scenario that enhanced his position. Now the flip side of that is that he did not want to open up the supply-side argument that you can grow your way out of the deficit. Politically, he would say, 'We've got to get these guys on the Hill to do something.' And the way to do that is to be gloom and doom on the economy and blame the deficit. That was always his argument. My argument was that you reach a point where you get so gloomy and doomy that you create paralysis up there—there's no light at the end of the tunnel. You give them the sense of total hopelessness."

Indeed, Stockman did seem like the odd man out in 1983, or perhaps more like the boy who cried wolf. At an April meeting of the Cabinet he warned that $200 billion annual deficits "for as far as the eye can see" imperiled both the Reagan Revolution and the economic recovery. In a private interview with the author in June, 1983, he said: "Two hundred billion a year deficits scare me to death. You are borrowing five or six percent of GNP. This is not a banana republic. When the United States borrows five to six percent of GNP it's a major force in the credit markets. I don't know how long the effects take, but you can't assume that a government can borrow $200 billion a year indefinitely."

But no one seemed to be listening. The improving economy had taken the pressure off of the political system to do something, and foreign affairs were the dominant issues that year. Lebanon, Grenada and Central America were the big stories, not the budget.

"I don't know why he was staying then," says

Jennifer Stockman. "It didn't make sense to me. It didn't seem that what he was saying was having any effect anyway. It didn't seem like the President was listening to his briefings. He was only listening to what he wanted to hear, and David was not telling him what he wanted to hear. And David was continuing to work night and day, continuing to kill himself. His work ethic and attitude didn't change one bit. I saw him getting up at four in the morning, pouring out these documents, writing these presentations — in my opinion, to no avail. I knew what he was hoping to accomplish, but I saw it as much more futile than he did. He was determined. It was almost like he was the eternal optimist: 'The President's got to see it now.' Every little thing he would hang on to, so hopeful that the President would now understand or that, now, maybe Weinberger would be changing his views on something. He was always looking for that silver lining. And it was much easier for a person not closely involved to see it much more realistically, I think. I didn't really see any change. I really didn't, and I just saw David continue to get really frustrated."

Stockman did find some outlets for his frustration. One was in humor — of the practical-joke variety. After one particularly bad session with Pentagon officials he came out of the meeting and told an aide to find him a white handkerchief so he could surrender with honor. Another time, when painters working on his floor had draped a net over a large circular stairwell, leaving part of the well exposed, Stockman attached to the stairs a sheet of paper from his yellow legal pad on which he had written: "Social Security

Net — Before and After." During one light discussion in which he and aides were trying to dream up new euphemisms for tax increases, he suggested "fiscal prophylactics." He also liked to play an occasional joke on his co-workers, and not always so kind. One day he read a newspaper article about how he and House Democratic Leader Jim Wright had argued over an issue at a forum the previous day. "Stockman, Wright Disagree," the headline said. So he covered up the picture of Wright with one of his deputy, Joe Wright, who was out of town at the time, made a photocopy of it and left it on his deputy's desk. "I came back and I swear to God, my career flashed before my eyes," says Wright. "I just couldn't imagine what we had done, because I had not read the article. I walked into his office. He was stern-looking for about ten seconds until I started to read it and he started laughing."

Stockman also dealt with the frustration by shifting his own focus more to where the action was. Always one who liked to be at the cutting edge of policy, he told friends at the time that he was getting bored with the budget and was developing an interest in foreign affairs. He had never before shown much interest in foreign policy except for budget-related issues, and although he was entitled to attend National Security Council meetings he rarely did, sending a deputy instead. But he started going to some of the meetings in 1983 and came away shocked. Whenever he examined some facet of government closely, he came away with the same conclusion — and foreign policy was no exception: he discovered, of course, gross incompetence. "The quality of foreign policy

487

analysis was crap. Absolute, total crap," says one former White House official involved in the area. "Dave frequently would lament about the quality of the discourse that would go on and the quality of the papers on these rather fundamental issues that were being presented. The staff work was terrible, the people hadn't done their homework, the analytic frameworks were useless, if they existed at all, analysis was highly flawed. It was just junk."

Stockman was particularly upset with U.S. policy toward Lebanon. He saw a danger that the Administration was about to involve the United States in a war where it did not belong. He would come back from meetings about the Middle East shaking his head and telling aides, "They just don't understand." He found one NSC meeting particularly distressing. The discussion was focused on whether to get deeply involved in Lebanon militarily, and Schultz and Weinberger were studying a map of the region and arguing about whether known camps of armed fighters were "commingled" with civilian populations. Neither man seemed to know what he was talking about, they stumbled over the pronunciations of names of towns and their personal rivalry seemed to interfere with sound policy-making. In retelling the story afterward, Stockman said, "Now I know why I was against the war in Vietnam."

Stockman may not have spent much time studying, contemplating or discussing foreign policy, and friends say he is unsophisticated on a number of issues, but he has formed a set of opinions that combine both support and opposition to Reagan's basic positions. He argues for a strong national defense based on efficiency rather than on symbolic levels of spending. He opposes Reagan's Strategic Defense Initiative ("Star Wars") missile defense system as an enormously expensive proposition that probably can be countered by new technology developed by the other side. He also does not believe the case against the current deterrent system, MAD (Mutual Assured Destruction), has been made. Like Defense Department hardliners, he is skeptical about the value of an arms control agreement because he does not believe the Soviets can be trusted to comply with one. He supports George Schultz's advocacy of use of force as a tool of foreign policy, but not in Lebanon. As for Central America, he favors U.S. aid to the contras fighting the Nicaraguan government, but on a large enough scale to make them effective.

In late 1983 the Administration's attention did shift back to the budget. Reagan was running for reelection and needed a safe, noncontroversial campaign budget to run on. Donald Regan was pushing for an across-the-board spending cut, but that was rejected because it cut too much out of the Pentagon's budget. Deep cuts in popular domestic programs were out because of the election, and Stockman did not want "another fuzz ball" like the contingency tax, which he saw as more a hindrance than a help in getting deficit reductions. So he and Feldstein pushed for an actual tax, but the President would not go for that. He was not going to be called a tax-raiser in an election year. Stockman did win a small and amusing victory on the tax issue, though. In a draft of the President's budget message that accompanied the new spending plan, Reagan declared, "To those who say we must raise taxes, I say no." Stockman quietly changed it: "To those who say we must raise taxes, I say wait." And it got printed that way in the budget.

Still, Reagan was left with a budget that showed huge deficits into the future. Senate Republicans were warning that the White House could not simply ignore the deficit in an election year. Time for another Big Think. "In eleventh-hour desperation came the down payment negotiation, not a proposal but a process," Stockman later recalled. It was too late to change the budget, so Reagan proposed in his State of the Union Address bipartisan negotiations aimed at making a modest "down payment" on the deficit. Some domestic cuts, some defense cuts, and a little bit of taxes would be thrown together. And it actually worked. By mid-1984 Congress had reached agreement on a small package of deficit reductions that Reagan signed into law.

What the White House wanted most out of Stockman during the campaign was for him to keep his controversial mouth shut. He almost succeeded, but not quite. In an interview published in a February 6, 1984, issue of *Fortune* magazine, Stockman argued that federal spending had been cut as much as the public would allow and that big domestic cuts in the future were impossible. The unspoken but obvious inference was that the only way to narrow the deficit would be through tax increases. At about the same time he told the Senate Budget Committee that the only place left to find significant domestic savings was in popular middle-class programs, and he ticked off some of the obvious ones—Medicare, veteran benefits, farm subsidies, student loans, government pensions. After *that*, he kept quiet and began working on an ambitious plan that would prove the case he had made in *Fortune* magazine. While Ronald Reagan's sunny campaign was promising that economic growth would make the deficit vanish, David Stockman was putting together the biggest assault on middle-class programs ever attempted. He tried to convince himself that it would succeed, but deep down he knew it would fail.

Larry Kudlow says Stockman seriously considered leaving the Administration around Labor Day to take a job as chairman of Financial Corporation of America, which had been having financial troubles. But when Stockman consulted with Jim Baker, who was managing Reagan's campaign, Baker reacted with what Stockman described as "extreme angst." Baker did not want Stockman to leave then; it was bad politics. Stockman might say or do something controversial and people might read the wrong thing into his departure. Democratic nominee Walter Mondale had been charging that Reagan had a secret plan to raise taxes after the election, and Baker feared people would think Stockman, whose position on taxes was well known, had been forced out or had quit over principle.

Now that he was staying, Stockman agreed to do another mock debate with the Gipper, this time impersonating Mondale. As with his John Anderson impersonation, he was brilliant: and once again, he overdid it. After Reagan's poor performance in the real thing with Mondale, his campaign chairman, Senator Paul Laxalt, complained that the President had been "brutalized by a briefing process" that filled him with too many "facts and figures." It was obvious whom Laxalt had in mind.

On February 4, 1985, Stockman launched his final attack on the social pork barrel. The budget submitted in Reagan's name had no major tax increases, it continued the military spending buildup begun four years earlier, it did not touch Social Security and it projected large deficits for the indefinite future. That just left the domestic spending side of the ledger—and Stockman had come up with a doozy of a hit list. The budget proposed to reduce or freeze spending for many programs and to eliminate others outright, including the Job Corps, Small Business Administration, Legal Services Corp., Amtrak, and other mass transit subsidies and revenue-sharing programs. Targets for reductions or freezes included farm programs, federal civilian and military pensions, welfare, housing for the poor, Medicare, student aid, veterans benefits. And the list went on.

Political observers described the budget plan as one last attempt by Stockman to capitalize on Reagan's landslide victory and finish the job he began in 1981. But those close to Stockman say he had another purpose as well, one that touched him more personally than politically. He had prepared a lesson about failure. The budget he produced was his final exam for the nation, a test to demonstrate once and for all the limited capacity of the political system to cut down his perceived social pork barrel. He would exhaust himself showing it couldn't be done, and then leave in ultimate vindication. He would do it Reagan's way at the peak of the President's popularity, and prove him wrong.

Over the next three months Stockman engaged in tortuous negotiations to get the Senate to embrace some version of the package. He was pushing "big medicine," as Don Moran would put it, and the "squeaking wheels," as Stockman would put it, were going crazy. That was no more apparent than at the raucous meeting on Capitol Hill that Stockman had with a group of Senate Republicans involving Lowell Weicker of Connecticut, who has a child with Down's Syndrome and was fuming about cuts in health programs and aid to the handicapped. "Dave had an inkling he would have trouble with Weicker," says former OMB Associate Director John Cogan, who attended the meeting. Stockman's inkling was correct. "Weicker ranted and raved about the 'viciousness' of the cuts in handicapped and compensatory education, [and] NIH [National Institute of Health] research. He claimed we had 'devastated' these programs. He was going on like this for fifteen minutes. He was the only one standing up in the room, his face was red, and he said members of Congress 'are making a mistake following David Stockman.' "

According to several eyewitness accounts, Weicker concluded by shouting, "And I think you have your head up your ass."

Stockman listened quietly and then said with a smirk, "Despite my difficulty in talking due to the position of my head, let me try to point out what the facts are. . ." Some of the senators laughed, but Weicker was not amused.

Stockman then went around the room handing out briefing papers. "Make sure that Lowell gets one,"

Majority Leader Bob Dole said. Stockman walked up to Weicker, who has about eight inches and one hundred pounds on him, and pushed one at him. "Here, Weicker," he said as it fell to the floor. "That's *Senator* Weicker to you, bub," the senator replied as he reached down and grabbed the paper off the floor. "That's just what I'm talking about, that sassy attitude."

"Okay, Lowell," Alan Simpson of Wyoming, the assistant majority leader, interrupted, "Stop being a bully and sit down."

Later, despite their angry exchanges, Weicker and Stockman met privately to work out a compromise on a new NIH budget, and Stockman picked up a much needed vote. The following year, after private citizen David Stockman moved to exclusive Greenwich, Connecticut, he received a telephone call from a neighbor who lived a block away. "Welcome to Connecticut," the friendly voice said. It was Lowell Weicker, who also asked if Stockman would lend his name to a fund-raising drive for a Republican Senate candidate. "Sure, if you think it can help," an amused Stockman replied.

In a climactic ending worthy of a Ronald Reagan movie, the Senate passed a version of the Stockman budget on May 10, 1985, by a 50-49 vote. Vice-President George Bush had to break a 49-49 tie that was possible only after Senator Pete Wilson, a California Republican, was wheeled into the chamber from his hospital bed, where he was recovering from an appendectomy. The revised plan reduced Reagan's defense spending request, and it also included a one-year freeze on Social Security cost-of-living increases.

That last change doomed the whole package. House Republicans took one look at the Social Security provision and said no. It took just that one word, says Ed Dale, "and the whole package crumbled."

For once Stockman was not distressed: he had made his point and he was moving on, professionally and emotionally. A week before the final Senate vote Jennifer Stockman gave birth to their first child, Rachel Lauren. Stockman has always been fond of children, and her arrival dramatically changed his work habits and demeanor, according to family and friends. He worked fewer nights and weekends, started taking time off during the day and became very much the proud father, recounting every detail of his infant daughter's activities to his colleagues at work.

Even before Rachel was born he had begun putting out feelers for job offers and book contracts. It was a busy spring for him. At the same time he was negotiating a budget with Congress, he was negotiating, without an agent, a six- to seven-figure job for himself with Salomon Brothers and a record $2.4 million advance from Harper & Row for a book explaining why the Reagan Revolution he was still supposed to be pushing had failed. But he knew the outcome in February as surely as he knew he was leaving. His decision to leave his high-pressure budget post was reinforced on February 19 when he passed out at a private dinner party and was hospitalized overnight. Physicians attributed his collapse to a combination of too much work, too much coffee and too many cigarettes. His wife, six months pregnant at the time, was badly frightened by the incident and said it was time for a mellower and more affluent lifestyle.

Money was becoming a bigger factor in his life. Although his $75,100 a year salary was respectable, on an hourly basis it worked out to a construction worker's pay, and he was tired of being the poor kin in a millionaire's Cabinet. "It really started to bother him," says his congressional campaign chairman, John Globensky. "We would talk about it and he'd say that he wanted to make more money, that even his wife was making more than he was. He was worried about his economic base."

Stockman could not leave without one last public ruckus for old time's sake. He had given an "off the record" speech to a group of New York Stock Exchange officials in early June. But as always seemed to be the case, his remarks found their way onto the record:

"As the fiscal crisis has worsened and the political conflict has intensified, we have increasingly resorted to squaring the circle with accounting gimmicks, evasions, half-truths and downright dishonesty in our budget numbers, debate and advocacy. Indeed, if the SEC [Securities and Exchange Commission] had jurisdiction over the executive and legislative branches, many of us would be in jail. So it is incumbent on both sides to come clean with the numbers, and thereby the true choices."

On July 9, 1985, three weeks after he stirred up that last controversy, Stockman announced his long-anticipated departure after four and a half years as OMB director. It was the longest tenure for a federal budget director since 1946, the year he was born.

And, as he had hoped, he was remembered in the media as the architect of Reaganomics, not its demolition expert.

On July 31, his last official day, Reagan held a brief farewell reception for him in the Roosevelt Room. First, there was the customary exchange of formal letters. Each referred subtly and gracefully to their long-running differences and their famous private lunch on November 12, 1981.

"I will always cherish the kindness, consideration and patience you afforded me — sometimes under very trying circumstances," Stockman wrote. "Changing decades'-old habits and policies has necessarily given rise to contention and disagreements among all of us entrusted with the responsibilities of governance. But your unfailing grace, spirit and goodwill have made all those debates and battles more pleasant, rewarding and memorable than you can possibly appreciate."

In a response that had a ring of fatherly comfort to it, Reagan wrote: "Not many people, even here in Washington, could name our nation's budget director for the past twenty years. But just about everyone knows who has held that post for the past four and a half years. Your analytical intelligence and obvious devotion to the public interest quickly made you one of my most important advisers . . . Sometimes, in dealing with an issue as important and multi-faceted as the preparation of the federal budget, it is easy to become discouraged by the sheer magnitude of the task and wonder if you are really making any progress. But the public tributes coming your way from every quarter are proof that you have indeed made a difference. Future OMB directors will be measured against the standard of your performance. . . ."

As a parting gift, Reagan gave Stockman a cartoon that showed a frazzled-looking Stockman on the left and a well-groomed Reagan on the right, pointing to his budget director and saying, "Stockman here is my lightning rod." Underneath, Reagan wrote, "Dear Dave — always well-grounded, aren't you? It has been a shocking experience but obviously you took it right in stride. Best Regards — Ronald Reagan (I'm the one on the right)."

Stockman gave Reagan his cheap little hand calculator, the one supposedly with the broken minus key. This little Texas Instruments calculator is headed for posterity: The Smithsonian Institution's Museum of American History asked to include it in its collection of computing machines. Curators got the idea from a cartoon that showed the calculator among items from the museum's collection of entertainment artifacts such as Dorothy's ruby slippers and Archie Bunker's chair.

One guest at the farewell ceremony recalls being surprised at how little real warmth was shown at the reception:

"Don Regan gave Dave a present — some books on Wall Street — and was hinting that he knew more on that subject. You could sense the edginess in them. Dave gave Reagan his calculator. Reagan looked at it strangely and then handed it back to him. I had this tremendous sense of distance between the two of them. Reagan acted like Stockman was just an employee who was leaving."

And then, as suddenly as he had arrived at a

498

moment of destiny to shake up the establishment, he was gone. "Let me tell you something, he didn't leave me one note," Joe Wright said, breaking into laughter, although he did not find it quite so amusing when he had to take over as acting OMB director the following day. "Not one . . . I guess you could say that was a Stockman weakness. He would tend to be, a lot of times, a one-man band."

David Stockman, the lonely and exhausted crusader, had gone into battle vowing that he and Ronald Reagan, a real conservative, would change the face of government. Instead, he came out waving a white flag to the system and its powerful protectors, who ranged from the business lobbyists lined up along Washington's K Street corridor to the man in the Oval Office.

"He became disappointed with the leadership in the White House and on the Hill," says his long-time aide Fred Upton. "He saw decisions that made no sense being made for political favors. It appalled him. He felt used up."

"At first he was in awe of the White House," says Jennifer Stockman. "I mean, who isn't in awe of the President?

"Until you've been there."

CHAPTER 12

THE NEXT MOVE

He's up before dawn, just like back on the farm. while his Greenwich, Connecticut neighbors are still stirring in their designer sheets, his chauffeured Lincoln is gliding into the city. By 7:00 A.M., he's in his glass office, forty-five floors above Wall Street, ready to get an early jump on the competition. Old habits are hard to break. Look out, New York, David Stockman has arrived.

Each prior life change has been accompanied by a fundamental revision in his perspective on the world, and this latest change should be no exception. He has drifted from rock-ribbed Republican to antiwar activist to skeptical neoconservative to manipulative budget-cutter. What shift will this new life bring? Will he lose faith in capitalism and find the free-market as

500

inefficient as he found government? Will he develop as much contempt for the super-rich in New York as he did for the superpowerful in Washington? Will he stretch the rules of the money-making game or invent new ones for distributing and accumulating wealth? At this point, even he can only guess. It took until the fortieth year of his life for him finally to join the free-enterprise system he has always extolled, and he has a lot of studying to do.

But he picked a great place to start.

In the fall of 1985 he became one of 102 managing directors of Salomon Brothers, one of the largest and most aggressive financial conglomerates in the country, at an annual salary and bonus estimated at $1 million-plus, depending on how good a year the company has. Nominally he joined the corporate finance group; in fact, he came as a minister without portfolio. He was let loose to use his reputation to bring in new clients, his brains to create new markets for Salomon to enter, and his insatiable intellectual curiosity to learn everything he can about the company's far-flung business activities. Some colleagues assume he was hired as a "doorkeeper" to attract new customers. Others speculate that company chairman John H. Gutfreund brought him on as a possible successor sometime in the 1990s. No doubt those were factors, but he also has the talents and personality perfectly suited to Salomon's style of operation.

Consider this description of the company in the December 9, 1985, issue of *Business Week* magazine: "Merrill Lynch remains the best-known Wall Street house and Goldman Sachs the best-managed, but

Salomon Bros. is the firm most feared by its competitors. It is the prototype of the thoroughly modern investment bank—the not-so-benevolent King of the Street . . . Salomon by almost any measure is one of the world's most potent financial institutions. With $68 billion in assets, it is twice Merrill Lynch's size and roughly on a par with American Express Co. If Salomon were a commercial bank, it would be the nation's fifth largest. But no one, not even Citicorp, the largest U.S. bank, can match Salomon's momentum. It is on one hell of a roll."

Now, that is David Stockman's kind of place.

Friends and relatives describe him as excited and fascinated with his new job. Always the scholar who likes to put his knowledge to immediate use, he is getting that chance at Salomon, where the giant engine of global capitalism is reduced to a series of highly technical and complex operations. Every day Salomon is involved in transactions that shift billions of dollars' worth of capital around the world. Stockman has had plenty of experience doing that for Uncle Sam; now he finally gets to do it for a profit.

The new job has forced some changes that have not been too difficult to adapt to. He is not thrilled about the hour-long commute from home. His glass-enclosed office is much smaller and less private than his spacious suite of rooms at the old Executive Office Building. He has cut back his work to eleven hours a day so he can be out the door at six and home by seven. That was one of Jennifer's demands, but one he willingly accepted. "As you get older you slow down," he told some friends. His hair is a tad shorter—"he looks less like a hippie," jokes a

502

friend—and he has traded in his government-issue pinstripes for Wall Street's somber grays. He still smokes Salem cigarettes and drinks too much coffee, to his wife's consternation, but he also has struck friends as a little more relaxed. "I think maybe he's a little bored," speculates one of them.

Already?

Adjusting to a new, lavish lifestyle may be the most difficult change confronting him. He is still several parts: farm boy, absent-minded professor, and unpretentious guy. But few people have had trouble acquiring the taste for wealth when they have set their minds on it. In his first major market transaction he proved he knew how to sell at the top. Between his book and his job he negotiated $3.5 million for himself in his first year out of government, roughly a 5,000 percent pay increase over his OMB salary. Some friends believe he likes the money because it is society's principal measure of success, not just for the opulence it buys. Nevertheless he and Jennifer have not been bashful about acquiring the luxury great wealth brings.

Donald Regan would feel comfortable in their new surroundings. For $2 million-plus, they have a new house, tennis court and swimming pool built on two and a half acres that one friend describes as a "mini-mansion." Another close friend jokes that he wanted his own tennis court and pool because he is so competitive and shy that he doesn't want people to see him play tennis or swim in public until he can get into shape in private. When he comes to Washington he travels about in a stretch limousine, courtesy of Salomon, just like one of those hot-shot corporate lobbyists he used to fight while at OMB.

Even though they have no trouble making ends meet on his salary, the Stockmans are a typical baby-boom, two-earner couple. While a live-in house-keeper takes care of daughter Rachel, Jennifer runs an international technical advisory firm under the name Stockman and Associates. Sometimes, while he is studying international transactions, she is in Europe overseeing one.

Several people who have known them have observed that in some ways the Stockmans are a proto-type for the ultimate upscale Yuppie Couple. "I look at them as the Charles and Diana of the Yuppies," says former congressional aide Jack Strayer. "I don't think anybody's caught on to that. But if you look at their age and their accomplishments and their life-style, that says Yuppie to me. I mean, they have done it all."

Yuppies? Jennifer Stockman was insulted: "That's really appalling to think that we would fit into the Yuppie stereotype, buying all those gadgets and all." Then she started to laugh: "We did our anti-Yuppie thing by buying a Cadillac instead of a BMW. We just thought that would be so gauche, that no Yuppie would ever buy a Cadillac." Actually, she admits, he insisted on a Cadillac, a white one with a black vinyl roof. He wanted to buy American. It's also his taste. She wanted a Mercedes.

"We hope this new lifestyle won't change us," she says, turning serious. "There are an awful lot of greedy and terribly materialistic people here, and I just hope we don't get caught up in it. I don't think we would. We're not those kind of people. David's big thing about having money is that it buys him more time. You can have somebody pay your bills, you can have somebody drive you around. So they're not real luxuries. It's not that he wants to show the world, yes, I have money. It's just very convenient."

Friend Richard Straus says Stockman's financial bonanza is just one more example of his serendipitous life. "I don't think he ever dreamed that the book would bring him the kind of money the advance brought, and when he put himself on the open market he certainly wasn't thinking of himself in those seven-figure terms. But I think it has assumed an importance in part because the poor boy from the farm is going to be real successful. In government, you measure it by being thirty-some-odd-years-old and a Cabinet member who was running the government for six months. But outside government, how else do you measure your success except in monetary terms? So I think that's a large part of his motivation, because he's not greedy, he's not ambitious to have a huge cash flow."

No one could deny that David Stockman brought a lot of excitement and controversy to the Reagan Administration. Now that he's gone, there seems to be a duller edge to the government. But aside from his contribution in warding off Potomac boredom, what did he accomplish? What was his legacy? What was *his* bottom line?

From a purely green-eyeshade view of the government, he was a pretty dismal failure, and he will be the first to admit it. Under his stewardship the government ran up its largest deficits in history by far, and doubled its national debt from $1 trillion to $2 trillion. For someone who believes as passionately as he does in paying for what you get, that is a sorry record. Government spending as a share of the U.S. economy during his tenure actually increased, from just over 22 percent when he first arrived to a peacetime record 24 percent, and federal employment—excluding postal workers—rose from just under 1.9 million in 1980 to just over 2.1 million in 1985. For someone as antigovernment as Stockman, it is a disappointing pattern. According to OMB's final calculations of the domestic savings achieved in his first year, Stockman reduced spending by $36 billion in the 1982 budget, a savings that grew to $66 billion in 1984. It was an impressive achievement, but one that was buried by spending runups for defense and interest payments on the burgeoning national debt.

Nevertheless, buried within those gloomy numbers are some trends that developed during his tenure that he found heartening. When the effects of inflation are discounted, the growth of government "entitlements"—direct payments to individuals—slowed to 2 percent a year on average from 1981 to 1985, and spending for all other non-defense programs actually declined during that period. "We have changed the climate on government spending and activism. There's just not much of an impulse there anymore," he said in 1984. "There are huge forces of resistance holding on to what's left of the budget, but there isn't anybody around inventing new programs—Hubert Humphrey Juniors—out there. It's just sort of old business now. We are trying to finance what we have, and that is a major change."

However, the Administration's number one accomplishment in economic policy during his OMB years, he says, was the very change that destroyed his ambitious plan to balance the budget: "Ironically, I think the biggest success, for philosophical and ideological reasons, was that we supported a strong anti-inflation policy at the Fed. That was the fundamental ailment of the economy when we got here and that problem has been substantially reduced. Now if we can only maintain it . . ."

To many of the career budget specialists at OMB, Stockman is being modest. To them he is a hero and will become a legend as a man who took the time to understand the numbers as well as they did, who cared about the subtle technicalities of the budget and who had original ideas. Instead of putting together budgets based on proposals that floated to the top from the examiners, he was innovative, something new. And he would call budget specialists directly on the telephone to consult with them rather than go through a supervisor, an operating style that provided a big morale boost. Assistant director Carey P. Modlin, whose thirty-five years of service rank him at the top of OMB in seniority, says Stockman tended to get into too much detail, to the detriment of his cause within the Administration. "He probably turned people off sooner by telling them, 'Here's what I'm doing, here are sixteen charts to show you what I'm telling you, and here's a summary of why I told you.' " But at the same time Modlin praised Stockman for involving the White House and OMB in the congressional budget process to a much greater degree than ever before. "I don't think there ever will be a hands-off-Congress view again in the executive branch." Of Stockman's personal disenchantment with his efforts to cut back government, Modlin adds: "He did not fail. He just did not succeed as much as he wanted."

Another high-ranking OMB career official, Deputy Associate Director David K. Kleinberg, credits Stockman for inventing a positive argument for doing something negative—saying the check is not in the mail. "There's nothing to arguing for a budget increase," he says. "But the idea of cutback budgeting was created under Stockman. He came up with a reason for . . . someone on the Hill voting for those bills." His telling arguments were human-scale examples that demonstrated how unfair or exorbitant a program was. One was that it cost the government $35 every time someone stepped aboard an Amtrak train. Another was that it cost $15,000 a year for each disadvantaged youth enrolled in the Job Corps, more than the tuition at Harvard. And there was his $6,000-per-pound-of-fish case against acid-rain controls. "Our job at OMB is to find savings and cut out programs, and he captured the hearts of a lot of frustrated people around here who had been pushing these ideas without success in the Carter years," adds Kleinberg.

What his OMB subordinates view as a positive legacy, however, has been skewered by Administration critics as a cruel and grossly unfair economic program that has increased the gap between rich and poor. A 1985 study of the Reagan economic program by the Center on Budget and Policy Priorities reported that the gap between the richest 20 percent and poorest 20 percent of the population has become greater than at any time since 1947. The report, "Smaller Slices of the Pie," based on official government statistics, also reported that between 1980 and 1983 the combined effects of the Reagan budget and tax cuts and the 1981-82 recession reduced average after-tax income for all but the wealthiest 20 percent of the population. Another finding showed that the nation's poverty rate from 1982 through 1984 was between 14 and 15 percent, the highest level since 1966, when the rate began a steady decline to a low of 11 to 12 percent during the 1970s. A third finding showed that only one in four jobless workers was collecting unemployment benefits in the fall of 1985, the lowest percentage in the program's history. Other statistics showed that the minimum income required for a family of four to cross over the poverty line has been growing twice as fast as welfare benefits provided by the government. At the same time, federal taxes owed by the average family of four living at the poverty line nearly tripled between 1980 and 1985, from $460 to $1,147.

The charges have bothered Stockman, who prides himself on his sense of fairness in developing government policy. And he refuses to acknowledge that they have any merit. Instead, he claims that inflation and a large increase in taxes, particularly for Social Security, during the Carter years began making life worse for the poor, and that the 1981-82 recession added to their plight. The subsequent economic recovery and drop in inflation will have far more beneficial effects on the very poor and working poor than any increase in social-welfare programs, he maintains. He also argues that critics of budget cuts have exaggerated the reductions actually made in low-income programs. And there is some evidence to support that argument. Federal spending on the poor for medical care, housing, food and general assistance rose from $59 billion in 1981 to $74 billion in 1985 — a 25 percent increase, according to figures in the government budget.

Where Stockman is willing to accept blame is for the huge budget deficits he left behind. In that sense, says Jennifer Stockman, "he thinks he really contributed to the mess. I mean, he's not blaming anyone for this except himself. He will take all the blame." But there is also a rather self-serving flavor to his admissions. His chief failure, he has argued, was his inability to persuade the President and Congress to change course after he belatedly discovered the budget was headed over a cliff.

"There has been a breakdown of responsibility among our political parties," he charged during a Sept. 29, 1985, interview on ABC News' "This Week with David Brinkley," his first public interview since leaving OMB. "As far as I'm concerned, for a good while now both political parties have been faking on the number one problem of governance in this society, and that is paying our bills as a national household." His solution to the deficit problem: a $100 billion-per-year tax increase. He made the same argument in an interview he granted in the summer of 1985 and which appeared in the March 1986 issue of *Penthouse* magazine: "We've had a four-year shot at going after all these little mothers, and nobody around here will do it . . . When you go through these things over and over and you see how embedded the resistance is — and not just big-spending Democrats, it's the Republican Party when it comes down to parochial interests — then you realize how insuperable the task is." He went on to say that Republicans "get away with making these speeches about how spending's out of control, but when it comes to their own piece of turf, they say, 'Don't cut you, don't cut me, cut the fellow behind the tree.' The problem is us." If there is a sense of déja vu to that complaint, it is because he has been saying precisely the same thing for the last ten years, ever since "The Social Pork Barrel." He has said it as an outsider, as an insider, and now as an outsider again.

Yet two remarkable and truly ironic things have happened in Washington in the year since he left. One is enactment of the Gramm-Rudman-Hollings law, which mandates a balanced budget by 1991 and imposes a mindless, automatic process of across-the-board budget cutting if the political process fails to do the job through thoughtful, reasonable choices. The law was passed by Congress and signed by Ronald Reagan shortly after Stockman left office. Privately, Stockman has condemned the new law as "pretty awful," which is not a very surprising reaction inasmuch as it usurps the power the budget director wields. Were he still in office his brilliant analysis, numbers juggling and eloquent arguments for establishing budget priorities would be rendered useless; instead he truly would have been transformed into a numbers-cruncher, as his successor, James C. Miller III has largely become. Of course, were Stockman

511

still in office he would have found a way to keep Gramm-Rudman-Hollings from ever becoming law in the first place, his former OMB associates note with knowing smiles. One suspects they are right.

The other ironic turn of events is an emerging change in attitudes about the dangers of the deficit. While Stockman was in the Administration the opinion-makers accepted as a truism his argument that the country's future well-being was endangered by the prospect of $200 billion budget deficits "as far as the eye can see." His warnings were seen as the courageous cries of an Administration iconoclast lost in a wilderness of ignorance. Asked in 1984 to name the administration's top priorities for a second term, he replied, "Usually priorities are something that you choose and try to get accepted on the agenda and then you try to execute. There won't be any choices of priorities. There will be an overwhelming fact of fiscal imbalances that will haunt the second administration from day one until day last." In 1985, however, that common wisdom was challenged by a new not-to-worry school of thought. Suddenly one-time critics of Reagan's big-deficits' policy began singing his optimistic lyrics that the country could grow its way out of the deficit.

The revisionist view about deficits derived from new forecasts by the Administration, the Congressional Budget Office (CBO), and private economists that showed a gradual decline in the size of the deficit over the next five years without further changes by Congress. Relative to the size of the economy, the deficit in 1991 would drop to one-third of what it was in 1985, according to the CBO forecast. One reason for the optimistic trend was that the new forecast assumed a leveling off of the military buildup rather than the continuing rapid defense growth assumed in Stockman's earlier estimates—Stockman could never beat Caspar Weinberger, but Congress ultimately did. The CBO and Administration projections also had a big "if" in their forecasts. The deficits would decline IF the economic expansion that began in mid-1982 continued at a healthy clip through the end of the decade. This in turn would make the recovery of the 1980s one of the longest economic "up" cycles in history, a possible but not probable outcome.

There is, then, still a gloomy note buried among all the cheerful news in those forecasts: if there is a recession over the next five years, the deficit could soar, this time into the $300 billion to $400 billion range.

Stockman is convinced things can still come crashing down, but in the spring of 1986 . . . who wanted to listen to a pessimistic Chicken Little explain why he was right? Oil prices were plummeting, interest rates were dropping, the stock market was on a historic bull run. The near-term economic outlook was sunny. Reagan's optimism had infected the markets.

At the very time Stockman was releasing his book, subtitled, "Why the Reagan Revolution Failed," many former Administration critics were beginning to think that perhaps it had succeeded after all.

Nearly two hundred people who have known David Stockman—either as a family member, friend, mentor, colleague, ally or adversary—were asked in the course of preparing for this book whether they expected him to return to politics. Not surprisingly, the vast majority said, Yes. Their main uncertainty was how soon. After a number of years, they predicted, he would consider a run for the Senate (either from Michigan or New York), another Cabinet job, or maybe even Ronald Reagan's job. He and his wife and a few friends said, No. They claim he's had it with politics and has embarked on a new career. "Really," insists Jennifer Stockman, then she hedges her bets . . . "at least for the next few years." And despite his own repeated denials, Stockman may have politics on his mind more than he is willing to admit. In a recent conversation with a friend about his first congressional campaign in 1976, he made a Freudian slip by referring to his "presidential campaign."

His brother Steve says a group of wealthy business people were prepared to invest $3 million in June 1985 to start promoting him for President, but Stockman turned them down. "He might get back into politics sometime in the future, but right now he's looking to be on the outside for a while," Steve claims.

"I don't think he'll ever run for office again," predicts former associate Don Moran. "My guess would be that if somebody in the next eight to twelve years offered him a Treasury job, he would take it." But Moran also makes the best case for why Stockman, the man who always wants to be where the action is, might find enough excitement on Wall Street to make a career of it:

"He's a money man. He's very quantitatively oriented, although not highly trained quantitatively; he's a very facts-and-figures and numbers sort of person, and that's a portable trait. OMB is the place where all the money runs through in the government and Wall Street is the place where a lot of the money runs through in the private economy. So in one sense he's a financial guy. If he left OMB to manufacture automobiles, that would astound me.

"Now he's not only continually pursuing further refinements in his theory of how the world is put together, but he's also obsessive in the day-to-day sort of things. He likes large complicated problems that require a wide degree of different talents and skills that he can just immerse himself in, and maybe even wallow in the wonderful complexity and difficulty of it all. He likes hard problems."

And Don Moran thinks he knows why: "Because that really sets your mind to racing and gets the blood level up and the adrenaline going and you really feel most alive when you stand there at the wheel of the ship as it crashes through the rocks and the waves. He's that kind of guy, and there are few environments outside of Washington where you can get that feeling except in the heady let's-lock-the-doors-and-come-out-forty-eight-hours-later-and-merge-a-couple-five-billion-dollar-companies kind of world. It's that interaction between people and money and human greed and avarice and pride and big complicated financial analysis of numbers and slugging it out across the table negotiating and trying to outperform the other guy by knowing the facts. It's the perfect environment for the same personality traits that brought him to where he is, because that's what those guys do. If Dave were working on a ship, he'd want to be simultaneously in the engine room and on the bridge."

That's the minority view. The prevailing belief is that he'll be back in Washington before too long, possibly as a senator, Treasury Secretary, Defense Secretary, chairman of the Federal Reserve. And after that, who knows? "If there's one thing about Dave, he likes working on the budget. He likes it. He loves it," says his former deputy, Joe Wright. But Wright also thinks Stockman might come back through electoral politics. "I think he might run for the senate some day. And I guess if you say, do I ever see him running for President, the answer is, it depends on how well he does as senator."

Some of his former adversaries in the government see his forthcoming book as another *Atlantic Monthly*, but with ten times the impact. "I say he's finished here," said one of his most antagonistic rivals. "People around this town don't forget and forgive that much." Adds one former associate: "I think people are going to say, 'This guy is the most vain, self-righteous person I've ever known.'"

Fed Chairman Paul Volcker believes Stockman could be a suitable man for his post after five to ten years of seasoning on Wall Street. Stockman's friend, George Will, thinks elective office is out, but that Stockman would make a fine Secretary of Defense because of his budget background and his ability to develop intricate global strategies. What does Cap Weinberger think of Stockman in his job? After he stopped laughing, Weinberger said, "I would welcome the opportunity to rest. Would you like to be OMB director?" And another Cabinet official close to Stockman says, "Doesn't surprise me a bit that he wants to be Defense Secretary. He thinks he could go over there and save the country in mortal combat."

"Tell him Kemp said he wouldn't be HIS Defense Secretary," Jack Kemp replied to the same question. Fed Chairman? "That would be a continuation of Volcker—run it out of your hip pocket . . . We certainly don't need another dose of that. He would be on my Council of Economic Advisers." As chairman? "As a member. Tell him I smiled at all times."

Congressman Newt Gingrich still sees Stockman as a formidable political leader in the future even though Gingrich remains highly critical of his budget views. "He will be one of eight to ten leading political figures of his generation in the Republican Party."

They say a mother knows best: "Yes, I think he'll miss Washington. I think he has that Potomac fever in him," says Carol Stockman, turning to her husband. "Don't you?" Al Stockman nods in agreement. Could their son be President? "You know, that's a hard question. Who knows what kind of circumstances, what kind of opportunities are going to come along," she replies, noting that it's not the first time the family has pondered the question. "Half of what makes your judgments are what kind of opportunities you have." Al notes, "We've had mention of it," and Carol adds, "Oh yes. A lot of people said, 'Oh, Dave's going to be President.'"

"He knows his chances are pretty good," brother Dan says bluntly, as if the decision already has been made. "In twenty-five years he could easily be President. Now he'll have a chance to meet the people with money and clout to build up his financial base."

Political columnist David Broder is just as convinced of the opposite view. Maybe he has a future in New York GOP politics, but the presidency? "I don't think he is understanding of human beings . . . People like that don't become President."

One close friend in the Administration predicts Stockman will reenter politics as soon as he becomes disillusioned with Wall Street, which should not take too long. At the first sighting of a flaw, he'll reject the whole system: "I predict he will develop a contempt for the market in the same way he has developed contempt for the workings of politics. Unless he doesn't have the time to pull back and reflect on the world he's entering, his work and his personality could combine to keep him so occupied that it can become like gambling: the wheel keeps paying off and he stays up late at night collecting more and more winnings.

". . . The presidency is not totally unreasonable. He's a generational phenomenon, and that generation is just beginning to take power. Things like the *Atlantic* affair, which older style people view as devastating, will not be viewed that way by lots of people in the newer generation, which has an element of irreverence. So, bearing in mind that [in 1986] he's only thirty nine, he has thirty six years left to reach Ronald Reagan's age. That's nine presidential elections. But if he ever expects to be President, he will have to be willing to deal with a world that is less certain than he would wish."

World Famous Author? Billionaire Tycoon? President? Savior of Mankind? David Alan Stockman and destiny are probably not through with each other yet. He is a man of extraordinary intelligence, drive, idealism, calculation and good fortune. He has the talent to find at least an approach to solutions to megaproblems, such as world hunger and the nuclear threat, were he to dedicate himself completely to them. He also has the skill to amass a huge fortune should he choose to conquer the world of finance. He is still naive and idealistic enough to want to make the world a better place, and yet he is so skeptical about the prevailing political process that he believes it can't happen unless he is on the job. He loves being at the cutting edge, in the center of the social maelstrom, but seems oblivious to the ego drive that brought him here; he believes he is an instrument of fate, not realizing how he has created his opportunities. He can't resist sharing his views with the world and takes delight in the way he generates passionate support or furious condemnation. He has the ambition and competitiveness to be President and the capacity to develop the necessary stage presence. But he still doesn't trust the wisdom of the people he would expect to elect him, and he still has the radical zeal of youth in a political system designed to minimize social change.

David Stockman is at once a symbol of old-fashioned American values and the hip baby-boom culture. He is a unique American political hybrid, a complex man of extremes, contradictions and enormous energy. How time reshapes him will say much about how an entire generation will change as it takes control of the country. Whatever course he chooses for himself, Child of Light or Child of Darkness, he will pursue it in a fascinating, unconventional and immensely controversial way.

Bet on this: wherever the action is, David Stockman will be in the thick of it.

INDEX